Going to WINDWARD

ROBERT A. MOSBACHER SR.

Going to WINDWARD

A MOSBACHER FAMILY MEMOIR

with JAMES G. MCGRATH
Foreword by GEORGE H. W. BUSH

TEXAS A&M UNIVERSITY PRESS *College Station*

This paper meets the requirements of ANSI / NISO z39.48-1992
(Permanence of Paper).
Binding materials have been chosen for durability.
∞

LIBRARY OF CONGRESS CATALOGING-IN-PUBLICATION DATA

Mosbacher, Robert Adam, 1927–2010.
  Going to windward : a Mosbacher family memoir / Robert A. Mosbacher Sr. with James G.
McGrath ; foreword by George H. W. Bush.—1st ed.
      p. cm.
  Includes index.
  ISBN 978-1-60344-221-3 (cloth : alk. paper) 1. Mosbacher, Robert Adam, 1927–2010.
2. Mosbacher, Robert Adam, 1927–2010—Family. 3. Petroleum industry and trade—Texas—
Biography. 4. Capitalists and financiers—United States—Biography. 5. Petroleum—
Prospecting—Texas—History. 6. United States. Dept. of Commerce. Office of the
Secretary—Officials and employees—Biography. 7. Boaters (Persons)—United States—
Biography. 8. United States—Politics and government—1989–1993. 9. Texas—Biography
10. Mosbacher family. I. McGrath, James Gerard, 1967– II. Title.
  HD9570.M65 2010
  338.7'6223385092—dc22
      [B]   2010014181

Frontispiece and front jacket background: Mosbacher and crew at left "going to windward" during
the 5.5 Meter World Championship Series in Newport Beach, California in the summer of 1973.
(Mosbacher family photo)

Jacket photo, front: Mosbacher after winning the Mallory Cup in 1958. (Mosbacher family photo)

Jacket photo, back: Mosbacher and President George H. W. Bush at Malcolm Baldridge Hall, U.S.
Department of Commerce, on November 2, 1989. (Photo courtesy of the George H. W. Bush
Presidential Library and Archives)

RAM: *For my wonderful family. As Pop often said,*
"When all is said and done, there is nothing left but family."

JGM: *For my girls—Paulina, Anna, and Caragh Rose.*

CONTENTS

Acknowledgments ix

Foreword, by George H. W. Bush xi

Prologue 1

1 From Less Than Nothing 9

2 The Boy Plunger 20

3 The Breaks of a Dozen Men 27

4 Guys and Dolls 35

5 "Paint It Blue and Sell It to Mosbacher" 46

6 Luck in the Breeze 56

7 "From Little Acorns Oak Trees Grow . . . You Don't Have Any Acorns Yet" 65

8 Just Get the Crumbs 78

9 Three Cents in the Ground 92

10 Cover Boys 101

11 Stumbled into It 114

12 No Price on Life or Limb 126

13 Blessed Are the Gatherers 143

14 What Do You Win Versus What Do You Lose? 158

15 Do You Suppose They'll Believe I Stayed? 174

16 "Please, I Don't Like to Beg" 187

17 Mr. Secretary 198

18 Don't Screw It Up 224

19 Actions, Not Just Words 246

20 Don't Let Them Put You Out Front 260

21 When All Is Said and Done, There's Nothing Left But Family 277

Epilogue 305

Index 313

ACKNOWLEDGMENTS

This book has, at times, felt like a journey of a thousand miles—and we are indebted to what seemed to be a thousand friends and colleagues who helped us along the way. The memories and photos they shared—and the encouragement and guidance they offered—benefited this project in countless ways.

That starts, of course, with my wonderful family—my sister, Barbara; my wife, Mica; my kids Dee, Rob, Kathi, and Lisa; my in-laws Nanette Gartrell, Downing Mears, and Michael Wheeler; my stepchildren Cameron Duncan and Bobby and Lloyd Gerry; my cousin Stanley Stern; and my nephew Clint Smullyan. We simply could not have completed, much less started, this project without their full participation and cooperation.

We were also fortunate to benefit from the perspectives offered by two of Pop's former employees, Liz Carbone and Bob Gall, as well as Pop's friend Gerry Goldsmith. Betty Ackerman, who started with me so many years ago, also added some invaluable insights and memories dating back to my earliest days in Texas.

My esteemed friends George and Barbara Bush and Jim Baker were generous with their time and recollections reaching back almost to the start of my involvement in politics.

The interviews with my sailing compadres Tommy Dickey, George Francisco, Thad Hutcheson, Pete Masterson, and Buddy Melges reminded me that no sailor was ever luckier on or off the water. They are the best, as are my business partners and friends Jack Bowen, Denton Cooley, John Duncan, Wayne Gibbens, Patricia Hubbard, and Berdon Lawrence.

My trusted staff and advisors from the Commerce days also helped us piece together the ups and downs of three eventful years at the department: Wayne Berman, Tom Collamore, Evan Hughes, Preston Moore, Amb. "Rock" Schnabel, Bruce Soll, and Fred Volcansek.

My respected friend Fred Malek was kind enough to share his perspectives on both the 1992 and 2008 campaigns during which we worked closely together.

Here in this acknowledgments section, we also wish to note several invaluable resources we consulted repeatedly in piecing together the narrative for this project, including the Census records available through Genealogy.com; the Stadt-und Stiftsarchiv in Aschaffenburg, Germany; the comprehensive online Holocaust records maintained by Yad Vashem; and the online Open Collections

Program, "Immigration to the United States 1798–1930," maintained by the Harvard University Library. These and numerous other archival news stories and published works helped supplement the project's narrative.

Finally, I want to express my gratitude to my ever-loyal and efficient assistant, Becky Lundmark, for her tireless help keeping us on track and—usually—moving forward throughout this marathon process.

RAM

George H. W. Bush

In a lifetime filled with so many blessings, I am constantly asking Barbara, "Where would we be without friends?" So many wonderful people have helped us in so many ways through the years, but that question is easy to answer when it comes to Bob Mosbacher.

Without him, it's highly unlikely I would have ever been president of the United States.

Bob was by my side from the very beginning, as we started a journey that would lead to the mountaintop of American politics. Part sherpa and always loyal friend, he helped me avoid more than a few pitfalls along the way, celebrated our successes, and dusted me off when the going got tough. I valued his advice, which he freely and frequently provided—and usually with the "bark off" at that. Bob was as direct as he was charming, but here's the thing: his judgment in the heat of political battle, or business, was usually spot-on.

It is a fact of modern political life that to run for office, you have to raise funds—and nobody ever, in my view, did a better (or more ethical) job of that than Bob Mosbacher. Fund-raising, of course, is the bane of every candidate's existence, but Bob genuinely loved it, and it showed. He made the process fun.

In the wake of the 1988 election, appointing my friend to run the Commerce Department was one of the easier decisions I made as president-elect. Of course, Bob already had a sterling reputation as a business leader who somehow kept his very successful energy business going during the oil patch "bust" of the early 1980s—a time when many larger companies fell by the wayside. That proven skill, and the fact that he was one of the shrewdest dealmakers I ever knew, made him the ideal front man for the U.S. business community as we worked with some tangible success to close our trade deficit and open more foreign markets for American-made goods and services.

As an ardent advocate of free and fair trade, Bob was particularly effective in working with his counterparts and the various constituencies in Mexico to lay the foundation for the North American Free Trade Agreement. He also was an aggressive advocate for HDTV and other communications technologies twenty years before they became popular. And Bob was a tough negotiator on trade deals with South Korea, India, and the European community.

But as grateful as I am for his selfless service in government, and his loyal and valuable political help, I am even more thankful for what Bob meant to Barbara and me as a friend. For one thing, he was one of the brightest Points of Light I have ever known—helping so many worthwhile causes. Our families have both suffered deeply personal losses due to cancer, for example, and working together with Bob to help support our beloved M. D. Anderson Cancer Center has been one of the great joys of life after the White House.

The fact is I enjoyed any occasion to spend time with Bob. The casual observer who may have seen us play golf or hunt over the last fifty years might think we were wasting our time if our goal was to demonstrate any true proficiency—but they would have missed the point. The real goal, for me at least, was to spend time with a man who loved life, loved his wonderful family, and was patriotic to the core. If you found yourself in Bob's company for any period of time, in short order you would be smiling and laughing—unless he was giving you a piece of his mind.

And then, my friend, your luck had run out!

Barbara and I are delighted that Bob decided to share his family's story in this wonderful book, because it is, in many respects, the quintessential American success story. The immigrant's tale is often one of tremendous hardship, and Bob's grandfather, Louis, was no exception. From there, however, the family story that follows is nothing short of exceptional.

Most of all, we hope this book gives you a sense for the true heartbeat of one of the kindest—if not *always* the gentlest—men I have been privileged to call a friend. Bob Mosbacher made life in Houston, life in Washington (life, period) more fun and more meaningful for Barbara and me than mere words can describe.

Simply put, we would hate to think where we would be without him.

Going to
WINDWARD

Going to windward. If you don't sail, you might wonder what the phrase means. After all, there aren't nearly as many sailors in America today as there were forty, fifty, or sixty years ago. On top of that, it might seem nonsensical to suggest that a boat relying principally on the wind to propel it forward could also gain speed sailing *toward* the breeze.

But trust me, you can. If done correctly, in fact, you can actually generate more speed sailing to windward than you can going downwind. After you have maneuvered your boat and sails in a delicate but demanding dance to where the sail becomes an airfoil creating its own energy—its own "lift"—it is not unlike the wing of an airplane as it takes off into the wind.

Of all the aspects of sailing, I love going to windward most of all. Why? Because it presents the truest test of skill. It involves total concentration; but more than that, it also requires you to make a series of instantaneous judgments based on ever-changing conditions thrown at you by Mother Nature. At first, the wind might be coming at you from the north, but how strong and steady is it—and do the waves ahead have a more easterly slant, suggesting the breeze is about to change?

And about the seas that day, are you moving well through a light chop—or are the rolling swells and frothy white caps foretelling that rougher going is in store? One big wave ahead can help you generate momentum, but three or four in rapid succession will kill it.

How to read the signs and juxtapose your boat properly against these various elements as you simultaneously see and feel them in one instant can change in the next, and it's up to you to react as if a reflex, make quick adjustments, and find the best new way to make the wind work for you.

To me, going to windward is sailing's greatest art form because you rely much more on feel than on technique or training. You have to improvise, and trust your gut; when you make a mistake, as every sailor will, you have to correct it faster than your competitors if you want to have any hope of winning.

When you are going to windward and everything is going right, you feel the lift of the boat coming from a perfectly trimmed sail. And as you climb the face and then slice down the backside of a swell . . . well, there is just no feeling like it.

It's been said that successfully going to windward requires you to know yourself as well as your boat. In that respect, going to windward is a lot like life. In sailing—as with your family, your business, or another pursuit—there come moments of frustration and even failure. But the true joy in sailing, as in life, is overcoming those challenges, and finding the right way to move yourself, your boat, and your crew (or family) into position to succeed.

Know your boat, and yourself. That's pretty good advice, both on the water and off.

Of course, it also helps to have the wind with you—to have a little luck along the way.

That's a lesson I learned a long, long time ago, when my father and I were driving down a broad New York City boulevard in the back of one of his favorite cars. From the 1920s through World War II, the Isotta Fraschini eight-cylinder limousine served as Italy's answer to the Rolls Royce, and as such exuded panache—a certain exotic flair—even before the robin's egg blue paint was applied to my dad's particular model.

"Pop," as I had only recently started calling him, was lost in thought, staring out of an open window providing a welcome reprieve from a seasonal heat wave. Thousands of New Yorkers on that mid-Depression afternoon had escaped oven-like apartments seeking relief outdoors, and everywhere you looked the great city was pulsating with life.

Emil Mosbacher Sr. was forty-one years old, and despite his hardscrabble childhood and early career surviving the largely untamed jungle of the financial markets during the first half of the twentieth century, his jet black hair—always neatly combed back—had yet to betray any evidence of his personal and professional struggles. I'm biased, but even to the objective observer my father was an attractive man. Like many men of that era, he was always neatly attired in a coat and tie, with his fedora stylishly cocked to the side, and usually with a small rose adorning his jacket buttonhole. Pop had a firm jaw and a strong but trim build, but without question his dominant features were his intense, almost mesmerizing, steely blue eyes—eyes that sparkled in laughter, and could cut you to ribbons in anger.

We were passing through an intersection in Harlem that afternoon in 1938, when an eruption of young voices drew our attention to one of the cavernous side streets. There, we saw a group of kids of all colors playing stickball up against one of the tall apartment buildings—using the stair stoop as a backstop.

With Pop in the early 1930s. The lessons he taught would stay with me throughout my life.

We had been driving in pensive silence for a few minutes, but when Pop saw the kids, like a bolt out of the blue, he immediately ordered our driver Connie to pull over and stop the car.

As the car came to an abrupt stop at the curb, Pop turned to me and tightly clasped my face in his strong hands to be sure he had my full attention. Then he locked into me with those eyes, gestured to the street kids, and said intently: "The only difference between you and those kids is luck. You're lucky enough to have a father who is lucky enough to make some money."

The words he said that day, some seven decades ago, still ring in my ears.

Pop, I now realize, saw himself in those street kids. For all his success, he never forgot the dire circumstances that indelibly marked his earliest years. We had been driving through his old neighborhood that day, and clearly the vivid scenes of so much desperation, so much childhood hardship and sorrow, had come flooding back.

As a child, Pop knew all too well what it was like to *try* to go to windward . . . only to see his sails luff, or stall. He knew the hopelessness of being a young boy adrift, at the mercy of a big and unforgiving city, his fate beyond his control. Pop grew up the underdog, the son of an immigrant butcher who saw his mother die too young. To help support his struggling family, he dropped out of school in the eighth grade and went to work.

In stark contrast, there I was, a carefree boy born with the wind at his back—coasting along nicely in a blissful world of prosperity and opportunity despite the Great Depression and its aftermath. And there, that day, the man who made this idyllic life possible was teaching me in his powerful way to look at the other guy, and consider their circumstances.

His constant insistence that we be aware of our luck in life was one of the greatest gifts Pop could give me and my siblings. We couldn't help that we were born to a life of plenty, but he darn sure wanted us to understand the obligation we had to be kind, to try and help others, and never, ever to take our luck for granted.

Of course, Pop was right. I was extremely fortunate. Unlike him, I was born on March 11, 1927 into a family that was largely shielded from the abject misery that would soon capsize much of our nation. While so many other families were homeless, standing in bread lines, or eating at soup kitchens, my parents could afford to feed us, and send my brother, my sister, and me to great schools, and take good care of us if we got sick.

One of my earliest childhood memories is a series of car trips I took with my mother, and occasionally Pop, into Manhattan. This was around 1933, and as we drove down the city streets I remember seeing men dressed as neatly as Pop—with a coat, a tie, and a stylish hat. These men also looked like they were gainfully employed with one exception: they had a strap around their shoulder holding a tray of pencils, or apples, that they were selling on the street corner for a dime.

One day, Mom took me shopping with her in town. "Will you come in with me, Bobby?" she asked, as we pulled up next to Saks Fifth Avenue. I didn't want to, so I gave her one of my less credible excuses. "No," I said, "I'm going to stay here and do my homework."

As I was sitting there in that big car, however, I soon spied a crowd of sullen souls nearby. They saw the car I was sitting in, and what they'd seen, it was clear, was the money and security they lacked. Even as uninformed and young as I was, the desperation in their eyes haunted me. Just thinking about them can easily bring tears today.

What was the difference between them and Pop? What made him so unique? For one thing, it was his good luck versus their bad luck. He never forgot that, but sadly some people of means do forget just how blessed they are. They feel no guilt if they have financial security. That obligation they have to give back rolls off them like beads of rainwater on a duck's back.

Others, like my daughter Dee, give it all up and go to places like Guatemala to help the less fortunate. My friend George Bush and my son Rob are also like that. They think, "God, I'm so lucky. What can I do to help others?"

As for me, I do some but not nearly enough. Like Pop before me, I hope that by building a successful business I have helped enable some of my family's charitable activities along with my own; but as blessed and lucky as I have been, I don't think I will ever feel as if I have done enough.

When I first told my family that I wanted to write about Pop and our life together, enthusiasm abounded. After all, Emil Mosbacher lived the American Dream. He stood as our own Horatio Alger, with his own rags-to-riches tale. After his hardscrabble childhood, Pop survived religious discrimination on Wall Street and had the perspicacity to avoid the 1929 stock market crash. He went on to amass a considerable fortune, and along the way, he befriended some of the most famous and powerful people of that era from business, showbiz, politics, you name it.

Though he knew many of the top business leaders and showbiz icons, however, Pop was just as interested in the "little guy." He always stopped to visit with the doormen, superintendents, and janitors—and knew everybody's name. More than that, Pop knew all about their families. He knew their children's names, and when their children came around, Pop would discipline them, and give advice, and help them like they were his own.

He rarely gave directly to an organized charity, but if the elevator operator in his building got sick, for example, Pop would give them the cash he needed to get through the predicament. Afterwards, he would never let them thank him. "I'm sure you would do the same if our situations were different," he would say.

My sister Barbara and I—and all who came into contact with Pop—still comment on his unique mind. My father saw things a little differently than most people, and had his own way of expressing himself. For example, he once told me, "Never ever tell a lie. Besides the moral aspect of it, you're not smart enough to remember what you said if you do tell a lie."

And this: "Never do anything so that when you see somebody coming down the sidewalk you have to cross the street." In other words, keep your word and don't do or talk about anything that is not true and honest.

While everybody else had these high moral metaphors, Pop had the ability to strip every situation down to what we called the "nut cutting" in the oil field.

He thought quicker, knew what he wanted to do, and—just as importantly—he had thought through how to do it.

I never knew, religiously, whether Pop considered himself Jewish like his parents were. He never talked about his faith. At the turn of the twentieth century, the synagogue was the center of community life for most Jewish families; but growing up in the 1930s I never went to a synagogue as a kid, so it was up to me to follow my own spiritual path when I became an adult. When I later married a very wonderful girl, Jane Pennybacker, at the tender age of nineteen, she was a Presbyterian—so after we moved to Houston I joined the Memorial Drive Presbyterian Church in 1964 and was baptized. I've been going there ever since. Even today, while I feel strongly that my religion is Presbyterian, my heritage is Jewish—and I am proud of that.

I am not quite as intense as Pop was. For me, I had the pleasure, the luxury, of being as intense or as foolish as I wanted throughout much of my early life. Pop, on the other hand, had to focus on his survival for so long, it was hard for him *not* to be intense.

An eighth-grade dropout, Pop nevertheless was a voracious reader. Knowledge was everything to him, and he routinely consumed ten newspapers a day— clipping out articles and mailing them to family members, whether you wanted them or not. Though he frequently wore gloves as he read, his fingers were often as ink-stained as any pressman's. Pop was also big on the postal "special deliveries" that came directly to your door. I usually received two or three a week from New York. It was his way of reaching out and staying in touch.

Pop introduced me to business and to sailing, and many of his keen business insights helped me branch out from my family in the late 1940s, move to Texas, and build a successful independent energy exploration company. With Pop's encouragement, my brother, Bus, and I also enjoyed success in the world of sailing.

But when it came to politics, I completely discounted Pop's admonition to avoid all things partisan.

My friendship with two of my fellow Texans in particular, George Bush and Jim Baker, eventually led me into national politics—the high point of which was my service as Secretary of Commerce under the first President Bush. It still seems surreal that a century after my nineteen-year-old grandfather landed in New York harbor with a single suitcase, I had the honor of representing the American business community to the world as a Cabinet Member. And the catalyst in this unlikely development—the connection between the immigrant ghettos of the late nineteenth century and the corridors of U.S. power in the late twentieth century—was Emil Mosbacher.

I can see Pop holding out his hands and saying, "Don't get a big head!" He always wanted to make sure that you didn't get too caught up in, or full of, yourself. Pop also actively avoided being in the media throughout his life—so I'm fairly certain this book that covers his life as well as my own would upset him greatly. Coming from me, however, it would not surprise him that I did not *totally* respect his wishes.

Later in his life, before he died, Pop expressed the hope that he didn't do anything to embarrass his family. Looking back now, to see the obstacles he overcame and the tremendous success he earned, we know he did the exact opposite. He still makes my sister and me very proud, as he does his grandchildren.

Emil Mosbacher Sr. overcame tough odds to make his American Dreams come true, and he generously shared his success with everyone he could. But Pop wasn't the first Mosbacher to go to windward, to overcome hard challenges,and seize his moment of opportunity. Every family has their roots, and to understand mine is to appreciate the courage and independence of yet another Mosbacher who set our version of the American Dream in motion.

It's a story that starts—where else?—on the water.

Chapter 1   FROM LESS THAN NOTHING

A stifling, late-summer fog shrouded New York Harbor as the express steamship *Aller* gently banked into the Hudson River and steadily churned its way northward. Gliding serenely through the narrows, enveloped by land for the first time in nine days, nineteen-year-old Louis Mosbacher could see the lush coast of Staten Island to the west; to the east, he surveyed the countless masts of sailboats nestled into the docks and shoals of Brooklyn.

Also off the *Aller's* bow as they entered the harbor September 6, 1886, were two sailboats, the American *Mayflower* and the British schooner *Galatea*, which according to the *New York Times* were struggling that day in fluky winds to finish the first race of the 1886 America's Cup amid the oyster smacks, skipjacks, sloops, cutters, and other pleasure crafts of the day. The foreshadowing of this particular scene cannot be overlooked, as Louis' oldest grandson, my brother Bus, would capture the America's Cup for the United States 75 years later with the President of the United States looking on.

Even in 1886, the waterway approach to Manhattan was an imposing experience. It had been said that "not the Thames to London Bridge, the Mersey to Liverpool, the Seine to Paris, or the Lagune to Venice"[1] could match the grandeur of the New York skyline—a dense, unending forest of buildings and concrete stretching from Brooklyn in the east to the Jersey shoreline in the west.

Added to this breathtaking view, however, was a bizarre sight for my grandfather and his shipmates to behold. Small at first from a distance, then lording over the passing *Aller*, stood the partially completed Statue of Liberty rising up on what was then called Bedloe's Island. That day, the *Times* reported how "delicate veils of vapor . . . wrapped the mutilated torso of Liberty . . . " The story referred to the still-exposed skeletal-like iron bars that formed the statue's interior framework, over which cantilevered, rope-tied workers scrambled to affix the last of the 214 crates of Liberty's copper "skin." Just seven weeks after my grandfather glided past, President Grover Cleveland would officially dedicate sculptor Frédéric-Auguste Bartholdi's majestic creation.

---

1. *New York Times* Marine Intelligence Column, "Experiences of an English Emigrant," December 23, 1866.

Taken from the Emma Lazarus poem, "The New Colossus," the inscription on Liberty's 150-foot base read in part: ". . . give me your tired, your poor, your huddled masses yearning to breath free. . . ." As he stood in the shadow of the "mother of exiles" that day and was confronted with the realization of what was once but a distant dream— America—Louis felt a great sense of relief at having survived the tough journey, as well as hope at having an opportunity to build a new life. But as he surveyed the great city ahead, a knot of apprehension tightened in his gut.

Okay, I'm here. Now what?

Louis Mosbacher's reasons for leaving his family and his fatherland behind were varied. He always considered Bavaria, not necessarily Germany, his homeland; but when he was a child, Bavaria was absorbed into the Second German Reich. Prussia in the north dominated the new nation-state, particularly the military forces. Starting in the 1870s, moreover, all "German" men were forced to serve in the army for a period of several years—and many Bavarians like my grandfather considered this newly consolidated national force to be a foreign army. As a result, many chose to leave for America, Canada, South America— anyplace but Germany.

No question, my grandfather was also drawn to the seaport and emigration agencies of Bremerhaven by "wanderlust"—the innate urge of a German to explore "beyond the mountains of his Fatherland into all corners of the earth." Later in life, Louis would routinely sail the seven seas, constantly spending vast amounts of time on the water. Between 1925 and 1939, in fact, he made at least ten major voyages. Like many of us to follow, Louis Mosbacher loved being on the water.

Still, it could not have been easy to leave his family and the life he knew in Germany behind. In 1873, my great-grandfather Mendel Mosbacher, a horse salesman and trader, had seen fit to move his still-growing family from his rural hometown of Eschau, the cattle market where he had been born in 1831. A wave of crop failures had swept across that part of Germany in preceding years, so Mendel and Hannchen Mosbacher packed their belongings into a wagon and traveled to a much larger river and rail town, Aschaffenburg, 11 miles away. Mendel Mosbacher knew what it was to see the winds of fortune change. To save his family, he had decided in 1873 to tack in a different direction. So when his second-oldest son contemplated making his own move—to buy a ticket for America and find work there—Mendel Mosbacher must have been understanding of such a daring, and difficult, decision.

In late July of 1886, with his parents and his six siblings there to see him off, Louis Mosbacher set out for Bremerhaven, 210 miles away—and the difficult cross-Atlantic journey. Looking back, it is clear to see how Louis was the lucky one. In the months and years ahead, numerous misfortunes would beset members of the Mosbacher family in Germany. Five months after watching her older brother leave for America, six year-old Klara—the youngest of Mendel Mosbacher's children—succumbed to illness. Ten years after that, Mendel's oldest son, Louis' brother Felix, died, leaving his wife, Betty, a widow. And this was before Germany was plunged headlong into World War I and the dark evil of Nazism that followed.

America would certainly not be free of severe hardships, but by leaving his family and his homeland, we now know Louis Mosbacher started a streak of better fortune that gradually carried our family through some dark days.

First, he would have to survive the journey across the vast Atlantic.

I never asked my grandfather about it, but traveling in steerage as he did, and judging by every account of the era, that ten- to twelve-day voyage from Europe to New York could only have been hell. Fresh water, for example, was a rarity. The pungent odor of so many unwashed souls squeezed into such a tightly enclosed common area rapidly accumulated and permeated the entire space. During rough weather, moreover, the hatches were closed—further fouling the air. And the food was often a soapy gruel barely fit for human consumption.

After surviving the sea journey, my grandfather and his shipmates were then herded like cattle through Castle Clinton, the erstwhile army fort at the southern tip on Manhattan that preceded Ellis Island as America's first immigration station. There his luggage was checked for imported material, while he was personally examined for diseases such as trachoma, tuberculosis, syphilis, and even insanity.

Once he passed inspection, my grandfather was then essentially turned loose on the streets of New York—where street peddlers barked out their wares, boarding-house keepers offered rooms, and con men offering jobs preyed upon the unsuspecting new arrivals. One account described the experience of the nineteenth century German immigrant this way:

A lucky few were met by family and friends. Hundreds of thousands, on their own, were simply told to head up Broadway, veer right at Park Row, and to keep walking . . .

Trains on the Third Avenue elevated lines roared overhead, whiskey bars lined the sidewalks, huge theaters playing German and Yiddish shows and burlesque punctuated the run of flophouses, pawnshops, and clothing merchants. Sailors, tramps, prostitutes, and legions of street kids, layabouts, and roughs thronged the old street, many of them given to a gleeful ferocity that included the habit of pulling pious elders' beards and pelting bewigged Orthodox ladies with anything that came to hand. The newcomers could not get around the Bowery; the only way into the ghetto was to bravely pass over.[2]

Into these foreboding concrete valleys strode nineteen-year-old Louis Mosbacher, carrying a single suitcase.

He wasted little time in laying claim to at least a modicum of the American Dream. Upon entry, he had declared himself to be a "butcher," and soon found himself working in one of the 250 slaughterhouses in New York's meatpacking district. It was inglorious work to be sure—after all, this was in the days before Upton Sinclair's seminal work, *The Jungle*, exposed the filthiest practices of the meat industry. Still, this menial job offered the means for basic survival, and the ability to start the family that came with meeting Babetta Braunschweiger, a German farm girl who had emigrated in August of 1891 from Bremen aboard the steamship *Werra*. Shortly after the two immigrants met, they fell in love and were married some time around 1895.

Louis' assimilation into his adopted country continued the next year when, on February 13, 1896, he became a naturalized American citizen in a ceremony at the New York Supreme Court witnessed by his neighbor, a bartender named Fred Rather. Finally, on December 30 of that same year, Louis and Babetta Mosbacher welcomed the arrival of their first child, Emanuel "Emil" Mosbacher, into the world. A second child, a daughter named Johanna, or "Hattie," would follow three years later.

If my grandfather was able to start a family, however, he wasn't always necessarily able to care for it. Watching Pop in later life, it was clear that the severe circumstances of his early years had embedded certain truisms into his psyche. When he was still a young boy, Pop went to work at a fruit stand to help the family make ends meet. For that first week, at the end of every day, he would treat himself to an apple or a pear. At the end of the week, when it came time to get his salary, Pop's boss deducted the price of the fruit. "We came from less than nothing, and losing that money—however little it was—hurt me and my family," he later confessed.

That experience taught him never to expect a lot of kindness and gratuitous

2. Martin Gelfand, "Welcome to America," *American Heritage Magazine* 43 (April 1992).

My grandfather Louis Mosbacher. He was the original Mosbacher to "go to windward," and take to the water.

favors from anyone. If and when those favors ever come, be thrilled—but don't ever expect them.

To hear him tell it, Pop's family was usually a missed paycheck from ending up out on the street. With the margin for error so small, that experience at the fruit stand— which threatened his survival—taught him that family comes before his own personal needs. He never forgot the shame and the desperation he felt that day, but he and his family were not alone in their struggles.

Between 1855 and 1880, New York had the third largest German-born population in the world after Vienna and Berlin. Manhattan's Lower East Side was so packed with Germans, in fact, that it became known as Kleindeutschland, or "Little Germany." In 1896, the Mosbachers lived not far from the Lower East Side at 14 Varick Street, on the west side, in what today is known as Tribeca.

Varick Street was originally a narrow dirt road cut through the lower west

side in 1822. A private square at the end of what would be my father's block was laid out between Beach, Hudson, Laight, and Varick Streets by the vestry of Trinity Church,which owned much of the land in the area. Private houses were eventually built around the square, and for a time during the early to mid-nineteenth century, it was a highly desirable neighborhood.

By 1896, however, many of the private homes had been partitioned and transformed into tenements—makeshift "hotels" that were infamous for their dilapidated, varmint-infested, and horrendously overcrowded condition. Indeed, during this period, the Big Apple was home to many such "colorful" neighborhoods—Mulberry Bend, Bottle Alley, Bandits' Roost, Thieves' Alley, Kerosene Row, Hell's Kitchen, Poverty Gap, and Gotham Court most notorious among them.

Though it lacked the colorful moniker, the living conditions in Pop's first childhood neighborhood were nothing short of deplorable. For eight to ten dollars a month in rent, in fact, some tenement buildings in my father's neighborhood had no running water. Many of the older wood homes had warped and decaying roofs, and thus were genuine fire hazards. Those tenements that did have inside plumbing were susceptible to contamination, so old and leaky were the pipes. The rooms themselves, meanwhile, were more akin to jail cells than living rooms—mostly devoid of light, rarely any with access to fresh air, and all absent any kind of luxury.

For this reason, the typical immigrant "home"—the cramped, dank room where they cooked and slept—was the last place most wanted to spend what little free time they had. To escape the stifling situation, many German families in particular would head for the thousands of beer halls and wine gardens scattered throughout New York. There, they would drink, listen to music, and enjoy theatrical performances.

During the day, the broad avenues of the ghettos teemed with sights and activity— laundry strung from windows, horse-drawn wagons negotiating the crowded thoroughfares, street vendors hawking every imaginable kind of food, and gangs of dirty-faced kids playing in alleys. Even the tenement hallways, which were usually so dark for lack of light that frequently adults tripped over children lying on the floors, were preferred to the rooms. If you were lucky enough to live in a building with an iron fire escape on the side of the building, that, too, would be crowded—particularly on a hot summer night.

Of course, tenement life was hardest on the children. Parents with little or no means frequently tried to give their children to relatives or friends that could provide a place to sleep and a chance at survival. Regardless of the weather, moreover, the poorest of these street urchins ran around in a loose gown and no underwear of any kind. The typical daily meal for such children, if they were lucky to get one, consisted of bread without butter, usually eaten in the hallway. Many tenement children did not know what it was like to sit at a table, let alone to eat there.

Near the dawn of the twentieth century, New York was witnessing an intra-city migration, as many Jewish families left the slums and ghettos of the Lower East Side for Harlem in the north—where a glut of newer, and sturdier, brown-stone homes were being built. The growth of these new residential areas further from the business centers of lower Manhattan was facilitated by the extension of the New York and Harlem Railroad, which was built along Park Avenue. By 1880, its elevated tracks stretched into Harlem—giving the borough's residents the ability to access jobs and opportunity at the southern end of the island.

In 1900, my grandparents and their two children joined this northerly exo-dus and settled in on East 106th Street, a block east of Park Avenue. There, their neighbors included many Irish- and Russian-born immigrants with names like Dunlavy, Schlossen, Aronofsky, Murray, and Cohen—with occupations such as furrier, machinist, insurance agent, plasterer, mill worker, clerk, laundress, and salesman. A decade later, my grandparents had moved still further north—to East 136th Street—where again they lived among other Irish, Jewish, and Ger-man families.

As hard as he tried, my grandfather Louis' good faith efforts to improve his family's circumstances did not immunize him from hard times—and outright tragedy. Around 1909, Louis lost his job as a butcher; Pop, then all of twelve years old, quit school in the middle of the eighth grade to deliver newspapers to help the family make ends meet. He never returned to school, and would frequently refer to his modest "8A education" the rest of his life. "Here's why you're wrong," he would often say, punctuating his critique with ". . . but don't listen to me and my 8A education."

Two other issues collided a few years later in April of 1917 that would have a lasting impact on my family. The first transpired on April 6, when the United States declared war on Germany. The 1915 sinking by a German U-boat of the *Lusitania* had fully ignited the nativist sentiment that had been smoldering in the United States against newcomers in general—and Germans in particular. Many Americans of that era were, sadly, unwilling to distinguish between the actions of the German government and its former subjects who had risked all to escape its tyrannical grasp. As World War I took hold, it gave rise to a new movement called "Americanization."

The Louis Mosbacher family circa 1910. Pop, right, and Aunt Hattie, left, flank my grandfather Louis and the grandmother I never met, Babetta.

In short, a nation that had become so full of immigrants—so full of hyphenated-Americans, as it were—was in the midst of an identity crisis, and the war in Europe only inflamed the emotions on all sides of a complicated debate. No doubt, for most Germans the ties of family and traces of old culture held firm here in the New World. Some anarchists went so far as to try and advance the Kaiser's goals here on American soil. The by-product of their perfidy tended to subject anyone with a German surname or accent, like my grandfather, to discrimination.

As long as I can remember, in fact, Pop was always after his own dad to get rid of his German accent. It evolved into a lifelong debate between the two. "You've been in this country so long, can't you talk without that German accent?" Pop would ask repeatedly. "Son," my grandfather replied, usually prompting giggles, "I don't see vhat ze problem is—I don't hov ün accent."

The other tragedy to strike my grandfather, Pop, and Aunt Hattie in April of 1917 was the death of my grandmother Babetta from tuberculosis. "Consumption," as it was then called, had not been prevalent among Jewish families as it had been among other ethnicities because of the cleanliness attributed to Jewish eating habits. Bad meat from cows was one of the main causes of the tuberculosis, so if you "kept Kosher" you were less apt to contract this particularly insipid malady—which was New York City's leading cause of death just a century ago.

Despite evidence to the contrary, however, tuberculosis was widely considered a "Jewish Disease," in much the same way that Italians were blamed for the polio epidemic that broke out in 1907, and the Irish were tagged with a citywide cholera outbreak in the mid-nineteenth century. It seems that newcomers to America in a given time period, whoever they were, were considered "unclean" and diseased, and thus blamed for whatever ailment plagued the city.

Eventually, the drastic deterioration of living conditions and onset of multiple epidemics prompted New York City health professionals to research the problem, and they soon found that an appalling number of tenement dwellers had little, if any, access to fresh air. That investigation led housing officials to mandate the construction of airshafts in buildings where not enough ventilation was deemed to be available. In short order, however, the new airshafts also came to be called "foul-air shafts." Many buildings had as many as sixty windows that got their air from these shafts, and some occupants used them as a convenient trash dumps—with all sorts of filth allowed to decay and rot in them for weeks on end before being removed.

My grandmother's death left a permanent scar on her family, and it affected Pop in two particular ways. First, while my father was a moral man, after my grandmother died I think he was angry at God for a time. He eventually grew out of that, but he never wanted to talk with anyone about his faith or what he believed. He always encouraged everyone who broached the subject with him to hold fast to their beliefs—"whatever gets you through the night," as my daughter Kathi described his attitude. Still, you simply couldn't draw him out on the subject of religion. After a time, most in our family simply stopped trying.

The second way Babetta's death affected Pop was that, for the rest of his life, even after he had earned great success in his investments, he always kept his apartment window open—no matter the temperature. "New York has the best air possible," he explained. In the dead of winter, during the dog days of summer, it mattered not—the window was open. I often suffered from asthma growing up in White Plains, and Pop always insisted that I sleep on what we called the "sleeping porch" right over the porte cochere to get all of that great air—hot or cold. Bus and sometimes Pop slept out there also, but I have to say the arrangement did little if anything to help my condition.

For Pop, losing his mother served to reinforce the other hard lessons that he had learned at the hands of the immigrant ghetto. He had been conditioned to expect the worst— or at least he had experienced so much of it firsthand—and that experience informed his decision-making as he moved through life. Pop referred to it as his "survival instinct," and for him that was always about remembering what he came from— despite being a wealthy man many times over.

He never lost the notion of being a survivor at a time when there was no social security—with a small "s" on social security. In his day, life was very much a high wire act, and there was no net to protect you. You had to fend for yourself. When Louis Mosbacher lost his job as a butcher, survival was very much a part of what Pop instinctively did—taking on the paper route, for example. And much of the wisdom and skill he had was honed from being driven as a survivor. That's why he never drank— because alcohol, as he saw it, clouded his judgment and interfered with survival.

I caught a glimpse of this survival instinct many years later when one of our family members approached Pop with a business idea and asked for his support. "That's the craziest idea I ever heard," Pop thundered in response. "In fact, that's so crazy that one of us is going out the window—and frankly, my survival instinct is stronger than yours!"

Argument over.

Chapter 2   THE BOY PLUNGER

On paper, it shouldn't have been a fair fight.

The mustachioed sixty-four-year-old legal lion at the height of his public powers—the national and even international counsel of choice when a host of business titans battled, a graduate of Columbia Law School and a millionaire many times over— moved in for the kill against his youthful prey, a witness who didn't finish the eighth grade.

June 9, 1922 found Pop sitting on a very hot seat.

"Why should you do such a thing?" demanded Samuel Untermyer, the Special Assistant Attorney General for the State of New York, as he paced the floor before the witness stand in New York's City Hall. "For the fun of it?"

"Probably to make a living," shot back twenty-five-year-old Emil Mosbacher.

"Do you make a living by gambling?" asked Untermyer, wearing his trademark three-piece suit despite the unseasonably warm eighty-five-degree weather.

"If you want to call it such," returned Pop. "Trading I call it."

At issue this contentious day was *not* a proposed merger of three steel companies—Inland Steel Company, Midvale Steel and Ordinance Company, and Republic Iron and Steel Company. Rather, Untermyer had zeroed in on the fact that stock traders like Pop were buying and selling shares of the newly merged company, called North American Steel, on the New York Curb Market (the precursor to what today is known as the American Stock Exchange) before the stock actually, technically existed.

In keeping with Curb Market rules, Pop had applied to "specialize" in the new North American Steel stock, and had indeed been present at the creation of this new market on Friday, June 2 at Post Number 8. As the stock opened at 1:00 P.M. at $50 per share, Pop testified, excitement ran high.

Over the next two hours of frenetic activity, until the close of trading at 3:00 P.M., my father made thirty-five different transactions on the stock—buying 7,672 total shares, and selling 3,400 on that first day (in addition to the trading he did for his own account). By Wednesday of the next week, in fact, he was a total of 6,000 shares "short" of the market—betting that the stock would go down. At nearly $50 a share, Pop was controlling shares worth $300,000.[1]

1. Roughly $3.3 million in 2006 dollars.

If that wasn't stressful enough, seven days later, on June 9, he found himself sitting on the witness stand in City Hall getting grilled by one of the best lawyers in the country.

The problem, as Untermyer saw it, was the fact that while the North American Steel stock had been authorized for sale, the paper stock was not yet issued—so Curb Market traders like Pop, in essence, were trading stocks that technically didn't exist yet.

As the testimony continued, the verbal combat between Pop and Untermyer became more of a running skirmish.

"Isn't it gambling?" Untermyer demanded.

"I call it trading."

"What is the difference between this kind of trading and gambling?"

"I don't know."

"There isn't any?"

"You can tell me that, Mr. Untermyer."

Untermyer had already earned national renown in 1912 when he led a congressional investigation into the concentration of wealth and political power in what Untermyer dubbed the "money trusts." That investigation led to the Federal Reserve Act, the Federal Trade Commission Act, and other legislation designed to curb excesses in the finance industry.

Ten years later, however, Untermyer was examining the steel supply and other issues that contributed to the housing shortage during World War I—not irregularities on the securities markets. The combined resources of North American Steel would produce 10 percent of America's ingot metal; thus, Untermyer was taking a decidedly curious detour to investigate the Curb Market's trading on this proposed steel merger.

For his part, after Pop dropped out of school in the eighth grade, he started delivering newspapers for the *New York Commercial*.

Fate soon interceded, because his paper route eventually included many of the brokerage houses in lower Manhattan. Pop was captivated by what he saw during his daily rounds—particularly the chaos and commotion caused by the group of men who gathered every trading day outside on Broad Street, regardless of the weather, to flash peculiar hand signals, shout furiously and endlessly among themselves, play pranks on one another and, most importantly, make money.

Timing is everything as they say, and when Pop started sniffing around for work in 1911, the Curb was experiencing a period of robust growth. As the number of brokers surged, so too did the demand for runners. An added lure for Pop were the nonexistent barriers to working at the Curb: he didn't need a formal education or references to get a job as a runner, just a willingness to hustle.

Another factor that made my father a viable candidate for success at the Curb was his ancestry. In those days, if you hailed from Irish, Eastern European, or Jewish heritage you *could* join the New York Stock Exchange—but you also should not reasonably expect to rise quickly, if at all, through its ranks. The Stock Exchange at that time was more of an aristocratic, closed club in that respect—considered by many to be the "blue bloods" of the industry.

The Curb Market was just the opposite. There, the Irish and Eastern European traders formed a close, fraternal clique that transcended the societal woes and divisions of that unsettled, xenophobic era.

By the time Emil Mosbacher Sr. appeared on the Curb scene, of course, the curbstone brokers had been trading outside for 120 years. Yet, even after so much time had passed, it was still called the "Broad Street Jungle," as it was still largely a self-regulated institution. The regular brokers had a way of imposing commonly accepted standards for behavior on those who showed up to do business in their midst.

Some brokers, for example, were known to steal signals between another broker and the clerk with whom he regularly conducted business. This was considered a major crime, because the Curb's business was routinely conducted in public view—the broker standing out on Broad Street used a series of arm, hand, and finger signals to communicate with clerks sitting in windows on the third floor of the Mills Building. If this system was somehow corrupted, the entire Curb—and its members—would be undermined. Thus, it was not uncommon for disputes, particularly those concerning unethical behavior, to be settled with a fistfight.

Later in life, Pop would tell me, "I was never physically afraid of another man." No question, his physical fortitude was due in large measure to this exposure to the Curb's prevailing sense of economic Darwinism: survival of the fittest.

Pop started out on the Curb as a runner, and quickly learned the ropes. He was always good with numbers, but was also motivated by the wages he was earning. At that time, a good lunch at the popular Exchange Buffet at 39 Broad Street cost 25 cents, and a Curb runner like Pop could make as much as $40 a week. A little further up the Curb food chain, a modestly successful specialist trader could take in the princely sum of $200 a week.

To a poor immigrant's son, my father later recalled, it seemed like a king's ransom.

The throng of hustling New York Curb brokers choke off all traffic on Broad Street in 1916.
Pop was moving up through the ranks and was almost assuredly in this crowd.

Pop learned the ways of the Curb so quickly, in fact, that the management waived the rule requiring a trader to be twenty-one, and permitted Pop to start trading on his own account in 1916, when he was still nineteen years old.

By then, he had watched, learned, and absorbed the oddities of the Curb. He knew that to succeed as a broker he had to juggle relationships with his clients, the banks, the police (who frequently accused brokers of blocking traffic on

Broad Street), and rival brokers out to take business away from him. Pop also appreciated that success on the Curb was primarily a young man's game.

In 1916, the Curb's move indoors was still five years away, and to do business you still had to withstand the outdoor elements—driving rain, searing heat, whiteout snows, whatever Mother Nature had in store on a given trading day. During the dog days of summer, the clerks on the third floor would frequently climb out of their office windows and perch themselves precariously on the ledge to escape their suffocating offices. In winter, when the temperatures plummeted into the teens, Pop recounted how he often had to layer newspapers beneath his overcoat to shield him from the biting winter winds.

Newspapers and his heritage couldn't protect him from what transpired in October of 1920, however, when charges were brought forward that Pop, age twenty-three and already a veteran trader, allegedly purchased stock at a discounted price and reported it to a customer at a higher rate—pocketing a profit of $3,700 on the transaction. The management essentially accused Pop of stealing from a client—a very serious matter, which was brought before the Curb's law committee. Following an investigation, on December 8, 1920, Pop was expelled from the Exchange.

The commonly accepted trading practices at the major exchanges during the 1920s were much looser than they are today. The worst of these practices— the scams perpetrated by "bucket shops" where investors bought stocks but brokerage houses never completed the transactions—expedited the demise of the Consolidated Exchange, which had the lowest standards for conduct of the three exchanges. There were occasional bouts of monkey business on the Curb and even the venerable NYSE as well. Indeed, this kind of misconduct in the financial industry continues to the present day—as exemplified by the breathtaking allegations made against Bernard Madoff in New York and R. Allen Stanford here in Houston.

What was specifically at issue for Pop in October of 1920 was a practice whereby representatives would come to a specialist with an order to buy shares "at market" and, given a choice between specialists, the rep would choose the one specialist who might be willing to sell at the actual market price—but report the transaction at a higher price. The two would split the difference, with the specialist keeping the difference in an "envelope" with the broker's name in his desk. The temptation to go along was great, because it was such a widely accepted part of the culture.

There's only one problem with Pop's expulsion in December of 1920 and the subsequent way it was recorded.

He didn't do it.

"I knew who did these things," Pop later said. "It was the old firmament of the Exchange, the very establishment. The deal was they would blame it on me; I would shut up about it; I would be off the Exchange for a year; and then I could come back."

In his book *The Curbstone Brokers*, financial historian Robert Sobel of Hofstra University also observed how "stories of Mosbacher's action appeared in several newspapers—a most unusual situation."[2] Normally such delicate matters were handled internally, Sobel noted, and not advertised to the outside world.

"I was a Jew in a world still dominated by WASPs," Pop summarized matter-of-factly, "and I was informed (by the Curb leaders) that that's what was going to happen."

Bear in mind that my father fiercely believed that "exaggeration is the same as lying." Not once did I ever witness him stretching the truth. To the contrary, he was always quick to downplay everything.

Pop went along and endured the public humiliation because he knew he had to take the hit in order to stay in business. And just thirteen months after his expulsion, in January of 1922, Pop was permitted to purchase a seat on the new indoor Curb, pass through the membership committee, and gain full reinstatement.

After he returned to the Curb in January 1922 and became embroiled in Samuel Untermyer's North American Steel investigation that summer, Pop was backed by none other than the Curb President, Edward McCormick—who defended the trading in North American, and for a short time said it would continue despite Untermyer's contentions. As I reflected on this, I found myself wondering why the Curb management would back Pop in that very public way? I do not know, but it appears to confirm what Pop was suggesting.

Enter once more Samuel Untermyer, who was no stranger to the world of securities trading. Thanks to his business acumen, Untermyer earned his first million dollars before turning thirty, and later purchased "Greystone" mansion—the 140-acre estate in Yonkers—from Governor Samuel Tilden, the 1876 Democratic nominee for president. Moreover, when he examined Pop on the witness stand, it was believed that Untermyer, a major stockholder in Bethlehem Steel, was worth $50 million.

---

2. Robert Sobel, *AMEX: A History of the American Stock Exchange 1921–1971*, (Frederick, MD: Beard Books, 2000), 13.

As he began delving into the North American Steel matter, Untermyer first questioned Mortimer Schiff—a principal at the venerable Kuhn, Loeb, and Co. investment banking firm. During testimony on June 2, Untermyer intimated that Schiff's firm was engaged in "washing" the North American Steel stock transactions—or conducting fictitious transactions to establish a disingenuous price level. Naturally, Schiff resented the suggestion and angrily denied it.

Next, Untermyer turned his attention to the principal traders who he thought were possibly leading a "bear raid," trying to drive the price of the North American Steel stock down, or at least trying to rig the action: two Curb brokers, Mortimer Altmayer and Pop; and one Stock Exchange trader, Philip Levi of Miller and Company.

Resuming his questioning of Pop, Untermyer pointed to a glaring, uncomfortable fact.

"You don't know anything about the companies, do you?" the counselor asserted. Pop had already testified that not only did he not know what the company was to be called, but he also didn't know what the capitalization of the company was to be.

"No, sir."

"And thereupon you proceeded to deal in the stock?"

"I applied for specials."

"Thereupon you qualified as a specialist, knowing nothing about the stocks, or what they represented, is that right?"

"That is right."

"Is that what is defined as a specialist on the Curb—a man who does not know anything about stocks in which he specializes?"

"A specialist does not necessarily have to know."

"The less he knows, the better?"

"Correct."

Untermyer also asked Pop how he came to decide upon 49¾ as the stock price unless he had someone tip him off. To this question, Pop pleaded a poor memory. When asked if he had a good memory generally, Pop gestured to the witness stand and said, "Not when I get up here."

"Tell me," Mr. Untermyer asked as his questioning wound down, "why should you go there and make a $380,000 transaction in the stock with respect to which no plan had been issued, of which you didn't know anything? Why should you do a thing like that unless someone was behind you?"

Untermyer continued: "You want the committee to understand that you are standing at the post dealing in the stock and that nobody is behind you?"

"That is correct," said Mr. Untermyer's twenty-five-year-old witness. "There is no one behind me."

A week later, Untermyer and Curb officials would agree to cancel the stock transactions related to National American Steel and drop the matter; but the exchange that day showcased the fierce independence my father exhibited throughout his life. He had been manipulated by the Curb management and taken the hit to his reputation—which privately haunted him the rest of his life.

Though he had been "fouled" (in the sailor's parlance), he never publicly complained. Instead, he used the humiliation as added incentive to work harder and smarter than his peers—and this drive, this extra motivation, would serve him very well in the challenging years ahead.

Chapter 3 THE BREAKS OF A DOZEN MEN

When Pop stepped down the gangway from the steamship *Bremen* to the docks of lower Manhattan on Tuesday, November 12, 1929, he was returning from a six-week European vacation to a vastly different New York City than the one he had left behind— one that, in many respects, was only beginning a free fall that would ultimately lead it, and the nation, into the depths of the Great Depression. Three weeks before on October 24, or "Black Thursday," panic selling on the New York Stock Exchange had spread like wildfire across the Big Board as scads of heavily margined investors—many of them millionaires on paper, who had borrowed heavily to finance their investing—tried, but failed, to escape the bursting market bubble and salvage what remained of their speculative wealth.

Fortunately for Pop, his trip to Europe was the final step in a planned sale of many of his stocks—to go with a superbly timed "short"[1] of U.S. Steel. By the time Pop arrived back home, the bellwether Dow Jones Index had sunk from its historic high of 400 down to 145. In two days alone, October 28 and 29, roughly $23 billion in stock capitalization had been suddenly cleaved from the markets as the Big Board, by itself, lost nearly a full quarter of its worth.

Action on the Curb Market was just as frenetic, and dismal. On Black Thursday, during the first wave of stampede selling, the Curb had seen a record-setting 6,000,000 shares traded during the violent sell-off. The Curb tally from that following Tuesday, October 30, however, eclipsed 7,000,000 as a second "hurricane of liquidation" sent shares spiraling downward. The intensity easily overwhelmed the heroic but failed efforts of some bankers and leading industrialists like William Durant, the founder of General Motors, to buy shares and try to contain the carnage.

In its coverage on October 29, the *New York Times* reported the morose scene from that Monday's trading session:

1. When you "short" a stock, you "borrow" shares of that security and then hope it goes down— whereupon you can repurchase the same stock at a lower price. This is done in an attempt to profit from an expected decline in price. Similarly, when you are short the market, you hold a number of bearish or short positions—not just a single stock.

It was in [the] final hour that the greatest damage was done. Terror reigned on the Stock Exchange, on the Curb and in the brokerage offices. A curious hush fell over customers' rooms in strange contrast to the pushing, whirling, shouting mob of brokers on the floor of the Exchanges who strove with might and main to execute their orders. Few men or women spoke. Most of them merely watched with fascinated eyes the jumping hieroglyphics. Most of them had been sold out. But they held to their chairs and watched the quotations as if hypnotized.[2]

Such a catastrophic coda to the Roaring 1920s had seemed so improbable just months prior. America had emerged from World War I with perhaps the world's most viable economy; and during the 1920s, the dollar reigned supreme on most foreign exchanges. The election of 1928, moreover, saw the popular Herbert Hoover follow the equally well-regarded Calvin Coolidge in the White House. In fact, such was the optimism of the day that, during the 1928 campaign, Hoover had audaciously suggested that the goal of eradicating poverty was within America's reach. Our country still faced plenty of tough economic problems, of course, but generally speaking the mood for most of the 1920s was upbeat and forward-looking.

And for good reason. While it seems meager by comparison to today's market levels, the period from 1921 to 1929 was nevertheless one of the great bull markets in history, as the Dow Jones Index soared from 60 to 400. As a matter of percentages, it was a breathtaking run; and like so many at that time, Pop had also profited greatly. In 1925, for example, our family paid nearly $60,000 in federal income taxes—which indicates the family income for that year came in at roughly $240,000, or roughly $3 million today.

I love the old saying: "Don't confuse brains with a bull market." Often, there is no sure telling what drives a market up or down, except raw emotions such as fear or greed. Looking back now, however, we know that much of what fueled the bull run of the 1920s was not just the confidence of the people but also the sheer manipulation of stocks. For example, there was an investment pool led by a broker named Michael Meehan that, with the help of "bought" journalists, ultimately drove the share price of RCA Radio from $2.50 to $500. The way it worked if you were a pool operator was, first you'd call your friend at the *New York Times* or *Wall Street Journal* and say, "Look, Charlie, there's an envelope

2. *New York Times,* "Stock Prices Slump $14,000,000,000 in Nation-Wide Stampede to Unload; Bankers to Support Market Today," October 29, 1929, A1.

waiting for you here and we think that perhaps you should write something nice about RCA." Thereupon, Charlie would write something nice about RCA.

After the crash, interestingly enough, a 1920s publicity man named A. Newton Plummer was discovered to have canceled checks from practically every major journalist in New York City.

To be sure, what we would consider unethical behavior today was largely condoned during the 1920s, but as long as the bull market continued, it attracted growing numbers of small investors. In turn, the rising tide of money on the markets lifted many middle-class Americans into wealth; and as it did the notion of investing and speculating in the markets became, for a brief period, akin to the national pastime.

The subsequent misery that the crash of 1929 cast across the country was as profound as it was stunning—and for Pop, the effect was a deeply personal one. Many of his friends on the Curb, who had bought into the thesis that the prosperity of the 1920s was a skyward-bound elevator with no top floor, were wiped out. Faced with ruin, many of his colleagues would approach Pop on the street, hat in hand, and tell him: "I need money to feed my family. I'm broke."

When asked, Pop almost always lent money to friends who were down on their luck. In fact, it wouldn't surprise me if the sum he doled out ran into the millions. The problem was: many of his friends would take that money, immediately head back into the market, and get wiped out once again. It got to the point that many of Pop's friends who couldn't repay their debts were too embarrassed to face him, so they avoided him indefinitely—and thus ended many a friendship. Adding to the heartbreak, Pop knew men who grew so despondent over what had become of their lives that they ended it all— jumping out of windows to commit suicide.

Many years later, Pop said he wished he had given the money to the wives and insisted it be used for household expenses. The wives, he reasoned, would not have been so addicted to the action, so blind to the dangers of the new market cycle. "Don't ever lend anybody money," he told me as he reflected on that painful time. "If they need help, just give it to them—don't expect it back."

Of course, not everyone who played the market in October 1929 suffered such dire consequences. Stock trader extraordinaire Jesse Livermore correctly forecasted the coming crisis, "shorted" the market, and reportedly made over $100 million during that period. Another well-known speculator of the day and friend of Pop's, Joe Kennedy, sold all his stocks before the crash because he allegedly overheard shoeshine boys and other novices speculating on stocks. Kennedy was smart enough to recognize that the price of common stocks in

1929 — like the so-called "dot-com" stocks that cratered in 1999 and 2000 — were not tied in any meaningful way to market fundamentals, but to the naïvety of the broader investing public.

For his part, Pop started to sense something was out of whack in July of 1929 when the price of a Curb Exchange seat soared $40,000 over five days to reach $235,000. The total value of the 550 Curb seats at this new price level placed the value of the Curb at $129,250,000 — or quadruple its value from just sixteen months before in January 1928. Again, it was sheer folly.

Thanks to these and other indicators, Pop foresaw the Crash; and like Livermore, he would short the market that autumn, betting that it would go down. One of his short positions was U.S. Steel, then one of the blue chip issues on the NYSE. On that infamous Monday, October 28, U.S. Steel — which had reached a high of $260 a share earlier in 1929 — lost 17½ points in a single session as the stock pounded down through the $200 level en route to the record low of $21.25 it eventually hit in 1932.

Another one of Pop's famous short positions — or infamous, depending on your perspective — involved Locomobile, a company that made some beautiful high-end cars in the 1920s designed to complete with Cadillac, Packard, and Lincoln. William Durant, the aforementioned founder of General Motors, acquired the company during the 1920s after GM deposed him from their board, and Durant brought in one of his right-hand men, Jack Bergen, to help advise the company.

Durant was a towering business figure, to be sure, but Bergen was also a force with which to be reckoned. He served in the navy during both World War I and World War II; and in between, he founded his own investment banking firm that, most notably, underwrote public offerings for Bank of America and the Grumman Aircraft Corporation. Bergen went on to run the highly profitable Graham-Paige private equity firm and the Hotel Corporation of America chain.

Many years later, my nephew Clint Smullyan was visiting with Bergen — who attained the rank of Rear Admiral following his dedicated service in World War II — and the late Sylvan Coleman, who was then the chairman and CEO of E. F. Hutton, when the subject of Locomobile came up at the lunch table. "Admiral Bergen, whatever happened to Locomobile?" Clint innocently inquired. "They made some beautiful cars."

Bergen, who didn't know Clint from Adam, replied: "We did make beautiful cars, but the crash came, followed by the Depression — and that was hard for everyone."

"We had an additional problem," he continued. "That sonofabitch Mosbacher sold our stock from $80 all the way down to zero."

That night, Clint relayed the day's conversation to Pop. Told that Jack Bergen had identified him as one of the leading architect's of Locomobile's demise, Pop said, "Damn! I didn't know *he* knew it was me!"

Pop once told me, "The very first money I made, I got two thousand dollars and put it into the bank. For a kid at that time, that was a lot of money, and I told your mother 'I just made two thousand bucks.' You know what she did? She went out and spent it all on shoes."

"That's why I keep working so hard," he concluded facetiously.

Now, the part about my mother spending $2,000 on shoes is probably a myth, but the part about my father working hard is definitely not. He did work hard—very hard. From the start of his career as a trader, he researched stocks at a time when there was no such thing on Wall Street. He dug through files, and reviewed the company filings before the SEC required them. He would talk to anyone familiar with the company's operations.

In short, Pop was the antithesis to the Thomas Edison phrase that "most people don't recognize opportunity when they see it because it usually comes dressed in overalls and looks a lot like work." At a time when information was even closer to money than it is today, Pop worked every resource at his disposal.

Incidentally, though not surprising, Pop was also something of a gambler—and he employed the same strategies when playing craps or at the horse track as he did at his "day job" on the Curb. He worked all the angles. At the racetrack, for example, he would talk to the jockeys, the stable hands, and other hangers-on. He did everything but talk to the horses. So by the time he did place a bet, he felt the odds were in his favor.

Later, when pari-mutuel betting was introduced in New York, and the state started taking 20 percent off the top of every race, Pop cut back on "playing the ponies" because he knew the odds were tougher. The point is: he wasn't gambling just because he loved horses. He was also gambling because, with greater information, he understood how to improve the odds of winning.

On the Exchange, Pop was a trader—not an investor—and the difference to him was very important. He would frequently hold stocks for a very short time to take a slim margin of profit. The Louisiana Land and Exploration (LLE) was one energy company he owned an enormous percentage of during the late 1920s. Pop would gamble big like that when his research or other sources of credible information led him to believe beyond a reasonable doubt that a stock would go up or down during a given time period. During the time he owned LLE, for example, it was benefiting from an extraordinarily generous contract with the Texas Co. (later Texaco), whereby LLE was receiving a remarkably high 25 percent royalty from Texaco while it drilled on LLE property for oil and gas.

Later, when Texaco went to renegotiate the contract to less favorable terms, Pop sold out of whatever he had left in the stock.

In the immediate aftermath of the 1929 crash, the Curb Exchange leaders—believing that the drastic, severe sell-off was nevertheless a temporary setback—tried to put the best possible face on matters and supported President Hoover's vain attempts to boost investor confidence. Some of Pop's fellow brokers had even taken to wearing buttons that read "For Better Business Be Bullish" and "Prepare for Prosperity."

Pop, meanwhile, had started preparing for prosperity a few years before the crash.

An interesting discovery was made as Pop's long-time assistant Liz Carbone reviewed some of Pop's real estate records many years later—records that included the history of each building my father owned, when it was purchased, and what the sale price was. As Liz went along, she noticed that Pop had started to take the money he had made in the market and buy so-called "taxpayer" properties, particularly in 1927, 1928, and 1929.

A "taxpayer" property is a city block where you theoretically put up a one-story building to pay the taxes until you generate enough income to build skyscrapers—or at least a much larger building. In the *New York Times*, there's still a Sunday column called "*Taxpayers*," and this concept of buying taxpayers made great sense to Pop as a surefire way to generate income.

Essentially, his real estate strategy was to follow the subway lines as they were built heading north into the Bronx. Every so often, the transit authorities would publish the figures of how many people used each subway stop, and these public figures helped Pop determine which subway corners he wanted to be on—or at least be close to. As it is today, location mattered above all else. Some properties back then would fetch two to eight dollars a square foot.

The rent for some of these same properties today can go as high as thirty-five dollars a square foot or more.

As Pop started to accumulate these taxpayers, he frequently counseled my cousin Stan Stern, "Own half as many buildings, but own them. No mortgages." Because he always paid cash, Pop was debt-free, with minimal exposure to the vagaries of economic cycles. He had seen enough people face a "margin call" at the Curb, and he clearly learned from that difficult experience. When tough times come, and tenants cannot afford to pay their rent, it helps to be debt-free. As it was, driving around the Bronx during the Depression, you could see rows of boarded-up buildings.

Pop bought these taxpayers all the way up into Westchester County; and today those properties are still good. They're still paying.

Some insight into Pop's real estate dealings and holdings came from a Tucson man named Roy Drachman, with whom Pop played golf during a visit there in 1941. Drachman remembered Pop this way:

> Emil was from New York City, was affable and played to a low handicap. We played nearly every day for a week and enjoyed each other's company. One day he told me he owned some property in Tucson and asked me to drive him by it so he could see it. I was surprised, and asked him when he bought it and where it was. He told me he had acquired it a few weeks before and he hadn't known where it was until he received the information in a telegram he had asked his office to send him. He explained that he had bought two Safeway stores in Tucson along with 123 other stores leased to that company for a little over five million dollars. He bought them as tax shelters, and for the security of the Safeway leases. We drove by the two buildings that he didn't even bother to go into. Until then I had no idea that Emil had that kind of money. He never spoke much about business activities.[3]

It was just like Pop to be so low-key, but another reason I put so much veracity in this account of my father is because it showed him practicing what he preached when he spoke of "safety of principal." He had incurred certain risks to make money on the Curb, but he also had the forethought to remove that capital from that arena of risk and volatility into a safer investment vehicle that would preserve and grow it.

This anecdote, to me, captures the essence of Pop—always thinking one, two, three steps ahead, always focused on "security" or survival, never forgetting where he came from or that day at the fruit stand when that family income was taken from him.

Safety of principal was a mantra, a creed, and one of his greatest lessons for the rest of us.

---

3. From *This is Not a Book: Just Memories*. Available from: http://parentseyes.arizona.edu/drachman/1201.html.

Chapter 4   GUYS AND DOLLS

Growing up, our family lived in what can only be described as a fantastic house in White Plains, New York—some twenty-five miles north from Wall Street, as the crow flies. A white Georgian mansion, it sat on a wooded, rolling, forty-three-acre plot that was divided by a babbling brook. Generally speaking, the grounds were the picture of bucolic serenity; but the furniture inside was very formal, and the atmosphere during family meals—even when guests were not present—was one of high expectations.

With his PhD in street smarts—having graduated magna cum laude from the school of hard knocks—Pop could always tell when he was being conned, but his B.S. meter always seemed particularly attuned when we were gathered around the dinner table. There, we would talk about our day, our schoolwork, sailing, whatever.

In accounting for our time spent on this earth for that day, however, it was imperative that we never engage in hyperbole, or even modest exaggeration. Pop would frequently probe our sources of information and our recounting of events for inconsistencies, and God help us if we were ever found to be passing him inaccurate or unfounded reports.

"Never say anything unless you are sure you can back it up," he often urged us.

When they first bought the house, it was much smaller than the thirty rooms it would eventually include. Perhaps most prominently, my parents added a big room for entertaining large groups called "the sun parlor." The room was thirty-five feet long with ten-foot ceilings, and was adorned with smoked glass tables, terrazzo floors, marquetry walls, and a crystal chandelier my mother bought shortly after they moved in. It was true art deco. The living room and wide entrance hall, meanwhile, were lined with walnut paneling, and inside there was an old stone fireplace.

It was in this civilized atmosphere that my parents threw a number of incredible parties, which earned them some renown. The irony here is that, though Pop routinely hosted these bacchanalian affairs, he never drank alcohol—for the simple reason that Pop felt booze interfered with his survival instinct. So the

Dinner at the Stork Club with my parents and sister, Barbara, in the 1940s. It was the heyday of New York City's Café Society.

morning after these parties, Pop would wake up clear-eyed and clear-headed and promptly head out for the office in New York.

"I have to work, you know," he'd say as he was stepping over the bodies passed out on the floor.

People who knew Pop would challenge my assertion that he didn't drink. "I went out for drinks dozens of times with your father," one of friends challenged me. "Of course he drank." What they didn't know was that Pop always ordered the same drink as they did, and when their drink got low he subtly switched glasses with them.

It was, no question, a maneuver he employed on countless occasions at perhaps his favorite place in New York—the restaurant 21, which was one of the most celebrated of the "speakeasies" to sprout up in New York after the onset of Prohibition.

In 1930, Jack Kriendler and Charlie Burns opened 21 at its current location on 52nd Street, and on that site their empire—in that day based on the finest black market booze—thrived. It was also during this time that the other playgrounds of New York's Café Society came into existence: Sherm Billingsley's Stork Club on 53rd Street, Joe Perona's El Morocco on 54th, and Gene Cavallero's Colony. Of these, only 21 still exists today.

The friendly Jack Kriendler, who minded the front of the house at 21, could also be a haughty fellow, and his elegant manners earned him the nickname of "the Baron." One 21 chronicler many years ago noted that, "To address Jack by his first name was a privilege; for him to address you by your first name became a definite mark of distinction." Pop was one patron to gain such distinction.

Just as the 18th Amendment led to the rise of 21 and other clubs, the passage of the 21st Amendment in 1933 also proved lucrative to Jack and Charlie, as they moved aggressively, and successfully, into the marketing and selling of fine goods from liquor to cigars. Because Pop was very friendly with both Jack and Charlie, in 1936 he helped the two get this new subsidiary, 21 Brands, listed on the Curb Exchange as a public company. It was not the first time he had helped the 21 with Curb-related matters, however. Years before that, Pop helped Jack's brother, Pete Kriendler, buy a seat on the Curb Exchange—which Pete sold in 1929 for $250,000, or roughly ten times the price he originally paid.

Ever since this close family friendship was struck, Mosbachers of every stripe and age have been fortunate to be classified as "friends of the house" at 21. In fact, in March of 2007, I celebrated my eightieth birthday there.

Not everyone was always so welcome inside 21, however. Jack ultimately decided who got in the club, and who didn't, and for this reason, one of the prized possessions for any man in that day was one of Jack's yellow business cards. If he wrote "OK" on the back, that meant you were one of the chosen ones who could enter at any time. However, if Jack wrote "OK" and then added "34," it did *not* denote a table number. Rather, it was Jack's discreet way of indicating the individual bearing that card was not to be admitted at all.

After they opened on 52nd Street, Jack and Charlie also determined that the privacy of their patrons was of paramount importance, so they let it be known that gossip columnists were not permitted to pass the iron gates that guarded the entrance. Most notably, the decree had the effect of barring the famed *Daily Mirror* gossip columnist, Walter Winchell, whose almighty pen back in that day was known to make and break careers—and lives.

Shortly after he was banned, Winchell ran a retaliatory column titled "A Place Never Raided, Jack and Charlie's at 21 West Fifty-Second Street," calling attention to the fact that the club had never been raided by Prohibition agents. The next day, as if on cue, federal agents stormed the restaurant and conducted a 12-hour inspection—seizing a large stockpile of illegal booze and arresting every member of the staff. (They were later pardoned.)

The raid, the first of only two raids visited upon 21 during Prohibition, prompted Jack and Charlie to install an ingenious system of pulleys and levers that would sweep bottles from the bar shelves and hurl the smashed remains down a chute into the New York sewer system. It was also during this period that 21's famous wine cellar was built behind a two-ton door that was unlocked by placing a meat skewer into a tiny hole in a certain brick. During Prohibition, Jimmy Walker, mayor of New York, had a private booth in a corner of the cellar, where he could often be found with his mistress, showgirl Betty Compton.

Pop's other favorite hangout, the antithesis of 21, was a place called Schraaft, owned by the Frank Shattuck family. One of the main attractions for Pop was the terrific ice cream they served. Pop loved ice cream—but only vanilla. Whenever he ordered a Baked Alaska at 21, for example, my siblings and I always hoped he would forget to order vanilla and that once, just once, we could try chocolate, or coffee, or strawberry.

Another draw to Schraaft's for Pop was the attractive Irish girls they hired. Pop loved women, and loved to sit at the counter at Schraaft's and to watch the girls everywhere in the room. "Spin those eyes," he would always say. "Use the mirrors." He never missed anything. Even many years later, Pop could identify a woman a city block away just by seeing her ankles.

To be sure, there was a certain "Guys and Dolls" aura that enveloped New York during the 1920s and 1930s, a time when gangsters and con men tended to be viewed more sympathetically—and even romanticized in print by writers like Damon Runyon and on TV shows like *New York Confidential*. It was a time and place in which these characters were known *not* by their given names, but by colorful monikers of every kind—"Spanish John," "Big Jule," "One-Eyed Eddy," and so on. Of course, more than a few purposefully carried several nicknames as a dodge to help them keep ahead of creditors, but the point is, everyone was a character. Everyone was on the make. And everyone had style—not necessarily great style, just style.

Style was very important.

What's more, everyone in that era seemed to speak what Walter Winchell called "slanguage"—a fast-paced, brash way of talking that became the vernacular used by journalists, bootleggers, gamblers, and showbiz types alike. It was a world of "dames and broads," one that particularly inspired dozens of bawdy Runyan stories.

If you say "Broadway Joe" today, most people would think of Joe Namath, not of a whole class of people. In his heyday, though, Pop knew a bunch of

Broadway Joes—a very sporty crowd. They made money, and spent it. They were very generous, and had a good time.

It was also a crowd that transcended, or maybe in some ways defied, the prevailing social strata of the time. It ranged from the top of the business and social scales, through the chorus dolls and singers, down to the gangsters, bootleggers, and rum-runners.

Pop's world also included a substantial amount of gambling. He was great at backgammon and bridge, but preferred games of chance. He had a particular fondness for horse racing. Whenever we went to Palm Beach, moreover, he frequently went with Mom and friends to Bradley's Beach Club Casino, founded in 1898 by the famed gamer and horseman E. R. Bradley.

One day Pop came home from Bradley's and confessed he had lost $25,000, and the only reason he had gambled that afternoon was because he was bored. "Never do that, son," he said to me, as if that was a lesson he needed to reinforce.

Pop loved gambling so much, in fact, that when my brother Bus became engaged to his wife Pat, my father brought his bookie to the celebratory dinner. It sounds amusing today, but my mother was not pleased at the time. In due course, Pop gave up gambling at Bradley's and most other forms of gaming. When he later caught Bus playing backgammon for what he thought was an outrageous sum of money, Pop read him the riot act—even though the total, which was maybe $1,000, was far less than he was known to wager.

Of course, Pop always paid whatever gambling debts he incurred immediately, so he never had to worry about mobsters or their henchmen paying an unwanted visit, but in the early 1930s a certain jarring event made him acutely aware of his personal security and that of his family.

On March 2, 1932, America awoke to the news that Charles Augustus Lindbergh Jr., the twenty-month-old son of the famous aviator and Anne Morrow Lindbergh, had been kidnapped the night before. The story caused a national furor; and the subsequent investigation led to the arrest and indictment of Bruno Richard Hauptmann, a thirty-five-year-old convict from Saxony, Germany. Hauptmann was ultimately executed in 1936, but not before the impact of his crime was felt far and wide.

After the Lindberg kidnapping, in fact, people in White Plains and other affluent suburban communities in the northeast became very nervous. My sister Barbara recalls how we had a lot of fireflies at night up in the country, and people were so on edge during that time that many thought the bugs were the flashlights of other would-be kidnappers.

Like a lot of other wealthy people, Pop took a number of security precautions. Our house in White Plains sat on forty-three wooded acres, with the nearest neighbor half a mile away. So Pop hired a night watchman, put a siren on top of the house that could be heard in White Plains three miles away, and had panic buttons installed in every room. Every time we had a new maid in the house, they would unfailingly mistake the panic buttons for the light switch and set off the alarm, which certainly didn't help everyone's nerves at the time!

The most memorable security measure Pop took was to buy a shotgun—but not your typical shotgun. This particular model was specially designed by the Ithaca Gun Company to be a sawed-off shotgun—with a shortened stock and barrel. It was a scary looking weapon, but it was also artfully inscribed on one side with "Burglar and Auto Gun" and a hunting dog engraved on the other.

Pop was great friends with the Gimbel family, who ran the largest department store corporation in the world, and Bernard Gimbel had a great house called "Chieftains" in Greenwich. Pop insisted Bernard have one of these Ithaca sawed-off shotguns, too. One night, however, Bernard heard a noise and in his panicked state grabbed the gun and shot a hole in the carpet. A few days later, the shotgun arrived back at our home, having been hastily packaged for return by Mrs. Gimbel.

Perhaps the most infamous incident involving "the gun" came courtesy of my nephew Clint. My mother was hosting one of her formal tea parties in our backyard one day, out under the huge chestnut tree where she had a deck so people could sit and visit. Mother was with her guests dressed in their finery when little four-year-old Clint walked toward the group waving the exotic Ithaca gun around. Of course, he innocently thought it was just a fun toy; but the sight of this four-year-old waving around a sawed-off shotgun sent all of mother's guests diving under tables.

Clint still has the gun, though he maintains he has not brandished it at any tea parties recently.

A few months after the Lindbergh kidnapping, when the furor died down and people started to relax a little, Pop joined a group of friends, including Bernard's brother Adam Gimbel and publisher Bennet Cerf, for a brief trip to Cuba. At that time, Havana was known as a playground for successful executives who needed a break from the rat race of business—and tagging along on this stag junket was another highly accomplished workaholic in search of some rest and relaxation, composer George Gershwin. By 1932, Gershwin had long since burst onto the American music scene and established himself as one of the most popular and prolifically productive artists. By the time they winged off to Havana together, Pop and Gershwin had already developed a very close personal friendship. In fact, Pop later recalled how Gershwin and Cerf were chasing after the same girl, and that Gershwin sank into despondency after the object of his affections stood him up for a lunch date.

The contingent took up residence at the Almedares Hotel in Havana, spent their days golfing or at the racetrack, and whiled away their evenings listening to the pulsating rhythms of the local music at the nightclubs that lined the Paseo del Prado. If they were in search of rest, however, their quest was disrupted that first night when a sixteen-piece rumba band caught wind of the famous American composer's presence and started "serenading" the group at 4:00 A.M. Pop recalled that, as groggy as they were, Gershwin was captivated by the special performance.

That episode, and indeed the entire trip, inspired Gershwin to start composing his own rhumba immediately, which soon became his *Cuban Overture*. The very next month, in fact, Gershwin came to our home in White Plains to finish the orchestration for *Overture*—working out of the small, gray fieldstone teahouse my parents had on the property.

The teahouse was far enough away from the main house that it was quite private. It had one medium large room with a great fieldstone fireplace and a remarkable, for those days, large curved picture window overlooking the brook. It was such a beautiful and tranquil setting that it may have even helped inspire a great composer.

A frequent weekend visitor, Gershwin could routinely be found sitting in our teahouse for hours before a baby grand piano, working on material for such classics as *Rhapsody in Blue*, or *An American in Paris*, and perhaps most notably *Porgy and Bess*. Gershwin's cousin, artist Henry Botkin, also lived in the teahouse for a time and painted several beautiful works while staying with us. Henry even gave my parents several pieces of his work, one or two of which now adorn the walls of one of my ex-wives' apartments.

As kids, my brother, sister, and I had no compunction about meandering down to the secluded teahouse and climbing onto the piano stool next to the composer as he noodled with a melody. Though I was very young at the time, I recall that he never seemed displeased by our company, and usually welcomed the break from his mentally engrossing work. My sister Barbara also remembers that when she was ten years old, Gershwin would teasingly chase her around the house proposing marriage to her.

In due course, Gershwin became such a fixture at our homes in both White Plains and Palm Beach that he ended up composing many other songs while staying with us—including "Summertime," the first song he wrote for *Porgy and Bess*. I still have a copy of the music score that Gershwin dedicated to my mother.

My parents eventually became so intertwined in Gershwin's life that our mother later confided how she was mad that the composer and his on-again off-again love interest Kay Swift, who frequently visited our home, never married. Kay's relationship with Gershwin had clearly led to the breakup of her marriage to Paul Warburg, and it would be a source of regret for both Gershwin and Swift that they never tied the knot. Near the end of his all-too-short life, the composer said he had made a "terrible mistake" in leaving Kay and going to Hollywood. For her part, Kay speculated that, had he lived, the two would have likely been married—and just as likely to divorce.

In early 1935, while the composer was completing the score for *Porgy and Bess*, Pop and Gershwin frequently traveled to Palm Beach together. The train trip from New York to southern Florida took longer than twenty-four hours back in that day, and while working on *Porgy*, Gershwin would occasionally stop midway through the trip in Charleston, South Carolina to consult with DuBose Heyward—the Charlestonian businessman who was working with Gershwin to bring his groundbreaking novel, *Porgy*, to the stage as a folk opera.

As a Charleston native, Heyward was intimately familiar with the under-privileged world from which he first created the storyline for *Porgy*, and was, by then, also a widely acclaimed writer known for the penetrating light he shed into the lives of the African Americans of that time and place.

During this particular detour, Heyward led Gershwin and a reluctant Pop to one smoke-filled, dimly lit bar after another to listen to southern roots music. Gershwin was determined to absorb the local rhythms and master their musical structure. After three or four days, however, Pop—never the most patient of people—finally left Gershwin and Heyward to their own devices and continued on to Florida by himself.

Many years later, my kids would experience this impatience for themselves. Whenever they were in New York, Pop would routinely meet them for dinner and take them to a show; but he would frequently leave dinner early—after paying the bill—and he never, that I know of, sat through an entire musical. After the first or second act, he would say, "Okay, let's go. We get the gist of it." My daughter Dee likes to joke that, thanks to her grandfather, she saw two-thirds of every great musical.

When Gershwin finally caught up with Pop in Florida, he privately fretted to my father over the finances for *Porgy*. The original budget had been $40,000, but Gershwin feared the actual cost could come in at as high as $100,000 — and that the Theatre Guild would balk. Pop counseled him: "George, handle it my way. Go to the telephone and tell the Theatre Guild that I, Emil Mosbacher, will put up half the money for the show. George, I'll bet you $100 I won't get any part of it, because as soon as they hear I am ready to come in on that scale, they'll go ahead with the show and do anything to keep me out."

In the end, Gershwin offered to put up 25 percent of the original $40,000 budget—including $4,000 from my father. Though the budget ended up running to $75,000, the Guild refused to entertain any funding formulas that included outside money . . . just as Pop predicted.

Looking back, you could say Pop and Gershwin were not an unlikely pair of friends. Both were sons of immigrants, who had experienced the hard life of the ghetto. Both entered the working world at a very early age, and by the dint of their work ethic enjoyed success early on. By the time he was twenty, in fact, Gershwin had penned "Swanee" for Al Jolson, another Jewish immigrant from Europe, which went on to be a huge hit.

And like Pop, Gershwin also considered his lack of formal education a shortcoming.

Nevertheless, both men were at the leading edge of the institutions to which they belonged—American popular music and the Curb Exchange—as they experienced historic transformations. Pop was there as the Curb moved indoors and continued to build its reputation as an international market; and Gershwin helped set the tempo as ragtime gave way to the age of jazz. Both men were also compulsively competitive, and would leave their mark on the world.

Still, for all Gershwin's success, he was known to be an unhappy soul—so much so that he consulted a psychologist named Gregory Zilboorg to help tame his inner demons. It was widely believed that Gershwin sought to monopolize the piano at parties because he was so shy and uneasy with small talk, and it was the only way he could draw attention to himself. But Pop recalled how the two were walking through Central Park one time, and Gershwin told him, "I was at this party last night, and they had me play the piano 'til late in the evening. I wish I didn't feel like I had to do that."

"But you're so great at it," Pop reassured him, "and besides, it's a great way to get the dames. I wish I had a talent like that. You have everything in the world going for you. You're incredibly talented, you're famous, you're rich—you can have any girl you want."

Gershwin dejectedly replied, "Emil, you're a businessman. I don't expect you to understand."

On July 10, 1937, renowned brain surgeon Walter Dandy of Baltimore was relaxing out on the Chesapeake Bay aboard Maryland Governor Harry Nice's yacht with the governor and his friends, when the doctor received an urgent message that the White House was trying to find him. A continent away, he was told, George Gershwin lay dying in Cedars of Lebanon Hospital in Los Angeles. The cause was a brain tumor, and Dandy was deemed Gershwin's best chance—his only chance, perhaps—for survival. Minutes later, a Coast Guard cutter came astride the yacht, collected the surgeon, and delivered him to the police escort waiting onshore. Dandy was then sped to a nearby airport, where a chartered plane was waiting to take him on the next leg of his westward journey.

The furious chain of events had been set in motion earlier that day, when Leonore Gershwin, Ira's wife, called Pop and another close Gershwin friend, George Pallay, and urged them to find a neurosurgeon to save her brother-in-law. They first tried to recruit a famous Bostonian, Dr. Harvey Cushing, but the aging Cushing had recently retired from operative surgery. Cushing recommended Dandy as the new top dog in that highly specialized field, so Pallay immediately placed a call to Baltimore.

When the duo learned that Dandy was away from his office and out on the Chesapeake Bay, Pop called Marvin W. McIntyre, one of FDR's key White House aides, and explained the life and death gravity of the situation. Pop had met McIntyre during the latter's stint in the motion picture industry, and was able to call in an admittedly unusual favor of having the Coast Guard intervene.

After contacting McIntyre, Pop also made arrangements for Dandy's police escort and the chartered flight.

The doctors at Cedars, meanwhile, had located another well-known surgeon named Howard Naffziger, who determined that Gershwin's condition required immediate action. Dandy, still on the east coast, was consulted by phone, agreed with the diagnosis, and Naffziger operated early the next morning, removing a large cyst from the front lobe of the composer's brain. In recovery, Gershwin's condition quickly deteriorated—spiking a high fever of 106 degrees and a dangerous pulse rate of over 180 beats a minute.

Gershwin died five hours after the surgery, at 10:35 A.M. on July 11.

George Gershwin's death, of course, was national news and a tragic loss for the musical world. His seminal works had helped to ignite, then define, then transcend the golden age of jazz—that uniquely American art form. But his passing also left a very painful and personal void for my family. He was one of Pop's best friends.

In addition to the Gershwins, Pop befriended many other showbiz executives and leading artists of the day. He always thrived being around talented people, and like anyone else enjoyed their celebrity status. It was a two-way street, however, as these same producers and artists were routinely looking for sponsors to help fund their next project.

Aside from this symbiotic relationship, like Pop many of these entertainers came from families of immigrants who also possessed a Jewish heritage—and this shared experience, this familiar background, maybe helped them gravitate together socially.

One such performer that Pop befriended was the incomparable Al Jolson. Jolson had actually been born Asa Yoelson in Lithuania in 1886. He came to the United States in 1894, and in 1911 launched a prolific career on Broadway lasting four decades, during which he was dubbed "the world's greatest entertainer."

On Sunday nights, which was the night Broadway was "dark" back then, Jolson would have a one-man show in one of the theaters, and a lot of his fellow performers along with Pop would show up to watch him—he was that good. So good, in fact, that Pop often stayed for the entire show!

Ethel Merman was another close family friend. She taught my cousin Stan to drive, and gave singing advice to my talented daughter, Kathi. One time, Ethel was traveling with my mother to Florida, when they stopped to see my sister at her boarding school in Maryland. Barbara had a terrible cold at the time, so my mother and Ethel decided on the spot to take her to Florida.

When they went to inform the head of Barbara's school of their plan, Ethel was wearing a tunic with a fox fur around the bottom. The school headmaster, meanwhile, was quite a sight herself—looking like Queen Mary, as Barbara recalls. "What do you do, my dear?" asked the headmistress.

Ethel Merman, a mega-star of stage and screen, simply said, "I sing."

Pop always maintained that California had the best year-round climate, so for a number of years running he would go out to the Beverly Hills Hotel every winter and take a cottage so he could see other showbiz friends like Jimmy Durante, and play golf with Bob Hope and Bing Crosby. Occasionally, we would accompany him and tour the Hollywood studios, meeting stars like Carol Lombard, Clark Gable, and other icons of the age.

Every once in a while, a Hollywood studio executive would pull my parents aside and suggest that maybe I should be in the movies—an idea Pop always and immediately snuffed out. As far as he was concerned, no son of his was going to be involved in such chicanery, and the conversations we had about my stillborn acting career were always the same: "I guess you should feel good that

A studio test shot for my stillborn acting career. This was as far as my Hollywood aspirations would get.

they asked," Pop would tell me, "but the idea that you could act in the movies is ridiculous."

In hindsight, I think Pop saw enough of Hollywood life to spare me the vagaries that went with it, but a part of me still wonders what might have been had that door been opened, however briefly—instead of summarily shut tight.

Chapter 5 "PAINT IT BLUE AND SELL IT
TO MOSBACHER"

Since the turn of the twentieth century, well-heeled Americans from every part of the country have migrated to the crown jewel of the "American Riviera," otherwise known as Palm Beach, Florida. It sprang to life in 1894 thanks to the vision and vast investment of Henry Flagler, the once-failed businessman who helped John D. Rockefeller launch Standard Oil a quarter century before. Flagler had become convinced of Florida's ability to attract out-of-state visitors during an 1878 visit to Jacksonville with his ailing wife, Mary, and soon began acquiring properties and rail systems to build a tourist-driven empire. In due course, he started carving Palm Beach out of the Florida mangroves, first building the Royal Poinciana Hotel that opened in 1894. The Breakers hotel quickly followed the Poinciana two years later—and instantly earned its enduring reputation as one of the finest resorts in the world.

With his first two resort properties opened for business, Flagler would continue working with Colonel Edward Riley Bradley and eventually the iconic architect Jim Addison Mizner to enhance both Palm Beach's cultural and architectural identity as we know it today. It is a unique corner of the world, to say the least.

Like Flagler's first wife, Mizner was driven to Palm Beach by hard luck and poor health. A struggling architect for much of his career, it was thanks to friend and sponsor, Paris Singer—the heir to the Singer sewing machine fortune—that Mizner was given a platform to build some of the most palatial, and fanciful, winter mansions ever built in the United States.

The architect started with the Everglades Club in 1918, and over the next fifteen years his portfolio included Villa Flora (built in 1921) for a banker at J. P. Morgan; La Guerida (or "bounty of war"), built in 1923 for the Wanamakers (Philadelphia department store heir); and Mizner's own home, El Solano, finished in 1925. La Guerida, incidentally, was reportedly purchased by Joe Kennedy for a paltry $120,000 in 1933, and would become John F. Kennedy's "Winter White House."

By the time Mom and Pop started going to Palm Beach in the 1920s, the red

Mediterranean tile roofs of Mizner's legendary creations already dominated the local landscape.

Like most everyone else, when my parents did go to Palm Beach for the season, they would rent a place to stay—and through the years, they stayed in a number of very fine homes. In 1928 and 1929, for example, they stayed in the Clarke Avenue villa belonging to Thomas A. Clarke, owner of the New Palm Beach Hotel. In the 1930s, they also stayed at a home called Earlham; and in the early 1940s, Pop and Mom took a home on Sea Breeze Road.

But it is the home located at 920 South Ocean Boulevard, dubbed the "Ham and Cheese House" for its unique coquina and brick exterior, that stands out in my memory today. The two-story Italian Romanesque house called "Casa Eleda" (named after Schiff's wife Adele spelled backward) was a Maurice Fatio design built in 1927 for renowned financier and philanthropist Mortimer L. Schiff. I loved the house because it included a 165-foot beach parcel accessed by a tunnel leading from the house under State Road A1A to the property's own private beach. The house also had a retractable ladder leading down to the public beach on either side, which provided hours of amusement for a young boy like me at the time.

Mom and Pop spent very happy winters there in the mid-1930s, entertaining a string of guests and visitors—from George Gershwin to business friends like George Bruce, the president of Aladdin Oil Company in Wichita, Kansas. In December of 1933, I recall, Pop dressed up as Santa Claus for a play put on by the pupils at the Palm Beach Private School. A few days later, my parents hosted a treasure hunt and supper for all our friends, then took everyone to the movies.

Palm Beach held other amusements for young and older alike.

On January 12, 1934, Mom and Pop flew down to attend the fifth annual All-American Air Races in Miami with friends Ned Grubbs, Howard A. Sykes, George J. Atwell Jr., Edward Block, and Charles Bromfield. It was one of five international races in the world that year; and of special note that day was the presence of Amelia Earhart and a death-defying incident after a half-dozen Marine planes came screaming down in a nosedive toward the airfield. Each of the planes pulled out of their dives except one piloted by Lieutenant Glenn M. Britt, which continued to shoot earthward at 300 m.p.h. About 250 feet above the ground, Britt jumped clear, and pulled his ripcord. His parachute barely billowed open before he struck the ground, just after his plane crashed in front of the grandstand. Lt. Britt picked himself up, hurried to a microphone, and greeted the crowd: "Hello, everybody! I'm not hurt, thank you."

I have a faint memory of my first plane trip in the late 1930s, a round-trip jaunt from Palm Beach to Miami with Pop on a passenger bi-plane built by the Waco Company out of Ohio. I felt like a kid on Christmas morning when I learned I was going, and remember what was, in hindsight, a mildly harrowing flight the way the primitive commercial plane bobbed up and down in the coastal breezes.

South Florida was a terrific place for young boys who liked the outdoors, and I often had the great fortune of being in the company of a great hunting and fishing guide named Bert Pruitt. Bert was such a popular guide, in fact, that in that day and age he could get away with murder—quite literally.

One day in the late 1930s, Bert found his wife in bed with another man and, in a rage of passion, shot the unlucky gent. Bert was sent to jail; but in what can only be described as an unusual arrangement, state officials let Bert out of jail every winter so he could tend to his steady roster of hunting and fishing clients.

Before and after his run-in with the law, however, Bert routinely took me out to the Everglades. One day, we went out into the brush with a guy named Sackett, who was from a very wealthy family in Philadelphia, and worked at the museum there. We were gathering specimens of snakes to send back to the Philadelphia zoo—collecting them in burlap gunnysacks, and then putting them in the back of Bert's old wooden station wagon.

Though he was a big guy, Bert didn't really like snakes much—as I soon discovered. During the ride home, we were driving along at a fair speed when all of a sudden Bert jams on the brakes, rolls out of the car, and shouts, "One of them got me! Grab 'em!" By the time I saw him, he was rolling in the grass, while the car was still moving.

Then Bert threw up.

Judging by his melodramatic reaction, Bert was convinced he was dying. He was sure he'd been bitten by one of the snakes, but it turned out that a hornet had gotten in the car and stung him on the back of the leg.

After we reassured Bert he was not at death's door, he drove us home. The day's drama was not over, though. When we pulled up in front of our house, Pop came to the door and I said, "Oh Pop, see what I got in here." When he moved a little closer, I reached into the glove compartment and pulled out a totally harmless 18-inch baby snake. "Isn't it cute?" I asked.

I thought it was pretty funny, but Pop was less than amused. Like 99 percent of people, he detested snakes. "Get that damn thing away from me," he shouted as he jumped back.

Another trip with Bert was equally memorable. One weekend Pop said, "I've got a couple of business friends I'm going to bring down. I want you to take them out fishing." Pop and his friend George Summers had bought a thousand acres at ten dollars an acre on the North Fork of the St. Lucie River, and they had put in a fish camp that they let Bert use. On this trip, I was to be Bert's assistant guide.

So after Pop's friends arrived at the camp, I took a man named Farrell with me in one of our canoes equipped with an outboard engine. I headed for a few of our regular fishing holes where I thought our luck might be good, but for whatever reason that day, the fish just weren't biting. When we finally decided to call it a day, I tried to start the outboard several times, holding the handle—but the engine wouldn't start. After several more failed attempts, I lost my temper and just pulled the motor without holding the handle.

Well, this time the engine started, but because it was turned sideways, it immediately flipped the canoe and dumped Mr. Farrell and me into the river.

Once in the water, which was only seven or eight feet deep, my first thoughts went to the equipment—so at first I was diving down to see what I could retrieve. When I saw Mr. Farrell, it appeared as if he was also diving down on the other side. After about the third time he surfaced, however, I could tell he wasn't diving down to help get fishing equipment.

He couldn't swim, and he was panicking.

By this time, I could only see his arms. All I had to do, which I did quickly, was grab his arms and pull them over the upside-down canoe. Once out of the water, he gagged and choked, and I felt horrible. So I dragged him over to the bank of the creek and got him up in the mangrove trees. It was a typically hot, muggy Florida day, but after a few moments I noticed that the trees were shaking, as if Mr. Farrell was cold. That's when I realized that Pop's friend was in shock.

"Don't go away," I told him—as if he was in a condition to do anything about our predicament. Then I maneuvered the canoe down to a shallow sandbar, emptied it out, and put back all the equipment I could find. By the time I returned to get Mr. Farrell, the other boat carrying Bert and the other guests was just arriving.

"What's going on?" they asked when they saw Farrell up in the mangrove.

I said, "Well, he's right up there." As I saw it, there wasn't much more to say. Mr. Farrell survived thankfully, but when I got home I wasn't sure I would.

"Goddamnit, you've been out there a hundred times," Pop railed at me after hearing what had happened. "You said you knew how to run all those things."

"Well, I do."

"Then how the hell can you start an outboard engine without holding onto the handle?"

Looking back, I would have to say I don't recommend it!

Interestingly, the decision to send Bus and me to school at the venerable prep school Choate also originated in Palm Beach. Pop often played golf with Joe Kennedy at the Palm Beach Country Club, and during one particular round, Kennedy confided to Pop: "I'm sending my sons [at the time meaning John and Robert] to Choate. Great place, great school, great people—and they'll educate him just correctly." By then, Joe Jr. had already graduated, and was off at the London School of Economics studying under economist Harold Laski.

Pop was sold on Old Man Kennedy's pitch, and essentially came home from that trip and said, "We're leaving for Choate in two days." Bus was eleven years old when he was first sent off; and while he was definitely not thrilled at the prospect of being sent to boarding school so young, he eventually graduated magna cum laude.

Another golf companion of Pop's was a fellow member at Quaker Ridge Country Club named Udo Reinach. As I recall, Udo was shorter and more slender than my solid-framed father; but like Pop, he was a securities trader, a sporty kind of a guy, and a really terrific golfer. Among Udo's many accomplishments on the links was playing in the 1948, 1949, and 1950 British Amateur championships.

Offering hope to golf hackers everywhere, Udo—like Pop—played to handicap of five even though Udo never hit a ball over 200 yards in his life. That used to drive Pop crazy. Once, they were playing a 160-yard par three over the water, and Pop said, "Udo, I'll bet you $1,000 that your shot won't clear the water." Udo nervously accepted the wager, but just as he started his back swing he blurted out, "No bet!" That turned out to be the wrong split-second decision, as Pop's friend proceeded to stripe his tee shot onto the green.

"Udo, opportunity just knocked," Pop said smiling, "and you couldn't answer!"

Pop, meanwhile, owed much of his respectable five handicap to his competitive streak and love of gambling. Pop was always a terrific money player, but he also always knew how to pick his partners.

Case in point: late in the afternoon of September 23, 1929, Pop and "the dapper" Johnny Farrell, who was the Quaker Ridge professional at the time, combined to shoot a 66 on the Gedney Farms course to win the pro-amateur championship, held as a precursor to the Westchester Open Championship that year. They edged out Winged Foot pro Mike Brady and his partner John G. Anderson, a former French amateur champ, who carded a 67.

Talk about a great partner. A year before, the ever-popular Farrell birdied the last two holes of a 36-hole play-off to achieve "the almost unattainable honor of beating Bobby Jones" by a shot and claimed the 1928 U.S. Open championship at Olympia Fields. In 1929, Farrell also was the runner-up in both the British Open championship, played at highly regarded Carnoustie, as well as the PGA Championship at Hillcrest CC.

During the 1920s, Farrell's popularity also helped Quaker Ridge—which had already established its reputation as a truly great course—attract a number of noteworthy exhibition matches. In 1920, Englishmen Henry Vardon and Ted Ray beat Johnny and Walter Hagen in a match there; and in 1922, Farrell and Gene Sarazen played an exhibition against two other Englishmen, Abe Mitchell and George Duncan. As a result, Quaker Ridge gained a reputation as a great course and club that endures to this day—though the club itself was once close to closing. Had Pop not paid his bills and then some during the Great Depression, I am told Quaker Ridge might not have survived.

Between the 1920s and 1940s, many prominent business leaders became Quaker Ridge members—including Bernard Gimbel and Samuel Bloomingdale, founders of the department stores that bear their names. Another Quaker Ridge member was George Gershwin. In fact, as Pop recalled, Gershwin was more nervous during a golf match than on opening night on Broadway. Despite the slice that sapped distance from his tee shots, Gershwin occasionally managed to break 90 on the strength of a solid short game—chipping and putting.

Pop, for his part, always complained about his putting: "I've got hands like a plumber. They're strong, but they have no feel, no feel." To remedy this, he was always putting in his bedroom. He loved to putt, and worked at it. When he practiced at home putting on the carpet or hitting balls at the club, he was always serious. I think it was a great outlet, a great mental release for him.

Though he had a car and driver waiting for him everywhere he went, to get to Quaker Ridge from his office near the southern tip of Manhattan or his apartment at 480 Park Avenue, Pop would often take the train. If he was staying at the apartment, he'd walk down to Grand Central, jump on the train, and take the thirty-five-minute ride to Scarsdale. My cousin Stan once asked Pop why he didn't drive like the others. "Because on the train you read," came the answer. Pop used his time on the train to relax and read. He was always reading and learning.

Pop was equally efficient with his time once on the golf course. When he played during the week, Pop would usually play nine holes—and often two balls on each hole. The unusual thing was, he managed to complete nine holes on foot in an hour. Mind you, this was also in the days before golf carts.

To achieve this breakneck pace, as he was teeing off Pop would have the caddy out in the middle of the fairway. If he hit an extra tee shot for practice, the caddy would pick up the second ball, leave two clubs by the first tee shot, then run up to the green. Then when you got to the green, the wedge and putter were waiting for you, and the caddy was already running down the next fairway. This way, Pop was constantly in motion—walking at a very quick pace, urging you to keep up. You didn't toss too many grass clippings into the air to check the wind direction when you played with my father.

Pop was so impatient when he played golf that one time his playing partner found him searching for his ball in the middle of the first fairway, getting frustrated.

"What are you looking for, Emil?" the friend asked.

"My tee shot—I can't find it," Pop said with growing exasperation.

"That's funny," the partner said laughing, "because you didn't hit a drive."

Pop had been so intent on getting going he forgot to hit a tee shot.

Pop loved to play on Sundays, because the course was technically closed and he didn't like crowds. He could get a caddy to take them out, however, because he was known to be a terrific tipper. "Don't be cheap," was a constant refrain of his, not only after a round of golf, but throughout our lives. "Give those caddies a good tip [five dollars in those days, for example, was a princely sum] and drive them home."

"Remember," Pop would add, "they have to live, too."

Incidentally, Pop was equally generous with respect to the golf pros with whom he played. Pop would frequently play them for big money; and though he was a five-handicap player, Pop also insisted on playing them "straight up"—meaning, my father would get no strokes from the pro. In essence, Pop wanted the pros to win; and on the odd occasion when Pop would actually prevail in the match, he would always pretend he wanted to let his bet ride. "I'm gonna get rich off of you," he would tease the pro, when in reality he had no intention of ever collecting.

I grew up liking golf, and love it today, but never quite became as engrossed as Pop or my brother, Bus, who was a low-handicapper like Pop for many years. In fact, Pop and Bus made it into the club championship one year; and on July 17, 1935, Pop—listed in the *New York Times* as a six-handicap player that year—played in the thirtieth annual New York State Amateur Championship held at Winged Foot Golf Club in Mamaroneck. Pop was happy that he and his fellow Quaker Ridge member, John Cadel, were the first in the field of 100 players to tee off at 9:00 A.M.—no crowds, no delays.

While in Palm Beach during the late 1930s and early 1940s, when Pop wasn't on the golf course or being "dragged" to Bradley's, as he put it, he could occasionally be found at the Taboo Club with a close friend, Dick Berlin, who by then was head of the vastly influential media giant, the Hearst Corporation. Berlin had started working for the Hearsts just after World War I selling advertising for their *Motor Boating* magazine, and was such a star salesman that he rose to be general manager of all Hearst magazines by 1930. During the Depression, Berlin continued his meteoric rise through the corporate ranks in part because he was generally credited with keeping the whole Hearst empire from foundering during the brutal economic downturn.

By 1941, Berlin would step into the presidency of the corporation and lead the empire's reorganization. A *Time Magazine* profile in 1951 described him as "nervous in temperament," as well as "an able executive, a master of office politics and the laws of power." Dick Berlin was probably the most powerful man in American media for many years, but the reason Pop liked Dick wasn't because the Hearst chief could get my father publicity. Quite the contrary. Given their close friendship, Pop often said to Berlin, "Now, Dick, I expect you to keep me out of the papers." To which the media executive, with a twinkle in his eye, responded, "If you stay out of trouble, Emil, I'll keep you out of the papers."

It was Dick who introduced Pop to William Randolph Hearst and his mistress, actress Marion Davies. Thereafter, Pop visited Hearst's famous San Simeon estate a number of times. In turn, Pop and Mom introduced Berlin to his eventual wife—a New York society girl named Muriel "Honey" Johnson, who also happened to be the daughter of one of my father's great friends, Harry T. F. Johnson. "Mr. Johnson," as I knew him, started with Pop in the real estate business and was the only partner Pop ever took, as far as I know.

Honey, meanwhile, was a great looker and a real character in Westchester—as was her brother, Warren Johnson. Both were very attractive, and used to ride around in convertibles. Honey had blonde hair and big blue eyes, and until she married Berlin in 1939 always had what Dick used to call "these phony princes" courting her. In fact, in 1937, Honey was forced to deny a rumor that she was engaged to a former Russian Prince named David Mdivani, with whom she had danced during her European vacation that summer.

Later in his life, Pop rarely left New York City. Instead, he went to Grand Central Station to watch travelogues or films about various cities and countries around the world. Thereafter, Pop declared that he already had "the flavor of the place without all the problems" of traveling to the country in question.

During the 1920s and 1930s, however, he was an inveterate traveler. He took several trips by sea to Europe (in May of 1920 and October of 1929), and to Bermuda (in April of 1934). But in 1936, together with Dick Berlin and their mutual friend George Summers, Pop also took the second trans-Pacific flight on Pan American airlines—which he later described as one of the most thrilling adventures of his life.

With their inaugural flight on October 21, 1936, Pan Am went from California to the Philippines with nine passengers aboard. Known as Pan Am Clippers, these Boeing 319 planes were essentially mammoth flying boats that flew from San Francisco harbor, skipping across the Pacific with stops at Hawaii, Midway Island, Wake Island, Guam, the Philippines, and then Hong Kong. Pan Am advance teams had prepared the stopover islands by blasting coral to make safe coves for sea landings and constructing luxury hotels for Pan Am's discerning clientele. The round-trip fare for this very special flight across the Pacific, from San Francisco to Manila, was more than $1,400.

On Pop's trip, the group stopped over in the Philippines, where Pop knew the president, Manuel L. Quezon. While in Manila, however, a torrential rainstorm caused Pop, Dick, and George to have a bad automobile accident. Summers ended up with a broken back, and had to return to the United States.

So Pop and Berlin continued on to China.

While in the Orient, Pop paid $10,000 for some natural pearls, which may have turned out to be the worst investment he ever made. By the time he got home, they were worth a tiny fraction of the price he paid, because the Japanese had figured out how to culture the same pearls.

Nobody got more fun out of telling that story than Pop.

One of Pop's other passions was cars, and he owned most of the high-end cars that were produced during the first half of the twentieth century—Dusenbergs, Packards, Cadillacs, you name it. No question, however, that the most spectacular car he ever owned was an Isotta Fraschini limousine. It was a big long car—the kind where, as my son Rob described it, "the driver arrived at your destination fifteen minutes before you as the rider did." In Manhattan, the Isottas were sold by the son of "potent Prince-Poet Gabriele D'Annunzio," and some of the early film stars who drove the Isottas were Clara Bow and Rudolph Valentino.

If you preferred to move anonymously through the streets of New York, however, the Isotta was not for you. Added to the car's extravagant appearance,

Pop's Isotta was painted robin's egg blue—the same color as some of the taxicabs in New York back then. So we would be riding along in this exotic vehicle, and people would try to hail us for a ride. They thought Pop's priceless car was a taxi.

We tended to cause a modest scene wherever we went, and it got to the point where Bus and Barbara would hide on the floor of the car and ask Connie, Pop's driver, to drop them off down the block from school—so they could avoid making such a splashy entrance in front of their school mates.

Parenthetically, Pop liked the color blue so much that people in Westchester gradually learned the secret to selling their unwanted assets. If they had a car or a boat they needed to unload, they adopted the same common philosophy: "Paint it blue and sell it to Mosbacher."

The only reason they did so was it occasionally worked like a charm.

Like any boy growing up, Pop loved to play baseball as a kid. For all of his enthusiasm, however, he was not generally known for his speed around the bases. "Actually, I wasn't that slow," he recalled, "but one day I was trying to stretch a single to a double and one of my friends yelled from the sidelines, 'Hey, Mosbacher! Get the piano off your back!'"

It's an analogy that also applied to Pop after he took up sailing as an adult. He loved it, and he sailed well, but my father was never considered the fastest or the most skilled sailor on the water.

Notably, the person most responsible for getting Pop into sailing was his friend, Cornelius "Corny" Shields Sr.—one of the great amateur sailors of the twentieth century. "If sailing were baseball," wrote *Time Magazine* in 1953, "Corny Shields would long have ranked with the Stan Musials and Joe DiMaggios; if golf, with the Ben Hogans and Sammy Sneads."[1]

Corny established his sailing pedigree early on, and continued to compete at the highest level throughout his life. After World War I, when he was stationed at Guantanamo Bay over the winter of 1918 to 1919, Corny skippered the winning boat in a fleet competition there. Thirty-three years later, in 1952, he would win the North American Sailing Championship to claim the very first Clifford D. Mallory Cup. In between, his triumphs were far too numerous to enumerate in these pages.

Like my father, Corny was a successful Wall Street trader who survived the crash of 1929; and like Joe Kennedy, Corny offered Pop some parental advice that affected my life—and my brother's. Corny convinced my father that sailing would be good for his kids. "It's clean and healthful," Corny would say, with a twinkle in those brown eyes set deep in his sun-beaten features. "Sailing teaches kids hard work, self-reliance, and good sportsmanship. It's a bug that gets you, and I can't think of a better one."

"I started too late in life to get really good," Pop later conceded, reflecting on his own sailing exploits. Pop was by no means devoid of talent, though. He had plenty of successes out on Long Island Sound, where he sailed in some of the

1. "Sport: Design for Living," July 27, 1953

toughest conditions and competed, and occasionally prevailed, against some of the finest sailors of the day.

For four or five years, Pop received instruction from a Scotsman named Peter Henson; but like a lot of parents, I think my father's ultimate dream was that his kids would surpass his own accomplishments. So he had Peter tutor Bus for a few years, then me for just about a year. Peter wasn't a great racer himself, but he was a good boatman. There wasn't anything that Peter didn't know about sailing, or about the wind. Peter was also very small in stature. In fact, my sister Barbara recalls that when Peter started tutoring Bus, all you could see were these two little heads sticking out of the boat.

Regardless of age, anyone who loved to sail was exceedingly fortunate to live near Long Island Sound. For one thing, it was one of the very first areas in the country where yacht clubs began to band together to sponsor interclub racing—around 1895. Before this, sailboat racing was almost exclusively a local affair. With the development of a network of competing clubs came the movement to start standardizing boats, rules, and equipment.

Then in 1911, the Sound became the birthplace of the Star Class, which was the first strictly one-design class to catch on regionally—meaning all of the boats were designed the same. The new advantages of the Star Class attracted a number of highly accomplished sailors such as Arthur Knapp (who won the Star Class world championship in 1930), Stan Ogilvy, Bill Lynn, Cooch Maxwell, Patrick O'Gorman, and Herb Hild.

Bus sailed a Star boat at first, which is probably one of the best one-design boats and is still in the Olympic classes.[2] He did quite well on the Stars for a youngster before he moved on to the Atlantic Class.

As for me, I started sailing at age five in Pop's 12-foot, flat-bottomed, cat-rigged, shell boat that resembled a small dinghy. More than anything involving actual sailing, my earliest memory is the great fun I had turning the boat over and watching the older fellows turn the boat back over and pump the seawater out. When they quickly tired of this antic and I had to right the boat myself, of course, it ceased being so much fun.

2. From http://www.boatingchannel.com/sailingnews107.html: All Olympic classes are International Yacht Racing Union (IYRU)-approved, have international organizations and controlled racing rules, and represent the best competition in the sport. The term "one-design" refers to a class boats' strict standards for materials and methods used in construction. Ultimately, each Olympic boat—built only by IYRU licensed boat builders to precise size and weight specifications—is identical to another in its class. The purpose of one-design class racing is to allow the best sailor—not the best boat—to win.

On my way, sailing in Palm Beach in 1938.

After getting our feet wet literally and figuratively, Bus and I—in succession—moved on to a Comet sailboat, which was a little bigger, at 16 feet long, and designed for two people. At age twelve, I then inherited the Star boat, which was longer still at nearly 23 feet. Twelve years old was pretty young to have a boat of that size. In fact, I was short enough that when I stood up in the boat—like Bus and Peter Hanson—you couldn't see too much of me. I'll never forget how a sailor passing by used to yell, "Hey Bobby, get off your knees!"

Like any child who is introduced to a new language during their formative years, learning to sail as young as Bus and I did helped us develop a natural feel for how a boat should properly respond in certain conditions—particularly as it related to going to windward. Most sailors will constantly check the sail and jib when sailing to windward, looking for signs that it might luff or stall. Because Bus and I were so young when we started sailing the Star Class boat, however, we couldn't crick our necks enough to watch the sails or the jib. Rather, we focused mainly on the angle of the heel, the look of the seas ahead, and the water passing by on the leeward or downwind side of the boat.

In this way, we learned to check a series of signs and develop an innate feel for getting the most out of our boat.

Early on, I also recall how, night after night, Bus would put small boats on the table and query me on what I would do given various situations. "What if the mark was here, the wind was from the north, and I was this boat here?" he would ask, presenting me with a hypothetical scenario. Sometimes I would get so sleepy at the table that Pop would cut short these tutorials.

As my older brother, Bus was also helpful to me before my first race in the Star Class. By then, I had been in a couple of good races, but nothing big. So Bus gave me some very wise advice. "See that guy in the green boat?" Bus said as we were getting ready. "He's Stan Turner, and he's one of our best sailors. Watch him. Watch what he does, and do the same."

Some time later, Stan, who unfortunately was killed in World War II, told my brother that not only did I keep track of him, but I also stayed within two boat lengths of him, right behind him, the entire race. "Geez, that kid brother of yours drove me crazy," Stan told Bus. "No matter what I did, I couldn't shake him." He ended up first or second in the race of about thirty boats, and I finished right behind him. I had never been in a Star boat race, and really didn't know where the hell I'd been or what I had done; but I knew if I followed that guy I couldn't be all wrong. So I took Bus' advice literally.

That same year, my Knickerbocker Yacht Club crew and I lost the Long Island Sound midget championship after a protest hearing brought by a competitor was decided against my team. The crew from Riverside, led by Charlotte Perry, claimed that we had fouled them on the starboard bow near a weather mark. A man named Jesse Smith headed the protest committee, and when he and his fellow conferees reached their verdict and ruled against us, it dropped our Knickerbocker crew, which also included Arthur Davis Jr. and Thomas Rickenback, from first place back to fourth.

My side of the story? We "was robbed" is what I think!

Of course, like any sport, there are certain rules when you sail. For instance, a starboard tack to the right has the right of way over port tack to the left. I can't tell you how many times Bus and I were fouled during the course of our racing careers on Long Island Sound, but we never filed a protest. Pop said, "You're not going to win races that way." It was the same theory he used during his own experience on the Curb, when he had been accused of doing something he didn't do.

Don't protest. Find another way to succeed by trying to outsmart, outwork—or in our case, trying to outsail—everybody else.

I don't think Pop's hard and fast rule against protesting necessarily made my brother and me sail with a chip on our shoulder, but I do think, in the end, it made us better sailors. Because he was holding us to a higher standard with respect for the integrity of our matches, we in turn held ourselves to a higher standard for our own performance.

In one golden week in August of 1939, I participated in two winning efforts of some note. First, I crewed for Bus as he won the Long Island Sound junior sailing championship, then a week later it was my turn at the helm captaining Knickerbocker Yacht Club to victory in the midget sailing championship of Long Island Sound. We took a first and a second in the last two tests of the fourteenth annual Scovill Cup to amass a total of 46 1/2 points at the matches conducted by Cold Spring Harbor Beach Club.

To win, we also had to overcome the handicap of a disqualification in the second race, which cost us second place and 11 points. The penalty was imposed for fouling, or hitting, a mark—an act by which we gained no advantage or hurt the chances of the other contestants.

As Bus had a few years earlier, I went on to defend our midget championship in 1940 by winning the first four of the five races in the series. That year I sailed with Arthur Davis and my cousin Stanley Stern, and we piled up a total of 40 points. Larchmont Yacht Club finished second with 28 points.

Then in 1941, at the tender age of fourteen, I inherited the Atlantic Class boat from Bus and moved up a class to sail in the "juniors," which was for kids fifteen to eighteen. Since I was fourteen years old I could have still competed in the midget class, but I decided I was ready to move up.

In one of my first junior races, however, I had a terrible series while Pop was out watching me in his 40-foot powerboat, *Ebb*, a Matthews. (The Matthews were great old motorboats designed and built by Scott Matthews in Port Linton, Ohio.) There was fluky or very light air that day, and I kept trying to get around a tugboat that would alternately go forward a little and stop. I made about three or four tacks, or come-abouts, and it was the worst thing in the world. I lost all the boats that I had led. During the fourth tack, from across this very quiet water, I heard a very familiar voice from at least a couple hundred yards away shouting, "Why don't you tack again you stupid little son of a bitch?"

Then I heard a crash. It was Pop. He was so mad, he threw his binoculars down and broke them. Then he zoomed off. That was the end of his watching me for that day. Bus recalled it this way: "When I saw the bow wave of my father's boat rise I knew I had done something wrong. It meant he was leaving me to watch Bob. If he was back a short time later, it meant Bob had also done something wrong."

Pop pushed us as hard as he pushed himself, and often was outraged by our mistakes. If Bus or I had screwed up really bad during a race, we took the precaution of arranging to have dinner at a friend's house that night—and on several occasions, we even stayed away for the weekend. By the time we got home and gathered around the dinner table, he was usually very calm. There he would ask us questions: why did it take two minutes to get the spinnaker up? Why did you tack at this point? Pop later suggested that he had "maybe added 1 percent to what they [Bus and me] found for themselves," but his probing questions forced us to think things through. Oftentimes at home, we got out little model ships right there at the dining room table to recreate various situations and talk through strategies.

Candidly, I did occasionally bristle under Pop's constant direction, and even openly disagreed with him a few times—which was always dangerous territory. He never hit me, but definitely came close a few times. Why he didn't still surprises me. There I was, a smart-ass kid sometimes arguing with him, which was something he was neither used to nor enjoyed.

One day, Pop was crewing for me, and we were coming down the home stretch with the chance to win the race—the finish line just a few hundred yards away. Over my shoulder I heard Pop say: "One of your jib sheet lines is fraying. I thought I told you to replace it." I guess I was too focused on winning at that point to pay too much attention to what Pop was saying, because I brushed his comment off saying, "Yeah, I'll get to it later."

Unlike Bus, boat maintenance has never been a passion of mine.

Even though we were so close to winning the race, after hearing my dismissive answer Pop took out his boating knife—everyone on a sailboat carries a knife—and cut the jib sheet (the lines that lead from the clew or back corner of the sail to the cockpit and are used to control the jib).

Instantly, I noticed the boat losing speed, and looked up to see the sail flapping harmlessly in the breeze. We were essentially dead in the water.

I lost the race.

When I saw what Pop had done, I was furious. It seemed an excessive thing for him to do to make his point; and yet gazing back through the looking glass of time, while so many other events from my childhood seem hazy, all these years later I can see clearly how he was trying to send me a message the only way he thought it might get through.

The jib sheet incident shows Pop taking action—drastic action—to make a point. It may have cost me the race, but if Pop told you do something and he thought it was the right thing to do, there was little if any patience with a failure to comply. He was not the kind of parent to cajole you, pleading, "Please do that. I've already asked you once."

That was not Pop.

Lady Bird Johnson once observed of LBJ: "He *stretched* people." Pop was the same way, I believe. He had the highest expectations for everyone around him—just as he did for himself.

As a teenager, for example, I went into the city one day for an asthma-related doctor's appointment one afternoon and did not return that night—staying with a friend in town instead. When I returned to our house on Rosedale Avenue the next day, Pop railed against such irresponsible behavior: "What are you doing with your life?" he demanded. "What could you possibly become?"

With a mischievous look on my face, I responded wryly, "Well, I thought I might try to become another Ted Bassett"—a widely known playboy. Pop looked for a second like he was going to kill me before breaking out in laughter.

Unfortunately, as a young prep school student I continued to test the outer limits of Pop's patience. In sailing, I always gave it my all when out on the water, but when it came to my studies I must admit I was anything but diligent.

I had started going to the Dalton School in New York City, but Pop felt it was too "progressive," or soft, and moved me over to Choate in Wallingford, Connecticut, where Bus and the Kennedy boys had gone. The stricter standards, however, did little to mold my behavior in a more agreeable or positive direction.

For example, I got caught a few times sneaking off the Choate campus with friends, and when I did Pop would dress me down. One time, he was reprimanding me in a restaurant—wagging his finger at me, in a not so friendly way. He was telling me if I didn't quit sneaking off from school and doing all of these terribly mischievous things and start applying myself to my studies I was never going to graduate, never go to college, and never get anywhere.

About that time, up walked one of Pop's great old friends and fellow stock trader, Ned Grubbs. Ned sat down at our table—without invitation—and started talking, when Pop cut him off short. "Mind your own damn business, Ned," Pop said. "This is between Bobby and me."

Pop was crazy about Ned—we all were—so Ned ignored Pop, and with a twinkle in his eye intervened anyway. "I know you're giving poor Bobby here hell about his work at Choate," Ned said. "But let me tell you, Emil, haven't I done alright on the Street?"

"Yeah, sure, Ned," Pop readily conceded.

"I think I'm pretty well respected," Ned continued, "and I play a pretty good game of golf." All true as well. In fact, Ned was a terrific single-digit handicapper.

"So let me tell you about my days at St. Paul. My father, first of all, was so old he never checked on me. He had been a colonel in the Civil War, so by the time I came along and started in school—in 1910 or thereabouts—I figured I was able to get away with murder, and I proceeded to do just that. I didn't do any schoolwork; instead, I had a lot of fun and concentrated on playing baseball. They would keep sending letters home trying to inform my father I was not doing well, but fortunately I had a friend who worked in his office intercepting these letters. But then, unfortunately, my old man came up to the graduation, and during the ceremony the headmaster got up and said, 'We now get to one boy in this class, who if you added all of his grades together would barely pass in one subject.'"

Finishing his story, Ned turned to Pop and said, "So go easy on Bobby, will ya? It's not *that* important."

Pop kinda shook his head as if he didn't know whether to laugh or strangle Ned for totally getting him off message in my case.

As for me, I wanted to hug Ned.

Another sincere attempt to help right my academic ship at Choate came from another friend of Pop's, Spyros "Spiro" Skouras. Spiro had come over from Greece with his two younger brothers, and they had gotten their start cleaning up a bar run by an Irishman. The owner said, "Look, I'll give you the job, but I am giving you one week to properly sing the 'Star Spangled Banner,' or I am firing your little butts."

So a week went by and when the big night came, the bar owner said: "Okay, let's hear it." Even though they couldn't speak much English at all, the Skouras boys were able to perform our national anthem to the satisfaction of their then-boss. They kept their jobs and went on to do very well for themselves, with Spiro becoming president of 20th Century Fox, while the family controlled roughly a thousand theaters around the country.

Occasionally, the three Skouras brothers—now wealthy men—would play golf with Pop, and after every hole, they would ritualistically turn to each other and say, "Pay up!" At which point Pop would interject, "Well, I lost that hole so here is my share."

The three of them would look at Pop and, refusing his money, say, "No, no Emil—you we trust. We just don't trust each other!"

I dated Spiro's daughter, an attractive redhead, and on several occasions when I was visiting at their house, Mr. Skouras would sit down next to me. "Bobby," he said with a thick Greek accent, "if you get to the head of the class at Choate, I will send you our newest movies."

I would always perk up when the offer came in, because it would have been quite the coup to have these movies before they hit the theaters—particularly back in that pre-TV day. I always thanked him profusely, but the truth is I never came near the top of class that year—or any other.

Though I never earned the movies per Mr. Skouras' incentive, one of the neatest things I had at Choate was a small, portable, transistor radio, which was a fairly rare commodity back in the late 1930s and early 1940s. Actually, it had been a gift of another rather well-known figure of the times—"Big Bill" Zeckendorf, who has been called New York's original real estate mogul. Zeckendorf was "The Donald" (as in Trump) of his day, who put together the parcel of land on the Upper East Side on which the United Nations plaza rose.

I had been out sailing with my friend Pat Davis when we came across Mr. Zeckendorf in his 35-foot sailboat. He was having a hard time picking up the mooring, and was clearly getting very frustrated. The problem was, he was also drifting perilously close to some unwelcoming rock outcroppings. So Pat sailed me over, and I jumped onboard to help get him under control. Mr. Zeckendorf was so grateful, it seems, that he sent me an early radio up at Choate.

One of the radio's features was that you pressed a button on top to turn it on or off. Another feature was its size. At roughly 2 inches high, 7 inches long, and 3 inches deep, I soon discovered the radio fit perfectly into a box of tissues— where it was, in turn, perfectly concealed. I kept this box near my bed, and at night my roommate Sandy Rubesemum and I would listen to the radio. If the hall monitor heard the radio and came into our room, however, I was able to tap the box on top, turn off the radio in a flash, and roll over to pretend sleeping.

"I heard a noise in here, I know I did," the monitor would declare each time he barged into the room, always with increasing exasperation. Then he searched high and low around our room.

"Wh . . . what," I would groggily respond as I rolled over, rubbed the pretend sleep out of my eyes, and stifled a fake yawn. It was a scene that played out on numerous occasions, and each time it got harder to suppress the laughter.

Chapter 7 "FROM LITTLE ACORNS OAK TREES GROW . . . YOU DON'T HAVE ANY ACORNS YET"

When it comes to sailing, I have always loved strong breezes and stiff competition. There is something both humbling and heady about challenging yourself, your crew, and your boat out on the open water against the best talent and the awesome force of nature. Sportsmen of all stripes frequently talk of being "in the zone," and to me there is no better feeling than being in those electric moments when you have harnessed the wind, sliced through a roiling sea, and surged past the rest of the fleet.

When the Atlantic Class championship came to a head in 1941, I had reached that point where hours of instruction and practice had started to morph into pure feel and instinct. This was a key development for me, because all sorts of great sailors were in contention for the title that year—including a future America's Cupper, Briggs Cunningham.

The key five-race series of the campaign took place in Southport, Connecticut at the Pequot Yacht Club. As I say, I have always loved a good strong wind; and for the first two days, it blew so hard— around 20 or 25 knots—that Pop insisted on crewing for me. He was scared to have us young kids out in a big wind, and called from his Rector Street office saying, "Don't leave the dock without me." In the end, all Pop ended up doing was bailing our leaky boat out as the seawater collected along the floorboards.

Meanwhile, on that third and final afternoon, I managed to navigate our boat, *Rhapsody*, across the finish line 15 seconds faster than *Shadow*, manned by the Gordon brothers, to capture the 1941 class championship at Long Island Sound. I was all of fourteen years old.

Winning that race, at that age, was really a high point of my young career as a sailor. The fact that we beat that particular field horrified everybody, because they were far more experienced sailors—many of them at least twice my age. They were among the very best sailors in the country, and my crew and I were viewed as mere upstarts.

I have heard sailboat racing of that bygone era described as a genteel, almost social affair where the greatest emphasis was placed not on the order of finish, but rather on the orderly manner with which the crews discharged their duties.

The highest compliment, or so it went, was to be considered a consistent skipper. As for results, some would brush those off, saying a certain skipper finished "there or thereabouts."

To be honest, all this business about stressing "good form over finish" was a mind-set with which I was wholly unfamiliar. Of course, both Bus and I were raised and taught by Pop to adhere to the highest standards for conduct on and off the water—but we both also liked winning. A lot.

Having tasted victory in the Midget and now Atlantic Classes, I was quickly discovering that that feeling of success never got old.

To show that our first Atlantic Class title wasn't a fluke, my crew and I successfully defended our title the next year in Greenwich. That 1942 campaign involved more luck in the end, because one of our top competitors—a very able sailor named Mrs. Van Wyck Loomis—was eliminated on technicality. She had hauled her boat, *Hound*, out of the water three days before the race, which was against the rules. Even though she had scored more points than I had, we retained the title. It was certainly not the ideal way to win in my view. Having been denied a Midget championship just a few years prior based on a similar technicality and judgment call, I could certainly empathize with Mrs. Loomis.

No doubt, the most significant family sailing event of 1943 took place when Bus was called up for the war effort and entered the Navy. As I was entering into early manhood, I recall how we had a highly competitive, brotherly relationship. Bus usually had little use for, or patience with me—and I frequently responded in kind.

But something changed when we saw my brother go off to war. It had been more than a year since Pearl Harbor was hit in December of 1941, and we were well aware that too many American boys Bus' age were not coming home. Both Pop and Mom were naturally very worried about what might lie ahead—we all were—and yet there was also a point of deep family pride to see Bus support the war effort.

First, Bus went to Notre Dame for what they called a "90-day wonder" class to become an officer. Because he did so well, the Navy powers that be sent Bus—quite against his wishes— to MIT for radar school. Bus did not enjoy that experience as I recall, and as a result, he did not excel at it. From there they sent him out to the Pacific, where he wanted to be in the first place. He served on a minesweeper for a little more than a year.

This was, of course, an entirely different kind of "on the water" experience. Minesweepers back then would go into an area—a potential Marine landing zone, for example—and try to clean out the mines. When they did, it was not uncommon for them to draw Japanese fire. "We were lucky they were lousy shots," Bus often joked, but one day there was one shot that came so close that it set off his lighter in his shirt pocket. The lighter started burning, and Bus thought, "Oh God, I've been hit."

Even though Bus and Pop could get crosswise, I can remember my father often saying during Bus' tour of duty, "There is only one thing I want in this world: bring my son home safely."

Sadly, I was away at college when Bus did finally arrive safely back home from the war, which I have heard was like a scene out of a Norman Rockwell painting—what with Bus barging through the door still in his uniform, and my parents and my sister there to smother him in hugs. There was great joy in the Mosbacher home that night.

Tragically, though, not all Mosbachers escaped the horrors of World War II.

On September 16, 1942, Nazi soldiers rounded up the last fifty-eight Jews in Aschaffenberg—the same river town my grandfather had left fifty-six years before—and herded them aboard "Transport XII/3," bound for the Terezin concentration camp near Prague. Included in this final group forced to leave Aschaffenberg, I recently discovered, was my grandfather's youngest surviving sister, then-sixty-eight-year-old Karoline Mosbacher.

Looking back, it is a wonder that my great aunt stayed in Aschaffenberg as long as she did. Nine years before, in 1933, a group of the elite Aryan black-shirted Schutzstaffel (or "SS") troops killed a number of Jews at the newly established Aschaffenburg concentration camp and were arrested by local police. In an ominous foreshadowing of things to come, however, the SS chief, Heinrich Himmler, and other Nazi officials insisted that these special forces were not subject to civil authority, and demanded that no charges be brought. When the charges in this Aschaffenberg incident were, in fact, dropped, many believe the decision set a precedent for the systematic genocide that took place when Himmler's "Final Solution" was set in motion just a few years later.

Not surprisingly, after the establishment of the concentration camp there, events quickly deteriorated in Aschaffenburg. Just two years later, in August of 1935, the first posters with "Jews unwanted" were publicly displayed in town. In June 1936, the Jewish cemetery there was desecrated for the first time, followed by the first arbitrary arrests. During the *Kristallnacht* (which means "Crystal Night" or "Night of Broken Glass") in 1938, moreover, some thirty

Aschaffenburg Jews were sent to the Dachau concentration camp, while that same night the historic synagogue was burned down along with its fifteen Torah scrolls. Jewish stores were also looted.

Before 1941, half the Jewish population from Aschaffenburg would leave town. Of the Jewish residents who were still there in 1942, 128 were rounded up in April and sent to the Izbica camp, a "transit ghetto" in the Lublin district of Poland. Then in September, the last two groups of fifty-eight total persons— including my great aunt—were shipped to the Terezin camp, which had been established in Czechoslovakia in November 1941, just northwest of Prague.

Of all the concentration camps they operated throughout central and eastern Europe, the Nazis designated Terezin as a propaganda tool—a kind of Potemkin village that they would eventually permit the International Red Cross to visit. They even constructed a fake cafe, a bank, and schools; planted flower gardens; and spruced up the park areas. In the wake of the Red Cross visit, moreover, they had the audacity to make a film using detainees that tried to portray life at Terezin as desirable. After the film was completed, of course, each of the "actors" was sent to Auschwitz to die.

For the Nazis, Terezin served two other central purposes. First, it was a transit camp—originally a holding pen for Jews being transported to the "ghettos" in Poland and the Baltic states, and later serving essentially as a waiting room for the Auschwitz death camp. Terezin's place in this horrific sequence was well understood to its inhabitants, and the possibility of being shipped "to the East" at any moment, and for any reason, cast a pall of fear and foreboding over the entire population.

In the final analysis, Terezin was also, in part, a death camp itself. Nearly one out of every five persons who entered its gates never left. By September 1942, the month my great aunt arrived, the ghetto reached its peak of 53,004 prisoners—all living in an area of just 150,000 square yards. That month alone, 3,941 evacuees died due to the deplorable living conditions—an average of 131 victims per day. Another 13,000 displaced persons were sent to the extermination camps in occupied Poland, mainly Treblinka.

Into this bleak, almost hopeless world, stepped an aged Karoline Mosbacher.

What was it like? Inhumane is the only word that comes to mind. After waking up with thousands of other women in a crudely prepared, rat-infested attic of one of the barracks of Terezin, my great aunt would go downstairs and wait in line at a sparse bathroom with only six toilets—one of three such bathrooms meant to serve tens of thousands of women throughout the camp. Usually, there was no water for flushing or grooming, or other bare necessities.

For breakfast, the food distribution center offered imitation coffee—brewed from grain and chestnuts. Rarely, if ever, was any other food offered. Despite there being one doctor for every seven detainees, moreover, medical treatment was virtually nonexistent. For one thing, the doctors were forced to do heavy labor like everyone else; but while my great aunt was there, before the establishment of a medical facility, the only so-called medication was a purple powder used for all sorts of purposes—including as a mouthwash agent. As a result, disease and every other form of malady routinely swept through the camp like wildfire.

Quickly, perhaps mercifully, the toll of such dire living conditions proved too much for my great aunt, who died in the camp on April 25, 1943—just two weeks after her sixty-ninth birthday.

Sadly, Karoline wasn't the only Mosbacher to follow the trail of tears into Terezin, or die in the Holocaust. All told, at least twenty-four Mosbachers— many of them from the region surrounding Aschaffenburg—fell prey to the systematic evils of Nazism, including another Emil Mosbacher (born in 1887). Of the twenty-four known victims bearing our family name, at least ten passed through or died at Terezin.

Half a world away, both Pop and my grandfather were aware of the cancer of hatred that had metastasized in Aschaffenburg. My grandfather had visited his family during the summer of 1933, and knew that a noose of evil was starting to tighten around the nearly 600 Jewish men, women, and children still living there. Thereafter, both he and Pop sent money and tried to help as many of our relatives as they could to escape Germany.

On May 29, 1937, in fact, Pop landed at the Alameda airport in California after returning from Hong Kong aboard the "Hawaii Clipper" with a German alien named Erwin Berghaus on board. Berghaus had been admitted "in transit," but his connection to my family is not known.

It is naturally a matter of considerable guilt to look back and realize that, while I was a fifteen-year-old boy living in an affluent setting, preoccupied with the relatively trivial matters of sailing and the fairer sex, one of my most vulnerable relatives found herself, through no fault of her own, a victim of Hitler's madness.

Like the lead character from the movie *Life is Beautiful*, Guido Orefice, Pop tried to shield his children from the evils being directed at Jews of every age in

Europe. Again, my father and grandfather were aware, but right or wrong we didn't ever discuss it at home.

So, yes, it was a charmed childhood in many respects; but I was also lucky when it came to life's basic needs, too. For example, when I got sick as a child with "double pneumonia," or was suffering from asthma, my parents could afford to get me the best medical care—and hire a nurse named Grace Howland to live with us.

I have only a sketchy recollection of this, of course, but such was the primitive state of medicine back then that Grace—I called her "Howie"— would put an umbrella over the bed, then a sheet over the umbrella, and finally have a kettle with steam coming out of it with camphor and other herbal remedies. That's how they treated pneumonia and asthma back then.

Two good things came of my asthma, incidentally. First, I developed a life-long habit of doing chin-ups to develop my chest, which also instilled in me the importance of staying fit. The second, and more immediately gratifying, thing asthma did was get me out of going to school at Choate, in New England, during the grim winter months when my condition acted up the most.

Pop checked into the matter and initially decided the best place for me to be was Arizona, with its warm but dry climate— better air for the asthma sufferer. So off I went, my mother by my side. We ended up spending exactly two days in Arizona, however. The day we arrived and enrolled me in school there, I was introduced to what was to be my new best friend for the semester: a horse. Now, personally I have nothing against horses; and if I hadn't been deathly allergic to them I am sure I could have forged a deep and meaningful relationship with that particular steed.

Instead, Mom and I left the next day by train for Florida. This was in 1942, just weeks after the Japanese sneak attack at Pearl Harbor and the American declaration of war. So during our train trip, occasionally it was necessary for us to get off the train onto the sidings to make room for the troops.

All in all, despite any inconvenience, it was a wonderful trip. The patriotism of that time was brought home to us during our stop in New Orleans. We were eating dinner in a local restaurant when a band of musicians came in, and everyone stood up. It took us a while, but we eventually realized, "Oh my God, they're trying to play the Star Spangled Banner!" It was barely recognizable to my then-Easterner ears, what with the band playing it in that wonderful Dixieland style.

Eventually we did make it to Palm Beach and the Brazilian Court hotel, and that winter—and several successive ones—found me attending school in Florida.

As the Long Island Sound International Class started their third and final series of the 1944 season in mid-August, I found myself in the hunt for the overall championship. I was in third place overall with a .746 percentage, trailing Jim Sheldon's *Sheldrake* with .817 and *Bumble Bee*, which was sailed by Arthur Knapp, at .796. The seasonal championship was the grand prize in the International Class, yet there I was: a seventeen-year-old upstart, smart-alec kid sailing against some of the most capable sailors on Long Island Sound—and, in Knapp's case, the world.

It was about this same time that, despite the fact that a lot of my friends at Choate had enrolled at Princeton (where I had also been accepted), I decided New Jersey was not for me. Having lived and gone to Choate off-and-on in the northeast all my life, my thoughts turned more toward going to a southern school. No question, one of the driving factors in my choice of college had to do with the fact that Princeton started earlier in the fall, but the biggest factor was the fact that I thought I could win the International Class series again. There I was, something like .003 of a point behind Arthur Knapp for the title—which was like the Holy Grail for me.

So I called the placement officer at Choate, D. D. Walsh, and shared my interest in a warm-climate university with him. We discussed it for a time, and he mentioned three schools he thought would be good for me: Tulane, which was a little too far away; Duke, which was okay distance-wise but a little big; and then he mentioned Washington and Lee. I was intrigued, and once I learned more about the school, its location, and its size I decided to go there.

In the end, I lost the International Class title— but by deciding for Washington and Lee, I gained something far more precious.

It was the finest twist of fate that brought Jane Pennybacker into my life. By then, I had moved down to Washington and Lee, and was out with a friend named David Garland Brown. Jane, meanwhile, had come up from the University of Tennessee with a close friend of hers, Ann Stowers, who was part of the old Stowers Furniture family. Jane and David were both from Knoxville, so when Ann would come up, Jane would come with her.

I just loved Jane Pennybacker from the first moment I saw her. She had the brownest of eyes, in which I found myself immediately and hopelessly lost. Added to that, I was utterly charmed by her. She was pretty, to be sure, but there was more to it. She was totally without guile. There was an innocence about her, a sincerity that struck a chord with me.

One night, Jane was out on a blind date with my roommate Thomas Jefferson Lee. When we got home that night, I asked Tommy, "Listen, are you going with

Second from the left in the front row, trying hard to appear studious in this Washington and Lee class photo in 1947.

her? Because I think she's terrific." The second Tommy said no, I said, "I'm going to call her."

The lesson here is don't oversell. When you get the answer you want, close the deal.

Jane was a classic beauty, with features as soft as an Irish morning mist. As we spent more time together, I learned that she had quit the University of Tennessee to work as a dental assistant after her sixty-year-old father Claude, a retired dispatcher with Southern Railroad, had a stroke. Her family had a beautiful house in Knoxville, but they were just hanging on—and to help them make ends meet, Jane went to work.

After just a few months of seeing Jane every time she came to Lexington, I started driving to see her in Knoxville. If you do not think I was in love, consider that it was 320 miles down to her place . . . and another 320 miles back . . . with no freeways. I'd drive down there on a Friday afternoon after my last class, and then try to drive back during Sunday night to get there in time for my first class on Monday.

To borrow the old Texas fishing phrase, clearly I was gut-hooked—head-over-heels in love. Our courtship continued for another two years, and somewhere along the way it struck me that Jane was the woman with whom I wanted to spend the rest of my life. I could see myself having children with her, and growing old together.

Happily, she felt the same way about me; and on January 3, 1947, at the tender age of nineteen, I eloped with Jane and married her in the upper northwest Georgia town of Rossville—just south of Chattanooga on the Georgia-Tennessee state line. Why Rossville, some 400 miles from Lexington, Virginia? Because it was the closest place you could go to be married without being twenty-one years old.

For our honeymoon as newlyweds, Jane Pennybacker Mosbacher returned with me to Lexington—where I was still in the midst of my first year in law school. Knowing I had done something that would definitely NOT please Pop or my mother, I didn't tell anyone in the family about the marriage until the end of the semester—six months later.

So there we were in the meantime, living in Mrs. Eichelberger's small boarding house, man and wife to all our friends—thankfully none of whom were from New York. Everyone else who had heard about it, I later came to understand, was too terrified to be the first person to tell my father.

When the moment of truth finally came in late May, I walked into Pop's study, and when he looked up from his desk, I said rather matter-of-factly, "Pop, I thought you should know I married Jane Pennybacker a while back." I continued to explain how my newfound status in life came to pass; but with each syllable to escape my mouth and register in his mind, I could see a vesuvial outburst building behind those piercing eyes.

"I suppose you got the poor girl pregnant," he angrily charged.

When I quickly denied it, thus removing the only plausible reason for such a rash act in his view, exasperation visibly overtook him, adding a new layer of disappointment to what was a roiling fury. "Damn, you are even stupider than I thought you were! What a dumb thing to do."

As the fuse on this confrontation continued to burn, Pop asked, "Just what do you think you are going to do now?" Of course, I had this master plan that was somewhat faulty in hindsight, but at least it had the virtue of being true. I was going to get a job in a law office in Lexington, where they promised me some associate work; and Jane was going to continue working as a dental assistant. We were going to work our way through graduate school, and then I

With Jane shortly after we disclosed our marriage to Pop and Mom in 1948.

was going to be a lawyer in Virginia—and I knew I was going to do alright. To be sure, I was not lacking confidence back then. I didn't have much sense, but plenty of confidence.

Upon hearing my rudimentary plan, the fuse ran its course. Pop was even more infuriated and exploded, "Get out of here. You're out of my life. I never want to see you again."

I had tasted the lash of Pop's temper many times in the past, but there was something different this time. Once I got downstairs, my mother told me, "Don't leave, Bobby. Just stay out of your father's sight." She was great with Jane when I brought her home, so Jane and I stayed in the little teahouse on the property—the one George Gershwin had used. Pop knew we were there, of course, but he had mixed emotions—and didn't particularly care to see us at that time.

If you're caught out on the water by a bad storm, the best thing to do is take down the sail and ride it out. That's essentially what we were doing out in the teahouse—waiting for the storm to pass.

Meanwhile, my mother stepped into this breach and served as the mediator, cajoling Pop to soften his stance even just a little. In time, her efforts paid off. About three weeks later, we went to visit Pop's partner, Harry T. F. Johnson, whose socialite daughter Honey met and married Dick Berlin after my parents introduced them. Jane and I were visiting at the Johnson house with Mom and maybe my sister, Barbara, when Pop drove up.

My mother was very soft, and rarely lost her temper. If she did, however, watch out! She was, after all, a redhead. But mostly she had a sweet, wonderful disposition. When she saw Pop pull up to the Johnson home in one of his convertibles, she turned to me and said softly, "Well, dear, I think you better take Penny out to see your father."

As we were walking out to see him, however, apprehension got the better of me and I not-so-chivalrously suggested to my new bride: "Sweetheart, honey, you talk to him first." Without missing a beat, Jane gamely hopped in to the car next to Pop, kissed him on the cheeks and said, "Oh Pop, I hope you're not mad at me."

"No, honey, I'm not mad at you," he said. "*It's that goddamn son of mine!*" He was still mad, but I could tell he was starting to break. A day or two later, he tracked me down at the house. "Alright, I want to see you. I want you in the office tomorrow morning, and you better work your ass off!"

I was out of jail, but understood I was still on probation with him. The deal was, like my cousin Stan and my brother Bus, I would go to work for Pop at Mosbacher Properties on a full-time basis—a deal I accepted.

Less than a year later, however, we were sitting out on the porch after dinner talking, when Pop told Bus and me, "The oil business has a tremendous future. One of you boys has to get down there and check into it. I think Houston is the best place, but Dallas and Midland are possibilities, too. One of you should go investigate what we could and should be doing in that industry." Then he added: "Don't come back in a week. You've got to stay probably a month or two and find out what's going on."

Then he turned to Bus. "What do you think?"

My wonderful mother, Gertrude Mosbacher. Pop affectionately called her "Red."

Bus recoiled. "Oh, I don't see any point in doing that," he said. My brother wasn't the kind to hop to a new adventure. He was exceedingly bright, to the point of brilliance in my view; but he demurred on Pop's offer. The fact is Bus and Pop rarely agreed on anything. If Pop had suggested that I go, who knows which Mosbacher might have ended up in Texas!

In contrast, I was totally game. "That's a great idea," I volunteered instantly, jumping at the chance to explore what many at that time considered an exotic part of the country and delve into an entirely new industry.

Part of my enthusiasm, I am sure, stemmed from a desire to strike out on my own. After all, from our earliest days in sailing my brother and I had been taught—encouraged, even—to take charge, chart our own course, and compete to win. Having spent so much time on the water in that environment, I guess I had come to revel in any level of independence.

Indeed, as the time for our departure drew nearer, the same feelings of ex-hilaration and anticipation that I had before my first Star race resurfaced, but absent any hint of hesitation at diving into the unknown. Self-confidence had never been my Achilles heel, and the year I had spent as a married workingman with Pop had groomed me, or so I felt, for the challenge ahead.

Finally, in the fall of 1948, Jane and I finally set out by car for the Lone Star State. Our journey that day lacked the drama and uncertainty of my grand-father's departure from Germany. I was backed with ample resources, for one thing, and we knew several folks in each of the cities we would be visiting. In fact, the only question mark in my mind as we set out on the first leg of our journey to see Jane's family in Knoxville concerned our impending parenthood. By then we had been married for nearly two years, and Jane was pregnant with our first child.

The next leg of our travels carried us to Louisiana, where I spent a week or so in Shreveport with Arthur Carmody, the man who ran North Central Texas Oil Company. Old Art was a very nice man, and respected in the industry. Like a lot of people back then, he used to call me "Bobby," and I used to hate it. But he was very generous with his time and his sound advice.

I was a neophyte, and at the time really didn't have a clue what was in store for Jane and me. As Pop would say, from little acorns oak trees grow, and we didn't even have acorns just yet. Art showed me the ropes by teaching me the basics of oil field exploration and how various deals were put together, but near the end of our week together he said something that was as important as any-thing else he taught me there in Shreveport.

"Bobby," Mr. Carmody said, "it takes a lot of patience in this business. Just remember: when something looks good, enjoy it, because there are a lot of times when things don't look so good."

In the months and years ahead, that proved to be very good advice.

Chapter 8 JUST GET THE CRUMBS

While I was first coming of age at twenty-one and getting ready to strike out on my own, Pop said to me, "Just get the crumbs of a big business—just get the crumbs. Don't be the first guy to make an item. Just get into business and get the crumbs." That was Pop's way of suggesting that I shouldn't start out trying to get too big, or to take on the core part of a business sector. Rather, he was suggesting, keep your overhead and risk minimal.

By the time I arrived in Houston in 1948, of course, I was far from the first person to get into the oil business. I was just hoping there were any crumbs left.

After all, it had been nearly half a century since the oil rush in Texas started on January 10, 1901, when Captain Anthony Lucas, a retired Austrian naval officer, drilled a new rotary bit 1,139 feet down through a salt dome and quicksand, and brought in the famous Lucas Gusher at Spindletop near Beaumont. For nine days, until the well was capped, crude oil shot 100 feet in the air.

For Texas and for the oil industry itself, of course, this was the shot heard round the world. "In no time at all, the Spindletop field was a jungle of drilling rigs and derricks," George Fuermann wrote in *Houston: Land of the Big Rich*. "It was said that you could walk across Spindletop without touching the ground, merely stepping from one derrick floor to another."[1]

As you might expect, Spindletop gave birth to many an oil company, and many a family fortune. The early oilers were the Hammils, the Blaffers, and the Abercrombies. Then came Hugh Roy Cullen and J. M. West, and their huge Thompson field. Then Hugh Roy went his own way, partnered with Humble Oil, and brought in the Tom O'Connor field in South Texas in 1934—with an estimated reserve of 500,000,000 barrels of oil, which at that time was worth at least a billion dollars. That discovery alone made Cullen the richest oilman in the world.

From a distance, Pop saw these wildcatters make these great discoveries. He had followed the earliest oil companies from his perch on the Curb, where

---

1. George Fuermann, *Houston: Land of the Big Rich* (Garden City, NY: Doubleday Books, 1951), 16.

he saw vast fortunes being made. One of the discoveries that captured my father's attention was the Old Ocean Field, which was located about twenty miles southwest of Houston in Brazoria County. Two drillers, Dan Harrison and "Mr. Jim" Abercrombie, developed the field, and in 1942 Harrison sold out of the partnership to Magnolia Petroleum Company for $27 million. Four years later, Abercrombie sold his share in Old Ocean to Stanolind Co. of Indiana for $54 million—causing a major rift between Mr. Jim and his former partner.

I guess Harrison didn't think $27 million was much of a consolation prize.

Pop also knew about Sid Richardson, Clint Murchison, and a young guy named John Mecom who was just getting started. He was just fascinated with the tremendous upside to the business. Of course, because of his thorough research, Pop also recognized the downsides as well—of which there were plenty.

For once, however, Pop was not ahead of the curve when he suggested that I strike out for Texas. At the time, a bunch of "carpetbaggers" were descending on the Lone Star State after the war. A lot of them were veterans, like my friends Leon Payne and Bill Kilroy. Another transplanted Easterner was a young war hero and Yale graduate named George Herbert Walker Bush, who originally settled with his wife Barbara and their first child, George W., out west in Odessa in June of 1948—just a few months before Jane and I made our way to Houston with our first child still "in the oven."

Without a doubt, Texas loomed large as the place to be, and it was an exciting time.

During our migration into Texas in 1948, Jane and I traveled to Dallas first and spent about ten days exploring what was happening there, oil-wise. Helping matters was that we knew quite a few people, and were introduced to others. One of our new friends, for instance, was the Marcus family of the Neiman-Marcus store chain. Stanley Marcus was running the show then, a fascinating guy I enjoyed getting to know. I also enjoyed meeting another young up-and-coming oil and gas operator named Ed Cox, who was fresh off his Navy service in World War II.[2]

Leaving Dallas, I drove to Houston while Jane flew, and we met at the old Warwick Hotel. The Warwick was a nice residential hotel built in 1926 near Hermann Park that John Mecom would acquire some years later. At one point, as I recall, we also popped out to Midland and saw a few friends there. The

2. Incidentally, one of my grandsons recently graduated from the Ed Cox Business School at Southern Methodist University—so it is safe to assume that Ed did eventually learn something about supply and demand!

area out West was experiencing a severe drought, but the people couldn't have been more welcoming and pleasant. Upon arriving back in Houston, Jane and I decided to settle there.

We immediately loved Houston. We liked the atmosphere. We probably hadn't talked to five people when we arrived at our conclusion, but we could tell Houston was a unique southwestern city. It was friendly, independent, and broad-based. Of course, the "Bayou City" also was warm—in every way—in the summer. But helping matters was the fact that it was, in true Texas fashion even back then, purported to be the "most air-conditioned city in the world."

Dallas, on the other hand, felt like an Eastern city. The denizens there were trying to build that image with the proper dress (which probably had a lot to do with Neiman-Marcus). Dallas was a very nice city, but it had a different feeling—more formal. This was nearly sixty years ago, and in my view, all those factors are no less true today.

We rented our first house, which was behind the newly completed Shamrock Hotel built by independent oilman Glenn H. McCarthy. Just months after we arrived, incidentally, the Shamrock was officially opened on St. Patrick's Day in 1949 in what was characterized both as a "flamboyant dedication ceremony," and the first "national media sensation" to originate in Houston. Some 175 film stars and executives from Los Angeles and journalists from across the country descended on Houston; and the event, to which the public was invited, was apparently so rowdy that a live network radio broadcast featuring Dorothy Lamour had to be canceled.

Jack Benny—another friend of Pop's—came to Houston for the opening of the Shamrock Hotel, and he called me at home just to say hello. Jane answered the phone, whereupon the actor introduced himself in that unmistakable voice, "Hi, this is Jack Benny."

Jane thought it was a prankster attempting a phony call, so she shot back: "Oh really? Well, this is Hedy Lamarr!"

Our first house at 2204 Dorrington had two big bedrooms upstairs, a living room, a little library, a small dining room, and a kitchen downstairs. Since I was only starting out in business, and office space in Houston at that time was very expensive at $200 a month, I also worked out of the house for a while.

Jane was very pregnant when we arrived in Houston, so we quickly tracked down a highly recommended obstetrician named Robert Johnston—who, by then, had already delivered about 10,000 babies. Dr. Johnston was a kindly old southern gentleman, and he immediately sought to put our mind at ease about the impending arrival of our first child: "Now, don't you children worry about a thing," he assured us in his gentle drawl. "Everything is going to be alright. Let me do all the worrying."

He was right. On January 13, 1949, I took Jane to St. Joseph's Hospital where she delivered our first child, Diane, without complication. After we advertised for someone to help take care of our new baby, a young African American woman named Cardella Smith, then still in her early thirties, answered the call. She quickly became a trusted member of our family. Most importantly, Cardella loved and cared for our kids like they were her own. She was nurturing, but in a no-nonsense, straight-talk kind of way. Later on, she took care of the children when Jane and I would travel, and there is no doubt that they were in as good, or better, hands than when we were home. On top of all of that, Cardella was a very good cook who specialized in all the southern classics of the time. Staying fit with Cardella in the kitchen was always a challenge.

So there we were: strangers in a strange but friendly land, and now a new family.

Though Pop didn't appreciate it at the time, getting married as early in life as I did was a blessing in many respects. Up to that point, I had been the freest of free spirits, but there is no question I also had to, and did, mature quickly with my new family and work responsibilities.

My son Rob thinks if I had remained in New York to start my career, I probably would have gone crazy working under my father and older brother—and he may be right. I may not be a terrific leader, but I'm much, much worse as a follower. What I wanted most of all, like many people, was to be my own boss; and going to Texas gave me that chance.

When I first set out, Pop said he would back me to some degree, but it was based on my not trying to do anything in the drilling area. I was only to buy royalties, which is simply a small percentage of every barrel of oil, or cubic foot of natural gas, produced by a well. One of the key features Pop liked about royalties was that they came free of all costs associated in drilling the well.

Pop was, throughout his life, inordinately risk-adverse—and at that time, it was estimated that only one out of every nine wells was a producer. For all the eye-catching stories of outrageous wealth in the industry, the Texas landscape in the late 1940s was also littered with plenty of dry holes—or "dusters."

By the spring of 1949, I acquired some office space in the National Standard building in downtown Houston, and began assembling a small staff. One of my first hires brought a young Betty Ackerman into my life. I wasn't sure I needed another full-time assistant so I told Betty I might hire her temporarily, but she said she really had to have a job because she had fibbed to her mother

Early days in business. I was fortunate enough to have talented professionals like Bill Mendell, left, and Dave Remick advising me from the beginning.

to leave her native South Carolina. Even though she didn't know what oil was at the start, we struck an unspoken deal. Technically, I never hired Betty, but she stayed with me for over forty years.

Two other folks eventually came down from New York, sent by Pop to help out. One was an interesting man named Ben Germani. Ben's dad, Tony, had emigrated from Italy and took care of Pop's garden, which had everything from orchids to corn. Ben was very bright, and Pop recognized this—so in typical Pop fashion he offered to pay for Ben's tuition to attend Brown University. As it turned out, Brown wasn't a good fit for Ben, so he soon quit school, started working for Pop, and became one of his most trusted employees. Shortly after I arrived in Houston, Pop sent Ben down to work with me—obviously to see what the hell Pop's son was spending all this money on. So Ben arrived by train, and like Betty Ackerman also stayed with me until his retirement many years later.

Another guy Pop sent to check on me was Dobie McDevitt. Dobie had been an assistant golf pro back at Quaker Ridge, and was roughly ten years older than me. Pop suggested that Dobie come down and help out as a landman, or "lease hound"— essentially someone who researches the owner of mineral rights on a given property and then contacts the individual to attempt to negotiate a mineral lease. Dobie was a sweetheart of a guy; and even though he didn't know a thing about the oil business, he was good at buying leases because everybody liked him. He was fun to have around, and it always seemed like we were laughing about something.

After he came on board Mosbacher Energy, for instance, Dobie liked to tell what happened after he decided to rescind his status as a professional golfer and become an amateur again. Though Pop got to know Dobie when he worked as an assistant pro at Quaker Ridge, Dobie had actually grown up in Houston and learned to play golf with the likes of golfing greats Jimmy Demaret and Jackie Burke. While Dobie's day job was working for me, he wanted to get back to competitive golf—and his only option was to do it as an amateur. This was a big and unusual step for a pro golfer to make, and to complete the process Dobie had to appeal to the Professional Golfers Association and visit with one of their representatives. This was all done as a precaution to make sure a pro golfer didn't simply want to go out and win a bunch of events against less talented, part-time golfers. At one point during the interview, the PGA man asked to see Dobie's golf swing so he picked up a five-iron and took a few swings.

"No problem," the PGA rep said after seeing Dobie's unorthodox swing. "I see no harm in letting you go back to being an amateur."

As a lease hound, Dobie routinely pulled a stunt on prospective sellers that still makes me smile. During the negotiation, he would sit there with a pen on top of the papers in his lap; and at one point during the conversation he would suddenly lift the papers up, in a premeditated spasm, causing the pen to pop into the lap of the prospect. Dobie made the whole thing look like an accident—and once the landowner naturally reached for the pen, Dobie would casually say, "Well, since you have the pen, why don't we just go ahead and sign this thing?"

As pathetic as it sounds, this gambit worked more often than it didn't.

Of course, the fact that Pop had Ben and Dobie come down to keep an eye on me didn't show complete confidence at the outset. At every step along the way, Pop was very interested in how we were doing—how we were growing. He called the office every day; and if I wasn't there or couldn't take the call, Pop would talk to Betty or Dobie. He liked to know what was happening. He didn't interfere, but he was very interested.

To give Pop a good sense for how business was going, we would also regularly send him copies of the logs that detailed the activities at each of our wells. The problem was: the copier we had wasn't a modern machine, where you could push a button and let the machine do most of the work. Instead, this was one of the first Haloid machines that had three solution tanks you had to fill. Then, you had to dry the pages on an attached dryer. If you burned the paper while drying it, you would have to start over. Even after all these years, Betty still remembers how maddening it was.

Recently, I found a copy of a memo that survived this draconian copying process. It was dated December 29, 1949, and detailed my first year of activity in Texas. My first foray into the business, for example, came on December 29, 1948 when I purchased 42.9 royalty acres at $25 per acre, or a total of $1,172.08, from Mrs. Adele Buss in LaSalle County, Texas. A driller named Lloyd Smith—a very formal man who would later become my father-in-law—was drilling a well just west of our purchase called #1 Reed, but he abandoned the well in March of 1949 so nothing came of that first investment.

Not a glorious start.

I partnered with Lloyd Smith on my second deal as well—this one in Wharton County. I bought the ten-acre royalty for $2,500, kept half, and Lloyd and his partner took the other half. They were going to drill a well on the property, and asked if I wanted in on the drilling side as well. I wasn't quite ready to assume that kind of risk, so I continued my legwork at the county courthouses reviewing property records—looking for more royalty leads.

Reviewing records at a courthouse sounds like dull, dry work—and it could be that. Helping matters in my case, as I saw it, usually there were very nice ladies in the courthouse who would help me—sometimes they were older ladies, and sometimes not quite so old. Young, cute women took the tedium out of the research; and once I found a good prospect I went out to see the rancher or the farmer.

Aside from pure luck, absolutely crucial to my early success buying royalties, I am sure, is the fact that I never admitted I was from New York. To help obscure this uncomfortable fact, I remember developing a Texas drawl fairly quickly. Some of it may have been natural, but I have to confess: much of it was pure acting. I also learned a little bit about rice farming and cattle ranching, enough to at least be conversant with the ranchers and farmers on whom I regularly called.

During my first year, I spent $54,863.33 to buy twenty-one royalties in different parts of Texas and Oklahoma—Leon, Grimes, Trinity, Polk, Victoria, Liberty, Dimmit, Jackson, Hamilton, Yoakum, and Zapata counties in Texas; and Harmon County in Oklahoma. Luckily, six or seven of them turned out to be good, so I wasn't just getting the crumbs of the business, but some real table scraps. I quickly came to appreciate that it's not the quantity, but the quality, that counts most.

Quality also describes the geologists with whom I was privileged to work,

Prowling for oil during a 1950s trip to Montana. From left to right are David Schaenen of Mule Creek Oil Co., W. R. Beam of Northern Pacific Railway, yours truly, and independent oilman Cy Tanner.

starting with Shapleigh Gray and Bill Mendell. Shapleigh studied geologic formations up and down the Gulf Coast, and was an encyclopedic resource on what areas had produced. I frequently worked with Shapleigh, usually to terrific results.

Bill Mendell, who later became one of my partners as well as president of Mosbacher Energy, was a Stanford graduate in geology; a graduate of the Royal School of Mines in Engineering; and a twenty-five-year veteran of Shell. He had left Shell just as I was getting established in Houston, so my timing was good.

As I say, I'd rather be lucky than smart.

In due course, I met another geologist named Dave Remick. Between Dave and Bill, then, we had two guys covering Louisiana and Texas. They had been just our consultants to start, and even after they moved in with us they still retained some of their independence. We had the big reception room, and a big conference room, and I had my own little office off the conference room. Pop had a duplicate guy in New York, who kept the maps up-to-date.

The plan called for me to work with the geologists to buy royalties under the plays they would develop or knew about, with the geologists getting a little piece of the deal as well. Early on, for example, I went in on a deal with Howard and Jimmy Boyles, a pair of small lease and deal brokers. Really nice guys. It involved a property located on a salt dome in Brazoria County, just south of Houston, which turned out to be very, very good. We split it fifty-fifty, and each paid $10,000—so it was a $20,000 royalty deal. Once it started producing, it paid out the original cost as many as six times a year for many years.

Before arriving in Houston, I only knew one oilman here. His name was Norman Boch—who is still around, now in his upper eighties. Norm was with his father-in-law's very successful company, Fraenkel Oil and Gas, and Pop had met them. Early on, Norm and I forged a unique bond, you might say. He had been the light-heavyweight champ of the Armed Services in Europe during World War II, but I had wrestled competitively at Choate—so I used to regularly challenge Norm to a wrestling match. I did the same thing with Hank Harkins, a star football player for the University of Texas in the 1940s, with whom I also worked in the oil business.

Norm and Hank were great big guys, very fit, and as strong as they come. They thought they were tough, but I knew how to wrestle, and they didn't, and it drove them crazy when I got them into a hold from which they couldn't escape—which I would do almost as a matter of routine. Looking back, I have zero doubt I annoyed the hell out of those guys—this little guy badgering them to wrestle.

It was the same thing when it came to arm-wrestling. I had pulled so many lines while sailing that my forearms were fairly well-developed, and since I wasn't a world-class tennis player I had resorted to arm-wrestling in my show-offy prep school days. That continued after I went into business.

To wit, I was in my office one day meeting with Bob Parsley, who worked with an oilfield supply company and was brother-in-law to one of the great early Houston oilmen, George Strake. Bob wanted my business, and when I was slow to give it to him he finally lost his patience. "Do I have to arm wrestle you to get an order?" he asked, somewhat impertinently.

I knew I could beat Bob arm wrestling, and maybe he did too, because before long he changed the bet. "Let's leg wrestle instead," he suggested. So we did, right there on the floor of the office. Not a very dignified or conventional sales call to be sure, but Bob beat me and true to my word I gave him an order for some of his pipe.

Around the same time, I was introduced to a distinguished art professor at the University of Texas named Charles Umlauf while visiting my dear friend Meredith Long at his home. Umlauf was a big and somewhat macho guy, and fancied himself quite the arm-wrester as well. "I can beat anyone," he told me in a matter-of-fact way, as if there was no debating the point.

Well, that didn't go over too well with me, so we got after it right there in Meredith's living room—on a beautiful cut-glass coffee table. We were huffing and puffing and straining with all our might when suddenly the table gave way—and all four legs shot out in different directions. The glass didn't fare much better. Curiously, all these years later Meredith remembers that unforgivable breach of etiquette even better than I do.

When I arrived in Houston, the city was buzzing with so much activity that meeting people with similar interests was never much of a problem. Everywhere you went, you ran into one guy after another with a series of maps rolled up under his arm, ready to tell you how he was going to make you and him rich.

My new office was also conveniently located near an old Houston institution, the Esperson Drug Store. Back then, the one place you invariably went if you were looking for someone to trade with—involving any kind of project—was the Esperson Building in downtown Houston. That was THE place to gather for deal brokers and would-be oilmen of all stripes—the place where so many of the earlier oil fortunes were made in Houston. I recall how many speculators just starting out, or veteran brokers trying to recoup a lost fortune, used the bank of pay telephones at the rear of the ground floor lobby as their "home office."

In those days, drug stores served nonalcoholic drinks along with coffee and ice cream sodas. You could also get a sandwich. But more useful to us, the Esperson Drug Store had a lot of zinc-topped tables with barstools where you could sit, look at maps, and visit with all the people who were buying, selling, or trading—essentially, trying to make a buck any way they could in the "awl bidness."

I bought a few leases at the Esperson, but just as important, I met a bunch of people at all levels of the industry there.

Another popular gathering place for business or just plain socializing in Houston was a restaurant called Maxim's, owned and operated by the irrepressible Camille Berman. I have always liked to cook, and enjoy a good meal, so Jane and I frequented Maxim's. Camille usually had flowers on his best customers' table, but he loved the ladies even more than steady customers. If an

Getting ready to tee off with friends at Houston Country Club in 1955. Hard to believe, but knee-high socks were in fashion back then.

attractive woman happened to walk in, it wouldn't take long before the flowers were whisked off your table to land on hers.

Once, when Pop wanted to send me a case of a wonderful red Burgundy wine called La Tache, we had it sent to Camille because only restaurants could receive alcohol—this was in the day before "liquor by the drink," or the even more liberal shipping rules of today. When I went to Maxim's to retrieve the wine, however, I could tell a bottle or two was missing. Camille had obviously sampled it, but I couldn't stay mad at him for long.

It was through Camille that Jane and I met John and Dominique de Menil. John helped run worldwide operations for the Schlumberger oil services company, and both he and Dominique were keenly interested in art. They were largely responsible for helping to guide and support Houston's blossoming cultural life. One day, they invited Jane and me over for cocktails and started pulling out canvas after canvas of paintings by a Belgian artist named Rene Magritte—who today is recognized as one of the great surrealists of the twentieth century. Offered the chance to buy as many Magritte works as I wanted for

At home with Jane and the kids in 1959. Kathi and Rob are holding the Mallory Cup, while Lisa (in Jane's lap) and Dee are more preoccupied with the Gold Cup trophy.

$10,000 each, I passed. I had never heard of the guy, and the work itself seemed a tad too avant-garde for my taste.

Today, Magritte's best works sell for millions of dollars.

So much for my art judgment.

All in all, though, I was off to a good start in Houston—meeting people, making modest headway with business, and clicking on all cylinders in regards to my young and growing family. Dee was a beautiful child, and Rob followed in short order. Life with Jane couldn't have been more idyllic or happier.

As I was raising the sail on my career and pulling out of the marina, Pop was

Pop with Ken Jamieson, who became Chairman of Esso about this time (1969) and eventually changed the corporation's name to Exxon.

drawing down the sail and tying off at least one part of his business activities to the mooring for good. He sold his Curb membership in December of 1951 to Gerald B. Nielson, some thirty-nine years after he first started on Broad Street as a runner. By then, Pop had without question become an integral part of that "firmament," as he put it.

That same year, in fact, both the old guard and the dissidents in the Curb community joined together to elect Pop's former clerk, John Mann, as chairman of the Exchange. Mann, whose career was closely tied to my father, went on to serve an unprecedented five terms.

When he left the Exchange, Pop also took several of his seats and gave them to his clerks, making them all specialists. Some time later, when my nephew Clint was working on the Curb as a summer intern, many of the very top specialists approached him, a mere clerk in the E. F. Hutton booth, and introduced themselves. These were big names on the Exchange, and one of them related to Clint how Pop gave away his stocks and seats, and left several million dollars in operating capital behind for his former colleagues.

Looking back at Pop's career on the Curb, it is hard for those who knew him not to admire the trails that he blazed. Because of what he did, and the way he did it, life for the rest of his family was smoother sailing.

Pop used to say, "influence is something you always have until you try to use it," but clearly Emil Mosbacher Sr. was an influential figure who left a mark on the New York Curb Exchange. After he retired, the Curb Market—which became the American Stock Exchange in January of 1953—dedicated a plaque in Pop's honor that reads: "In special recognition of Emil Mosbacher, whose vision and dedication were instrumental in transforming the American Stock Exchange from a curbside market to an international securities market."

Once manipulated by the Curb's management, he was in the end respected and perhaps even admired. Not too shabby for a poor immigrant's son—but don't worry, Pop never got the "big head." For one thing, he still had me to worry about in Texas, and I was about to take a risky step that would stretch his comfort zone.

After a few years of buying royalties, just as Pop wanted, I saw that the real money—maybe not net, but gross—was in putting deals together and drilling wells. That's what I wanted to start doing, much to the dismay of my father. His theory had always been, "Always do a deal where you can win a lot, but only lose a little—and always know the downside of your losses." In other words, know exactly how much you're risking before you shake hands.

What I was proposing to do in drilling wells definitely did not fit within Pop's risk-adverse formula. As usual, I was pushing him past his limits.

The difference between royalties and drilling is important. If you bought a royalty for $10,000, for example, you won maybe a quarter of an eighth or 1/32 of the production of the well. If you "promoted" a well or put the drilling deal together, however, you may end up leaving the same amount in it—but owning at least a quarter of the project, and as much as a half. Obviously, promoting a well takes a lot more work and risk, but also has more of an upside to it if you strike oil or gas.

Unfortunately, this new and riskier phase of my career as an oilman got off to a rocky start. My first well was in Duval County—about seventy miles west of Corpus Christi in South Texas. At age twenty-three, I guess I looked young enough that the drilling contractor felt compelled to ask me, "Are you old enough to sign a contract?"

I only had a quarter interest in that project, for about $10,000, and it turned out to be a dry hole. After that, somebody started calling me the "Envoy to the Duke of Duval County." (The real Duke of Duval County, George Parr, and his political machine were the closest thing to royalty in that part of Texas.)

After that first shutout, I worried my career might turn out like that of John Mayo—the wildcatter who distinguished himself by "promoting" or putting deals together to drill 117 wells over a seven-year period before he hit his first producer. John was able to survive this infamous dry spell because most of his deals were farm-outs from the majors, the big oil companies. He kept just a whisker of an interest and took some cash out of each deal, so he more than survived. Pop actually hosted Mayo in New York one time; and like everybody else he liked John because, despite his string of disappointments, his word was good. If John Mayo told you something, you could count on it.

Fortunately, I was luckier as a driller than John, as I discovered on my second deal in Colorado County, some sixty miles to the southwest of Houston. Bill Mendell knew there was a nice little structure that might contain a gas deposit. At first, Shell— which owned the rights to the project—said they were going to farm it out to other drillers. This brings me to an old industry saying that "no major oil company ever discovered any oil." They let all the independents like Mosbacher Energy take the risk, and then buy us out if we hit a producer.

In my case, Shell agreed to let us have this particular drilling prospect if we put together a "unit," or a lot of acreage combining leases from other people. The idea was that we would get them to agree to share proportionate parts of the royalty, and hold a 640-acre "unit" with one well.

As I was working on this deal, I was fortunate to recruit a big local guy named Homer Kolliba, a Czech who lived near the field—and who was key to our success. I say this because many of the lease owners we approached were local folks also of Czech descent, and Homer had an easier time connecting with them. In fact, Homer would get all red-faced, stamp on the ground, and argue until people would sign up just to get rid of him.

After we put the deal together, the Shell representative said, "You really put that block together?"

"Sure, just like you told me to," I said.

"We have been trying to do that for almost four years," came the reply. "We wouldn't have farmed this thing out to you if we had known you could actually put the unit together."

Having cleared that hurdle, I then recruited Hank Harkins, one of the old "Iron Men" from the University of Texas football teams, to do the drilling. Hank was with Kirkwood Drilling and had the equipment, and was offering to "turn-key" it for me—in exchange for which I gave Hank $40,000 and a 25 percent ownership of the deal. He later said, "Why didn't I trade you harder? I think I could have gotten you to $45,000!" We became very good friends and did a lot of deals together.

Involving Hank and his company was key to my being able to convince Pop to let me do this drilling deal. "Hank is going to turn-key for us," I reassured Pop. "There is essentially no risk. He'll take the fall."

"Well, suppose he goes broke?" Pop shot back.

"I'll go broke after he does in that case," came my less-then-totally-satisfactory reply.

Pop finally just threw up his hands.

Bill Mendell knew somebody who he thought that we could sell another quarter of the deal to for $25,000. So we had half of the well, for $20,000. That is a lot better than royalty. You wouldn't get more than a 1/32 for that money on a royalty, and we had half the total deal. As luck would have it, we drilled down to 9,000 feet and it proved to be a very good well.

Like an oil well, a gas well comes in with a tremendous roar—with a great big fiery flare of gas shooting 100 feet into the air, at a horizontal angle away from the rig. It's one of the most exciting things you can experience. As we were trying to bring this well in, however, I was walking around the mud pit with a camera getting ready to take a picture of this massive flame; but it never came.

"I wouldn't worry about it too much," Bill Mendell told me. "I think the cement job didn't hold right, so I think we got to squeeze it, do it again."

"Doing it again," however, meant we were starting to sink some real money into the deal.

On the second try, in an act of sheer superstition, I declared I wasn't going to take any pictures. And wouldn't you know, it came in beautifully! We were so happy, in no small part because we were getting seven-and-a-half cents per cubic foot for our gas—a great rate at the time.

Of course, the $40,000 we invested to drill this well was only the start. To complete the well would require another $50,000 by the time we finished the tanks, so our deal had nearly $100,000 in it—with my stake alone at just under $50,000 for our 50 percent ownership stake. The same well would cost ten times as much to drill today; but even back then at those low prices, the well paid out pretty quickly.

Then along came Michael T. Halbouty, who was a great showman and a really well-known geologist and oilman. Mike had drilled a well near ours. It wasn't nearly as good a well, but he had a well. We met one day at the Petroleum Club in downtown Houston, and Mike pitch an idea to me. "Bobby," he said. "You should sell your gas to this intrastate pipeline. They don't pay as much, but they'll take more gas and you'll make more money."

Something didn't feel right about Mike's offer, so I tried to put him off— unsuccessfully—by feigning interest. "Well, that is interesting Mike," I said. "Let me think about that and get back to you."

In those days, major pipelines, like Texas or Houston, would take gas at a rate based on your reserves. This particular well in Colorado County, for example, had ten billion cubic feet, so the pipeline would take one million cubic feet a day. That was the going rate back then: one million for every ten billion cubic feet of gas.

Speaking at a meeting of the American Association of Petroleum Landmen in the 1960s.
I was proud to have served as president of that vitally important organization.

Halbouty had less than half of our reserves, though, so the pipeline people would only take half as much from his well. That's why he was trying to talk me into going to his pipeline, because they would take equally from both wells. The trouble was: they were only paying five cents, and I didn't want to do that.

Mike was always very aggressive, a hard-charger—which certainly served him well during his highly successful career. But after three or four conversations with him, with Mike still not taking "no" for an answer, I finally stopped returning his calls, which was a mistake. I should have candidly asked him, "What is it about 'no' you don't understand, Mike?"

Instead, I ducked his calls and gave him the silent treatment.

When he realized what was happening, Mike got so mad that he wouldn't talk to me for a couple of years. At the time, I was a punk kid all of about twenty-five years old, and he was considerably older—maybe forty-five or fifty—and was, even back then, considered a pretty big deal in the industry. Eventually, Mike got over my ducking him, and we went on to be dear friends.

Fortunately, I had Bill Mendell advising me. I didn't figure this all out by myself. I learned a huge amount of geology and engineering from him, some from Shapleigh Gray, and some from other geologists with whom I had worked. Mostly I learned because I was a pain in the neck—or persistent—and was always asking questions.

In all my time in the energy business, for all of the success with which I have been blessed, I have never had a grand slam—which might be an oil field with over 100,000,000 barrels where I had a big interest in it. I've had a bunch of singles, doubles, and triples—and a maybe few home runs with men on base. But no grand slams.

One of the first ventures of grander significance for me was a royalty and drilling play we made down in Zapata County, on the Rio Grande just north of the Valley. It was, and still is, a mighty poor part of Texas—cactus country. I remember how the farmers back then used to take these converted World War II flamethrowers and blow the needles off the prickly pears so the cows could eat them. Even with that provision made, you could only put twenty cows on a "640" (or 640 acres), which was also a square mile.

Wally Jayred served as our promotion man for this particular project, the Cinco de Mayo Field. Wally's job was made all the more difficult because we were "shut in." We were so far south, at first we couldn't get a pipeline to come to us. There was one called the Rio Grande Pipeline down in that vicinity, and the guy who was head of it at that time was Bob Herring. Bob later became head of Houston Natural Gas. (After Bob died, Ken Lay took over and merged HNG with the Omaha, Nebraska-based InterNorth to form a company they called Enron.)

I had sold other gas to Bob, but the Cinco de Mayo field was forty miles from his Rio Grande line—and it wasn't feasible for him to build that much pipe. Upon realizing this, I started to do what every oilman would do: worry. Some people offered to buy that gas for one cent in the ground, which was absurdly cheap. That's when I remembered that Pop knew an associate of Clint Murchison's—who was one of the big, big Texas names along with Sid Richardson, H. L. Hunt, and Hugh Roy Cullen. Pop somehow connected me with Mr. Murchison. We talked on the phone a few times, and he finally said, "I'll buy your gas, Bobby."

It turned out Mr. Murchison had a power line near the Cinco de Mayo field that he wanted to connect to his power plant in Laredo. (His manager in that area, Jack Bowen, later became CEO of Transco and a very dear friend of mine.)

I thought, "That's great, he [Murchison] is going to pay three cents in the ground." That's what I had heard. So I went up to see him. I was going to take a 7:00 A.M. flight, so I got to the airport a little after five. I was so nervous and excited that about 6:15 I fell asleep and missed the flight. So I called a guy and got a little puddle-jumper and paid him what was then a hell of a lot of money, $250, at a time when the regular fare for flying to Dallas probably cost $20.

My first impression after entering his spacious office was that Clint Murchison, the legend, was actually a little man. He also had little squinty eyes, but a kindly voice. And after he invited me to take a seat, he said, "Bobby, I'm glad to meet you. They tell me you are doing so well; you're such a fine young man; and I'm just so sorry that I can't pay you more than two cents for your gas."

I said, "Gee, Mr. Murchison, don't you think that is less than the market these days?"

He responded, "Yes, Bobby, I do, but my boys think I am crazy to buy it at all, because we have an offset lease next to yours. They think we can drain the entire field with our own well, and we don't have to buy your gas. But that isn't right."

What Murchison was subtly threatening to do, in a kindly, avuncular way, was to "sidetrack" or drill from his adjacent lease into the pocket or proven reserve of gas I was sitting over. Looking back, I now realize, I had made it to the big leagues in a sense, and Murchison was trying to see if I could hit a major league fastball.

"Thank you, Mr. Murchison," I said, realizing we didn't have much more to discuss. "I'll have to think about it, but I really don't think I can sell it for less than three cents."

His reply offered little comfort: "Well you think about it, and I'll try and hold those boys off for a little while."

As Murchison's people got ready to drill, however, Bill Mendell assessed our drilling tests and the geology and surmised that they couldn't access the same pocket of gas we had. "That's off the structure," he insisted. "They can't get under ours."

At the same time, I had gotten to know the county sheriff, a very nice man named Gutierrez. Shortly after returning to the Valley from Dallas, I approached him about the Murchison crew, and said, "I know it's part of your job, but I hope you're checking to see if there are any of those trucks for sidetracking out there. If you see any, we sure would appreciate your letting us know."

Then I innocently added, as was the custom in South Texas in those days, "Incidentally, I want to do something nice for your reelection campaign."

Shortly thereafter, the Murchison crew started to receive daily visits from Sheriff Gutierrez. I'd like to think that part of the reason they didn't sidetrack the Cinco de Mayo field was because he was going out there to check on it everyday. The sheriff would tell the Murchison crew, "I'm just checking on you fellows."

It kept them on their toes, and just as Bill predicted, they drilled a duster.

Then, as if the answer to a prayer, the people at the South Rio Grande Valley Gas Company said, "We've got a market now, and we'll pay you three cents." So I sold it for three cents in the ground.

Pop always said, "Never stretch to make a deal. Deals are like buses: if you miss one, another will come along."

We calculated that we had 42 billion cubic feet of gas in reserves net to us, which was a small reserve in those days. Nevertheless, we closed the Cinco de Mayo field deal in 1956, and I was paid $1.25 million over two years. Even though we had over $200,000 in that well and the field—and our net was closer to $1 million—I thought I was the richest sonofabitch in the world.

Most importantly, I felt like a certified oil and gas man.

We developed that field from about 1953 to 1955, and except for buying Jane a few things, I made a few noteworthy acquisitions. First, in 1950, I bought a bigger house in west Houston on Memorial Drive for $45,000. I've always been a big believer that you make your money in real estate the day you close the deal; and that part of Houston was really starting to take off as a place to live. We were able to get an acre and a quarter at the corner of Buckingham and Memorial with some wonderful trees and space for our growing brood of children.

A few years later, you couldn't even buy the land there for that price.

Another really big personal expenditure was the $1,000 I paid for an air conditioner in my car—which was more than the car itself cost. It's been said that "most Houston oilmen would rather have a dry hole than an imported car," and I had paid $960 for my first Chevrolet. The new air conditioner, however, took up most of the trunk. It had two glass tubes in the corner behind the backseat through which the cool air flowed, but if you hit a bump and bounced around, it would throw little bitty round ice cubes and hit you in the head with them.

But boy, it was worth every cent—particularly when I drove from Houston to just south of Laredo for six hours.

Aside from the house and the air-conditioned car, the success of the Cinco de Mayo project elevated my profile within the industry somewhat, and I think people started to look past my youthful appearance to see that maybe, just maybe, I might amount to something after all.

To be honest, Jane noticed that people were maybe seeing me differently before I did. I had gotten used to the fact that everyone with whom I was wheeling-and-dealing at that time was older than me, and because of my stern upbringing would always show the proper deference when addressing anyone older than me.

One night after I got home from work and Jane and I were having a cocktail before dinner, she said: "You know, sweetheart, you're dealing with all of these people and calling them 'sir' when they really view you as a peer, a contemporary. Even though they might be twenty years older than you, I think they want to be on a first-name basis with you—so you don't have to 'sir' them anymore."

Until Jane made that very perceptive point, it never would have occurred to me that I should treat these older and much more accomplished businessman with any other than the formal, proper protocol. Growing up, Pop would have killed me had I addressed one of his friends by their first name—that sense of propriety had been deeply ingrained in me. Jane was right, as usual, but calling these older men by their first name was something I had to work on over a period of time.

In the meantime, I had been fortunate to develop some special relationships with some very special industry and civic leaders in Houston, and one of the most important people I met was E. O. Buck, the vice president in charge of oil and gas at National Bank of Commerce (what became Texas Commerce Bank, and then Chase). E. O. was a great character and a mentor to me until he died quite a few years ago at a ripe old age. He'd been a tool pusher and vice-president of Rowan Drilling Company way back, so before he went into banking he had some real oil experience. He was just a savvy old guy, and a wonderful guy at that.

I'll never forget how, after he retired from Texas Commerce some thirty years ago, E. O. agreed to serve on the board of oil and gas operator Oscar Wyatt's company, Coastal Corporation. When I asked E. O. why he would go to work with Oscar, who was known to be volcanic in manner, E. O. said: "Actually, it's not too tough as long as you remember that peace torments Oscar's soul."

No doubt, one of the great highlights from my earliest days in Houston was meeting E. O. Buck's boss, Jesse Jones. Mr. Jones had long since been known as "Mr. Houston" for the way he had, in the words of a 1940 *Fortune* magazine article, "built Houston up from a one-night stand on Buffalo Bayou into the second-largest and fastest growing metropolis in the South." The Port of Houston, the Rice Hotel, the *Houston Chronicle* building, and the 1928 Democratic convention all bore his stamp.

By the time I met him, Mr. Jones had also made a significant contribution to the country in several key posts. During World War I, he served as the Director of Military Relief for the American Red Cross—where he recruited combat nurses and doctors; organized hospitals, canteens, and ambulance networks throughout Europe; and established rehabilitation centers for the wounded. For his efforts, the Red Cross dubbed him the "Big Brother to four million men in khaki."

Following the collapse of the stock market in 1929, President Hoover appointed Jones to the Reconstruction Finance Corporation—but it wasn't until FDR made Jones chairman in 1933 that he made his mark. With that appointment, Jones had almost total autonomy to distribute $50 billion in federal money to help reverse the financial decay of the Great Depression. Jones did not just give out grants, however. Rather, he would buy stock in struggling companies—which, in a very similar manner to what we see happening with the Obama administration today, gave the government a say in how those companies were run. So absolute was Jones' power and influence during those bleak times that he was referred to as "a fourth branch of government."

Of course, most interesting to me today is the fact that Jones also served as FDR's Secretary of Commerce from 1940 to 1945—during which time Jones wielded his tremendous influence to make sure American businesses were able to support the war effort to the fullest extent possible. He was a remarkably effective and widely admired administrator, so it is noteworthy that FDR would sack him in 1945 after Jones' feud with Vice President Henry Wallace.

Even though ours was a fairly brief courtesy meeting, I remember Mr. Jones' stately manner and large presence—both literally and figuratively. Naturally, I had no idea I would follow in his footsteps to serve as Secretary of Commerce many years later, so it is in hindsight that our very brief meeting took on added meaning. I wish I could say Mr. Jones looked into my eyes and said, "Son, I see great things ahead for you."

In reality, he said something perfectly polite and innocuous like, "Well, you sure seem like a nice young fellow. I wish you lots of luck."

Everybody, I suppose, has their own list of who they would invite—living or not—to a dream dinner party, and after my tour of duty in Washington, DC there is no question I would put Jesse Jones on the short list for mine.

Chapter 10   COVER BOYS

Pop occasionally remarked that he was "never physically afraid of another man," which—given his hardscrabble childhood and Darwinian climb up the ladder of success at the Curb—I never doubted for a second. He had been on the streets for so much of his life, and he had to fight his way up the ladder. In his day, who was going to get to do what in the neighborhood or on the Curb was often settled with a fistfight, so Pop learned to fend for himself.

My father was more than just an intense man, however. In many ways he was fearless—and he imparted that same indomitable spirit onto his sons.

Of course, viewed from a different perspective, you could also say Bus and I grew up to be just as stubborn and hardheaded as Pop was. Added to this, Bus was never one to suffer fools gladly. So when we found ourselves in 1953 as young adults on the brink of our first fistfight, it's a wonder either of us backed down.

The issue was sailing, naturally. During the summer of 1953, Jane and I—with Dee and young Rob in tow, and brand-new Kathi in our arms—went to New York to see Mom and Pop; and while there I ended up competing in the Manhasset Bay Race Week. This was my first official foray back into competitive sailing in eight years— during which time I had finished college, completed a year of law school, started a family, and launched a new business.

Despite this prolonged absence, however, the competitive juices still coursed through my veins whenever I got close to the water. The trouble that week was that Bus wanted to sail in the Manhasset Bay event as well, so we agreed that we would both sail two races—and whoever did better would get to sail the last race. After four races, I had a better record; but when I asserted my right to sail the last race, those competitive juices reached the boiling point. It almost came to blows between Bus and me.

Looking back, I understand my brother's reaction. Bus was still very active— and exceptionally successful—on the local sailing circuit. He did not like his kid brother showing up from Texas and stealing his thunder; and if the shoe had been on the other foot, it is highly doubtful I would have taken such a turn of events very well, either.

Taking a dip with little Kathi. I worked hard to build Mosbacher Energy, but always tried to make time for my family.

Part of what fueled that squabble was also the fact that, after eight years, I didn't realize how much I missed sailing.

Fortunately, two friends with deep oil roots in Texas as well as ties to New York and Long Island Sound were helpful at facilitating my reentry into sailing: Lawrence S. Reed and Herman F. "Swede" Whiton. In business circles, Larry was widely respected as the guy who, with his brother Gordon, had been running Texas Gulf Producing Co. since 1941. Among other achievements, Larry brought in the Headlee Field in West Texas' Permian Basin and landed the first American oilfield production deal in Libya.

Swede, meanwhile, was the grandson of the man who invented the frasch system of mining—which involved pumping very hot water into the earth to extract sulfur.

Both Larry and Swede were aware of my Jewish heritage, which could be problematic to some people back then. Undaunted, they encouraged me to join the Texas Corinthian Yacht Club—which Ernie and Al Fay and two other families had established along the shores of Galveston Bay in Kemah, just southeast of Houston. As it turns out, the "TCYC" was modeled after the Seawanhaka Corinthian Yacht Club in Oyster Bay, New York—a very fine club where I had sailed many times as a young man, and that had a great reputation for promoting amateur sailing at the highest level.

Thanks to Larry and Swede's backing, I ran the gauntlet that was the membership committee to become a TCYC member; once in, I started sailing Larry's boat.

Unfortunately, while I was still a very new member, I repaid Larry and Swede for their kindness by nearly getting thrown out of the club. During a club race, I employed a legal, but also very aggressive, tactic against Albert Bel Fay—one of the earliest Republican national committeemen from Texas. I turned into the wind to "luff" or block Al (and another sailor, Pete Masterson, with whom I would sail a great deal in the years ahead) so he couldn't get around a mark or even head toward it, which I had the right to do as long as I didn't then go around the mark at the same time. When I stopped the luffing match, I immediately popped my spinnaker and sailed back down to the mark leaving Al behind, all mixed up. What I did was fair, if not entirely kind and gentle, and when he realized his predicament Al became so mad he didn't talk to me for days afterwards.

I don't know why they didn't kick me out of the club right then and there.

In 1950, Ernie and Al sought to burnish the TCYC's growing reputation when they commissioned Olin Stephens of Sparkman & Stephens yacht designers in New York to conceive a one-design boat more suitable for the shallow depths, short waves, and strong breezes of Galveston Bay. The final product was a 21-foot sloop keelboat with a 500-pound keel, and was named *Corinthian*. Platzer Shipyard, located on the south side of Clear Creek near Houston, built the first boats until Ernie and Al established their Seabrook Shipyard.

After that, the Fay brothers spent what seemed like a huge sum of money at the time, maybe $5,000, on an Olympic 5.5 meter boat and a subsequent model, the *Flame*. To keep pace, Larry and I wanted an equipment upgrade as well; fortunately, Larry had some connections in Norway. He found us a good boat for $1,000, and I agreed to split the cost with him.

In a strong breeze, this older 5.5 meter boat could be very competitive. Once in a while, we even beat the Fays; but their boats were newer and better all-around performers, and as a result we usually found ourselves finishing our races staring at their sterns.

The following year, 1956, Larry and I went to the Olympic trials, which were being hosted by the Beverly Yacht Club in Marion, Massachusetts. The field included George O'Day, who would win the Mallory Cup the year before I did and sail with Bus as an assistant helmsman in the successful 1962 America's Cup campaign; Ted Hood, who would capture his own America's Cup and become a world-renowned designer of boats and sails; and of course, the TCYC's own Fay brothers.

For my part, showing wisdom beyond my years, I set aside all sibling rivalries and got Bus to come up and crew for me. Without a doubt, he was the hottest sailor on Long Island Sound at the time, yet it still amazes me that we somehow won the first race of the Olympic trials. Helping our cause tremendously was the big wind that blew that day, which is when both Bus and I were at our best.

Once again, however, my mischievous, overly competitive side emerged and nearly scuttled our triumph. After we finished first, instead of putting the American flag on the stern to show we'd finished the race, I flew the Lone Star of Texas. A fellow named Julian "Dooley" Roosevelt, from the old Roosevelt family in Oyster Bay, was head of the judge's committee. When Dooley saw what I had done, he was livid. He stormed up to our boat and, with all the bluster he could muster, declared: "We're throwing you out."

Recognizing that my impish antic was about to cost us an important victory, I immediately backpedaled and contritely pleaded for mercy. "Alright, I won't do it again," I told Dooley. "But it wasn't in the race, and had nothing to do with the outcome." Dooley wasn't entirely satisfied. As he saw it, flying the Stars and Stripes at the end of the race was part of the decorum of sailing, what we were supposed to do, and what I did was improper. He was right, but he eventually relented and our first-place finish stood.

We ended up placing fourth overall.

The year after our encouraging finish at the Olympic trials, I competed in my first serious race in foreign waters—traveling to Helsinki to represent the United States in the Scandinavian Gold Cup. The Cup had been established in 1919, and had only recently (in 1953) changed the rules of the competition and switched to 5.5 meter boats. From the beginning, I was excited at the prospect of going, because it meant I would have a chance to race against the best crews from Great Britain, Italy, Norway, France, Sweden, and Finland.

But first, I would have to qualify.

As it turned out, Ernie Fay loaned me his boat because he was unable to participate in the trial races that year. It proved to be a very good bit of fortune for me, because I won that elimination round with Ernie's brother, Al, coming in second. After our earlier "luffing" encounter, you can be sure Al was doubly chapped that I beat him with his brother's boat!

Following the qualifiers, however, a boatyard mishap nearly ended my first foray into international competition. The Fay brothers had taken their boats to Bermuda, and Ernie's boat, *Sabre*, was dropped in a shipyard when they were moving it. The mishap broke a lot of the bow sections, and the end result was I didn't have a boat to sail.

That's when Al Fay, who could be a bit cantankerous but was fair to the core, called me up and said, "I want you to sail *Flame* in the Gold Cup."

"No, you were next," I protested. "You should get to go."

Al was not to be deterred. "No, you beat me fair and square," he insisted. "I'm going to let you have my boat."

It was maybe the finest display of sportsmanship I have ever seen.

One of the most unique features of the Gold Cup is its formula: only the winner of at least one of the first three races continued racing; the first boat to win three races is the overall winner.

I started out the competition sailing with Peter Masterson and Larry Reed; and though we had a very fine boat, we didn't do so well in the first two races. Part of that may have had something to do with the fact that Larry, at age fifty-two, fatigued easily. To his credit, Larry recognized what was happening and suggested, "Why don't we give Don McNamara a call?" We knew Don was a very good sailor, and after he joined the crew we won the third race to advance.

We then went on to score two quick wins in the championship round to win the whole shootin' match.

Near the end of what was to be the decisive race, we had shot out front and had a fairly commanding lead. As we were nearing the end, however, I was trying to figure out where the finish line was. There had been three different starting lines in recent days; and Pete, Don, and I couldn't remember with certainty where we should be finishing. We were in unfamiliar waters, and each of us was convinced that a different line was the right one to use.

As the skipper, I made the executive decision to go for the third line, but when we crossed we didn't hear the cannon fire telling us that we had won. Instead, there was dead silence. So we tacked over and crossed the second line—and again, nothing happened. Not a sound.

In the meantime, our closest competitor was rapidly closing the gap.

By the time we tacked back, we were just barely ahead of this guy. We crossed the line just a few feet ahead—at which point we heard all the guns go off, horns blowing, and every American in the area was cheering. It was one of the most nerve-wracking finishes to a race I had ever experienced, and set among the craggy Norwegian fjords made it all the more special.

Incidentally, by the time Jane heard the final cannon fire, she was so nerve-wracked by my misadventures and the closeness of the race that she mistook the sudden burst of sound for gunfire—and thinking someone had been shot, she fainted.

Before the races, a well-dressed man in a double-breasted yachting jacket with a club tie came walking through to review the competing boats that were out of the water at a shipyard. I didn't know who he was, but could tell he was important—possibly the commodore of the club. As he got closer, I was cleaning something up on top of the boat. Larry, meanwhile, was down on the ground working on the keel. As he saw this distinguished figure approaching, Larry shouted, "Hey, friend!" As the gentleman returned the greeting, I realized there were several people trailing him.

Then it dawned on me: "Oh God, I think it's the king."

Larry had missed these trappings of power and, before I could alert him, asked his regal visitor, "Hey friend, do you think you could get somebody in this yard to help us fix this keel? We've got a spot we need to fix." King Olaf V had this high giggle; and I recall him chuckling, "Hee hee hee, I think so." Instantly, after Larry's request, seven or eight workers immediately came streaming in to help on our boat. By this time, I had ducked my head and tended to the floorboards, not wanting His Majesty to think Larry and I were associated.

After we won, the king handed out the trophies in a part of the yacht club that had a slotted deck, the kind of decking with little gaps in between the planks. As Jane and I were introduced to the king, she sort of half-curtsied. As she did, however, her heel got caught in the deck, and she fell into his arms. Again, His Majesty giggled. He couldn't have been nicer.

Sweet Jane, meanwhile, was just mortified.

Though I wasn't sure of it at the time, looking back now, 1958 has to stand out as a banner year in my sailing career.

For one thing, in February, we finished second in the Miami-Nassau leg of the Southern Ocean Racing Conference, or the "Southern Circuit." I borrowed a 40-foot yawl, or two-masted sailboat, from a Houston friend, Jake Hershey, called *Ca Va* (meaning "it goes" or "it goes well"). The *Ca Va* was a terrific Sparkman and Stephens design, and during this particular Miami-Nassau jaunt our seven-man crew covered 200 miles in forty-six hours.

A few days later, while still in Nassau, we took first place in the Governor's

After winning the Mallory Cup in 1958 with crew members Pete Masterson, left, and George Francisco.

Cup—which was a thirty-mile course that we finished in four-and-a-half hours.

In March, we won another Southern Circuit race called the St. Petersburg-Miami Handicap—a 370-mile trek around Key West to Miami. Traditionally, the race went to Havana, but was diverted to Miami during that winter of 1958 as Fidel Castro was in the process of consolidating his takeover in Cuba. By winning the Handicap in March, we also won the overall 1958 Southern Ocean Racing Circuit.

Without a doubt, the top achievement of the year, and maybe of my entire sailing career, came in September of 1958 when together with my crew—Pete Masterson and George Francisco—we won the seventh men's North American sailing championship to claim the Clifford D. Mallory Trophy. That was really the big win, because the Mallory is recognized as the overall sailing championship of North America. To compete, everybody had to go through the local quarterfinals, regional semifinals, and sometimes club eliminations before that. Added to this: although they were one-design boats, or essentially built to the same specifications, we changed boats after every race to ensure there was no advantage to any boat. The outcome relied solely on the skill of the crew.

I've often been accused of being a risk-taker on the water. On the starting line, if I thought the first wind was going to favor the left side of the line, I would tend to go for the pin at the left side. Usually, there's only room for one boat right at the pin; and usually, there's a lot of people that try to be right in that same spot at the same time. If you don't do it exactly right, it can be disastrous. You would get shot back out the back of the fleet. On the other hand, if we got a really good start—shooting out in front of everybody—we could be tough to beat.

It was the same thing when it came to going around marks on a course. Oftentimes a lot of people get to the mark at the very same time, but I was never all that fond of going around outside of the pinwheel. If you did, you would have to travel a much greater distance, ending up on the leeward side and in a poor position. So I would always fight to get right in there, and I guess more often than not we came within inches of the marks themselves—and other boats. Judging by the reactions of my crewmates, it could be harrowing at times.

All of these experiences came together the week the Mallory Cup was contested in 1958 off Rye, New York. With one race to go and a good lead over my nearest competitor, Norman Freeman of Ithaca Yacht Club, I only needed a seventh place finish to win. Instead of playing it safe, however, I covered Freeman the entire race, moving ahead after we passed the second mark of a twice-around flat triangle course.

To that point in my sailing life, the Mallory Cup had been the brass ring for me—the one competition I really wanted to win, even more than the Atlantic Class as a teenager. After we won it, though, I had a terrible downer coming home. It was sort of like that Peggy Lee song, "Is that all there is?"

I've heard my friend George Bush say that he is a goal-oriented person, and I think this had something to do with my post-Mallory letdown. I always like to have another destination on the horizon; and for a time after winning the North American, I wondered what could come close to the ecstasy of that triumphant moment.

In the end, all I could do was to keep sailing, keep charging the mountain. I was eliminated from the Mallory series in 1959; but I made it back to the finals in 1960 and 1961—both times finishing second to Buddy Melges. On paper, Buddy made for an unlikely champ because he lived and worked in Wisconsin, which is thousands of miles from any coastal water, and with a highly compressed sailing season at that. I hate to lose; but as time wore on, I felt less poorly about losing twice to Buddy for the simple reason that he became what I, and many others, believe was the most outstanding sailor in the world.

Another interesting character with whom I routinely crossed paths, or wakes, in the Mallory Cup qualifiers was a fellow out of Atlanta named Ted Turner—who I understand went on to have some modest success in the broadcasting business. I raced against Ted several times in the semifinals, where all of the different teams in the South—Florida, Georgia, Louisiana, Texas—came together to see who would represent the region in the finals. Ted was always a hard charger and competitive, but we always managed to beat him—and it drove him crazy. As a result, we developed a sharp, teasing relationship.

In the Mallory semifinals in New Orleans one year, we covered Ted all the way up to the finish on the last leg, which was upwind. As only Ted could, he kept yelling, "I'm gonna get you! I'm gonna get you!" At one point, when I was on a port tack and he was on a starboard tack, in an uncustomary lack of gentlemanliness on my part, I shouted, "Try to hit me, you dumb shit!" Which he did try to do, but missed—and it slowed him down. He fell back quite a bit.

Someone watching from the Southern Yacht Club front windows counted roughly 50 tacks we made on that leg, an unusually high number to say the least.

During another Mallory semifinal, which was held at my home club—Texas Corinthian—we were well ahead of Ted and the others going into the final race. There was no wind that day, unfortunately, so the judges and the committees declared that they were calling off the last race, which meant I would win and advance to the finals. Ted immediately accused the judges of bias in favor of the hometown boy and ruining his chances. Somehow, he managed to talk the judges into going out and trying to start the race in no wind. They ended up calling it off—but for the record, we were ahead of Ted when they did.

Some years later, we were sailing in another Southern Ocean Racing Circuit race, and Ted had pulled out to a good lead—while I had fallen off the pace and was near the back of the pack. During an onshore break in the action, Ted walked up while I was visiting with a mutual friend who was on my boat and, speaking to our mutual friend, said: "Why don't you get off this loser's boat, and get on a winner's?"

I sweetly replied, "Ted, I'm glad you were finally able to buy yourself a fast enough boat where you could win something!"

He just walked away.

A new era dawned in America's Cup racing when the matches were brought back in 1958 from the brink of extinction by the leadership of Henry Sears, Henry Morgan, and Harold "Mike" Vanderbilt. Because of World War II, the races had not been held since 1937—at which point every available resource in the country was devoted to building and maintaining a two-ocean navy. Such was the state of global affairs in the war's aftermath, well into the 1950s, that most assumed the Cup—which continued to be proudly displayed in the trophy case at New York Yacht Club—would never be competed for again.

Sears and Morgan changed that when they successfully petitioned the New York Supreme Court for certain modifications in the Cup's "deed of gift" that governed the qualifications—including the move to the smaller, and superior, 12-meter designs to replace the J-class boats of the 1930s.

With the Cup races brought back to life, the next step was identifying which team would represent the United States in its first defense following the twenty-one-year hiatus. Many accounts of that year's Cup suggest that the finals of the first selection trials—which pitted Pop's friend Corny Shields and Briggs Cunningham in the state-of-the-art *Columbia* against Bus in the pre-World War II designed *Vim*—was the finest racing of the entire campaign. Many of the races were marked by masterful tactics and decided by mere seconds.

In fact, according to his obituary in the *New York Times*, Bus "won world attention for his handling of the aging 12-meter yacht *Vim* in the America's Cup selection trials in 1958, gaining greater fame in a lost cause than any yachtsman since Sir Thomas Lipton."

It's still hard to believe; but for my brother's remarkable efforts in the '58 Cup trials, and my success that same year in winning the Mallory Cup, *Sports Illustrated* decided to feature a picture of my brother and me on the cover of their May 19, 1959 issue. There we were: two tidy, serious-looking yachtsmen, dubbed the "Kings of the Class-Boat Sailors." (I cannot confirm if this is the cover that forced them to scramble for better-looking swimsuit models!)

Not surprisingly, four years later, shipping magnate Henry Mercer asked Bus to take the command of Mercer's *Weatherly* in the 1962 America's Cup trials. The *Weatherly* to that point had a reputation as a mediocre vessel; but upon taking her command, Bus began a transformation that would take *Weatherly*, and her crew, to victory.

Of course, the 12-meter sloops that were the mainstay of the competition during that era were designed to an international mathematical formula that dictated length, girth, and sail area. But Bus did some calculations and removed what he considered to be excess weight, from a 2-pound wind gauge that had been perched atop the 90-foot mast, to the previous skipper's pipe rack. This

MAY 18, 1959
America's National Sports Weekly

25 CENTS
$7.50 A YEAR

SPORTS
ILLUSTRATED

THE $74,000 BOY WHO 'FAILED'
by Mark Harris

KINGS OF THE CLASS-BOAT SAILORS
by Carleton Mitchell

BOB AND
BUS MOSBACHER

Sharing the May 18, 1959 Sports Illustrated *cover with my brother Bus, who went on to captain* America *to two consecutive victories in the prestigious America's Cup races.*

ended up saving more than half a ton, which enabled Bus to put lead in her keel for greater stability in strong winds.

In July of 1962, leading *Weatherly* into battle in the "wind-rippled waters off Newport, Rhode Island," Bus would not be denied his chance to take the defense of the Cup on his shoulders. As skipper of *Weatherly*, an okay yacht but not necessarily a great boat, my brother captained his crew to four victories in a row against the roughest competition U.S. yachting could offer.

The '62 Cup finals against Australia's *Gretel* skippered by Jock Sturrock was, itself, a statistical rout, but several incidents stand out. The first came on September 16, 1962, when President and Mrs. Kennedy, then aboard the destroyer *Joseph Kennedy Jr.*, were among the spectators who watched *Weatherly* win the first race "under fair skies and a fresh wind." When Bus finished 3 minutes and 46 seconds ahead of the *Gretel*, the president's destroyer reportedly gave two blasts of her horn. After the *Gretel* finished, President Kennedy ordered the destroyer to move close for a salute with five blasts of the horn. The *Gretel* crew responded by waving and dipping the Australian colors.

Weatherly and her crew went on to win the America's Cup after taking a crucial fourth race by 26 seconds, the smallest margin in the race's history. The United States prevailed four-to-one to retain the Cup; but the months of trials, plus the pressure of the four-of-seven series, took their toll on Bus. When asked about a second try at the Cup, Bus firmly declared, "Never again."

Maybe Bus felt the same letdown after his triumph as I did following the 1958 Mallory; but whatever it was, he too, would be back—taking the helm (successfully) of the *Intrepid* five years later, in 1967.

Today, I am somewhat sad to note, the America's Cup races are dominated by professionals—not amateurs. In one recent holding of the Cup, out of sixteen men on the defending Swiss crew there were many Australians, New Zealanders, and even a few Americans all "representing" Switzerland. If you looked at any other boat, you would see the same thing: a team of hired guns, most of them professionals. My concern here is that too much money is having a negative impact on sailing, just as it is in many other sports. Maybe it is a sign of the times; maybe I am guilty, like others, of thinking things were better when I was younger.

But there was a purity to sailing back when more people did it simply for the love of competing out on the open water, and that may be why the sport doesn't receive more public attention these days.

As the stunned silence fell around the long, Texas-sized conference table in Dallas, I wasn't sure if I should be elated or deflated. It was fall of 1967; and only moments before, I was sitting across the table from Richard Milhous Nixon as he addressed a blue chip group of Texas businessmen gathered to gin up support and enthusiasm for his '68 campaign for president. The assemblage included such venerable figures as H. L. Hunt and Sid Richardson, who were akin to Texas royalty at the time; and the former vice president was dutifully making the early rounds trying to lock up some of the top tier financial support. As part of Nixon's Texas team, I had flown up from Houston with Bill Liedtke, Roy Winchester, and several other players to help introduce Nixon to some of these key business leaders.

It's hard to describe just how bitter the political environment was during this time. With the Tet Offensive just months away, the Vietnam War was nearing its deepest throes, and President Johnson had already seen much of his political support erode as a result. Here at home, meanwhile, widespread unrest over race issues had also engulfed a number of major cities in flames and riots—from Washington, to Los Angeles, to upstate New York, to Detroit. Simply put, it was a divisive and—as we would see in the traumatic months ahead with the assassinations of both Martin Luther King Jr. and Bobby Kennedy—dangerous time in American politics. Owing to the turmoil, even Texas' own LBJ would be forced, albeit voluntarily, from the White House in the coming months.

After eight years as Dwight Eisenhower's vice president, and his razor-thin loss to President Kennedy in 1960, Richard Nixon was already widely known to the politically astute people in the room. Still, going into this meeting, the plan called for the candidate to say a few words about his plans and his campaign; and when he was done, I was supposed to get up and get the financial ball rolling. Specifically, I planned to get up and appear so moved by what I had just heard that I was pledging $5,000 to the Nixon campaign right then and there. I was all of forty years old, so I could be forgiven my youthful earnestness.

It helped that, back during the 1968 campaign cycle, there were no limits on what you could give to someone running for president. To be sure, $5,000 was a sizeable contribution—but not so large as to be considered excessive or even

Jane with Richard Nixon, when he launched his 1968 presidential campaign in Houston.

obscene. More importantly, I knew most of the thirty-five or so men at the table could easily one-up me and, to be candid, that was part of our calculation. We hoped the subtle clash of Texas-sized egos and bank accounts would lead to a spirited game of one-upmanship—all to the benefit of the Nixon campaign.

After the vice president laid out his vision for the country, he left the room before the conversation turned to money. As the door closed, it was time for me to play my role as the Lead Shill. I was halfway out of my seat, however, when I heard this high-pitched, almost squeaky voice seizing control of the floor from the other end of the long conference table. As it did, all attention fell on this very young-looking, short, and trim fellow, neatly dressed in a crisp white shirt with thick dark-rimmed glasses.

While this unknown figure started talking about how much he liked and respected Richard Nixon, I sat there stewing a little, wishing he would shut up. I had no idea who he was or what he had done, but I was getting ready to pledge some real money to the campaign—or so I thought.

As he wrapped up his comments, however, this young fellow kind of sheepishly said, "And so, I'd like to give $100,000 to the vice president, and my brother Charles here would like to give another $50,000."

Cue the stunned silence.

The voice belonged to thirty-five-year-old Sam Wyly, already a veteran of IBM and Honeywell, who had only a few years before launched University Computing Company—a software and computer company. Together with his brother Charles, the Wyly brothers had already experienced terrific success with UCC; and, as would be their custom throughout their lives, when the Wyly brothers got involved in a project they gave it their all.

The problem in this particular instance was that their amazingly generous offer had the effect of sucking all of the oxygen, or momentum, out of the room. All of the folks that Bill Liedtke and Roy Winchester had managed to gather—the "big dawgs" we were hoping would pledge their $5,000, $10,000, or $25,000 after I got the ball rolling—essentially sat there in disbelief. No one was prepared to match the Wylys, and no one wanted to be upstaged by so large a margin.

The meeting was over before it really got going.

Don't get me wrong: a quick $150,000 in pledges was a really good problem to have, but I was still feeling somewhat jolted by the turn of events. I was already planning to follow up with the other prospects in the room when H. L. Hunt—one of the old-school oil tycoons who had topped *Fortune Magazine*'s list of the wealthiest Americans in 1948—said, "Bobby, come by the office. I've got something for you." Like any fundraiser worth their salt, I naturally accepted the invite on the spot, expecting to collect another contribution for Nixon's cof fers In fact, I was salivating at the prospect.

When I arrived, however, H. L. handed me a large envelope filled *not* with money, but with pamphlets concerning his beliefs about what was right for America. Throughout the 1950s and 1960s, Hunt had been distressed about what he viewed as a communist threat to the United States—and had invested much time and treasure in disseminating his conservative views in newspaper columns, books, radio programs, and even TV shows.

To say I was disappointed to receive political propaganda from Hunt instead of a check would be putting it very mildly. I didn't like drilling dry holes, but this was nothing but.

That one day in Dallas, I suppose, encapsulated the experiences of anyone who has ever raised money for a major political candidate—the highest of highs, rubbing elbows with the powerful and influential, mixed with frustration.

Like anyone else who cut their political teeth in Texas in the early 1950s, my personal path to the role of Republican activist came at a time of severely managed expectations. George and Barbara Bush, who were out in West Texas at the time, are fond of recalling how they conducted the first Republican primary ever held in Midland in 1952. That year, native son Dwight David Eisenhower (born in Denison, Texas) clashed with Senator Robert Taft of Ohio for the GOP nomination.

As George tells the story, a sparse three Midlanders voted in their '52 GOP primary: George Bush, Barbara Bush, and a drunk Democrat who wasn't entirely sure of his whereabouts.

Things weren't much better for the Texas Republicans in Houston, meanwhile. When Eisenhower first ran for President, I had been in Houston just three or four years, and was invited to a poorly-attended county level GOP meeting at Albert Fay's house. That night, the crowd was so thin I ended up spending quite a bit of time with an impressive man named Thad Hutcheson Sr., whose son is a terrific sailor and would become a good friend—on, and off, the water.

For his part, Thad Sr. would rise in party prominence after winning a surprising number of statewide votes in the 1957 U.S. Senate race to fill the unexpired term of Price Daniel, who had taken over the Governor's Mansion.

No one questioned the supremacy of the Democratic Party of Texas in those days, but there was a clear liberal-conservative split among the Democratic ranks—which is not to suggest that we Texas Republicans didn't have our own divisions with which to contend.

In 1952, for example, a lot of Texas Republicans, particularly people who had been involved in the party, tended to be far more supportive of Senator Taft—then known as "Mr. Republican"—than they were pro-Eisenhower. Fortunately, the GOP activists who supported Taft were a minority, and the rest of us "liked" Ike enough to help him win the nomination—and the presidency. General Eisenhower was a perfect symbol of strength coming off a great victory in World War II. Added to that, he always had this engaging, wonderful smile; he looked like a leader, and he was, in many ways, a great president.

But the general popularity of the Eisenhower Presidency, and the seminal importance of his carrying the state in 1952 to the resurrection of the GOP from the ashes of Reconstruction, wasn't enough to keep some Lone Star Republicans from adopting the extreme and intolerant views of the John Birch Society. Today, some in the Birch Society believe there is a conspiracy to create a "North American Union" where the United States, Mexico, and Canada will someday merge together to form a kind of European Union—which is absurd in the extreme. As hard as it may be to comprehend, though, the group's views in the 1960s were even more exotic. They tended to view any proponent of "globalism" as an agent of the Communist Party—including such noteworthy "sell-outs" as

Dwight Eisenhower and FDR (who Birch Society founder Robert Welch accused of being aware of the Pearl Harbor attacks before they happened).

Another target of the Birch Society in its early years was a fellow oilman and new friend of mine named George Herbert Walker Bush. I had first met Barbara and George Bush at a backyard barbecue at the home of a mutual friend of ours, Fred Chambers, and we instantly hit it off. We quickly got close enough that, in 1962, George approached me about partnering with him in offshore exploration with his company, Zapata Offshore—looking back, I wish I had done the deal. As it was, however, I was just taking Mosbacher Energy into the Canadian oil play—my first international foray—and concerns about overextending the company led me to pass on the Zapata Offshore offer.

At that time, offshore drilling was a risky business, but so was the world of Texas Republican politics. What apparently threw the Birch people for a loop was the fact that George's father, Prescott, was a United States Senator from Connecticut during this same period. Nothing gets the conspiracy nuts going quite like someone with a background in the energy business, East Coast ties, and a familial connection in Congress. The fact that Senator Prescott Bush was also a frequent golfing partner of President Eisenhower's could have only fueled their conspiratorial fires.

As he had done in the oil business, when George Bush got into politics, he started on the ground floor and worked his way up. He was approached in 1962 to run for chairman of the Harris County GOP to defeat one of the Birch Society people poised to take over the county party. Houston and Harris County had been the largest metropolitan area to go for Richard Nixon in 1960, and there was widespread concern that ceding control of the local party to a Birch loyalist would squander the clear gains that Republicans were starting to make in Texas.

Fortunately, George worked like a dog and won election as GOP chairman; and in very short order, made such a fine name for himself that in 1964 he was widely sought by state party chairman Peter O'Donnell and many others to challenge the liberal Ralph Yarborough in the Senate. George took the plunge, won the GOP primary against John Cox, and was mounting a terrific general election with the help of Barry Goldwater, Nixon, and other national leaders.

As George headed into the home stretch, in fact, he was starting to close the gap when two developments staunched his momentum: first, though it was widely known in Harris County that George was on the Birch Society hit list, in the last week of the '64 general election Yarborough came to Houston to charge that George was actually "the darling of the John Birch Society;" and second,

President Johnson was personally campaigning on Yarborough's behalf to make sure the Republicans didn't pick up their second Senate seat from Texas.

Yarborough won with over 56 percent of the vote, just as LBJ also won with a landslide over Barry Goldwater. It was a bitter defeat when we had so much hope going into the home stretch, but that's the way politics works sometimes.

The best man doesn't always win.

It was in the early 1960s that, like George Bush, I started to catch the political bug. It started in earnest during the 1960 presidential campaign, when my dear friend Bill Kilroy and I cochaired the "Democrats for Nixon" in Texas. I had never been a Democrat, but the idea for this came from former Governor Allan Shivers, who we had gone to see in Austin at his invitation. Though he was a Democrat, Governor Shivers—himself a veteran of North Africa and Europe during World War II—had split with the national Democratic Party and helped to deliver Texas for Dwight Eisenhower in 1952 and 1956. He was out of office at the time, but the conservative Democrat was working to help Nixon in 1960. During our meeting, the Governor said, "Boys, here's what we need you do, and this is the way to do it." As young and impressionable as we were, we never questioned whether we ought to do it as Republicans or Democrats.

Incidentally, it was probably a similar level of naïvete that led me to give some money to LBJ in 1960. John Connally, who I always found to be a charismatic figure, had gathered a large group of us together to make a pitch for Johnson's presidential aspirations. Connally told us it was imperative to help our state's favorite son against a northeastern liberal like Jack Kennedy who was, horror of horrors, a Catholic and—if elected—would be taking orders from the Vatican. I frankly found that part of Connally's appeal distasteful, but it was impossible to get out of that room without making a commitment of some kind.

Looking back, I view that single dalliance with LBJ the same way Bill Clinton later explained his brief encounter with marijuana: I did it once, I didn't like it, and I never "inhaled."

Immediately after Nixon lost and LBJ ascended to the vice presidency, I signed on to help a political science professor named John Tower in his second bid for LBJ's Senate seat. Tower's campaign chairman was an old, dear friend of mine named Jimmy Bertron—a good guy, but a little off the wall.

It was through Jimmy that I stumbled into political fundraising.

Johnson had drubbed Tower in 1960, despite running for vice president at the same time (and despite Tower's clever campaign slogan: "Double your pleasure, double your fun, vote against Johnson two times, not one"). After LBJ became vice president, Governor Price Daniel temporarily appointed a conservative

Democrat, William Blakely, to LBJ's seat. Given the aforementioned rift in the Texas Democratic Party, this appointment caused an uproar with liberals who refused to turn out for Blakely—and Tower effectively capitalized on this opening to become the first Republican elected statewide in Texas since 1870.

From helping the Tower campaign, I went on to serve as the general chairman for Desmond Barry's campaign, a business owner running for Congress in Galveston. Desmond had defied the unions and kept his midsized trucking business nonunionized; and to many of us, that made him a bit of a hero. I still don't know how he found his way to me; but I was happy to help him—and though he lost, he made a good showing as a Republican.

Along the way, about 1966, I met another man who, like Bill Kilroy, would become one of my very best friends in the oil business, in politics, and in just plain old life itself. The phone rang in my office one afternoon, and the fella on the other end introduced himself as Chesley Pruet of Arkansas. Chesley had a drilling company and was an operator to boot—which means he operated and drilled wells for his own account, and acted as a drilling contractor for others. He drilled primarily in Mississippi, and was well-connected there, but also took action in Louisiana and a few other states.

Through his network of friends, Chesley had heard that I was taking a couple of deals in Mississippi, which was true. Pop had bought some mineral royalties in Mississippi with our old friend Arthur Carmody of the North Central Texas Oil Company, and these minerals never got more than a $25 an acre bonus, along with an eighth royalty if we wanted to lease them. Early in 1966, however, some folks called me about two areas where we had minerals and offered us quite a bit more—a $100 an acre bonus and a quarter royalty. Immediately, I hopped on a plane and went over there, figuring any place that's getting that kind of activity is getting hot. So I went over to Mississippi, spent a few days, and made a deal to drill a well.

Chesley heard about all this, and called me when I got back to Houston. He wanted to come meet me in Texas, but I was on my way to New Orleans to defend myself against a South Louisiana Cajun landowner who claimed we didn't pay our royalties in time, and wanted to take our lease away from us. Chesley said, "Alright, I'll meet you at the courthouse after your lawsuit." So I told him where it was and what time.

At the appointed time and place, I came out from the lawsuit testimony, and we said hello. "How did it go in there?" he asked.

"I think we're going to win," I told him.

"How can you be so sure?" Chesley inquired.

Chesley Pruet was one of the finest, and funniest, oilmen I ever met.

"Well, it's a strange thing," I confided. "The foreman of the jury is a nun—a great big lady. I was staring at this guy who was giving his testimony, which I knew were full of lies. Then I happened to glance over at the nun, the nun glanced at me, and she winked. That told me she knew he was lying too, and so that's why I think we are going to win."

And in fact, we did win—something Chesley teased me about for years. But out of that first encounter, a strong professional and personal friendship grew. Everybody, I soon discovered, was crazy about Chesley. He was a live wire—bright, quick, a great doer, and recognized as one of the kings of the wildcatter community. After I got him into politics, he also became a terrific fundraiser. We had a lot of fun traveling together, drinking too much whiskey, and telling big lies.

Though he had lost an eye early in life, Chesley was a good pilot and usually flew himself wherever he needed to go. One time, he was flying himself to New Orleans and fell asleep while the plane was on autopilot. When he awoke, as the story goes, all he could see around him was the blue of the Gulf of Mexico. Fortunately, he had enough gas to make it back to dry land.

Everyone who knew Chesley has a million stories like that, but what drew a lot of people to him, I think, was his energy and upbeat personality. Even during the hard times, Chesley was fond of saying: "The drilling business is pure pleasure and pure profit."

In his book *Drilling Ahead: The Quest for Oil in the Deep South 1945–2005*, author Alan Cockrell said that I "respected no boundaries when hunting for oil and gas, but [I] had a fondness for Mississippi and Alabama, partly because of [my] good pal Chesley Pruet."[1] No question, after we became friends in the mid-1960s, working with Chesley was, in itself, a draw to any project—but I also enjoyed working in that part of the country because it was often a productive use of our time and resources.

In 1968, for example, Chesley had a piece of the action when Mosbacher Energy went in on a deal for two wildcat wells in Clarke County in southeastern Mississippi with Getty Oil and Love Petroleum out of Jackson, Mississippi. This particular venture was based on a new theory about soil conditions and drilling techniques in and around the so-called Smackover Play—a known area where oil had been discovered for years.

I remember meeting in my office with a landman named Jim White who explained this new drilling theory and the information they already had on the site, and while White's explanation made sense, somewhere in the back of my mind I also knew no matter how good a pitch sounded, failure was always a distinct possibility. At one point, I saw White admiring a couple of my English fox hunting paintings, so I threw an added incentive at him: "I'll give you that painting if we make a discovery."

"What if we make two discoveries?" he shot back.

I smiled.

In short order, we spudded or broke ground on two wells, and both struck oil. Jim White got his two paintings.

In addition to the Deep South, we had also expanded north into Canada in the 1960s, drilling fifteen wells there in 1965 alone, in Alberta and Saskatchewan.

1. Alan Cockrell, *Drilling Ahead: The Quest for Oil in the Deep South 1945–2005* (Mississippi Geological Society Books: University Press of Mississippi), 125.

I really felt as if Canada at that time was where the Gulf Coast was exploration-wise in the early 1950s—namely, a hot place to be.

At the same time my drilling activities with Chesley Pruet was starting to pick up pace, my political involvement with another friend, George Bush, was likewise heating up. In fact, for some people, you could say it reached the boiling point in April of 1968.

Just six days after Martin Luther King Jr.'s assassination, George—then a second-term House member from Texas's 7th congressional district—went against the overwhelming sentiment of his district and voted for the Open Housing Bill, which was essentially an extension of the landmark Civil Rights Act of 1964. His constituent mail on that issue ran roughly 500 to 1 against his position, and George knew he would have to explain what he did and why to many of his angry supporters back home. As he wrote one friend as he prepared to come back to Houston following that vote: "I am being fitted for my lead underwear."

As a close friend who had helped George raise money for each of his congressional races, I had a good sense of the pressures he would face. Many of the people who had given money to him sought me out to express varying levels of antipathy toward Congressman Bush's action. The only good news seemed to be that the only ones who were *not* pledging to oppose his reelection with every fiber of their being were nevertheless threatening to withhold any future financial support.

It was plain ugly.

Before he got home, I had arranged for a key group of supporters to meet with George—most of whom were preparing to go into that meeting and tell George Bush how the cow ate the cabbage. The group included Larry Reed, Dudley Sharp, and Butch Butler—all independent, tough-minded businessmen. Before the meeting, I also offered to spare George of their wrath and talk to them myself, but he instantly cut me off, saying he had to do the talking.

As he started out, he thanked them for their support and told them that, if his vote had caused a rupture in their friendship, he would understand—but that he was not going to change his position. George confided he did have several technical problems with the legislation—questions about its constitutionality, for example—but he steadfastly reiterated his support for most of its provisions.

Then he changed the subject to Vietnam, and talked about the African and Mexican American soldiers he met during his fact-finding trip there. They were fighting, and many were dying, for the ideals of this county, he said, and they ought not have the door slammed in their face when they get home because of the color of their skin—or the fact that they might speak with an accent.

By the time he left the meeting, George Bush had won over everyone in the room.

It was the same when he went to a town hall-style of meeting in the Memorial section of his district. The place was packed; and when he was introduced, a deafening chorus of boos and catcalls greeted him. But as he made his case, you could tell that he was changing a lot of minds—not all, but a lot. And when he walked out of that meeting, the same crowd that had seethed with anger only minutes before gave him a standing ovation.

I don't think I've ever seen a political scene quite like it before or since.

"There were a lot of people who thought my vote was going to alter their lifestyle and diminish their property values and all this kind of stuff—which never did happen, of course," George said as he reflected on that tumultuous time. "But as I saw it, if you're good enough to fight for your country, you ought to be good enough to buy a decent house when you got back. And that was kind of the theme I struck—speaking to the fairness of it."

I had already been sold on George Bush the candidate; but for me and many others, that impossibly tough week where we saw our friend fearlessly plunge into action, standing up to his critics and appealing to their "better angels," cemented our undying respect for George Bush the man. And as word spread of his remarkable stand, George's national stock soared to the point that the second-term congressman eventually, and remarkably, made Richard Nixon's short-list as a potential vice presidential ticket mate in the fall campaign.

By then, I guess I had amassed enough of a political resume that Richard Nixon's people felt comfortable asking me to chair their efforts in Houston. In 1968, mind you, they still did politics the old-school way, because they didn't separate the political side of the operation from the fundraising like they do these days. I ended up doing both for Nixon. As a matter of fact, typical of those days, I was driving into work one day and I saw some buses that had kind of scratched over signs on the back that had been ads for some company. Looking at them, I thought it would be a great place to put up the sign saying, "Nixon's the one."

This was after Labor Day, so I called the bus company and asked how much would it cost to have these signs on all those buses for the remaining two-and-a-half months. The man told me it would be some huge amount, like $12,000. I told him, "Okay, I'll take them." Then I called three other guys, and we each put in $3,000 to cover the expense. I don't think I kept any record of that transaction; and if I did, I would have had a hard time finding it. The point is nobody thought about those kinds of things very much back then; and at one level, it was really a lot more fun because you were free to do anything that was legal and moral to get your guy elected—whether it was a rally, getting stories in the newspaper, or anything else that would help.

I remember having a conversation that year which, in retrospect, is the same conversation Republicans and Democrats seem to have every four years. A friend and I were talking about the upcoming election, when this fellow said, "Geez, I wish we had a candidate that we could all get behind this time—a really good man—instead of all these lousy politicians."

In hindsight, the "lousy" candidates in 1968 turned out to be Richard Nixon, Ronald Reagan, Nelson Rockefeller, and George Romney. Regardless of what you think about Watergate, Richard Nixon was a very smart man, very able, and really a moderate on most matters—not very conservative at all. Reagan, of course, had smartly positioned himself to be the candidate of the far right; but in his heart I don't think he was the hard-core conservative many depict him as these days. Rockefeller was a wonderful, colorful character who was very able, very attractive, and—as it turned out—very liberal. And George Romney was a very successful businessman who had also been a very effective, and popular, governor in Michigan.

I was naturally thrilled that my candidate, Nixon, had prevailed; but the truth is no matter who won, I think our party, and more importantly our country, would have been in fine hands. Of course, it was fun for our family that Nixon had indeed prevailed, because Bus became the first Mosbacher to enter a presidential administration on January 21, 1969—the day after President Nixon's inauguration. He had been appointed as chief of protocol for the United States.

It was a fairly big deal because, since 1961, the job had carried ambassadorial rank and required Senate confirmation. Moreover, after he was confirmed, Bus was in charge of planning, hosting, and officiating ceremonial events for visiting chiefs of state and heads of government, as well as coordinating logistics for the visits. And of course, he managed Blair House, the President's guesthouse, and oversaw all protocol matters for presidential or vice presidential travel abroad, working alongside the White House.

When I heard of the appointment, I teased Bus. "What the heck do you know about protocol?" I asked when I saw him.

"Little brother, whatever I say or do *is* protocol!" came his prompt rejoinder.

The following year, sensing that Ralph Yarborough was more vulnerable than ever, George Bush was once again being heavily recruited by President Nixon and the state's GOP leaders to take on an incumbent senator. It was a tough decision to leave a very safe House seat and his position on the influential Ways and Means Committee; but just as he showed from his days in the oil business, George Bush never shied away from a challenge because he thought it was too risky. He launched his second Senate campaign in 1970 with the heady sense that Yarborough's time was nearly up. I was happy to head up the finance team with Fred Chambers, while our mutual friend and recent Democrat-turned-Republican Jim Baker was heading up the Harris County political operation.

Once again, however, events beyond his ability to control moved against him. In fact, before George could declare his own candidacy, another attractive, successful businessman and war hero from Houston named Lloyd Bentsen officially announced he would challenge Yarborough in the Democratic primary. Lloyd had a solid business background as the man who started Consolidated American Life Insurance Company, a financial holding firm that eventually grew into Lincoln Consolidated. He said he intended to challenge Yarborough from the right; and the move paid off.

George later told me: "In 1970, we didn't think we were going to be running against Houston's own Lloyd Bentsen. Barbara Jordan told me, 'Well, if Bentsen beats Yarborough, you can go pick out your seat in the U.S. Senate. The minority voters in Texas will be so outraged that they'll vote for you instead of Bentsen.' But that didn't happen."

Another development that helped to torpedo the 1970 Bush campaign was the fact that a measure banning "liquor by the drink" was on the ballot that year. George didn't support such a restriction, but the measure was hugely popular in East Texas—where the devout Baptists were thicker than the piney woods. It proved to be a huge issue in turning out straight-ticket Democratic voters in East Texas and other rural parts of the state, and helped to seal our fate.

Even as the disappointing returns came in on election eve 1970, George never lost his sense of humor. At one point, he turned to me and said: "You know, Bob, now I understand how General Custer felt when he asked, 'Where did all those *#&@%# Indians come from?'"

It had been a tough campaign for our candidate, to be sure; but the fact is his two top lieutenants, Jimmy Baker and I, had suffered far worse that year—the loss of our first wives. And out of the profound sadness of that time, a unique bond among three men, three personal friends, was made all the stronger.

Chapter 12 NO PRICE ON LIFE OR LIMB

It should have been the best of times.

In October of 1969, Jane and I traveled to Spain for the Dragon Class[1] World Championship. At that point, we had been married for twenty-two happy years, and had four beautiful, healthy children, with the addition of our wonderful Lisa in 1959. The kids had done well at sailing and, more importantly, were doing better in their studies than their old man.

With four kids, of course, Jane had plenty on her plate as the manager of the house, as was the custom at that time. The division of labor was that I was the disciplinarian, while Jane was the soft touch—the nurturer. She was perfectly cast in that role.

In addition to supporting our kids in every way, however, she also was devoted to her volunteer work, which included the Junior League and the Houston Zoo, even chairing the annual Zoo Ball event on several occasions. To me, she was what George Bush would call a "Point of Light" long before the term existed.

With great pride and love, I had seen Jane Mosbacher blossom over the years into a fantastic mother, an attentive wife, and certainly a caring and involved citizen in her community. But more than that, she was a true friend to me, her kids, and all who gravitated into her orbit.

Plainly put, Jane was fun to be around.

At the Texas Corinthian Yacht Club, for example, Jane won an annual award called the "Frivolity Cup" one summer—but not because she was a cutup, or someone who became more animated after a few drinks. That honor was simply an acknowledgment of the fact that Jane loved to laugh, and people

---

1. An Olympic class sailboat from 1948 to 1972, the Dragon features a long keel and possesses spars and sails that are easily adjustable while racing. The boat's features allow a crew to adopt it to any condition, and remove the need for an optimum body weight that characterizes so many other sailboat classes. According to the International Dragon Association's website: "Dragon races cannot be won by brute strength. The Dragon's design philosophy has made it a class where extremely close racing is the norm, and where races are won by the crew's mastery of the conditions and tactics on the course rather than by speed advantage." Available at: http://www.waida.com.au/site/about -dragons/aboutthedragon.html.

The calm before the storm. Attending a charity event with Jane in 1968, the year before she fell ill. (Photo courtesy of the Houston Chronicle)

loved her for it. She saw the humor in life that, if you look for it, is there in abundance.

Shortly after we moved to Texas and she joined the Junior League, she came to me a tad perplexed. "I can't figure it out, darling," she said one night, referring to some women at the Junior League she thought she should know. "I went to UT, and was an Alpha Delta Pi, too—so how is it possible that I don't know these girls?" She went on to mention the orange and white school colors, and it was really bugging her. We had a wonderful laugh together when we realized that "UT" in Jane's case was the University of Tennessee—not the University of Texas. Being the smart aleck that I am, I naturally teased her about that for quite some time afterwards.

In short, that innocence and sincerity I had detected in her so many years before when I met Jane as a mere undergrad at Washington and Lee was still very much intact.

Forget the oil and gas business. For the grace and goodness and love she brought into our lives, Jane Mosbacher was, by far, the most important discovery of my young life. Long story short: as 1969 was drawing to a close, life was good. In a family sense, I could feel the lift of our family sails as kids and parents alike were moving well through a light chop—with a following sea at our back.

In Spain, meanwhile, I skippered my boat at the time, *Aphrodite*, to a narrow one-point victory in Palma de Mallorca (together with my crew of George Francisco and David Saville) over a sailor out of Seattle named G. S. "Buddy" Friedrichs. That we bested the field of thirty-eight other Dragons in Spain made that win all the more meaningful, because on hand to witness our triumph were two fairly new friends of Jane's and mine, Crowned Prince Juan Carlos of Spain and his beautiful wife, Princess Sofia. I had hosted the prince at a sailing event in Houston the year before, at which time I also introduced my visiting dignitary to a peculiar American invention unknown to many Europeans: the speed trap. I was racing the prince back from the Texas Corinthian Yacht Club forty-five minutes south of Houston to a speaking engagement at the Rice Hotel in downtown Houston, when a highway patrolman pulled me over and accused me of exceeding the speed limit by a considerable margin.

Not knowing how else to get us out of this predicament, when the patrolman approached my window and asked for my driver's license, I blurted out: "Officer, I have Prince Juan Carlos, who will be the next King of Spain, in my car."

The patrolman glared back at me and said, "Look buddy, I didn't ask you for a passenger list. Just show me your driver's license."

So we became good friends, the Prince and I, and naturally it was a great treat for Jane and me to celebrate with the royal couple the night we won the 1969 Dragon World Championship in his country. After we retired for the evening, however, Jane and I were in our room getting ready to go to sleep when I heard Princess Sofia's sweet voice through the balcony window.

Accepting the 1969 Dragon Class World Championship cup from my new friend, Crown Prince Juan Carlos, in Spain.

"Yoohoo, Bobby," the princess was calling out in innocent, dulcet tones. "Where are you?"

The royal couple was staying in the room just above ours, so I assumed she just wanted to congratulate me one more time. But when I put my head over the balcony rail and looked up in her direction, Princess Sofia, the eldest daughter of Greece's King Paul I and Queen Federika, dumped a cold bucket of water on my face.

Royal decorum it was not.

Afterwards, I came home to get back to running my business while Jane stayed in Europe with a few girlfriends to do some sightseeing. It was while she was in Europe that she first noticed a loss of energy, a general lethargy.

Jane rarely, if ever, complained. As long as I had known her, she was always upbeat—the kind of person who always managed to see the good in people, and in life. So when she sheepishly told me, "I don't feel very good, dear" in October of 1969, that was my first sign something was not right.

From the moment Jane uttered those words in our bedroom, however, that idyllic world we had known as a family started to slip from our grasp. First came the blow that she had a rare form of leukemia. When I first heard the horrible news, it was if someone had swung a baseball bat into my gut. In fact, the first doctor we consulted said Jane would be gone within six weeks.

All things considered, we were fortunate to live in Houston, which was, and still is, home to one of—or maybe THE—most advanced cancer treatment facility anywhere in the world, the University of Texas M. D. Anderson Center. The M. D. Anderson Center was conceived in the 1940s to push the envelope on cancer research and treatment, so once we were confronted with what we were told were very bleak prospects, with time quickly running out, it didn't take long to realize I had to get Jane in there to do everything we possibly could.

Maybe other spouses and loved ones feel the same way, but looking back at Jane's illness it sometimes felt as if I was going through a train wreck in slow motion. Throughout my life, I had always been in control. On the water, I learned to control a boat and take advantage of the wind and sea conditions as I found them. It was the same thing in business: control the terms, don't "stretch" to make a deal.

Now, even if I didn't appreciate it at the time, I was not in control—not even slightly. I naively thought I could regain control of events and save her life if I simply worked the problem harder, but nothing I did, or that we did, seemed to work for long.

Pop was often fond of saying that there's "no price on life and limb," meaning where your health is concerned you should never skimp or settle for second-rate care if you can avoid it. Get a second opinion, or a third. Information, as always, was key for him. If Pop showed up for a doctor's appointment and the nurse informed him the doctor was busy, Pop would say, "No problem, I can wait all day."

I took Pop's lesson to heart in admitting Jane to M. D. Anderson and consulting every doctor I could. For a time, I was convinced we could turn this heart-wrenching situation around. First, we had the top doctor in that specialized field of leukemia, Dr. Emil Freireich, on the case. As president of the Gulf Coast chapter of the Leukemia Society I knew he was up on the latest developments on that still-emerging field of treatment.

In May of 1970, I also threw a big fundraiser for M. D. Anderson at the Shamrock Hotel's Emerald Room that was attended by Congressman George Bush, Houston Mayor Louis Welch, singer Nancy Ames, and guest speaker Art Buchwald—along with Bus and my sister-in-law Pat, and a bunch of personal friends too numerous to mention who turned out to support Jane and the cause of fighting leukemia. It was a very moving night because Jane had suffered a setback and was not able to attend, but her indomitable spirit permeated the room.

As our campaign to save Jane continued, we tried a series of experimental treatments, including one where they placed her in a purified oxygen room with all kinds of tubes running in and out of her frail body. The clock was starting to run out, and we had started to throw a bunch of Hail Marys—looking for the miracle I was sure would come, but in the end never did.

During the spring and into the summer of 1970, the reality that Jane might not make it started to seep into my mind. The thought of her no longer there was too sudden, too jolting; and I went into denial. I went to the hospital every single day, but to try and cope—or more likely, to keep from dwelling too long on Jane's mortality—I played more tennis, worked harder, whatever I could do to distract myself. I simply couldn't accept such a painful, totally unacceptable possibility.

Jane, meanwhile, accepted the difficult cards she had been dealt with the same serenity, grace, and faith with which she lived the rest of her life. She kept to her passion for reading, and would frequently call friends from the hospital recommending new books. After Jim Baker's first wife, Mary Stuart, passed away from cancer on February 18, 1970, we tried to hide the news from Jane. The Bakers were our neighbors and friends, and we were devastated by Mary Stuart's illness. In hiding that news, we were simply being protective of Jane and her state of mind. We wanted to keep her outlook as positive as we could.

Despite our efforts, however, Jane read about Mary Stuart in the paper— which I hated—and she called Betty Ackerman in my office to send flowers to Jimmy and the boys. As time went on, Jane tried to start talking to me about her own funeral plans, but I simply couldn't listen. It was completely unrealistic, but I was still pushing, still holding on. I was going to hold Jane in my arms until someone, some way, somehow took the sickness out of my sweet wife.

Finally, after nearly a year where her body was ravaged from the inside and constantly probed and prodded, she could withstand no more. To me, Jane never stopped radiating beauty, but even I could see that the light in her soft eyes had started to flicker. One day, as we were sitting in her hospital room, she gently took my hand in hers and quietly said: "Bob, let me go."

I was utterly powerless to deny her this request, and so on August 6, 1970, at age forty-five, Jane Pennybacker Mosbacher closed her eyes for the last time. My kids and I miss them, and her, still. She was my soul mate, and a guiding star for our children. It still hurts to think about it.

After Jane died, we gathered our family and friends together at Memorial

Drive Presbyterian Church for a memorial service. There, our dear friend and minister Charlie Shedd—who later moved to Georgia and launched a modest media ministry before it was so in vogue—said something that Rob remembers well. Charlie said, "Jane Mosbacher was the kind of person who, when she walked into a room, and you started talking to her, she never broke her gaze from you to look around the room and see who else was there."

Following the service, we had a very well-attended wake at the house, and my daughter Lisa remembers there was a lot of laughter as family and friends reminisced about the many good times had with Jane. Afterwards, I got the kids together and we took a trip to Bermuda, where I rented a house. Dealing with my own grief didn't come easy, and as a result I probably wasn't as good as I should have been about helping the kids deal with our shared loss. No question, I worried most of all about Lisa, my youngest daughter, who was still at home. She was so sensitive, so vulnerable.

But somehow my kids and I stuck together, and looking back nearly forty years later we're as close as we've ever been. I was far from perfect as a dad back then or even today, but I genuinely love my kids and grandkids—and, happily, they reciprocate.

When our kids were younger, of course, I was scrambling to build a business. While my head was at the office, my heart was at home. I loved being a dad, but like Pop I was probably too impatient at times, and too strict at others. Nevertheless, we had fun too—lots of fun.

Halloween stands out as a fun holiday. Dee and Rob usually tried to scare Lisa and sometimes Kathi, too—and on occasion I got into the act as well. One time we were out trick-or-treating when we passed a large tree with a low-hanging branch. I quickly and quietly hopped up on the branch and started making scary sounds. When the kids couldn't find me, they started to get anxious until I hopped down.

Years later, while she was in medical school at the Baylor College of Medicine, Dee got me back when she came to my house dressed as a very little girl—standing on her knees, with a long dress that went down to her "ankles." When I answered the door, she innocently said "twick or tweet," and I had no idea who it was.

"Of course, sweetheart," I said as I extended this large basket of candies out to her.

As I was extending the basket, however, Dee reached down under and—bam—knocked the entire basket out of my hands, candies flying everywhere. Mind you, I still didn't know who it was, so for a split second I wanted to strangle

Our kids (sans Kathi) and spouses with Cardella Smith, their "second mother" who was with us from the beginning in Texas.

this small creature. Then Dee started howling with laughter, and once her true identity was known I joined in.

So as a family, we did have the base of trust and love to fall back on after Jane died. Fortunately for all of us, as we grieved and then tried to pick up the pieces, we also had Cardella Smith with us. She had been with us for so long she was like a ballast that helped steady our family ship in a stormy sea. True,

Cardella gave us a connection to our past, a happier time, but she also helped us get on with life.

Two other dear friends also rushed in, picked me up, dusted me off, and got me back in the game—George and Barbara Bush. A few weeks after Jane died, even though he was in the midst of a tough Senate race, George called me up, and together the three of us went out for dinner. It was so typically thoughtful of them, when they had so much going on in their own lives. In fact, fifteen or twenty years later, I finally shared their kind act with Jimmy Baker. It turns out the Bushes had done the same for him after Mary Stuart passed away.

No wonder we love and admire them.

After Jimmy and I were named to President Bush's Cabinet in late 1988, a *Los Angeles Times* reporter surmised—correctly, I think—that the deeply personal trauma Jimmy and I faced in 1970 and the way the Bushes reached out to us in our hour of despair helped the three of us forge a friendship that was deeper and more personal than you tend to see between a president and his Cabinet members. Even though ours isn't a generation known for sitting around and discussing our deepest feelings, we know that friendship is there.

During the early 1970s, another family development was beginning to bubble up to the surface that would challenge us in the years ahead.

During the late 1960s into the early 1970s, a series of overlapping political and social issues collided and set off a chain reaction of radicalism across the country. It started within the civil rights movement, as the peaceful intent and inclusive tone set by Dr. Martin Luther King Jr. and LBJ was gradually co-opted by more divisive figures like Malcolm X and George Wallace, and militant groups like the Black Panthers. Then, tensions over our escalating engagement in the Vietnam War erupted, opening a new rift in our society; and a flourishing counterculture encouraged young Americans to "tune out" from their disillusionment, and numb themselves with drugs.

Against this backdrop of urban riots, mounting casualties in Southeast Asia, the tragic shootings at Kent State, the spectacle of Woodstock, the insanity of the King and RFK assassinations, and more, a network of varying student movements took root on campuses across the country. My daughter Dee was attending Pitzer College in southern California during this troubled time; and like many students, she embraced the rebellious nature of the times.

Like her old man, Dee is terribly competitive and has a fierce independent streak. Unlike me, perhaps, she also possesses a brilliant mind. We raised all of our kids to think for themselves; and in short order, Dee would indeed strike out on her own path as a political activist.

In fact, while she was still in college in the late 1960s, Dee demonstrated there was a sharper edge to her activism when she joined a group of students who took over and occupied a campus building for a short period of time. Of course, college kids angrily protesting anything during the Vietnam era was almost a daily occurrence—and the Claremont consortium of schools, of which Pitzer was one, was no exception. In 1969, for example, roughly 300 student-members of the Claremont Liberation Army stormed an administration building and demanded the removal of the ROTC program from campus. A year later, 1,500 students and local residents marched to protest the U.S. invasion of Cambodia.

So student protests around the country—and at Pitzer—were fairly routine, but to be honest I was troubled, embarrassed, and angry when I heard what my Dee had done.

Another more fundamental revelation came over the Christmas holiday in 1971, when our family got together in Aspen. Dee told me she was heading to New York for a big New Year's Eve party. She casually mentioned she had a new date for the affair, and when I asked who the lucky guy was, she said, "Sarah."

I had no idea Dee was gay. Growing up, she could almost certainly be found playing sports with the neighborhood boys, or dissecting frogs, or digging for snakes in the woods—but it would be absurd to suggest an interest in medicine or sports predetermined her sexual identity. (I am proud to add that while Dee is short in stature—like Pop and me—she has always excelled in sports, whether it was tennis, basketball, skiing, or sailing.)

What's more, growing up Dee always dated boys and even had a fiancé for a brief time while at Pitzer. So to say the news that she was dating a girl took me by surprise is putting it mildly, and looking back I have to say I didn't handle the situation very well.

Shortly thereafter, we had a strong argument on the phone about her lifestyle—as if anything I might say could change it—at the conclusion of which Dee said, "Fine, Dad, if you feel that way I'll change my name. That way you won't have to be embarrassed by me anymore." Then she hung up.

As I heard the line go dead, I instinctively thought of Pop and our fierce argument in his study after Jane and I first came home as a married couple. I recalled how upset Jane and I were, maybe disappointed was the word, at Pop's reaction. Then it hit me that, here I was treating my oldest daughter in much the same manner for following her own path, just as I had in marrying Jane when I did. Something about that didn't sit right with me, so I called Dee back five minutes later and said: "Whether I agree with you or disagree with you, you're still my daughter—and I love you."

If you make a wrong move while going to windward, you can feel it immediately—the loss of speed. My reaction to Dee's news was a case where I had tacked in the wrong direction, and made a mistake. Fortunately, I recognized the problem and acted quickly to address it.

I can't pretend it was all peaches and cream between Dee and me from that point forward, but our biggest disagreements since then have tended to have more to do with politics. A lot of these arguments stemmed from the fact that, shortly after she left college, Dee moved to Washington, joined the Young Socialist Alliance, and started organizing marches against the Vietnam War. This was a particularly sensitive matter for our family since my brother Bus was still serving as President Nixon's chief of protocol, and I was chairing President Nixon's fundraising efforts in Houston.

Moreover, our family always had a deep vein of patriotism running through our ranks. As an immigrant, my grandfather impressed upon Pop how blessed he felt to have come to America, and as a result Pop always had a deep appreciation for our country and the opportunities it afforded him and so many others who worked hard and saw their own American Dream come true. So it was unfathomable to me that Dee or anyone else would protest against our country—and just as she was not shy about sharing her strong feelings with me, I tended to respond in kind.

Meanwhile, Dee brought home some girls that I wasn't particularly crazy about; and for all of us as a family, including Dee I suspect, there was a growth period after she "outed" herself. But when Dee finally met a dynamic young woman named Nanette Gartrell in July of 1975, something clicked. Like Dee, Nanette has a brilliant intellect, a wonderfully engaging personality, and is a thoroughly principled human being. The fact that Nanette was studying to become a doctor no doubt helped at some level to reassure us that this was the stable relationship we wanted for Dee. They've been together ever since, and well over thirty years later can rightly boast the longest relationship in the family.

While I spent a period of time continuing to grapple privately with the guilt and the questions that confront any parent who discovers their child is gay— Did I cause this? Did I do something wrong?—I think Pop was mostly fascinated by Dee's epiphany. He had hired at least one gay man named Matthews to work for him back in the 1950s—a progressive thing to do at the time. Just as my father was agnostic with respect to a person's religious views, his was an equally laissez-faire attitude regarding sexual orientation.

Pop was no doubt doubly welcoming of Nanette because, particularly after he suffered a heart attack in the late 1960s, his fondness with doctors grew to be something of an obsession. Doctors had already saved his life once, and he wanted them to continue saving his life—so Nanette instantly went on a pedestal.

The heart attack, incidentally, slowed Pop only temporarily. He didn't go back to work right away because he had to recuperate, so every day one of the office girls would be dispatched to bring him papers at his somewhat secluded apartment at 480 Park Avenue. Pop's place was all the way in the back of the building, and to get there you had to run a modest gauntlet consisting of about five elevators. Once inside, his apartment was fairly large, with three bedrooms and a large dining room. Thanks to Mom, the apartment was tastefully appointed with fine French furniture; but the most prominent feature in his bedroom were the papers you would always find stacked everywhere.

Each day, my office in Houston would send Pop a drilling report, and he would pore over all the wells, the partners, the percentages, the producers, and what the reserves would be. Together with a geologist named Bob Gall, they would go over this detailed information. Pop loved having access to this inside information so he could follow our progress, but he didn't try to run my business. He used to say our drilling reports simply gave him "a rooting interest."

"I'm rooting for you," he would constantly say.

Once a week, usually on Thursday, I would convene what I called our "early birds" meeting in Houston. It would begin at seven in the morning, and over breakfast we discussed all the prospective different plays that were in progress—things we would like to explore, possible projects we might want to do. Afterwards, when we sent Pop a copy of our meeting notes, Bob Gall would gather up all of the maps on the different areas, circle the prospective acreage, determine who had the adjoining acreage as far as neighbors were concerned, and so forth.

On the weekend, Bob would lay out all of these maps for Pop, so he could ask any question on any prospect—at which point Bob would do more research.

Pop was all about the percentages, which he said he learned from the biggest gamblers in the world. Pop taught me never to do a deal unless the percentage was in our favor. Conversely, if the percentages were against us, I stayed out. It sounds like an easy thing, but Pop used to talk about the vigorish—also known to bettors as "the vig," the "juice," or the "take." It is an old term. Anytime you were going to do a well, he would always want to know, "What is the vigorish? What is it going to cost in the long run?" Pop attributed a lot of his success trading securities and in real estate to this attention to percentages.

Conducting one of our "early bird" meetings at Mosbacher Energy. We worked hard, but had fun too.

Pop was always very generous with his employees—routinely sending them on cruises of Long Island Sound, dinners, shows, you name it. But like any successful manager (as my siblings and I could readily attest) he was never the least bit hesitant to insist that people follow certain rules. This fairly routine June 1972 memo Pop sent to the employees at Mosbacher Properties in New York, which I didn't see until recently, gives a little glimmer into his management style:

> I would like to see everyone happy here; however you must consider my side. Business First Always. I am very disappointed, disturbed and frustrated with the lackadaisical way work is being done. Or rather the work that is not being done. And the lack of production. Our punctuality record is poor. Late arrivals, early departures. Our attendance record is poor. Lunch period has been extended by some well beyond the 45 minute period, socializing a great deal within the office, lengthy telephone conversations, if everyone were to put in their regular weekly hours, thirty-three and three quarter hours, excluding lunch time we would not run in to the problem of falling behind, trying to catch up and keeping the work on a current level. It is almost imperative for the business, therefore, that I ask the following of you. To make up time for any lateness, early departures or personal time off. This may be done either by shortening your lunch hour, lengthening your day or reducing your vacation. Time for

time. It is important that everyone work together so that all phases of the work to be done be completed on time. I would like to see an increase in the production of the work being turned out and not all personal business and relaxation done on my time. I look forward to your cooperation and understanding.

The early 1970s was about the time that a young woman named Liz Carbone started helping Pop prepare his tax statements, and throughout the Byzantine process Liz recalls how Pop would frequently tell her, the attorneys, and anybody else involved in the process: "If I go to jail, you're going with me." He would constantly remind them that they would be signing every document he did, so accuracy and adherence to the rules were of paramount importance to him.

When the time came for Liz to submit her first tax statement, however, she gave Pop his state returns. Each state had its own numerical code, and when the time came to file his income tax for state number six—which might be Michigan, or Montana—Pop reviewed the statement and stated defiantly, "I don't have oil there."

Liz felt she was on very solid ground when she responded, "Well, here's the report."

"I don't care what the report says," Pop repeated, "I don't have oil there. You better check with them because something is wrong."

So Liz went back and checked it out—and sure enough, a number had been transposed. Pop was right, and it just showed how his mind was still humming along several clicks faster than the rest of us.

After Jane died, meanwhile, I tried to keep up my competitive sailing—trying to stay a few clicks ahead of everybody else—and for a time continued to do well.

In October 1971, together with my fantastic crew of Tommy Dickey and Thad Hutcheson, I was very fortunate to beat fifty-two other top-flight teams from fifteen nations to claim the Soling[2] World Championship held in Oyster Bay. Before the start of the race, we were surveying the prerace favorites including Paul Elvstrom, known as "the Great Dane;" Lowell North, who had won at least one Olympic gold medal as well as a world championship in the Star Class; and many other top sailors from around the world. A friend of mine sized up

2. The Soling was introduced in 1965. It has room for two crew and one skipper and possesses controls for every aspect of sail and rig trim—jib tack, halyard, sheet and traveler, main Cunningham, outhaul, sheet, vang and traveler, spinnaker sheet and guy, jibstay, backstay, and upper and lower shroud cars.

the competition before the start and said, "Boy, I'd be thrilled to finish in the top ten."

So to win that was another high point in my sailing life. This was *the* important warm-up race before the Olympics the next year in Munich, and it really gave me a shot in the arm coming off Jane's death.

The next year, we entered both the Dragon Olympic trials and the Soling Olympic trials that were being held on San Francisco Bay within a few days of each other. We finished second in the Dragons, which meant we could go to Munich as an alternate. I very much wanted to go to the Olympics and represent my country, but I was not a good fit as an alternate. They needed a professional sailor more suited to the maintenance type of duties that might be required, so I suggested—and the organizers agreed—to tap another person.

From there, it was on to the Soling, where our hopes were high, only to be dashed in short order. We broke our mast right at the beginning of the series and never seemed to get going again. My other excuse for doing badly was that I pinched a nerve, and that sidelined me for a time.

Soon after that, I was tired and disgusted with racing, and stopped all competitive sailing for a while. Competing for my attention by then was a lovely lady named Sandra Smith, with whom I was spending an increasing amount of time. I had done a few deals with Sandy's prim and proper father, Lloyd, and Sandra also knew my kids. As I saw it, I thought that familiarity would help with my kids. Emotions were still very raw after Jane's passing, and I hoped the fact that I wasn't dating a stranger might help matters.

Like any widower, I suppose, I was grappling with the guilt of starting a new relationship with someone other than the mother of my children; but as a realist, I also knew that I had to turn the page and start a new chapter. Life somehow had to go on.

Besides that, like most men, I readily confess to being putty in the hands of women.

My brother Bus was still serving as President Nixon's chief of protocol at the time and tried to help me turn the page when he introduced me to the Italian actress Gina Lollobrigida. Gina was lovely in every way and, not surprisingly, a favorite of the Italian papparazi—as I discovered during a brief trip to Rome to visit her. We had good fun dodging the photographers staked out around her apartment as we would come and go.

Back in New York, I discovered that my stock went up with Gina on my arm. When we went to 21 for dinner, for example, it seemed I suddenly had friends that I didn't know I had—and, in some cases, just flat out didn't know.

The same was true just a few years ago when I ran into Gina again at a New York restaurant. After she bounded up to our table and we briefly caught up, my lunch partner seemed to treat me with a little more consideration and respect.

I think highly of Gina even though things did not work out between us.

As it was, I found myself falling in love with Sandy. She was younger than me by some fourteen years, and I found her beautiful and fun-loving. When we weren't in Houston, we spent a good bit of time in Aspen, and gradually our conversations started to include talk of marriage. We married in March of 1973.

Like me, Sandy and been previously married—and she had two very fine young boys, Bobby and Lloyd, from her first marriage. Bobby was seven when I married his mom, and Lloyd was four. Both were adventurous like their mother, and I was crazy about both of them.

One of our great highlights came when we camped out on Snowmass Creek in the summer of 1973, on a property I had only recently acquired. At the time, the only structures on the ranch had been abandoned for many, many years, so we pitched our tents next to a grove of large cottonwood trees flanked by small Aspens. We also had a set of styrofoam coolers for our food that I lodged between rocks on the bank of Snowmass Creek in the shade of the cottonwood grove. We later found that some sort of animal, possibly beavers, had gnawed into the styrofoam to get at some of our food.

We spent about twelve days camping out. During that time we hiked all over the property though large meadows of sagebrush and rocks and into enormous, dark, cool groves of aspens in pine trees. When we sent the boys off to shoot their BB guns and explore, they were equipped with whistles that they were instructed to blow if they got lost.

Two other memories stand out. I remember catching a trout using a piece of silver foil from a Wrigley's gum wrapper that I made into a little ball to put on a fishing hook. Believe it or not, we actually caught a number of trout for our dinner—and there are witnesses to vouch for this claim!

During this camping trip, incidentally, I never shaved. I let my beard grow out, and arrived back in Houston looking rather unkempt. That first Monday back to the office, I decided not to shave that morning. Instead, I put on a cowboy hat and jacket, and headed into work. Before walking into the reception area, I pulled the hat down low over my eyes, went up to the receptionist, and in a western twang kind of half-shouted, "Hey there, Little Missy. I'm looking for Mosbacher."

The ruse worked as the receptionist clearly didn't recognize me, and as she struggled to figure out what to do I finally lifted up the hat, and said, "It's me!"

Together with my own kids, Sandy and her wonderful boys helped to fill the vast emptiness left by Jane's passing. Later, as Sandy and I sailed the Windward Islands during our belated honeymoon, I was still hoping, trying, searching to get some wind back in my own sails. I couldn't turn back the clock, but I could see if it was possible to start all over—and find a new happiness. At the very least, I was going to give it a shot.

Jane would have wanted no less.

The first time you enter the Oval Office, your mind has a hard time processing the fact that such a stately, but relatively modest, space could already possess such a vast history. The mind's eye becomes a mental newsreel filled with touchstone moments of national trial and triumph that have transpired between its gently curved walls.

For that reason, it is perhaps the most powerful symbol of the presidency itself, and has been referred to as the "greatest home field advantage in the world" given its propensity to strike awe in the hearts of visitors. Many a person has arrived at the White House intent on giving the president of the United States a piece of their mind, only to find themselves suddenly weak in the knees and tight in the throat upon entering the Oval Office.

Since FDR relocated the office to its present location in the southeast corner of the West Wing in 1936, each succeeding occupant has put their own stylistic imprint on that space—choosing everything from the desk they use, to smaller details such as the décor, artwork, and personal mementos on display. Looking back, the Oval Office as I found it during my very first visit on December 16, 1975 offered an apt reflection of the thirty-eighth president of the United States—with its rich salmon, gold, and green hues projecting a warm, inviting atmosphere.

"Hi Bob," President Ford said as I was escorted in, making my way across the pale gold rug accented with blue florets. Though I was hardly a member of his inner circle, the president's avuncular manner made me feel instantly at ease.

Like George Bush, Gerald Ford was without a doubt one of the nicest, most decent—and most capable—men ever to occupy the Oval Office. I found him unfailingly kind and calm in demeanor. What's more, Jerry Ford had an amazing work ethic, and was an ardent practitioner of the politics of inclusion. During his career at both ends of Pennsylvania Avenue, his natural political instinct was to reach out, and to try and find common ground with allies and adversaries alike.

The occasion for my fist visit to the Oval Office actually had as much to do with my brand new duties as the national finance chairman of the President

Talking politics and the oil business with President Ford during my first visit to the Oval Office in December 1975.

Ford Committee (PFC)—his 1976 election campaign—as it did with my regular day job in the energy business.

In the wake of the OPEC oil embargo of 1973—an event that shocked the national psyche and caused high fuel prices and long lines at gas stations—Congress in December 1975 passed the Energy Policy and Conservation Act that called for establishing the strategic petroleum reserve and mandating vehicle fuel economy standards. Both of these measures were fine. The objectionable part of the bill, however, was that it also called for gradually phasing out price controls on domestic oil over a forty-month period ending in 1979.

In his low-key manner, President Ford referred to this last provision as an "inadequate measure," but it struck me as both economically irresponsible and politically lethal when I first heard about it. As it turned out, President Ford's top economic advisors, Treasury Secretary Bill Simon and Alan Greenspan—then heading the Council of Economic Advisors—also wanted an immediate end to the controls, and were actively urging the president to veto the bill.

Why not deregulate immediately? Congress was predictably wary of the political fallout because removing the price controls would have led to rising energy prices. Those of us who favored a veto on economic grounds, meanwhile, believed that keeping prices at an artificially low level would deprive energy companies of the capital they needed to find and develop new sources of fuel. Immediate deregulation would, as we saw it, foster greater energy independence the nation needed while enabling U.S. companies to produce a greater, and more stable, supply of fuel that would lower prices for consumers in the long run.

Unfortunately, most of President Ford's political advisors shared Congress' shortsighted concerns—wishing neither to see rising gas prices at the pump, nor to engage in a divisive debate with Democrats over deregulation in the run-up to the 1976 election. At least this protracted, phased-out deregulation called for in the bill was better than no deregulation at all, they argued.

That might have been sound strategy as it related to the general election, but to me, in December of 1975, it didn't make any sense politically when the president first faced a daunting primary challenge from the right in the form of Ronald Reagan—and states like Texas would loom large in deciding who won the nomination. Even though I had been with the campaign a scant week when the bill was sent to the White House, I asked to see the president to voice my concern.

So there I found myself on December 16 ready to make my case as the president politely listened. We exchanged a few brief pleasantries about the campaign and how my new situation as finance chairman was working out, but quickly got down to business. After I had my say, I summed my case up as respectfully as possible: "If the price controls remain in place, Mr. President, I'm afraid Texas will go for Governor Reagan."

"Bob, I don't like these controls any more than you do, but we're probably not going to get a better offer from the Hill," the president responded, alluding to the firm Democratic majorities in both houses of Congress. Few men alive at that time knew how to count votes on Capitol Hill better than Jerry Ford, so once I heard him lay that reality on the table I knew my cause was doomed. President Ford signed the bill six days later; and as feared, six months later Governor Reagan soundly defeated the president in the Texas GOP primary to keep his insurgent campaign alive, heading into the Kansas City national convention that summer.

Looking back to that first meeting in the Oval, the fact that I was able to see the president on fairly short notice was somewhat noteworthy. This was in the immediate aftermath of Watergate, when many still viewed fund-raisers as second-class political animals. True, I had served on the Republican National

Finance Committee, and as chairman of the Texas Congressional Boosters. I also had attended receptions at the White House and in Texas with President Ford, but ours was still an informal friendship.

What helped my credibility with the Ford camp was my close friendship with two men in particular: George Bush, who had been on Ford's short list for vice president after he succeeded Nixon and was then serving a Director of Central Intelligence; and Max Fisher, who was a fellow Michigander like Ford and had been a close friend of Pop's since the 1940s. In fact, I remember how Pop used to walk with Max in Central Park after Max's first wife, Sylvia, became ill with heart disease. I think talking to Pop helped Max cope with his feelings of sadness and hopelessness; and together with their many business dealings together, that helped them forge a family friendship that holds strong to this day.

By the 1970s, Max was one of the most trusted American businessmen not just on Israeli relations, where he had strong relationships throughout the government and the private sector, but a whole range of issues. Like Jerry Ford, Max was a stout supporter of, and leader in, the Michigan Republican Party, and he recognized Ford's national potential early on. In turn, Ford invited Max to DC for consultations the day President Nixon resigned from office in August of 1974. The mutual trust, and respect, between Ford and Fisher was deep and enduring.

Not surprisingly, then, it was Max Fisher who was among the very first not only to recognize that the Ford campaign's 1976 fund-raising operation was in deep trouble, but also to do something about it. Five days after President Ford headlined an October 1975 event that Max organized for him in Detroit, with 4,000 attendees paying $50 per person to attend, Max went to Washington to encourage the president and his top advisors to address what was already an acute problem.

Earlier in 1975, the Ford campaign had rightly thought they scored a coup when they landed David Packard, of Hewlett-Packard fame, to run the fund-raising operation. David was a conservative from California, had ties to Governor Reagan, and a network of rich friends around the country. The fact that he chose to go with the Ford campaign over Reagan helped the president's effort in terms of perception, but in the end it proved less than optimal from an execution standpoint.

In the spring of 1975, David publicly declared a $10 million fund-raising goal by the end of 1975, but was quickly forced to scale it back to $5 million by the campaign's lack of performance. By the time Packard left the campaign in November, only about $950,000 had been banked—and the campaign's "burn rate" of expenses had started to exceed its income.

That's when my phone started ringing.

What began with a casual few chats to feel me out was quickly followed by a call from Commerce Secretary Rogers Morton, who was one of the president's most trusted advisors and would eventually end up replacing Bo Callaway as campaign chairman—and was, in turn, replaced by my pal Jim Baker. Rog asked me to come to the campaign headquarters in Washington, which was located just a few blocks from the White House at 1828 L Street.

I could tell the campaign was interested in my being involved at some level, but when Rog asked if I wanted to run the national fund-raising operation for the president, it sounded too exciting to pass up. Of course, while my four kids were heading off to college or had already struck out on their own, I still had to consider Sandy and my two stepsons, Bobby and Lloyd, at home. I also had a day job running a business, as well as plans to buy a new boat and possibly make another run at Olympic sailing in 1976. At least the sailing would have to go on hold.

Despite my best efforts to reassure her it was only a temporary arrangement, Sandy was not happy about my wanting to take an assignment that required me to be in Washington four days a week. But she also recognized it was a unique and important opportunity, so I called Rog, accepted the job, and the campaign announced my appointment on December 3, 1975.

Upon arriving back in Washington, I discovered the situation was as bad as the rumors had suggested. Just $238,000 was left in the PFC (President Ford Committee) bank account, and our cash flow was, frankly, flowing the wrong way—going out faster than we were taking it in.

David Packard was a brilliant man, but he never adjusted to the post-Watergate fund-raising rules—which for the first time limited political giving in federal races to $1,000 per person, and $5,000 per political action committee. As White House staffer Fred Slight had presciently observed in an early campaign memo to scheduling director Jerry Jones, the enactment of the Federal Election Campaign Act Amendments of 1974 essentially meant "the days of the 'fat cat' contributor are over."

Slight was alluding to the fact that no longer could you get a group of rich guys to write big checks for $10,000 or more that directly supported a candidate—as I had tried to do during that 1968 Dallas meeting with Richard Nixon. Instead, you had to dramatically expand the donor universe by reaching out through direct mail, phone solicitations, and other mass communication methods that enabled the campaign to "touch" more people.

For whatever reason, David didn't do that. After he talked to all the obvious big money people, the "low-hanging fruit," he apparently didn't know what to do next. As a result, he became totally frustrated, threw up his hands in disgust, and quit.

When I took the job, I started by calling key people I knew in every city, or key friends of friends, to create a network of capable people devoted to collecting $1,000 contributions. The idea was to get someone in every city, and certainly in every state, who would contact their friends, associates, and neighbors. The key thing to note here is this was in the days before the Internet. We had to work the old-fashioned way, by working the phones, going person-to-person, and asking for the sale.

When you sell a president to a prospect, of course, you have to be a good listener—as well as a good salesman. Almost everyone who contributes to a political campaign has a pet issue, or policy recommendation, that they think can change the world; that's what motivates them to get involved. Some of these ideas make sense, but many do not—and in the latter case it helps if you have either a high threshold for pain, or a good pair of hip-waders.

Either way, however, you have to be able to patiently, persistently focus on the strengths of your candidate, keep steering the conversation in that direction, and above all keep your sense of humor.

Once we had our various state and local leaders in place, I told them I would try to get President Ford to their city for a fund-raising event; but if I couldn't get the president there, we would be sure to send a high-ranking official. At worst, I would go.

At the time, I knew many of the Cabinet members—many of whom became surrogate speakers for the campaign. Secretary of the Treasury, Bill Simon Sr., was excellent at this kind of stumping. My friend Henry Kissinger also helped, but frequently intoned in that deep German accent: "I don't want anyone to know I am dabbling in politics and money." Mel Laird, Secretary of Defense, was also sensitive to this perception of partisanship. He got plenty mad at me because he went to a fund-raiser, and it somehow leaked.

I was a convenient target for his wrath.

In his memoirs, President Ford referred to me as a "blunt-spoken Texas oilman," and I plead guilty to the charge. Early on, in fact, I shocked some of President Ford's advisors when I asserted the only way I could ask people for money is if I knew what was going on in the campaign. So I often sat in on senior staff meetings, which several of the top strategists didn't like. After one meeting, I remember one guy asking another about me: "What's HE doing here?"

"He's the new finance guy."

"Well, hell, I don't care—get him out of here."

I would hear these complaints, and at first tried to ignore them. Before long, however, the griping got under my skin so I decided to handle it in my own sweet, lovable way. "Who the hell do you think it is in all these cities who builds the hospitals, and the universities, and the like?" I asked one of the main offenders. "They're not the hot shot political pros—they're the same smart, successful business leaders we're asking for money. If we want their support, I am *sure* you can appreciate that I need to know what's going on."

After a while, they stopped griping—or at least, they stopped griping in front of me.

There was another disagreeable office element with which I had to contend, and it came in the form of a staffer I inherited from Packard. His name was Bob Mathias—the same Bob Mathias who won the gold medal in the Olympic decathlon in 1948 at age seventeen, and then became the first to repeat as gold medalist again four years later.

Bob was so popular after his Olympic exploits, that his life at the tender age of twenty-three became the basis of a 1954 movie, *The Bob Mathias Story*, with Mathias himself in the leading role. He was "the epitome of the all-American boy," as the *New York Times* later described him.

My main problem with Bob centered on the fact that he was still extremely popular in 1976, particularly with the ladies in our campaign office. As a result, it was not uncommon for him to take three or four hours for lunch, usually in the company of one of our female staffers, before the two returned appearing somewhat disheveled. I had no problem with socializing on the job, or office romances carried out off-hours, but I did have a problem with losing not one, but two, staffers for half a day when we had too much to do. As a result, I appealed to the president to have Bob reassigned, and this time my request was granted.

Fortunately, we had plenty of hard-working men and women who were dedicated to the president. We had folks like Bob O'Dell, Margaret Alexander, and Fred Bush. Fred was not related to George and Barbara, but was instead a talented young man who did a superb job running the PFC phone bank. Together as a team, we kept after it; and slowly but surely, we started to see some positive results in our corner of the store.

It was a lot of hard work, but we also had fun, too. Helping my situation was the fact that my youngest daughter, Lisa, was attending Mount Vernon College

in the Washington area—and I got to see a good deal of her. In fact, with Sandra back in Houston, Lisa often served as my "date" at White House functions.
(Funny how some things stay with you: it was at one such reception that I recall
seeing Alan Greenspan positively gorging himself at the buffet table as if he
wasn't sure where or when his next meal might be.)

It was also during the 1976 campaign that I learned a key lesson involving
presidential motorcades. I was with the president at a fund-raiser in some hotel,
where I have no idea, and after the event we both stopped to use the washroom.
President Ford walked out just as I was washing my hands—maybe thirty seconds ahead of me. When I arrived at the hotel exit, however, I was just in time
to see the last vehicle in a twenty-car motorcade speed past the entryway.

The important takeaway there is: the president waits for no one, even those
who practice solid personal hygiene.

Most of all, however, that experience in the Ford campaign taught me:
"Blessed are the gatherers; not just the givers." I got a lot of undeserved credit
for turning the PFC's financial fortunes around, but the truth is the really hard
work was done by a lot of citizens with busy lives—who also cared deeply about
America, and our collective future, and who got involved with all their heart
and soul.

Much has been written about the Ford campaign of 1976—how disorganized
it was, how little political judgment it demonstrated, and so on. At the end of the
day, however, what counts in politics above all else is results; so what does it say
that President Ford was first able to overcome the hard-charging primary challenge mounted by Ronald Reagan? The former governor of California had been
a national political figure for twelve years by the time, had a better campaign
organization, and was certainly more adept at using the media.

To me, if there was a reversal of fortunes, it started at the top, with President
Ford himself. Despite his calm and gentle manner, Jerry Ford was also a determined competitor who was true to his values—and to himself. I firmly believe
that, in 1976, the American public started to recognize this. Even if President
Ford was never the most scintillating orator before the cameras, I think the
people understood he was a trustworthy and capable leader when the TV klieg
lights were turned off.

I'm biased, of course, but there's no question another Texan who had come
on board the PFC also played a significant role in righting the 1976 political
operation—my friend Jim Baker. Like me, Jim's political experience before arriving in Washington was almost exclusively local and Texas in nature—which

President Ford greets Sandra and stepsons Lloyd and Bobby Gerry during a Houston campaign stop in 1976. Jimmy Baker is to the President's left.

made what happened to him in the summer of 1976 totally unexpected to the Washington pundits.

In May of 1976, Jim moved from the Commerce Department (where he had served under Rog Morton and Elliott Richardson) over to the PFC, starting out as the chief delegate hunter. All summer long, he did such a remarkable job helping the president prepare for, and then win, the nomination during a dramatic convention floor fight in Kansas City, that Ford decided to promote Jim to campaign chairman—running the entire show—when Rog Morton became too ill with cancer to carry on.

As I recall, Baker took his new post around Labor Day, and made his big debut before the national media with the president and his team of advisors, who had gathered to strategize for the general election in Vail, Colorado. Before the press conference, I was nervous for Jim because, from that point forward, the national press would be adversarial at every turn. Of course, I needn't have worried because he was terrific as always, appearing calm and collected with answers for every question.

Still, even with the highly capable Jim Baker on board, the Ford campaign faced gale-force political headwinds going into the fall campaign. The economy, which had showed signs of improving earlier in 1976, softened as the year progressed. In fact, some of us had, only half-kidding, suggested replacing the administration's less-than-inspiring "WIN" or "Whip Inflation Now" PR campaign with a more direct message: "Jesus, get the economy going."

In the end, though President Ford battled like a warrior and erased Governor Carter's significant lead to a razor-thin margin, he still lost one of the closest elections in American history. In fact, had Ford picked up just a few thousand more votes in Ohio and Hawaii, he would have won one of the greatest come-from-behind victories of all time.

Sadly, it seems one of Jerry Ford's very first, and finest, acts as president—the pardoning of President Nixon—had combined with concerns about the economy to seal his electoral fate. I reflected on that cruel irony again some thirty years later in the aftermath of President Ford's death. As our thirty-eighth president was being laid to rest, he was universally lauded as a good man and noble leader who helped America usher in "a time to heal" following the betrayal of Watergate.

So hope does spring eternal that the media, and historians, do eventually get it right.

Coming off the bitter disappointment of the Ford campaign, I returned to Houston to discover my marriage to Sandy wasn't faring much better. She wasn't particularly happy, and one night told me she needed to leave Houston, and me, to try and "find herself." I protested, but she left shortly thereafter for a yearlong hiatus in Florida, taking Bobby and Lloyd with her. Sandy did invite me to visit—which I did once or twice—but to be honest, I was too angry that she left in the first place to go more often.

Eventually they came back to Houston, only to leave against my hopes and wishes (again), this time for Europe. After I heard that she had taken a flat in London, I was out of patience—something I never had in abundance to start.

In fairness, and in hindsight, Sandy and I had different expectations for the marriage. When we were dating, I'm sure she didn't realize I was a workaholic when it came to business or politics. In hindsight, I think she really wanted someone who would take more time away from the office and campaigning to travel with her and enjoy life. The fact that I wasn't cut out to do that—at least not to the degree she wanted—was certainly not Sandy's fault. Our priorities were just different, and recognizing that reality led us both to realize the marriage wasn't working. We separated shortly thereafter, and divorced in 1983.

I am happy to report that, today, Sandy and I are still friends, and I feel very close to my stepsons Bobby and Lloyd. They are wonderful young men.

Sadly, while Sandy and I were separating, another family break was in the works. In 1978, my brother Bus and I decided it would be best if we severed our business ties.

There were several reasons for this unhappy development, starting with the "older brother-versus-younger brother" dynamic. Added to that, Bus and I were too different. I was business-oriented, and though Bus had served on numerous corporate boards he didn't have the same firsthand knowledge of the nuts-and-bolts of what made a company tick. He frequently phoned people in my office, for example, and asked questions that often distracted our people from their daily responsibilities.

By then, I had spent thirty years in Texas building a reasonably successful company—and had managed to do all of that and more without Bus' input. So I naturally chafed when he made these unwanted, and unhelpful, inquiries. The best thing for all of us, we eventually realized, was to "unscramble the eggs" as Bus put it—which meant buying Bus out of the family business. It was best to dissolve the part of our relationship that seemed to cause the most friction.

So in fairly short order, I had to grapple with the demise of the Ford campaign, my marriage to Sandy, and then my business ties with my older brother.

But life wasn't all bad.

For one thing, on January 28, 1978, my youngest daughter Lisa married Arthur D. "Downing" Mears Jr. in Houston. Downing is a University of Virginia grad, a remarkably solid and honorable man, and I cannot find the right words to describe what it means to have him not only helping run Mosbacher Energy, but more importantly, in our family. He is a devoted husband, a great dad, and a darn good sailor in his own right.

Perhaps the greatest seal of approval, though, came from Pop himself. After Lisa and Downing were married, Downing and Pop stayed up a few nights talking about business, and life itself. Pop quickly took Downing into his confidence, and taught Downing the "code" Pop used when discussing the family's various business deals.

The second development helping me through this rough patch was the discovery that being a bachelor did have its compensations. In fact, when my daughter Kathi married a wonderful man, Michael Wheeler, in November of 2006 my kids came up to me after the reception to tease me about all my former girlfriends from this period who had been in attendance.

To be sure, the late 1970s to the early 1980s was an active and fun time for me socially, but it was also a productive time for my business.

In the late 1970s, for example, a local real estate developer, Vincent Kickerillo, approached me about selling the north end of Cinco Ranch—a fairly substantial chunk of land that stretched from western Harris County into eastern Fort Bend County. I originally bought the 6,500-acre tract in the late 1960s from William "Fishback" Wheless of Gulf Oil, who along with "Mr. Jim" Abercrombie and three other prominent oil families had bought the historic Blakeley Ranch in 1937 and renamed it Cinco Ranch. The Wheless family was the only one to live on the vast expanse of scrubby pastureland, rice fields, and a few dense thickets of overgrown oak, pine, and holly. However, the property also had a wonderful old lodge with a beautiful stone fireplace where the other families could congregate as well.

Ol' Fishback didn't want his kids fighting over the land when he was gone, so as he was sitting there—an elderly man in "heaven's waiting room"—he decided to sell. Pop, as I recall, did not like this land play of mine, so to help placate him I brought in a few partners, including "Mr. Jim" Abercrombie's only daughter, Josephine, Jim Elkins Sr., and a few others. We bought the property, putting up 10 percent, or roughly $5 million, and I kept a half interest. After that, throughout the 1970s, we did some pretty terrific duck hunting out there, but not much else.

A few years later, when Kickerillo and I first got together he said, "You put down a number, and I'll put down a number." So we did, and when we compared figures we were too far apart, and that first attempt to strike a deal fell through.

Vincent came back some time later and struck a deal for $84 million—which was, at the time, the largest raw land transaction in Houston history. It's been said that the three key factors to success in real estate are location, location, and location—but good timing doesn't hurt either. Helping our valuation in Cinco Ranch was the fact that, because of Houston's growth, the state of Texas wanted to build a highway construction project known as the Grand Parkway in the area; and where major roads like that go, developers like Vincent Kickerillo are sure to follow.

As I say, I'd rather be lucky than smart.

I didn't do this with Vincent in the case of Cinco Ranch, but in many other situations when I have disagreed with someone over a business deal we have settled it by flipping a coin. For example, when my nephew Bruce sold his inherited interest in a gas well, we couldn't agree over the interest we would pay the purchaser. So I flipped a coin, and when I won, Bruce—to his credit—stood by the deal.

This method, I found, was much cheaper than calling in the lawyers.

Another venture that came to fruition in the mid- to late 1970s involved the barge business and a friend named Berdon Lawrence—who I met in 1974 while he was building a towboat and barge company called Hollywood Marine. Our mutual friend Jon Roberts introduced us, as Berdon needed investors in three push-boats or towboats, which would be used in moving drilling rigs for inland oil and gas exploration.

During the mid-1970s, because of the long lines at service stations, you could buy gasoline only on certain days based on whether your license plate ended with an odd or even number. As a result, there was political pressure to expand refinery capacity in the United States. About 150 small refineries or "tea kettle refineries" sprung up across the Gulf Coast, from Brownsville, Texas to Mobile, Alabama. To meet the demand, they had to have crude oil barged or shipped in to them—but they also needed products such as gasoline, diesel, and the dense and viscous #6 oil shipped out, all using barges. As a result, the demand for barges shot up.

I could see the market was moving Berdon's way and his barges were a good investment, so I signed on and brought a few friends, including Jim Baker and George Bush.

Ten years later, when then-Vice President George Bush was running for the presidency, *Washington Post* reporter Bob Woodward came to Houston to investigate this particular barge deal. Bob was under the firm impression that we had "given" George his interest in Hollywood Marine—that despite the fact George had been a pioneer in the offshore oil business, he had not had enough knowledge to invest his own money in the deal. Woodward changed the thesis of his story when we were able to produce George's canceled check.[1]

Happily for all of us, Hollywood Marine turned out to be a good bet.

In response to the oil crisis of the mid-1970s, the Carter administration passed a law designed to get more gasoline and diesel fuel into the market. Called the "small refinery bias," the law required major oil companies to sell crude to small refineries at $2 under market price. Hundreds of independent refineries sprouted up between New Orleans and Houston, and all of them relied

1. Unfortunately, in the same series Woodward and the *Post* ran in August of 1988, Bob cited me as the source of a fabricated quote he attributed to George Bush, where after the 1976 election George supposedly offered not to run for president in 1980 if President-elect Carter kept him on as CIA Director. The idea of George Bush suggesting such a thing didn't even make for good fiction—it was that absurd. Still, I was so livid Bob made this up that I wanted to respond publicly and call him on it. Jimmy Baker calmly, and wisely, suggested that we wait and see if the story developed any legs. It didn't.

on tank barges to transport gasoline and heavy oils. In the five years that followed, the tank barge industry almost doubled in size.

During this same period, business was also good for Mosbacher Energy. We
made a few new discoveries, perhaps most notably—or infamously—in the
Philippines.

I had gone to Manila with Sandra to meet with Ferdinand Marcos in 1973
or 1974, and it was a fascinating visit because he invited us to stay at the Mala-
canang Palace—the official residence of the President of the Republic. During
our stay, the First Lady, Imelda Marcos, came to the guesthouse with a huge
box filled with elaborate jewelry—so much, in fact, I recall thinking (wrongly)
that some of it must have been fake. Imelda had stopped by just to show off
her dazzling wares, which struck me as an odd thing to do. She was a strong
woman, to be sure, but I also came away with the distinct feeling that she was
not trustworthy.

More importantly, we also came away with the first license, or concession for
a foreign company to drill for oil there. That's when I decided to bring Pan Am
Production Co., a sister company to Standard Oil, into the play. The mistake I
made, however, was making them the operator.

After we found some oil, Marcos' Agriculture and Energy Minister accused
us of "promoting" under false pretenses, saying our company didn't have any
money invested in the project, so they essentially took the well away from us.
In response, we had no choice but to send our lawyers from Vinson & Elkins
over, along with the Arthur Anderson accountants, to show where we had put
money into the project—not taken it out, as had been alleged.

In due course, it became apparent that Marcos' plan was to take our well over
using the government as his foil. By then, Marcos' "friends" had formed a little
oil company that offered to buy the well from us for next to no money, and we
took the offer because we realized it was the best we could do. I have zero doubt
that my erstwhile host, President Marcos, had a piece of the action on that,
maybe even the biggest piece.

In the end, we took the risk—and they took the well.

What that experience taught me in dealing with suspect foreign leaders is
to make sure you always keep the operations end of an oil or gas deal. If you
merely put the deal together, you're expendable. But when you do the drilling,
they need you. They can't kick you out. In the late 1970s, the Filipino government could kick Mosbacher Energy off the deal, but they had to keep Pan Am
Production Co.

As luck would have it, after the election of Corazon Aquino in May of 1986, the Marcos family was forced to flee Manila and seek exile in Hawaii with help from the U.S. government. During the Marcos' exodus, I heard they had a vast sum of cash and jewelry on their plane, so I called some friends in the government to arrange a special U.S. welcoming party that included federal agents with the proper paperwork to seize twenty-two crates. These crates were identical to the ones confiscated from a brother of Mr. Marcos' wife, Imelda, that contained 110 million Philippine pesos, or about $5.5 million, in cash.

I am not a vengeful person, but in Ferdinand Marcos' case I was only too happy to try and see a modicum of justice served.

After Corazon Aquino assumed the Filipino presidency, she made me and my other partners in the Filipino project "whole" by paying us the $2.5 million we were still owed. I subsequently split this payment per the agreement I originally made with my partner and friend at Florida Gas, Chairman and CEO Jack Bowen, as well as Jack's executive vice president—a man named Ken Lay. They were thrilled to get their half, but the truth is, had I been anything other than a "blunt-spoken Texas oilman," I might never have told them.

My friend Chesley Pruet told his two sons-in-law after they joined his business that if you did anything unethical in the oil business, everyone in Houston—and throughout the industry—would know about it before the sun set the next day. That might still be true. Even today, in this age of lawyers and escrows, many of us still believe that a Texas oilman's word is his most solemn bond.

Chapter 14 WHAT DO YOU WIN VERSUS
WHAT DO YOU LOSE?

During the 1960s and the 1970s, few Texans loomed larger over the
state and national political landscape than Governor John Connally.
War hero, lawyer to Texas legend Sid Richardson, savvy political in-
fighter, and close confidant of President Johnson's, Connally appeared to have
been picked for the role of Texas Governor "right out of central casting," as the
saying goes. He cut a dashing figure, and could be a mesmerizing speaker.

Of course, Connally's place in history was assured on November 23, 1963
while riding in President Kennedy's limousine on that fateful day in Dallas.
However, after he left the Governor's Mansion in 1969, the governor had ambi-
tions to make his own history. Connally forged a close alliance with President
Nixon, who appointed him Secretary of the Treasury in December of 1970 despite three politically uncomfortable facts for the White House. First, Connally
was still a Democrat; second, in the 1970 Texas Senate race Connally helped
Lloyd Bentsen beat George Bush, who ran for the Senate after President Nixon
recruited him; and third, just weeks after his 1970 defeat, George also lobbied
the president for the Treasury post. George ended up "settling" for the United
Nations posting with Cabinet ranking, while the Nixon-Connally relationship
grew stronger.

In the wake of the Vice President Spiro Agnew's resignation in October
1973, Nixon made it known that he intended to appoint Connally—who had
switched to the Republican Party just a few months before—as Agnew's successor. As others have noted, this would have put Connally in a strong position to
run for president in 1976; but jilted Democrats still miffed that Connally bolted
from their party threatened to fight the appointment, forcing Nixon to name
Jerry Ford instead.

After the Ford appointment, Connally returned to private law practice but
soon faced a criminal prosecution over bribery and conspiracy charges involving a milk price scheme during his stint at Treasury. He was acquitted after a
trial in federal court, but in 1977 once again found himself under attack for a
bank partnership he had struck with two Arab sheiks.

Still, as the 1980 campaign neared, Connally was by far the best-known Texan in the country—even if, for many, his reputation was tinged with notoriety. Relatively few people outside Texas or the Washington, DC "Beltway," meanwhile, knew my friend George Bush. In March of 1977, just two months after Jimmy Carter took office, *New York Times* columnist Bill Safire named Jimmy Baker and me—along with Senator John Tower and Anne Armstrong—among those who would be quietly working to build support for a Bush candidacy. In Houston, where both Connally and Bush lived and started their White House quests, few were impressed with George's chances as 1980 neared. More than a passing few asked why I was backing the darkest of dark horses against more formidable candidates like Ronald Reagan and John Connally.

By 1978, Connally was back at work at the prestigious Vinson & Elkins law firm in Houston—the same law firm that handled legal affairs for Mosbacher Energy. That summer, he had one of his partners call and invite me to lunch. So I went, and together with a few other fellows we had a great time at the Ramada Club—which in those days was right above the Vincent & Elkins offices. Governor Connally pretty much dominated the conversation, but I found him an engaging and charismatic figure.

After lunch, Connally intoned in that deep drawl of his: "Bob, if you've got a few minutes, I was hoping you might stop by my office for a visit."

Once we were seated, Connally started talking about his plans for the country—and for the world. Clearly, he was signaling to me his all-but-declared intention to run for president, and as he talked about his grand plans I found myself thoroughly captivated. It seemed like he had everything figured out. For example, I recall him suggesting that he would retaliate against Japan for their unfair trade practices by letting their cars "rot on the docks of Yokohama." He was really going to stick it to the Japanese on trade, which was very popular with many business leaders at that time.

Connally was a charmer—part snake-oil salesman, part visionary statesman, part cold-eyed realist and dealmaker. He made a very compelling case for his candidacy, or so I thought sitting in his office.

Connally then paused for a breath and launched into how he wanted the fund-raising part of his campaign to work. He had been around politics more than thirty years at the time, had managed LBJ's Senate races, and knew a great deal about the machinery of politics. Added to that, he served on the boards of numerous major companies—so he had an enviable network of influential business leaders ready to write checks, and get others to do the same.

Still, after he spent five or six minutes talking about raising money, I thought, "Isn't that strange?" Even though I had just managed fund-raising for President

Ford, and knew a little bit about how it worked in a national campaign, it dawned on me that Connally clearly had no interest in my views on the matter.

Right then, the halo that I had envisioned around Connally's head came off, and I sort of snapped out of this political spell he was casting upon me.

I am ashamed to confess this; but if Connally had stopped at the right moment, he might—might—have seduced me in a political sense, and talked me into working for him. It is very painful for me to admit I was tempted because I love George Bush like a brother. It took a great deal of political courage for George to run for president in 1980 when nobody thought he had a chance. Nobody risked more or worked harder, but those of us who stood with him early on also felt the sting of being totally discounted—as if we were a bunch of Sancho Panzas being led by a modern Don Quixote to go tilt at political windmills.

Whatever explains my contemplating such an indiscretion, I am grateful Connally never "closed the sale" that day in his office. He talked too long—long enough for me to come to my senses. When the conversation finally wound down and he expressed an interest in having me on board, I thanked him for sharing his vision, said I would think about things, and made for the door as quickly as possible. I never looked back.

A few months later, the first George Bush for President campaign started cranking into gear. After Jim Baker lost a very respectable bid for Texas Attorney General to Mark White in November of 1978 (the 44 percent he garnered was the second-best showing for a down-ballot Republican since Reconstruction), George started rounding us up. In my case, he invited me to drop by the sparse campaign office, where he told me in the low-key way George Bush does things, "You know, it would be really good for us if you became national finance chairman."

With everything else I had going on in my life—personally and professionally—I wasn't sure I could afford to take on such a demanding assignment. As we say in the South, it took me some time to "wrap my mind around" the prospect.

In the end, of course, I was as incapable of saying "no" to George Bush back then as I am today—and ended up taking the job. We had already set up two political action committees (the Fund for Limited Government, and the Congressional Leadership Committee) to help lay the groundwork for a 1980 run. On January 5, 1979, we filed the necessary papers with the Federal Election Commission to permit us to raise money for a Bush candidacy, opened an eight-

Starting the climb, still an asterisk. An early event to raise funds for the 1980 Bush candidacy for president of the United States.

room office in west Houston, established a catchy phone number GOP-1980, and started to build up a national organization.

That was just the beginning.

By the time George pulled to the starting line and officially declared his candidacy for president on May 1, 1979, we had already set up committees in nine of the first eleven primary states, appointed finance chairmen in forty states, and raised $825,000—more than enough to obtain federal matching funds. This first wave of support came primarily from close friends, former Yale classmates, and a bunch of former colleagues and peers in the oil business. Added to that, many of the top campaign leaders and grassroots activists who had supported President Ford in 1976 were already in our camp.

I also had some good connections to help form the nucleus of financial support, but enthusiasm for the candidate and his remarkably diverse record of service at his various posts—the United Nations, the Republican National

Committee, Ambassador to China, director of the CIA—is what helped us grow quickly. "There were always doubts at the beginning whether he [Bush] was up to these jobs," the venerable *New York Times* columnist Scotty Reston wrote the day of the campaign declaration, "but applause for his record at the end."[1]

During his morning campaign announcement speech at the National Press Club in Washington, George called for a "new candor" in our political dialogue and promised to deliver "the principled, stable leadership we need in the decade of the eighties. . . . My practical experience in foreign affairs and national security qualifies me. . . ." Defense spending needed to be increased, he argued, along with looser government regulations and tighter controls on federal spending—all standard Republican fare. He also took pains to note he had been a lifelong Republican, which was a not-so-subtle jab at his fellow Texan, John Connally, and Governor Reagan. "I understand this party," he added. "I worked in the precincts."

Quickly warming to the task of campaigning, he earned a standing ovation at a luncheon speech in Hartford, Connecticut later that day, declaring: "I am tired of apologizing for this country. We are the fairest, we are the most decent, we've been the most generous, we should hold up our heads."

George's travels over the next week also took him to Massachusetts, New Hampshire, Florida, and Alabama—a grueling pace that, particularly for George and Barbara and their kids, wouldn't let up for the next year.

We were on our way.

Meanwhile, as this new campaign for president was born, my sweet, frail, sick mother was nearing the end of her life's journey in New York City. She had fallen ill in the early 1970s, suffering from what my sister Barbara thought was a series of strokes, while I maintained she had Alzheimer's disease. Either way, Mom was incapable of communicating with us. Most days she could be found sitting quietly in her room with her empty eyes wide open—staring off into the distance, a prisoner in her own skin.

Though Mom and Pop had become somewhat estranged during a period of their marriage, after she was admitted to Lennox Hills Hospital and then the Mary Manning Walsh Home, Pop went to see her every day, usually in the afternoon. "I'm off to see Red," he would tell friends, using his nickname for my mother. Pop would sit there and hold her hand, and after a time was convinced he was able to get through to her. "She can hear me, she just can't respond," he often claimed. Perhaps. I still think that was wishful thinking on

---

1. Scotty Reston, "George Bush for President?", *New York Times*, May 2, 1979.

*Pop and Mom at home in the early 1960s with, from the far left, Susan Smullyan
(daughter of Barbara and Clint), Dee, Clint Smullyun, Rob, Trip Mosbacher (Bus and
Pat's oldest son), Bruce Mosbacher (Bus and Pat's middle son), John Mosbacher (Bus and
Pat's youngest son), Kathi, Ben Smullyan (Barbara and Clint's youngest child), and Lisa.*

Pop's part. My daughter Kathi, who was living with Pop at the time, also used to
visit Mom (who she called "Nanna"). The nurses would always make a point of
telling her how sweet Pop was—constantly dropping in, bringing Mom food,
and showering the nurses with Yankees tickets and other tokens of his sincere
appreciation.

Looking back, my parents were two very different people. Mom was a cul-
tured lady who loved the arts, while Pop had a harder edge to him. He was
pretty definite in what and how to do things—and like all of us, Mom occasionally bristled under his firm guidance. It got to the point where, for a few years,
theirs was not a happy marriage. Growing up, Mom often seemed somewhat
withdrawn to me. I later found out that, during the 1930s, Mom thought about
going her own way—and getting a divorce. Eventually, my parents worked their
differences out, or at least stopped fighting over them.

My brother, Bus, and Barbara often accused me of being Pop's favorite, but in turn, Pop always said that Bus was Mom's favorite. If so, I never could tell because she always treated me so warmly and sweetly. In the end, I hated to see illness reduce someone I loved deeply to a mere shadow of her former lively and intelligent self. So it really was, in some ways, a blessing when Gertrude Mosbacher died in October of 1979.

Back on the campaign trail, meanwhile, the Bush campaign's prospects continued to improve with each passing month. The September 30, 1979 finance reports showed us just behind the Reagan campaign's $2.7 million, while Governor Connally had more than lapped the field with $4.3 million raised at that early stage. Having successfully executed his strategy to raise money first and foremost from executives and the business community, it dawned on me then that maybe Connally knew something about fund-raising after all!

More importantly, that fall also saw the Bush campaign getting steady traction in the Iowa polls, as the Bush organization in New Hampshire also gained strength. An upset win in the Maine straw poll in November 1979 and a stronger-than-expected showing in the nonbinding Florida beauty contest the same month "reinforced the growing impression among politicians that he [Bush] is a far more serious contender for the Republican nomination that was apparent a few months ago," as the *New York Times* reported that November.[2]

Though it may appear insignificant at just 466 votes, or 35 percent of the nonbinding straw poll ballots cast, the Maine win was really important because Senator Howard Baker of Tennessee had just announced his candidacy the week before and was making a big push to win in Maine—where his Senate colleague Bill Cohen was spearheading his campaign.

The Baker candidacy was also a long-term threat to us in several important ways. Howard Baker was a down-to-earth campaigner with an undeniable southern charm. When he was on his game, the courtly legislator could also be a great speaker. Most importantly, though, we viewed the senator as our main competition to become the "lead challenger" to Governor Reagan. Both Howard Baker and George Bush were aiming to be the last man standing against the California governor. The fact that we scored such an unexpected win there in Maine, during what was essentially Senator Baker's big debut on the national stage, was a blow from which I am not sure his 1980 candidacy ever recovered.

That John Connally, meanwhile, was viewed to be the "oratorical star" in

2. Adam Clymer, "Maine Republicans, in Informal Ballot, Give Bush a Victory," *New York Times*, November 4, 1979.

Maine while still finishing a distant third in that state proved an apt metaphor for his entire campaign. When he started out in early 1979, Connally possessed a great deal of support in America's boardrooms—but far less support, it turned out, in America's living rooms. No question, Connally's ballyhooed history as a Democrat cut against him in the GOP primary. Most of the media reports from that campaign refer to his celebrity status; but as one reporter noted, his candidacy seemed based on "excitement over organization," where Connally's star power was supposed to make up for his lack of political infrastructure.

For all the money he raised and spent, which totaled well over $10 million by the time he withdrew, Connally won only a single delegate from Arkansas.

Meanwhile, the November straw poll results in Maine and Florida, followed by the stunning caucus results in Iowa on January 21, 1980, showed that George Bush had both a broad appeal and common touch. Just as important, the win in Iowa showed the value of getting organized and working like hell. Aside from the candidate, Barbara Bush traveled to each of Iowa's ninety-nine counties while son Marvin practically lived in the state with political director Rich Bond and everyone else who sacrificed so much to get us across the finish line first.

Coming out of Iowa, we started to pick off a lot of Connally supporters. By the end of January, as a result, we had raised over $5 million. Though we had raised half of Connally's war chest, it was a respectable tally—enough to make us viable.

Just as important as money was political support; and in the wake of the Iowa win, one national poll showed us running even with Reagan. The "Big Mo" that George had claimed to have coming out of Iowa looked like it just might last. On February 13, in fact, we scored a strong second-place showing in the Mississippi straw poll despite the fact that we didn't have a campaign organization there—and our candidate hadn't spent a day in the state.

It was the same thing a few days later in Puerto Rico, where we racked up 59 percent of the vote to 38 percent for Senator Baker in second-place. If we could win the New Hampshire primary two weeks later, there was no question in my mind that we would have broken through and captured the nomination.

The day before the good news from Mississippi, however, George had started to receive the kind of attention from the media, and scrutiny from his Republican opponents, usually reserved for political front-runners. For one thing, given the polls consistently showing he and Governor Reagan running first and second in New Hampshire, the executive editor of the *Nashua Record*, Jon Breen, invited the two front-runners to appear in what would clearly be a pivotal two-man debate just three days before the February 26 primary.

That was the good news.

The bad news was that George was starting to draw enemy "political fire" of varying intensity. For starters, Senator Baker, acknowledging his third-place position in New Hampshire, went on the offensive against both Reagan and Bush—highlighting his ability to get elected statewide in Democratic Tennessee, while he and a campaign aide named Rob Mosbacher were pressing the point that George had failed at his two statewide Senate runs in Texas. The Baker campaign's gambit was certainly a "kinder and gentler" attack by the MoveOn.org standards of today.

An added complication for me personally was the fact that the Rob Mosbacher cited in news stories was, in fact, my capable twenty-eight-year-old son, who had worked for Senator Baker on his Capitol Hill staff before jumping over to the 1980 Baker campaign.

This was a different family complication than the one involving Dee's protests against the Vietnam War at a time when my brother Bus and I were tied so closely to the Nixon administration. Rob knew and admired George Bush, was friends with the Bush boys, and had worked on the Bush campaigns in Texas. By 1980, though, he had also worked for several years for another good and decent man. These days, in fact, Senator Baker refers to himself as Rob's "second father."[3]

In February of 1980, however, tensions started to build between the Bush and Baker camps—and for a short time, in the heat of political battle, things got a little frosty between Rob and his "first father" as well. After all, we are both competitive, and loyal, individuals.

A few days later, on February 16, the next shoe dropped for the Bush campaign. Word leaked in a *Washington Post* story that a former Nixon operative named Jack Gleason had testified in 1974 that he gave George Bush an undeclared $6,000 donation during his 1970 Senate race from a secret White House campaign fund that came to be known as the "Townhouse Operation" fund. This was in addition to $106,000 in other contributions that the Nixon-directed fund gave the 1970 Bush campaign. The difference was, according to Gleason, that George never declared he received the $6,000 contribution. Never mind

---

3. File this under the "six degrees of separation," but our family would have another Howard Baker connection in time. Before I married her in 2000, my wife Mica (née McCutchen) lived in Memphis during the 1960s and helped put up yard signs and go door-to-door to help get Howard elected. Mica was in sixth grade at the time, and Howard Baker was the first of many terrific political candidates to benefit from her help.

that Gleason also testified that the handing of money directly to Senate candidates was Nixon's deliberate "scheme for obtaining leverage over the candidate himself"—provided the candidate failed to report the donation.

As for Gleason's allegation, let me answer this way.

First, I never saw George Bush, in the nine campaigns in which I was involved from his 1962 run for Harris County Republican Chairman to his 1992 reelection run for president, accept a direct contribution from any donor. Dealing with money—be it a check or cash—was something he simply didn't do, so anytime a donor offered George money directly he always suggested the donor give it to me or another staffer.

The most definitive way I know the Gleason story never panned out as alleged is because I took the contribution in question and filed it in with other donations, as the campaign laws at that time allowed. I suggested as much at the time the old news leaked in the *Post*, but either I wasn't a big enough name for the Beltway headhunters to go after in 1980 *or* they understood what I had done in 1970 was legal—because the "new" Gleason revelation died almost as soon as it flared up.

So we dodged a few bullets early on in New Hampshire, and even after the first multicandidate debate on February 20 our confidence was running high. But that's about where our luck in 1980 started to run out. The Nashua debate three days later where Ronald Reagan famously asserted, "I paid for this microphone, Mr. Green" is so much a part of political lore, and covered in so many other accounts of the 1980 campaign, that there is little to add except to say I agree with the view that we were set up. I also agree that Ronald Reagan was on his way to winning the nomination following that exchange.

Even though I was not present for that event, everyone throughout the entire campaign felt the jarring effect as the momentum we had established instantly went over to the Reagan camp. Without a doubt, that may have been the lowest point of the 1980 campaign—watching erstwhile supporters and even a few campaign workers abandon us.

To his everlasting credit, though he came out of New Hampshire badly bloodied, George Bush was unbowed. The point has been made by others that running for president of the United States is a marathon; but to me, it also resembles a heavyweight prizefight. Every night George would arrive at the hotel bone tired; but every morning, he also answered the bell and came out "charging like a bull," as one reporter observed.

Following New Hampshire, of course, the very full field that once also included Senators Bob Dole of Kansas, Larry Pressler of South Dakota, and Lowell

Weicker of Connecticut; Illinois Congressmen Phil Crane and John Anderson; Minnesota Governor Harold Stassen; and businessman Ben Fernandez—the first citizen of Hispanic descent to seek America's highest office—started to thin out. Senator Baker was the first to go, on March 5, after finishing fourth in the Vermont and Massachusetts primaries. Connally exited soon after his crushing loss in South Carolina, where he had invested so much time and money. Soon, the GOP contest was the two-man race we had hoped it would become, featuring our candidate versus Reagan.

Time and money were running out, however.

George pressed gamely onward and, on April 22, won the Pennsylvania primary. We won Michigan on May 20, too, but that same night Reagan won two other states—which according to most, but not all, news reports *appeared* to give the former California Governor enough delegates to win the nomination. As long as there was a chance of winning, any chance at all, George felt a deep obligation to his supporters who had rallied to his candidacy to give the race everything he had—which he did each of the 391 days he was formally in the race.

The Pennsylvania and Michigan victories did not produce the level of new contributions we needed to keep moving forward, and as a result, by late May we were $300,000 in the red. With a few encouraging signs of political support in the Ohio and New Jersey primaries next on the calendar, George was bent on pressing ahead—but many of us had reached the point where we didn't want to see his chances for being on the ticket spoiled.

In fact, Jimmy Baker and another Bush loyalist, Vic Gold, had already taken a run at George about dropping out, and after Jimmy asked me to make my opinion known I felt obligated to join the chorus, advising him to bow to the political reality as we saw it. George didn't want to hear what any of us were saying, though, and it was one of the few genuinely tense conversations we've ever had. George told me he felt an overriding sense of obligation to everyone who was working so hard in those late states to not let them down. "These folks have taken a chance in supporting me, and helping us get this far," he explained. "I can't just abandon them."

Still, George also knew that time had essentially run out, and that according to ABC and CBS Governor Reagan already had the 998 delegates he needed to clinch the GOP nomination. Dreams die hard in the Texas oil patch, and it was no different for us in politics. We had done well to get to 266 delegates, but there was no way to torture the numbers in a way that kept the Bush candidacy alive. The time had come to "suspend" the campaign, which was a technical decision that allowed us to receive federal matching funds that we needed to retire our campaign debt.

"I am an optimist, but I also know how to count to 998," George conceded to the media and roughly 200 supporters at the Marriott Hotel in Houston on May 26. It had been "the toughest decision of my entire life," the then-fifty-five-year-old candidate concluded with Barbara, son Jeb, Jeb's wife Columba, and the Bushes' two oldest grandkids standing by his side. He added that he wanted to "go pleasantly about decompressing." Then, in typical George Bush fashion, he invited members of his traveling press corps to his home—where he traded stories and laughs, lounging barefoot in his canary yellow slacks and a light blue shirt.

Chivalrous to the very end.

Whenever I approached Pop with a prospective deal, he always counseled, "Do what the gamblers do: make it so you either win big or lose little." Though this first Bush campaign did not prevail, we had done just that in my view. We had lost this first nomination fight—a fight that nobody expected George to win—but we had also succeeded in further elevating his stature as a national political leader.

Between the suspension of the Bush for President campaign in May and the GOP Convention in Detroit in July, we were all busy shutting the campaign down. Maybe it was the businessman in him, but we had an extra challenge in that George wanted to be sure that every campaign worker, even those who had offered to work for free or at reduced wages, received full payment for their work on the race. This took extra time and effort, but he wouldn't have dreamed of ending the campaign feeling like he still owed someone something.

In the meantime, July and the GOP convention finally came. As we boarded the planes for Detroit, however, we certainly did not feel as if Governor Reagan owed the VP nod to George. We were hopeful that something, somehow might be in the political cards—but George's fate was out of our hands. The 1980 nomination fight in both parties had not been without its sharp elbows on all sides of the contest, and we were holding our breath that the antagonistic feelings that every primary fight engenders had subsided by the time the victorious Reagan camp arrived at Joe Louis Arena, site of the 1980 GOP convention.

These days, of course, political conventions are essentially infomercials where each party tightly controls the scripting and images being broadcast of their national meeting to present as much of a unified, positive, and inclusive image as they can to the rest of the country. Any drama coming out of these four-day confabs is either totally unintended—or completely manufactured.

Gone are the contentious floor fights over the party platform, which most candidates these days ignore anyway. Gone, too, is any uncertainty over who will be heading the ticket.

The 1976 GOP convention in Kansas City—where Jimmy Baker did such a masterful job of helping President Ford fend off the Reagan insurgency—is rightly remembered as the last meaningful convention, where the nominee was picked by the delegates on the convention floor. But Detroit in 1980 was not without its own feeling of suspense, mainly over who would fill out the Reagan-led ticket.

Together with the other Bush surrogates, we fanned out to the various meetings at the Detroit Plaza hotel where the Reagan camp was staying, the Ponchartrain Hotel where the Bush forces were mustered, and convention proceedings at Joe Louis Arena. Then, in what felt like thousands of one-on-one and small meetings, we would advocate, cajole, and generally push the idea of a Reagan-Bush ticket. It was, really, a mini-campaign—with Reagan-Bush signs made, endorsements being quietly tallied, and designated spokesmen spreading our message to the media.

As the week progressed, it was hard to gauge whether we were getting any real traction. The Reagan inner circle was playing the cards very close to the vest, but we had high hopes for that Wednesday night when George was scheduled to address the convention. A great reception from the delegates and a great speech could—just maybe—tip the balance in his favor.

I was honored to be one of a handful of people there in the Bush suite that pivotal night, and like everyone else I was crestfallen when news of the "Dream Ticket" comprising former President Ford and Governor Reagan hit the airwaves while George was on his way to the arena to give his speech. Even if George lit himself on fire that night, I realized, he would not be able to shift the media attention back to him and his qualifications. In a political sense, the line to our jib sheet had been cut—and any sense of momentum evaporated into the evening air.

In his usual calm and analytical way, however, I remember Jimmy Baker expressing his doubts that the "copresidency" President Ford had suggested during an interview that night with Walter Cronkite could work.

"I don't think that's constitutional," I remember Jimmy saying, as we chewed over the latest in a series of twists that day.

Fortunately, we didn't have to put that theory to the test because later that evening the phone rang, and upon hearing Governor Reagan was calling, George stepped into the bedroom just off the suite's main sitting room. He was

Sharing a private word with Jimmy Baker at the 1980 GOP convention in Detroit.

silent as the phone call started, but when he turned to us, smiled, and gave a thumbs up we knew it was a new ballgame.

What was, for us at least, a "dream ticket" had in fact come to pass. Reagan-Bush it would be.

We were elated, but not totally surprised, so our celebration was not a wild one. As many of us saw it, biased as we were, George Bush was the obvious choice to round out the ticket. He had the second-most delegates, proved he was an able campaigner and organizer, and his call for party unity earlier that night set the right tone in Detroit.

A few months later, after the assassination attempt on President Reagan in March of 1981, George showed the world his calm judgment under fire when he insisted his helicopter take him back to the vice president's residence—rather than the White House. "Only the president lands on the South Lawn," he told the pilot. But well before that, in the privacy of his hotel suite on the verge of his nomination for vice president, George validated the wisdom of Reagan's choice with his first words as the vice presidential nominee. The wide grin still on his face, he reminded us: "Our campaign positions are over. Reagan's positions are ours now."

There had been a sharp disagreement over economic policy during the primary. We had denigrated Reagan's supply-side platform as "voodoo economics," to cite the most memorable example, but now George was telling us the time for debating was over.

It was time to fall in line.

Heading out of Detroit, I participated in a few Reagan-Bush efforts to raise money for the state PACs, but it was mostly a Reagan show from that point forward. Both the Reagan and Carter general election campaigns received public financing, which back in that day and age meant my work as a fundraiser was mostly over. Besides, I had to get back to my business—which provided an interesting postscript to 1980, and a foreshadowing of a campaign to come.

It was around the time that we were winding things down on the 1980 campaign that Ross Perot came to see me.

"I've decided to get in the oil business," Ross told me, "and I've picked you as my partner, because all of my research shows that you know the most about the oil business and do the best job." I had the distinct feeling Ross was "blowing smoke," but listened on.

"Let's make a deal," Perot continued. "I want to join you."

I didn't want any partners in my company per se, but told Ross that we were always looking for partners on our various drilling deals. "Good," he replied. "I'll be your partner." So we agreed in principle to a two-year stint drilling a few wells together.

Before we closed the deal, my close friend Randy Smith, who was also my lawyer with Vinson & Elkins, called me and said, "I've got bad news for you. Perot and his people say that they want to be able to stop this agreement, even though it is a two-year agreement, any time after sixty days with sixty days notice."

Randy added: "I know that's not what you two discussed."

"Well Randy," I replied, "from what I know of Ross, if he's unhappy with a deal and he's going to make life so tough, you might as well let him out. *Just make sure it's reciprocal.*"

So we amended the agreement, funded the partnership, and got to work. Immediately, Perot had his people in my offices all the time—and asking a bunch of questions. Why did you pick this one contractor? Why does the pipe cost so much? Did you get three bids for the pipe? That kind of stuff.

Eventually, we drilled two wells—one dry hole, and one producer. Not a bad start for wildcatting out there. Despite this good start, however, Perot's people were bugging all of us—and at one point, one of Perot's top managers called me. In what I thought was an accusatory tone, the manager demanded to know why we were doing things a certain way. I wasn't too happy about the nature of the call, but tried to explain what was going on.

After about three or four months of that, however, I went back to Randy and said, "Don't we have the right to get out of this thing?"

"Yes, the same way they do."

"Let's write that letter and cancel this thing. I've had enough of this."

So we prepared the formal letter; and after Ross received it, he called me, very upset. "Let's meet and talk about it," he suggested.

My enthusiasm for the partnership had totally waned by then, so I said, "No, Ross, I think it's better if we don't try to do that. It's not just you and me—it's all these people coming into the office all the time. Let's just end this and stay friends."

A few days later I received a call from a familiar voice. "Bob, how are you? This is John Connally."

We exchanged pleasantries, but Connally quickly got down to business. "Bob, I can't believe you are going to treat Ross Perot like that."

I immediately defended my actions and explained what had happened, at which point Connally said, "Well, ol' Ross is still not going to like it." I had already decided that was a chance I was willing to take, so the phone call ended on a slightly disagreeable note.

Years later, after we heard Ross Perot had entered the presidential campaign in 1992, I told George Bush about my failed partnership with the newly minted independent candidate. "Now that you got Perot into this race," the president teased, "what are you going to do about getting him out?"

Chapter 15 DO YOU SUPPOSE THEY'LL
BELIEVE I STAYED?

While Pop was alive, he never carried a wallet, and he never carried $20 or $50 bills. Rather, in different pockets he kept $1, $5, $10, and $100 bills—all arranged so he knew where the different bills were without having to look. He did this because my streetwise father understood that flashing cash in New York City back then was likely to get you mugged, but there was more to it.

"I never want to embarrass anyone by pulling out bills," he once explained to his assistant Liz Carbone. One time he saw me keeping different bills in the same pocket and mildly chided me. "Well that's dumb," he would say. "You might as well pull out a $100 every time in front of everybody. Why the heck would you do that?"

In a word, Pop could be eccentric. My daughter Dee recalls how during the summer his attire, while in his apartment, always consisted of white silk boxers, a couple of layers of silk undershirts, and often an old-fashioned golf cap. During the winter, meanwhile, he wore gray down-feather booties with long silk underwear covered by gray sweat pants, a gray cashmere sweater, and the same wool cap.

When he did venture out, Pop always walked briskly—and always near the curb, so nobody could mug him. As he churned along, he would shout instructions over his shoulder as he walked: "Keep your hands out of your pockets. I know somebody who had his hands in his pants, and he was hit by a cab and dragged down the street because he couldn't defend himself. And don't walk over grills because I know somebody who fell in a grill. Everyone knows the manholes in Manhattan are totally unsafe."

During the 1960s, Rob frequently visited Pop at his Park Avenue apartment during a break in his studies at Choate, usually bringing a friend. New York City back then was not the relatively safe and tourist-friendly city it is today, and while giving Rob some spending money Pop would routinely implore Rob and his buddy to take every precaution while moving around Manhattan. "Now, Robbie, there are more drug addicts, dope fiends, and street muggers within a square mile of here than you'll find probably anywhere else in the world," he said, adding, "They don't fight fair, so don't mess with them."

Upon hearing this warning, Rob's smart-alecky friend piped up, "Don't worry, Pop, we'll choke 'em with our heel dust." In other words, if attacked the boys would run away—very fast.

"Goddammit," Pop would sharply reply, not understanding Rob's friend. "I told you not to fight them."

In addition to his extreme impatience and constant advice, my kids also vividly recall Pop's extraordinary generosity. He loved shopping at Bloomingdale's on Lexington Avenue, for example, and if you expressed an interest in a particular shirt he would insist you get a couple in the same color. "Don't get one," he'd say. "Get half a dozen."

If anyone could cut a deal with Father Time, it would have been Pop. He was such a forceful, dynamic presence in our lives for so long—who took his health and exercise seriously even into his eighties—I was convinced he would end up outlasting us all. If someone could find a way to crack the code on mortality, to pick the lock on longevity, it would have been Emil Mosbacher Sr.

Try as Pop might, though, Father Time didn't cut deals or play favorites. Right around the time we lost Mom, Pop started complaining about recurring migraine headaches and dizzy spells. Sadly, ironically, these same symptoms also plagued his good friend George Gershwin during the last weeks of his life in 1937, after he lapsed into a coma and was rushed to the hospital. Pop had suffered from dizzy spells as a younger man, but never with such intensity—or regular recurrence.

It didn't take long to discover my father had a brain tumor.

Upon reporting their diagnosis, however, the doctors said they might be able to operate—though they also cautioned it would be a very difficult procedure and they were not overly optimistic as to Pop's prognosis. Not surprisingly, Pop balked at that course of action. "They're not going to make a vegetable out of me," he declared. He had watched helplessly from afar when George Gershwin had died on the operating table, and that was simply *not* a risk my father was going to take.

He never said so, but I also think his daily visits to see Mom—to see the helpless condition she was in, not in control—struck him as a far worse fate than the tough and painful fight he accepted against the sizeable mass inside his head trying to kill him. As he had become accustomed to controlling the circumstances of his life, Pop opted to try and control his death.

After he learned he was sick, Pop asked my cousin Stanley to get him a motorcycle helmet. None of us were ever allowed near motorcycles, so Pop's request confused Stan at first. At the motorcycle shop, they naturally asked what size, and remembering Pop's admonition "don't be cheap," Stan bought two of them.

"I fell and hit my head going into the bathroom," Pop explained when Stan gave him the helmets. "If I fall again, I want to have a helmet on." It seems so random, perhaps, but this anecdote shows how he always played the odds—always exerting control.

Stan also recalls the day Pop was in bed and dropped a pencil on the floor. The home nurse, thinking she was being helpful, picked it up and handed it to him. Pop lost his cool, however. "I'll tell you when I want you to pick it up," he yelled. He was mostly very sweet and generous with his caregivers, but this incident showed that my father still had his pride, and had great trouble forfeiting the independence he had achieved—and guarded so fiercely.

In the fall of 1980, Pop became fixated on changing the rug in his room, and wanted us to measure the space. My sister Barbara and I didn't think much of his idea, and were dragging our feet on the project—hoping he would change his mind or forget. Finally, Pop lost his patience: "Damn, both of you went to college and had all sorts of degrees, and neither of you can measure a rug!"

He was his feisty self to the end.

In fact, when someone in the family suggested getting medicinal marijuana to help ease Pop's pain and revive his appetite, my drug- and alcohol-adverse father laid down the law. "If you try to bring me pot," he proclaimed, "I'll throw it—and you—out the window!"

During the last few weeks of his life, Pop's hearing went bad so I offered to get him a hearing aid, which I had started to use myself by then. "No chance," he protested. "Didn't you tell me they were no damn good?" As always, Pop had a better idea. "Get me one of those old-fashioned horns," he said—referring to the antiquated "ear trumpets" more commonly used in the eighteenth and nineteenth centuries. It took some searching, but we finally found one that enabled Pop to hear us during his last days.

Happily, while some brain tumors can cause a sharp change in behavior and cognitive ability, Pop's mind was clear and working until the day he died—October 26, 1980, a Sunday. The problem was the rest of his body shut down. The day before, we had noticed his breathing and general condition deteriorating quickly. On Sunday afternoon, Dr. Allen Tanney, Pop's physician since 1967, stopped by the apartment. "It won't be long," he said forlornly when he left at 5:30 P.M.

With my father teetering on the edge of consciousness, I told Pop I loved him one last time. Then all we could do was wait. Even in death, however, Pop had little patience. At 8:30 P.M., he gasped a final groan—as if a muted roar—and then he was gone.

Pop died the way he lived, like a lion.

There were no tears when we realized he had passed. For one thing, I think part of us was still afraid of making him mad. Pop always said, "If you want to cry, cry when you can do something about it. Otherwise, move on. Be positive. What's the next step?"

That's an important lesson, because a lot of people dwell on what has already happened to them while Pop instilled in us the importance of focusing on what happens next. "What's to be done now?", as he put it. Whether it is something as catastrophic as your father dying, or something in business, or a divorce—you can't live your life always looking in the rearview mirror. It's best to keep your attention on the road ahead; what's still coming at you through the windshield.

Of course, losing my parents within a year of each other hurt a great deal, but watching Pop slip away cut deeper. First, he wasn't taken from us following a prolonged illness like Mom, but there was more to it. Pop was more than the man who raised my siblings and me, and put us through school. He wasn't just the man who married my mother, and did all the other things fathers do. To me, he was also my mentor; my closest and best advisor; and my toughest, most honest critic.

If Pop had the "breaks of a dozen men," then I had the good fortune of a hundred more to have someone of his unique qualities in my life. I could say the same about my best friends Chesley Pruet, Pop's and my mutual friend Max Fisher, and Randy Smith—to say nothing of George Bush and Jim Baker. Yet my relationship with Pop was something totally different and unique. The influence he had on me was orders of magnitude larger than anyone else outside my family.

While he was alive, I never had the conscious feeling that I was trying to escape from Pop's shadow and establish my own place or identity in the world. Moving to Texas had helped me do that to a degree, as had my own success in the business world. Yet, his passing left a void I still feel today. I wish he had seen his youngest son go into the president's Cabinet in Washington, help take on big issues, and represent our business community to the world. I wish he had seen how Mosbacher Energy managed to survive a severe downturn in the industry and come out stronger on the other side. That would have made him proud, too. And I think he would be very proud of his grandkids—Dee, Rob, Kathi, and Lisa—who have all turned out to be remarkably successful and decent in their own right.

But most of all, I'm like any son who just misses talking to my dad.

After he died, I not only dreamt about Pop a lot; I also felt his presence. Many nights I talked to him in my sleep—to the point where, occasionally, I'd wake up startled. The same thing happened after Jane died, incidentally. Maybe that's how the mind deals with such a painful loss; but in both cases, even to this day, when I look at my kids, or hear myself repeating yet another one of Pop's sayings, I still feel both he and Jane are a part of my life.

So yes, as the song says, there is "laughter after pain . . . [and] sunshine after rain. . . ." You have to wait a while sometimes, but the cycle of life goes on.

Barely a week after we said goodbye to Pop, the phone rang at my house in Houston. The unmistakable voice at the other end of the phone said, "Mosbacher, where the hell are you?" It was election eve 1980, and if anything could bring me out of the funk I had sunk into following Pop's passing, it was seeing George Bush help Ronald Reagan carry forty-four states en route to being elected the forty-third vice president of the United States.

Unfortunately, I was under the weather that night, suffering from a stomach problem, and while George's thoughtful call boosted my spirits, it couldn't get me out of bed to join the celebration. Nor did his going to Washington in January of 1981—along with Jimmy Baker, who had landed a huge job as Reagan's White House chief of staff—entice me to join their northerly migration and go into the government, as both casually suggested I might do. The energy business was piping hot at the time, and after helping manage two national campaigns I was determined to focus on Mosbacher Energy and other interests.

Still, I visited DC often and stayed in touch with both George and Jimmy, but early on I discovered that George's gatekeeper, a woman named Jennifer Fitzgerald, was trying to shut some of the older Bush-backers out of the scene. Every time I called, she would tell me, "I'm sorry Bob, but the vice president is busy and can't take your call."

Somehow, after several attempts, I managed to get in touch with George directly, and when he came on the phone he immediately asked, "Where the hell have you been? Why don't you come see me?" He wondered if we had had some kind of falling out. When I did visit him and explained what Jennifer had been doing, the vice president got as mad as I have ever seen him. Loyalty to family

Moving through the receiving line for the March 1981 state dinner honoring my friend, King Juan Carlos of Spain.

and friends is the most precious coin in the Bush realm, and the idea that one of his staffers hadn't clued into that was more than he could calmly abide.

With both George and Jimmy in Washington, I once again found myself a frequent visitor to our nation's capital. One of the most memorable visits during the first Reagan term came when I received an invitation to the State Dinner that the Reagans hosted for my old sailing companion and very dear friend, King Juan Carlos of Spain. As I approached the president and the king in the receiving line, His Majesty leaned over to Reagan and said, "Mr. President, I regret to inform you that this next gentleman is a son of a bitch!" Fortunately, the White House photographer captured the three of us enjoying a hearty laugh.

Not all of my visits to the White House were social in nature, though. During the first Reagan term, I was identified, along with Arthur Leavitt of the American Stock Exchange—Pop's old haunt—and a dozen or so other entrepreneurs, as the "new face of business leadership" in America with "access to the Reagan Oval Office." When I did get to Washington, most often it was related to my involvement with business and policy-related groups like the U.S. Oil and Gas Association and the National Petroleum Council (which I chaired from 1983 to

1985). After more than thirty years in the business, I felt I had gained enough perspective to help the industry as a whole confront a series of tough problems. At the very least, I was not shy about expressing my opinions to my industry peers or the Secretary of Energy—whether it was strategic reserve, methods of enhanced recovery, conservation, or a whole host of esoteric issues that might make the average citizen's eyes glaze over.

Sometimes, the collective views of our industry prevailed in the Reagan administration—but not as often as you might think. In 1985, for example, I was one of several industry figures trying, yet failing, to gain tax breaks aimed at increasing domestic energy production. This was when the oil industry was in the middle of a historic collapse.

While these leading organizations sought my advice, during 1981 to1982 my various joint venture partners were mad at me because we only invested half the $100 million we had set aside for exploration—while the market was white hot. By that time, the prices for every facet of drilling were so absurd that I didn't think the market parameters were right. I saw too many crazy markups and deals taking place.

Some outfits, for example, were paying all the costs to drill a "wild" wildcat (very risky) well all the way through the tanks—meaning a fully completed well—but for only half the interest. Nobody in their right mind before, or since, would think to agree to such terms. Yet the market had been so hot so long it brought to mind an old Max Fisher saying, or "Max-ism" as we called it. In his low, slow voice, I can still hear Max saying, "Bobby, when times are good, people think they'll never turn bad. When times are bad, they think they'll never be good again."

The situation in the energy business in 1981 reminded me of the people who paid so much for Curb seats back in 1928 and 1929 before the crash. It was totally unrealistic, and in no way tied to market forces. Things got so out of hand that I went to my doctor's office one day and found a sign: "Closed. Gone into the oil business." Now, that story is apocryphal, but in 1981 I could tell something wasn't right—and that it was time to get on the sidelines for a spell.

That same year, as it turned out, the price of oil slipped from $40 a barrel down to the mid-20s. Suddenly my joint venture partners, who had been so mad at me, started treating me with a little more deference. They were grateful that we had not been fully exposed to the risk of a down-bound market.

I prophesied this falling market at an Arthur Anderson meeting in Houston in late 1981—suggesting that prices were likely to go down. After that was published, some people didn't like it, but that reaction was mild compared to what followed in January 1982, when I flew to Midland to talk to the "Young Producers." When I repeated my gloomy outlook there, the crowd of thirty-something dealmakers got very angry at me for daring to say prices might come down. Luckily, some of the members were sons of my friends in the industry—otherwise, I'm not sure they wouldn't have tarred and feathered me.

That's how irrational the atmosphere had gotten.

I didn't make the same hay out of the bear market that Pop had managed in 1929, but I did pull back Mosbacher Energy operations and avoided letting the company go into serious debt. As Pop always said, "make sure you protect your 'nut,' your principal base of capital." Hearing Pop's voice, I did that, but too many others did not. By 1983, the so-called "Jacuzzi tub operators" went under, and by 1986—when the price of oil had sunk to $10 a barrel—many of the independent operators were out of business.

To be sure, it was a tough time to be a driller. Complicating matters was the fact that a lot of people, including several of my fellow board members at Texas Commerce Bank and me, had loans on our drilling rigs. These were nonrecourse loans, however, meaning the rigs were the sole collateral—not financial or other assets. So during this time when the industry essentially froze up, and drilling came to halt, many drillers stopped paying the banks back and simply gave them the rigs—all perfectly legal. Of course, some genuinely couldn't afford to pay back the loans, but others with stronger balance sheets than Mosbacher Energy took this easy way out because they thought it was smart business.

Though I had roughly $5 million in these nonrecourse loans at the time, I couldn't do that. Having served on the bank's board since my early thirties, I felt a moral obligation to make good on my word. I told my friend Ben Love, the much-respected banker who ran Texas Commerce, that I would repay my debt, but would need a longer period of time and a break on the interest rate. He readily agreed. Just recently, in fact, a man who worked with Ben Love approached me at a luncheon and informed me I was the only driller who paid them back during that dark time in the industry. That included the bank's other board members.

While we managed to weather these tough times, we were far from immune to the pain of the bear market. Between 1982 and 1990, Mosbacher Energy gradually went from 235 employees down to 35. Without a doubt, being forced to call employees into my office and let them go is the worst experience I have ever had in all my years in the oil and gas business. We always tried to treat our employees like family, and it just makes me sick to my stomach all these years later even thinking about it. What I was doing was a matter of survival, but that didn't make it any easier.

Happily, today, more than 70 percent of our employees have been with us twenty years or more. As a result of that terrible experience during the 1980s, moreover, instead of growing internally we've outsourced more operations—so we can grow as the market permits. Yet when the market contracts, as it did once again in the late 1990s and oil hit $10 again in 1999, we didn't have to cut our internal staff, but rather consultants whose services we no longer needed. That way, I didn't feel like I was cutting off my own arm in terms of our company family.

While I was making such dreadful decisions to keep the business alive, during the mid-1980s, my family was going through its own transition.

Although I had separated from Sandra in the late 1970s, we didn't get around to finalizing our divorce until 1982. In the interim, I dated several ladies, including an adorable blond from Houston and a princess from the Middle East. Both were steady relationships, and I cared deeply for both women—but I was always very careful about not telling someone I loved them unless I thought marriage was in the cards. These women were remarkable people, but the breakdown of my second marriage had me a little gun-shy in terms of another commitment.

Then, sometime in 1982, I met a woman named Georgette Paulsin-Muir, and something just clicked. A two-time divorcee, Georgette was in Houston when a mutual friend got us together. I found her very attractive—a ravishing redhead—and we enjoyed each other's company. Before long, we were an item.

In fact, while Georgette and I were dating, my friends John Duncan and Gerry Hines chartered a boat in Europe, leaving from the coastal town of San Remo, Italy—near Monaco, and the Italian Riviera—to sail through islands. I couldn't get there when they were leaving San Remo because I had a meeting, so John kindly said, "Well, let's just pick an island, and we'll pick you up."

So we picked an island, which one, I forget. At the appointed hour and place, I saw the large boat motoring into the harbor. No other boats coming in were the same size, so it was easy to point out.

Standing at the edge of the pier with Georgette, we should have stood out, too—or at least, so I thought. As the boat carrying the Duncan party neared the dock, however, nobody made eye contact, nobody waved. Then they started to make a U-turn as if to head out to sea, which is when I started jumping up and down and shouting, "Over here!"

Still no sign they had seen us.

Finally, the boat turned around, and we could see everyone on board laughing at my expense. They had seen us all along, but were pulling a gag. Suffice it to say I greeted my good friends Gerry and John with an expletive-laced salutation!

During a subsequent trip to Europe, in September of 1984, another friend of mine convinced me in spur-of-the-moment fashion to charter a 12-meter boat named *France III* and telephone my friend Buddy Melges (who was then the reigning world champion in the Star Class, gold medal winner in Soling) to come to the Costa Esmeralda Yacht Club in northeast Sardinia for the 12-meter world championships. Eight teams on similarly configured 12-meter boats competed in the month-long event, and a bunch of well-known America's Cup sailors, including Dennis Conner (who lost the cup in 1983) and Alan Bond, the Australian entrepreneur whose syndicate won it.

"The usual lines that separate syndicates by nationality during an America's Cup campaign have given way in Sardinia to a level of camaraderie," reported the *New York Times*. "The significance of this world-class regatta is in the people who are here, the ideas that are traded and the plans that are made. Talk of the next America's Cup leaves room for discussion of little else. . . ."[1]

At the time, I had little experience aboard 12-meters other than occasionally sailing with Bus aboard the Weatherly in the early 1960s, and while we didn't win we ended up doing okay. It was one of my first forays back into racing since the 1970s, and after a substantial layoff, the heat of combat on the water at such a high level seemed to rekindle the competitive fire within. "I was supposed to meet with the Secretary of Energy, and had all sorts of business meetings back home," I told a reporter during the competition. "Do you suppose they'll believe I stayed to sail a 12-meter?"

While I was rediscovering the joy of competitive racing—and enjoying life with my new bride Georgette, who I married in March of 1984—my son Rob was making his own first serious foray into elective politics. Seeking to follow in the footsteps of his U.S. Senate mentor, Howard Baker—and his earlier mentor, George Herbert Walker Bush—Rob challenged a recent Democrat congressman-turned-Republican named Phil Gramm, and the libertarian in Republican clothing Ron Paul, for the U.S. Senate seat being vacated by Texas' John Tower.

As a fiscally conservative Democrat, Gramm cosponsored President Reagan's budget-cutting legislation in 1981 and 1982, and converted to the GOP in

---

1. Barbara Lloyd, "12 Meters Meeting in Friendly Waters," *New York Times*, September 24, 1984.

1983. Gramm ran on his "proven record as an effective leader," and had a distinct advantage of appealing to conservative Democrats and independents. Rob, meanwhile, was widely viewed as Gramm's strongest primary opponent.

Unfortunately, Rob finished third in the primary, but the loss did nothing to diminish his standing in the state party. He was soon made finance chairman of the Texas GOP, and Republican leaders like Jack Kemp were describing Rob as "not only a rising star in Texas politics but a rising star in national politics." He was a sought-after speaker for the Gramm campaign that fall. Helping Rob's cause, he also organized a very successful fund-raising event after the primary for Gramm that raised $100,000—a terrific sum.

In 1984, my friend George Bush and President Reagan were in the process of rolling to reelection following a recession that, just a year before, had seemed to spell doom. That year's GOP national convention in Dallas went smoothly, as did the 1984 reelection campaign.

We awoke the morning after election night 1984 to the sudden realization that, by virtue of his role as a trusted Reagan confidant and vice president—to say nothing of his own credentials—my friend George Bush was the leading contender for president in 1988. We had everything to lose, while maintaining such an advantageous position would require all of us to help him negotiate a political minefield where disaster lurked with each step forward.

Within three months of the second Reagan inaugural, in fact, we took our first steps down the 1988 campaign trail when we established a political action committee to help us raise funds in the event George decided to run. At the time, George said he would wait until after the 1986 midterm elections before making a final decision, and accordingly the first function the PAC would serve would be as a "multi-candidate committee" helping to support Republicans running for the House and Senate. Of course, it could raise contributions for a Bush campaign if and when he formally declared his candidacy for president.

Fortunately, the fund got off to a very encouraging start. Within the first two months, we raised $800,000—mostly coming from oil and gas interests. Many of these energy producers were George's longtime friends, some dating back to the 1950s. A year later, in 1986, our fund was sitting on $5.5 million, a remarkable sum when you consider that the price of oil in April 1985 was roughly $28 a barrel—and a year later, the price was roughly half.

In fact, given the domestic developments in the industry, Mosbacher Energy was one of several U.S. companies that started looking to Canada as an attractive place to operate. During the mid-1970s, we sold our Canadian holdings—like other U.S. drillers—after the liberal government in Ottawa tried to nationalize the energy industry. Nearly a decade later, under the capable leadership of Prime Minister Brian Mulroney, Canada started relaxing the rules for foreign ownership of projects while cutting taxes and opening more areas for exploration. As a result, I helped put together an investment group to start investing in new reserves and assets in Canada.

Looking for oil and natural gas in Alberta was cheaper than here in the States, and was comparatively unexplored, with more areas of potential discovery versus the well-drilled areas of Texas and Oklahoma. Estimates at the time placed the cost of finding a barrel of crude oil in the United States ranging from $10 to $15 a barrel, while the cost of exploring for crude in Canada back then was about $6 a barrel. So, no, you didn't have to be a math whiz to understand the allure of Canada at that time.

Amidst the hustle and bustle of a new national campaign and a new series of oil and gas plays, the most meaningful personal development for me during the mid-1980s was the great gift only my kids could give me—that of making me a grandfather. On July 11, 1983, Rob and his wife Catherine welcomed Peter Clark Mosbacher into the world. Peter was followed later that year by Lisa and Downing's twins, Parker and Whitney. Rob and Catherine then had Jane in 1985 and Meredith in 1988, and Lisa and Downing gave us Bayly in 1991. As our family grew, seeing the birth and growth of my family's next generation gave me a profound sense of happiness. As I've gotten along in years, I think that happiness comes from the knowledge that not only the names but also the hopes of my ancestors, those who scratched out a living in rural Bavaria, would live on.

I was immensely proud the day I heard of Peter's birth, and the pride I feel in him—and indeed, each of my grandkids—has only grown with time. Most of all, I am grateful to have been blessed with enough years to see them grow and mature in wonderful ways, and have more time to enjoy them now in their adulthood.

As it was, when the 1988 campaign neared, life was so hectic that the opportunities to stop and smell roses were few and far between. From mid-February 1987 to the end of April, for example, the Bush campaign raised what the *New York Times* called "an impressive $4 million," with most of our support coming in through our network of influential donors. Helping us build such a formidable war chest were well-known finance and business leaders Ted Welch of Tennessee, Robert Galvin of Motorola, Richard Wood of Eli Lilly, and David Kearns of Xerox. Each of these respected leaders would, in turn, talk up the campaign to their friends and colleagues, and the collective success they and all of our finance team had put us in an excellent position to reach the $27 million maximum.

This, in turn, would give the campaign ample funds to invest in the critical early primaries and caucuses. Even though we were to have troubles early on, unlike 1980, we would have the resources we needed to compete for, and win in, the later state primary contests.

But the greatest thrill of 1987 had nothing to do with politics, because in September of that year I managed to win sailing's Scandinavian Gold Cup for the second time—the first time being thirty years before, in 1957. I had not spent nearly the same amount of time getting ready for this 1987 effort, but we had a good boat named the *Gorgi* and a terrific crew—and once again we found a little luck in the breeze.

Most of the folks I have sailed with know that I have no appetite for boat maintenance. Over the years, sailing in different classes, I have rarely developed a strong emotional bond with any particular boat. As a result, I have never been very good at fixing them. Lots of sailors are different, of course. They revel in cleaning the fixtures, fixing the lines, and the like. Not me. Normally when it is time to clean up and fix things, my fellow crew—fearing I will just get in the way—usually say, "Mosbacher why don't you go have a drink?"

In late 1987, the last thing I needed was dealing with getting the *Gorgi* home, so I just sold her after the race. I had the distinct feeling I wasn't going to have much time for sailing, or anything else, over the next few years. It was time for me and everyone on Team Bush to batten down the political hatches for the rough seas ahead—to prepare for a challenging, frustrating, and ultimately satisfying ride.

Chapter 16   "PLEASE, I DON'T LIKE TO BEG"

The saying goes that desperate times call for desperate measures; and while neither I nor anyone else on the Bush campaign was exactly desperate in August of 1988, the situation was unusual enough that I found myself in a New Orleans hotel room dancing on a table in front of a group of prospective donors.

Perhaps I should explain.

A month before, the Democrats had convened in Atlanta to nominate Massachusetts Governor Michael Dukakis after one of their most protracted and turbulent primaries in modern history—with Dukakis outlasting a crowded field that originally included Senators Gary Hart, Al Gore, Joe Biden, and Paul Simon; Congressman Dick Gephardt; Arizona Governor Bruce Babbitt; and the last man standing, civil rights activist Jesse Jackson. Although their primary was surely more drawn out than their party's strategists would have preferred, by the time they rolled out of Atlanta, the Democratic ticket—which now included a dear and respected friend from Houston, Lloyd Bentsen—had achieved a seventeen-point advantage over the man who had long ago sewn up the GOP nomination, my friend George Bush.

Of course, a seventeen-point deficit in national opinion polls was less than ideal, but we had yet to have our convention and felt we still had time to make up the deficit. In an odd way, in fact, news of the Democratic lead may have even been helpful—a wake-up call that erased any sense of complacency and underscored the tough road we would have to travel in the upcoming fall campaign.

The development coming out of Atlanta that troubled me even more, however, was the announcement that, in addition to the $46.1 million in public financing each campaign would receive, the Democrats would also try to raise an eye-popping sum of so-called "soft money."[1] As the *Wall Street Journal* reported shortly thereafter, "Michael Dukakis's chief fund-raiser, Robert Farmer . . .

1. In 1978, the Federal Election Commission amended its Watergate-era inspired rules and permitted unregulated or "soft" money in federal elections for campaign activities such as voter registration drives and get-out-the-vote efforts that also had implications in state and local elections as well. The FEC also let the parties determine the acceptable mixture of such federal-state-local funds, provided it was done on a "reasonable basis."

stunned the political community by announcing his intention to raise a total of $50 million in party funds, including much soft money, to be spent in addition to the . . . public funds to be spent directly by the Dukakis campaign."[2] In both 1980 and 1984, by comparison, the two national parties combined raised a total of about $20 million in "soft money"—which is money you can raise without regard to federal limits because those funds are used for campaign activities that are not necessarily tied to, nor divorced from, a federal or presidential election. Statewide voter registration drives and local get-out-the-vote efforts are good examples of such nonspecific party-building enterprises you can fund using soft money.

Still, what Robert Farmer proposed to do in the summer of 1988 was the fund-raising equivalent of exercising the nuclear option. It immediately changed the rules of political engagement, and escalated the stakes—particularly for those, like me, whose chief job was to make sure my candidate had the funds he needed to be competitive.

At first, the Bush campaign's response upon hearing of the Farmer program, called "Campaign 88," was one of moral indignity. Rich Bond, one of our top political directors, said the effort was "illegal on its face." Another unnamed GOP official huffed that the Democrats were "breaking the law . . . just asking for a lawsuit."

Whether the Democrats' "Campaign 88" program set an illegal precedent is still, to this day, a matter of debate; but one thing I did know with crystal clarity in August of 1988 was that we had to find an answer for it. If we pursued a strictly legal strategy and challenged it only through the courts, the best we could hope for was a largely empty legal victory many, many months down the road—during the administration of President Michael Stanley Dukakis.

The hardest sell on this point, however, would be my candidate.

George Bush is the most conscientious and decent man I have ever met. Having known him for five decades, I have watched firsthand and with great personal admiration the way he has conducted himself in both his public and his private affairs. Without fail, he hews to the strictest standards for integrity— trying always to avoid even the appearance of impropriety.

I hasten to add that "Number 41," as he is known today, is also one of the most competitive men I know, and he is a realist.

The vice president and Barbara had barely arrived at the 1988 GOP convention

---

2. Brooks Jackson, "GOP Is Aiming New Fund Drive at Big Donors," *Wall Street Journal*, August 17, 1988.

in New Orleans—making a picturesque entrance by way of river steamboat along the Mississippi River, and announcing his selection of the young and energetic Indiana Senator Dan Quayle as his choice for the vice presidential nomination—when I felt the urgent need to stop by his hotel suite at the Marriott. The next event on his schedule that afternoon was a Victory '88 reception for major donors, and before we went over I wanted to discuss our response to Farmer's "Campaign 88" strategy.

As we settled into the couch in his spacious living room area, campaign aides buzzing about, I suggested that we had to match the Dukakis-Farmer effort. George clearly had a lot on his mind, but the reason the idea seemed to almost catch him off-guard at first had nothing to do with the campaign or the convention. Rather, it was the vice president's sense of propriety that led him almost instinctively to deflect my proposal. Then I showed him a news article that detailed how the Democrats' soft-money drive had already raised $17 million—including about 100 checks for $100,000 from individuals. Farmer was quoted in this same story saying they had commitments to contribute or raise at least another $10 million in $100,000 amounts, along with thirty fund-raising events and direct mail, to bring the total to $50 million.

I had been carrying the newspaper article in my pocket for a few days by then, and remember how the clipping itself was frayed and gnarled at the edges. After the vice president read it, he let out an expletive or two that harkened back to his days in the Navy. "I worry that some people will get the perception that they can buy influence," he added, chewing on the end of his reading glasses—a telltale sign that my friend was torn between two difficult choices.

I hated to add to George's many concerns during one of the most important weeks of his political career; but one of my traits, for better or for worse, is a tendency—not unlike a dog with a bone—to latch onto an idea, keep pushing for it, and then drive it home.

Put another way: I can sometimes be a pain in the ass.

"We have to do this," I argued. "We cannot disarm unilaterally. We'll be left at the starting gate." I was mixing my metaphors, but my point was not lost on the candidate.

After ten or fifteen minutes of hearing me spout off, reassuring him that what I wanted to do was aboveboard, the vice president reluctantly relented. Thus, the GOP answer to Farmer and his soft money program was born. Now, we had a chance of pulling to the starting line of the fall campaign in a competitive financial position.

In fairly short order, things started to fall into line politically as well. Two nights later, George Bush officially accepted the Republican nomination for president of the United States of America—and gave what many consider to be one of the greatest political speeches in modern history. Thirty minutes before his big speech, our pollster Bob Teeter and I visited with him in his holding room, which in 1988 was under the massive podium at the Louisiana Superdome. Bob and I were nervous wrecks, but not George Bush. "Hey Mosbacher," he kidded me at one point, "I think that double-breasted jacket you have is pretty snazzy—maybe I should go with that tonight."

Of course, minutes later he was onstage, effectively transforming himself before the American people. The loyal vice president and affable no. 2—the ultimate wing man—assumed a distinctly presidential bearing before the nation. I would say it was a masterful performance, except it wasn't a performance. Anyone who knew George Bush knew he could be tough as nails. We knew he was his own man. We damn sure knew he was no "wimp," as an infamous *Newsweek* magazine cover earlier in the '88 campaign had alleged.

Never one to indulge in what he calls "flowery speech," or soaring rhetoric, near the end of his speech the vice president brought his audience to their feet as he declared: "I will keep America moving forward, always forward—for a better America, for an endless enduring dream and a thousand points of light. This is my mission. And I will complete it."

All great convention speeches give the audience a chance to interact with the speaker, and make their voices heard. Given the patriotic themes we were using to highlight the contrasts with Dukakis—who proudly embraced his liberalism—I had suggested that George put the Pledge of Allegiance in at the very end to make sure he closed the speech in unison with the delegates, firing them up to go home and work their hearts out for a GOP victory. You never know if a speech element will work the way you intend, but fortunately, this one did.

Rolling out of New Orleans, we learned that what had been a narrowing 49–42 Dukakis lead just before the Republican convention became a 48–44 Bush advantage after it—an eleven-point bounce, giving us a lead we would never relinquish.

To be sure, we had come a long way in just the last year.

Early on in the primary season, we had suffered an embarrassing third-place finish in the Iowa caucuses—the scene of our thrilling win in 1980. Senator Bob Dole from neighboring Kansas won the 1988 Iowa caucus as expected; but the real shocker was who finished second. In what proved to be the debut of the Christian Coalition, televangelist Pat Robertson rode a wave of previously undetected churchgoer support to an improbable second-place showing. Former Congressman Jack Kemp and former Delaware Governor Pete DuPont trailed the vice president.

No doubt, that third place finish took a layer off the Veep's veneer of inevitability; but if he was down, George Bush was never out—not by a long shot.

Fighting back, he reversed his political fortunes in New Hampshire—where the 1980 Bush campaign had seen our hopes dashed. Pulling out all the stops, the vice president brought out baseball legend Ted Williams, the former Boston Red Sox star who was like a demigod throughout New England. Also creating a buzz with New Hampshire's no-nonsense primary voters was the conservative icon, former Arizona Senator Barry Goldwater, stumping for the Bush campaign.

Looking back, there are so many indelible moments that stand out from what turned out to be a pivotal week; but I share the view of many that the decision to run the "Senator Straddle" TV spot put us over the top.

The night we arrived in New Hampshire from the lowly Iowa defeat, our adman Roger Ailes worked until dawn to create a blunt ad asserting that Senator Dole had waffled on tax hikes, oil import fees, and arms control. Roger's idea was to start running the ad immediately. As with the "soft money"/Team 100 question I raised with George months later, the vice president's instinct for decency and civility led him to demur when the idea of running such a tough ad was first broached.

A few days later, however, we were still slightly behind Dole—who had just picked up the endorsement of former Secretary of State Al Haig—as we headed into the weekend before the primary vote.

Again, the idea of the "Straddle" ad surfaced.

Like George Bush, I don't like negative ads; but in the rare circumstances where they might be appropriate (i.e., necessary), I also believe they should be factually accurate—and based on public issues, not personal ones. "Straddle" hit hard on the issues, but it was above the belt.

That Saturday, as the team assembled to discuss the matter, Lee Atwater assured us the ad was factual—and pollster Bob Teeter and Ailes made the case for running the ad. When the vice president asked my opinion on the matter, I said, "You *have* to run this ad, as long as it is truly factual."

Hearing a chorus of advice encouraging him to proceed, the vice president approved the spot; and within hours, thanks to New Hampshire Governor John Sununu's contacts in his home state's media market, we had bought every remaining thirty-second slot through Tuesday's primary vote.

As it began airing that night, "Straddle" caught the Dole team flat-footed. They didn't have time to produce a new ad of their own, and even if they had time to make a response ad there wasn't a single available time slot in the New Hampshire media market before voters went to the polls. All of the TV ad time had already been sold.

That Tuesday's election results gave the Bush campaign a convincing nine-point win in New Hampshire, while dealing the Dole campaign a near-fatal blow. In a sense, George Bush had reestablished a more durable "Big Mo" (short for momentum), as he had memorably described it coming out of the 1980 Iowa Caucus. Having broken through in the Granite State this time, and boosted by Lee Atwater's great work and ties in South Carolina, the Bush campaign ran to daylight in the tough weeks ahead—and the GOP nomination in New Orleans.

Along the way, what started as an informal gathering of six senior Bush campaign advisors came to be known as the G-6—Group of Six. In addition to yours truly, the group included pollster Bob Teeter; strategist Lee Atwater; the VP's chief of staff, Craig Fuller; media guru Roger Ailes; and former New Jersey Senator Nick Brady, who was then chairman of the Wall Street investment firm of Dillon Read & Co. Each was clearly skilled and knowledgeable in their area of expertise, but Nick and I—along with Jimmy Baker, who while at Treasury was privy to many of the campaign's early operations and later came on board as our ringleader—shared a particularly lengthy friendship with the candidate.

Given our long-standing affiliation with George Bush—and *possibly* owing to our relatively older age—the other younger campaign consultants and staffers dubbed Jimmy, Nick, and me "The Adults." As 1988 progressed, it was observed that we were "at the tip of a massive collection of advisers—hundreds, maybe even thousands—available for on-demand policy advice to the man who will be the 1988 Republican presidential nominee."[3] To be honest, fielding all of the advice that came our way (meant for the candidate), was like trying to get a sip of water from a fire hose. But one memorable encounter came when I was leaving Washington with the vice president one day, riding to Andrews Air Force Base outside of Washington from the DC campaign headquarters. Bob Teeter and Lee Atwater were in the car, and finally Lee said: "You want your friend to be president, right?"

I responded—somewhat sarcastically—that, no, I had spent the last quarter century of my life dedicated to this man to see him lose.

---

3. Rudy Abramson, "Brady, Mosbacher and Baker: Three Early Disciples Cap Legions of Bush Advisers," *Los Angeles Times*, May 19, 1988.

The so-called "G-6" group of political advisors gathered in August 1987 for a meeting in the Bushes' Kennebunkport living room. From left to right are Nick Brady, Craig Fuller, David Bates, Roger Ailes, yours truly, and pollster Bob Teeter. Then–Vice President Bush and Lee Atwater have their backs to the camera.

Lee continued: "Then we have to rule out a tax increase in his administration. He has to say 'Read my lips.'"

As a matter of principle, I was against "Read My Lips," and can tell you that George Bush feels the same way today. Why? Because, if elected, George knew better than anyone that our nation was going to have to face some very difficult decisions regarding the federal budget; thus, it was smart politics but bad governing to use such hot rhetoric like "Read My Lips" that, in effect, handcuffed him, boxed him into a corner—choose your metaphor.

As it was, "read my lips" became a mainstay of George's 1988 stump speeches.

I pride myself in having a pretty good political antennae, and knowing when I am being manipulated by others. Looking back, I am disappointed that I went along with "Read My Lips." For some time, I have been convinced that Lee and Bob "played" me on that element of the campaign. They won the political battle in 1988, but in the long run it may have cost us the war for the president's political survival in 1992.

At my end of the campaign shop, in the meantime, our finance operation was reaping the benefits of more than a decade of hard work and national campaigning—starting with the candidate, his wife, and his family. For ten solid years, and even before then, George and Barbara Bush had crisscrossed the country innumerable times; and had earned respect and loyalty from countless allies for the way he handled some tough, demanding political appointments—such as chairman of the RNC during Watergate. In fact, it was during the RNC days that George met such stalwart supporters as builder Alec P. Courtelis of Miami; restaurateur Wally Ganzi Jr. of the Palm chain; industrialist and dear friend of mine, Max Fisher; and in New York we had my close friends Don Marron, head of Paine Weber; Jack Hennessy, head of CS First Boston; and Henry Kravis.

Thus, by the time 1988 rolled around, George Bush had a substantial list of capable and committed political supporters in most every city—ready to go to work.

Many is the politician who knows how to make friends; but few are the ones who know how to keep them—and George and Barbara Bush have a gift for keeping friends. Armed with the Bushes' unceasing propensity for friendship and their 20,000-plus person Christmas card list, we were positioned for success long before 1988 when we started recruiting community and business leaders to man a 350-man finance committee for a second run at the presidency.

Many of them were old-line Republicans, who were drawn to George Bush not so much because they shared a philosophical bent—but more often out of personal loyalty. They came from New England; some attended Andover or Yale, where George was a genuine "big man on campus;" still others like Bobby Holt came to the campaign from Midland, Texas and the all-important oil circles where I also had many friends.

As a result, the gang we assembled had as diverse a background as you could have, from small business to big business. And the glue that obviously held everyone together was the strong respect and affection for the candidate.

That helped most of all.

It also helped our operation that both George and I felt you had to find ways to make the onerous job of fund-raising fun. At one of our 1988 finance meetings, for example, I had maybe 200 people in the room—all serious executives, influential people. Before the candidate came in the room, to lighten things up and give him a little surprise, I had everyone in the room put on the same gaudy looking t-shirt that read "President George Bush" on the front of it.

After the vice president entered the room and caught wind of the gag, he asked me before the assembled audience "where the heck those t-shirts came from?"

"I don't know," I said, facetiously looking skyward. "Maybe from heaven."

One area where George Bush didn't help so much, however, was when it came to one-on-one solicitations. I've helped a number of candidates raise money through the years, but George Bush is the only candidate with whom I have worked who never—not once—asked a prospective donor for a contribution. No matter how hard or how much I cajoled him to make the ask, he would always leave a donor meeting saying, "I did my part, now you do yours."

Whatever the formula, it worked—and worked well. During the 1988 primaries, thanks to a hard-working finance committee, we raised the maximum of $29 million—of which, 70 percent came from fund-raising events or one-on-one solicitations. The rest came from PAC contributions and telephone contribution drives. By May of 1988, we had received donations from some 75,000 donors, with an average contribution of $220. We also persuaded 17,000 individuals to give what was then the maximum $1,000 donation, a record $17 million that surpassed even Ronald Reagan's fund-raising prowess.

And as always, George Bush also took the time to sign thank-you notes to each of these and about 3,000 other donors of $500 or more.

As we headed into the summer of 1988, however, something was noticeably different from 1984. During the summer of 1984, Walter Mondale's presidential campaign found itself $7 million in debt, whereas in 1988 the Democrats were already well on their way to raising over $20 million on their own.

Which brings me back to why I was dancing on that table in New Orleans in August of 1988. I had just received approval from the then-vice president to launch our Team 100 program, and went almost directly to Don Bren's hotel room. Don was the chairman of the Irvine Company, and was the key leader of our finance team in California. I had Don get a group of people together so I could share the news—and make my first pitch.

We had settled in around a large coffee table in Don's suite when I laid out the new initiative, why it was necessary, and the urgent fact that we had to get the ball rolling. "The Democrats already have these big checks coming through the door," I stated, "and we have to match them."

Then I turned to Don Bren and said: "Don, as one of our key leaders, I need you to write the first $100,000 check."

As the audaciousness of my request registered in the ears of those gathered, an uneasy quiet settled in across the room. Even today, $100,000 is a tremendous sum of money—all the more so back in 1988. I knew we had a few fantastically wealthy people for whom such a sum was insignificant; but for the vast majority, what I was asking would require them digging deeper than they ever had. In fact, many subsequent donors to the Team 100 program told me they had to steady their hand while writing all of those zeroes.

The quizzical look on Don's perpetually tan and quintessentially Californian face said it all.

"Bob Mosbacher, have you lost your mind?" he blurted, his voice dripping with disbelief. "I'm not going to do that. Why, you'd have to dance on that table before I'd even consider it."

Whenever Pop was putting the squeeze on someone—trying to get them to do something that person really didn't want to do—I often heard him say, "Please, I hate to beg." It was certainly a dignified way of pleading his case.

Don Bren's offer might have been an empty one, but seeing how it was the only one I had at the time I seized it. The next thing I knew, I was dancing a little jig on the coffee table.

It worked—and by that, I do not mean the quality of the dancing. The ice had been broken, and by the time we headed out of New Orleans, I had 100 commitments at the $100,000 level.

As the midwife to the GOP program that responded to Robert Farmer's soft money program, I will candidly confide that our program moving forward from New Orleans was remarkably unoriginal. Save for its name and its targeted audience, Team 100 was almost identical to Farmer's effort on the Democratic side. We tried to reach as many supportive individuals and companies as we could, and my goal—at least as I mentioned to the press—was to match the Democrats "plus one dollar."

When the dust from the fall campaign settled, we did even better than I dared hope. On our side, 249 individuals made contributions of up to $100,000 to the Bush effort, while the Democrats' "$100,000 club numbered 130 individuals."

A few weeks after the election, I found it slightly amusing when the *New York Times* noted how Bob Farmer "won praise" for leading the Democrats' effort to raise millions in soft money just days after it opined that it was I who somehow needed to "come clean" on the tactics employed in the 1988 campaign.

To beat this dead horse for the final time, the American Association of Retired Persons *and* the public interest group Common Cause, certainly no sycophants for Bob Mosbacher or the Republican Party, filed a joint amici curiae brief in support of the constitutionality of the bipartisan Campaign Reform Act of 2002. In that brief, they observed that "the spiral of soft money fundraising began with the Dukakis campaign which, led by its treasurer and chief fund-raiser Robert Farmer, initiated a program to solicit $100,000 contributions from wealthy individual donors."[4]

There is no question that the Farmer decision eventually led to a series of unfortunate, unintended consequences. Eight years later, for example, President

---

4. Donald J. Simon, *Brief of Common Cause and AARP as Amici Curiae in Support of the Constitutionality of the Bipartisan Campaign Reform Act of 2002,* August 5, 2003.

Clinton dramatically expanded the use of this same "soft money" leading up to his 1996 reelection campaign. Under that Clinton-Gore reelection effort, money that had previously been used exclusively for "ground war" tactics like voter registration was suddenly being used in the "air war" as well—for TV ads favorable to the president and his policies. Estimates differ widely; but during that particular election cycle, 1996, the soft money raised by the two political parties exploded to an estimated $271 million.

As I write, we have come through an election cycle where President Barack Obama chose to take the heat for violating a political pledge and opting out of the public campaign finance system en route to raising a jaw-dropping $640 million between the primaries and the general election. The days of the billion-dollar campaign are near at hand.

Clearly, no matter how well-intended, the various legislative and administrative attempts to reduce the role of private money in presidential elections have failed miserably; and like Robert Farmer, I believe the system has gotten out of hand. But at the time, in the heat of battle in August 1988, none of us possessed the enlightened perspective that only time would bring.

In 1988, George Bush overcame early setbacks in both the primary and the general elections, stood out there on the line as his own man, and the nation responded in resounding fashion. On November 8, he carried forty of the fifty states and, most importantly, earned 426 of the required 271 electoral votes to become president-elect.

I will confess there was a lump in my throat when I first addressed my friend as "Mr. President." After so many years of hard work, after the roller coaster ride of heartbreak and ecstasy too, it was an honor to be there when he finally reached the summit—to what he calls the mountaintop of American politics. The view from that rare vantage was as breathtaking as the challenges we faced ahead were daunting.

In the final analysis, while there is cause to question the methods instigated by our opponents, I still feel like dancing on a table to celebrate that the better man won in 1988, and that I had a chance to help him change the world for the better in the years to come.

Chapter 17   MR. SECRETARY

As the athletic, angular figure of the new president approached the podium and launched the ceremony that would end with my becoming the twenty-eighth secretary of commerce, I looked out into the expanse that is the Department of Commerce's great hall—aptly named for my predecessor Mac Baldridge. Gathered amid the Indiana limestone walls and Vermont marble flooring, I could see my dear family, loyal friends, and colleagues—old and new—all there to offer their support and friendship, and to size up the new boss.

It was February 3, 1989, three days after the United States Senate had unanimously confirmed me as secretary of commerce, and I was ready to get to work. First came the constitutional formalities, and as I listened to the president speak, my wife by my side, I found myself wondering what Pop would make of the spectacle.

"I trust his advice," President Bush said. "I respect what he's accomplished in business . . . He's a savvy international businessman, an entrepreneur who built his own extraordinarily successful business and kept it on solid footing even during tough economic times. . . ."

No doubt, Pop was looking down on the scene and reminding me: "Don't get a big head!" But there could be no escaping the pride of the moment, as I realized that just a century before my grandfather had stepped alone onto the docks of lower Manhattan carrying his worldly possessions in two suitcases—and the hope of a better future.

Of course, it was also deeply moving to me to have George Bush there presiding as my president—and Jim Baker there to administer the oath of office. Not lost on me that day was the improbable journey the three of us had traveled together over the preceding nineteen years—from a tough 1970 Senate loss during a year of deep personal grief, to the pinnacle of American power. In the annals of presidential history, it is not clear that three political allies, who started out originally as personal friends, had ever risen to such heights together.

George and Jimmy were old Washington hands by then; and though I was not exactly a stranger to our nation's capital and the people who made it run, I had a more low-key profile thanks to the fact that I ran a privately-held business.

"Mr. Secretary." Secretary of State Jimmy Baker administers the oath and President George Bush looks on as I assume my Commerce Department duties on February 3, 1989.

That would change—in fact, even before I was sworn in. I understood that increased media scrutiny of my family went with the territory, but Rob put my frame of mind best when he told the the *Los Angeles Times*, "The only reason he's willing to enter the Washington fishbowl is because of his devotion to George Bush. I'm sure there are going to be days when he regrets it."[1]

Rob was right on both counts—though fortunately, the days I regretted going into government were few and far between. It might have been different, however, had the first administration post offered to me panned out.

A few days after the 1988 election, President-elect Bush had suggested that I might come on the White House staff to help lead the economic team—as a "senior advisor" to him, as he put it. I was naturally honored by the thought of working so closely with him in the West Wing. Everyone who enters an administration serves "at the pleasure of the president," and had George insisted that I

1. Tom Redburn, "Death of Oilman's Wife Was Crucial Turning Point Bush-Mosbacher Ties Forged by Tragedy," *Los Angeles Times*, December 7, 1988.

To Bob Mosbacher —
On this special day in our lives with thanks —
All Best G. Bush

Accepting my friend's nomination as Commerce Secretary on December 6, 1988. Also nominated to the Bush cabinet that day were, from left, William Webster at CIA, Michael Boskin for the Council of Economic Advisors, and Carla Hills as the U.S. Trade Representative.

take the White House posting I would have had to do it—but instinctively, the idea of running a department of my own had a stronger pull.

I have long maintained that I may not be much of a leader, but I am a much worse follower. In 1989, I had essentially been my own boss for forty years, except for answering to Pop during those earlier days. As a result, I knew I had to be in a job where, first, I had some knowledge and, second, some autonomy. Though the West Wing of the White House is the most cherished political real estate in Washington, the only way I could go into government was not to be reporting to someone else—but to be working, instead, with and for a president and personal friend I admired.

Of course, given my background in the oil and gas industry, you might think that the Department of Energy would be a good fit, but that's a curiosity of our system. In Washington, it seems the more you know about an issue, the less qualified you are to assume any responsibility for it. I would have had too many conflicts, as Congress and the media saw it, to take the energy account—so the next feasible option for me was Commerce.

One of the great pastimes in Washington is speculating who will get what Cabinet job after a presidential election, and several other serious names had surfaced as possible contenders to head the Commerce Department's 38,000 employees and manage its $2.6 billion budget—most notably Peter Ueberroth, the Major League Baseball commissioner and Los Angeles Olympics organizer, as well as Hewlett-Packard's CEO, John Young.

The parlor games and guessing over who would get the Commerce post ended in early December, on the eve of his historic mini-summit in New York Harbor with Mikhail Gorbachev and Ronald Reagan, when the president-elect stepped before the media and declared his intention to "submit the name of Robert Mosbacher, a friend of long standing, a very successful leader in the business community, as my nominee for Secretary of Commerce. I've known Bob for longer than he'd like to admit, but for more than thirty years. He's built a very successful business. . . . He is a leader, not only in the energy industry but in the business community nationally."

When the Department of Commerce and Labor was established back in 1903, Congressman Charles Cochran described what he saw were the necessary qualities of the person who led that vast bureaucracy. "Above everything," Cochran said, "[the secretary] should be a man of affairs, acquainted with the vast subject with which he must deal, vigilant, enterprising, resourceful, and possessed of the sagacity which distinguishes the American man of business from all others."[2]

I will leave it to others to judge if I possessed some, or even any of these varied characteristics. As far as I was concerned, the only quality I truly needed to possess was the full faith and confidence of the forty-first president of the United States—which he generously conferred on me that cold winter morning.

Also nominated that day were two other key members of the economic team: Carla Hills, who had served as secretary of housing and urban development during the Ford administration, was put forward as the new United States Trade Representative; and Dr. Michael Boskin of Stanford was tapped as chairman of the Council of Economic Advisors.

The *New York Times* seemed to approve of my selection, noting in an editorial that I shared ". . . President Reagan's sensible views on free trade. . . . President-

2. President George Bush, remarks at the swearing-in ceremony for Robert A. Mosbacher as secretary of commerce, February 3, 1989.

elect Bush continues to put together a team of moderate Republicans who can work in harmony with a Democratic Congress. His choices so far . . . suggest a healthy preference for non-ideological, practical people."[3]

The six weeks between the president-elect's nomination and my confirmation hearings were chock full of meetings with business leaders, courtesy calls on members of Congress, holiday events, and issues briefings with my staff. In the midst of all this hustle and bustle, one of the nicest letters came in from my friend Jose "Pepe" Fanjul—a successful leader in the sugar industry whose family left Cuba and moved to Florida during Castro's 1959 upheaval.

"Bob," Pepe's letter read, "if we in Cuba who had some success were willing to get involved directly with politics—to get our hands dirty, and run for office win or lose, or be involved with the government—we never would have had Castro. So I admire what you are doing, somebody who didn't have to do it." Pepe's kind letter touched a chord, and yet I felt very fortunate to be able to serve in some constructive way in government.

It was with a tremendous sense of pride, mixed with trepidation and a keen appreciation of the hard work ahead, that I placed my hand on the Bible and repeated the solemn oath of office. In laying out my agenda for advancing the president's vision of helping American businesses compete in the global economy, my first comments as the new secretary focused on the big picture:

> We must ensure that trade is a two-way street for American business by expanding overseas markets for top U.S. goods and services while ensuring fair competition through effective enforcement of our trade laws. . . . Another vitally important mission is to improve the beauty and quality of our oceans, shorelines, and estuaries. . . . We must also enforce our national capability to develop the best in modern technology. We must pursue policies that will speed commercialization of technology. Our new technology administration will be in the forefront of this effort.

I would be less than forthcoming if I tried to suggest that tackling the job in running that massive, diverse department was anything other than daunting. Commerce is a collection of miscellaneous agencies and bureaus that do an extremely wide array of things. Many people are familiar with the Bureau of Economic Statistics, and other economic functions that produce some of the key reports and numbers that help us understand how the economy is doing.

Then you have the other high-profile function dealing with international

3. *New York Times*, "Mr. Bush's Practical Choices," December 7, 1988.

All smiles at my Commerce desk with, from left to right, Peter and Jane, Rob's kids; and Parker and Whitney, Lisa and Downing's twins.

trade. Even today, I will wager that most folks in Washington think those two functions—economic statistics and trade—encompass your entire job as secretary.

They don't realize you have to manage the census, which is a political and bureaucratic nightmare. You're also responsible for, of all things, the weather—or at least predicting hurricanes, and launching satellites. Additionally, you oversee one of the last vestiges of pure political pork in America, which are the government weather stations located all over the country. And if you even begin to *think* about closing one of those weather stations down because the technology has been improved, then one congressman, two senators, and a governor are sure to become your mortal enemy.

There's more. As commerce secretary, you are responsible for deciding the politically sensitive issues regarding allocations of fish catches. How many lobsters can be harvested off the coast of Maine? How many shrimp can be taken in the Gulf of Mexico? How much salmon can be caught up in Alaska? No matter what you say, someone is going to be mad—count on it like the rising sun.

Finally, there's the patent and trademark office, telecommunications issues dealing with spectrum allocation, and the minority business development group. This last agency brings you into the middle of a long-running rivalry between African and Hispanic Americans over which is the more important minority group, and what they ought to be getting in terms of federal assistance.

To think any one person can walk in and manage the place requires you to focus your energy—because, frankly, not everyone in the building wants you to succeed. Some, but not all, career bureaucrats won't bother to warn you when you're about to walk into a brush fire as you check the box, sign your name, and move onto sexier issues such as trade agreements. Their attitude is: *We'll outlast you. We know what's best.*

Even before I was sworn in, I discovered that some bureaucrats in that big building were out to trip me up. It was during my confirmation hearings that Lloyd Bentsen, my friend and home-state senator, introduced me as the hearings opened. We'd been friends for years, during which time we occasionally had lunch and played tennis. According to Senate tradition, Lloyd was given the courtesy of asking the first question. After his genial introduction, the niceties ended abruptly as Lloyd then gently turned on me and asked a very technical question that seemed to come in from left field: "What are you going to do with those airplanes that the Air Force is going to turn over to NOAA for the weather surveillance?"

For weeks, I had been scouring two thick briefing books for details, and talking with department experts about the major issues I might face. And during that time, I had never heard a single word from anybody about Air Force planes going to the National Oceanic and Atmospheric Administration (NOAA). Lloyd had me cornered; and as a personal policy, when all else fails, I try to be truthful. "Senator," I sheepishly confessed, as I instantly felt the beads of perspiration collecting on my brow, "I'm not fully up to speed on that, but I'll check it and I'll get back to you within two days."

What I was really thinking was: *That's the first friendly question? This is a sucker punch. You know I don't know "shit from shinola" about that.*

In due course, I found that the NOAA bureaucrats had planted that issue with Bentsen's staff. After so many years of liberal dominance on Capitol Hill, the agency had very strong relationships with the Democrats. On top of that, they had their own Admirals and their own Navy—so they thought they were totally independent.

Still, coming in from the private sector, I was pleasantly surprised to find that the majority of the career people at the department were not only very smart,

With my home state senators, Phil Gramm (left) and Lloyd Bentsen, preparing for the start of my Senate confirmation hearing in January 1989.

but dedicated. I quickly discovered that if you motivated them and brought them into the inner circles of planning, they could and did make substantive contributions.

To help me preserve and enhance the department's clout, I was very lucky to assemble a group of young Turks on my inner office staff, and to recruit some terrific professionals to the other top posts. Some of the key members included J. Michael Farren, my undersecretary for trade administration. Mike was a trade expert who we referred to as "our best bureaucrat." Wayne Berman served as my senior counselor, and I constantly leaned on him for advice. I grew fond of telling Wayne he was my right arm, even though I am left-handed.

For my general counsel, we had Wendell L. Willkie—former general counsel of the Education Department, a Rhodes Scholar, and grandson of the 1940 GOP presidential candidate by the same name. As my assistant secretary for trade development, Michael Skarzynski proved a very good technical advisor; to be director of the U.S. and Foreign Commercial Service, I hired Susan Schwab, who had been a key aide to Senator John Danforth (R-Mo.) and would eventually rise to become the U.S. Trade Representative under President George W. Bush; and Tom Collamore, a veteran Bushie, came onboard as my assistant secretary for administration.

Once the key slots were filled, to help drive a sense of teamwork deep down into the department's ranks, I conducted a weekly Saturday morning meeting with all the appointees—which is something, I am told, my predecessors had not done. These very large meetings started at 9:00 A.M. with thirty-five or forty people around the table representing the various parts of our "alphabet soup" department. At first, there was some grousing about coming into the department on Saturday mornings, and I made only modest headway telling everyone how lucky we were not having to spend the morning running errands. "Instead, you have the joy and privilege of helping to move the ball forward for the country," I said to the expressionless, groggy faces gathered around the large conference room table.

There was a serious purpose to these meetings, however. I thought it was important to give every person a voice, an opportunity to tell me something I needed to know. "Face time is king," as the saying goes. Those meetings empowered those appointees to take responsibility for what was happening throughout that vast building.

Every once in a while, we would encounter bureaucratic inertia of one form or another. When we did, being as stubborn as I am, we would fight back—sometimes with mixed results. I recall once when our front office sent out a department-wide memo requiring that my office approve every single bit of travel. Did I mention the department had over 38,000 employees at the time? That was what you might call a stupid idea.

Another idea someone raised involved switching our vast nation of 280,000,000 citizens over to the metric system—using meters and grams, instead of yards and pounds. Happily, that idea also died a swift death. I told the folks who pushed the metric proposal I could fight all the built-in resistance to that idea for the next four years, or we could get a number of other matters of great importance accomplished.

Most importantly, I never lost sight of why I became the secretary of commerce. Principally, I was there to make sure the president's agenda was carried out. In the end, it didn't matter if I or anyone else in that massive building thought we had a better idea—after the president made his decision, I was determined that every single employee, be they an appointee or a career bureaucrat, would salute and do as the president had directed. You could come in and maybe question others, but never the president (unless you had a damn good reason).

Without a doubt, the first major challenge on my plate dealt with Japan. Indeed, if there was a main antagonist during my time as secretary it was our

As commerce secretary, I never forgot whose agenda I was in Washington to carry out. The only time George Bush had to look over his shoulder, I hope, was to share a light moment like this one.

trading partners and competitors in Tokyo. They proved a constant source of frustration.

At that time, the Japanese had startled many Americans during the late 1980s by acquiring iconic American properties such as Rockefeller Center in New York City and the Pebble Beach Golf Club. The hysteria that broke out in these cases was particularly foolish because the Japanese couldn't take this real estate and move it—but that maybe gives you a sense of the raw feelings that many harbored. Some back then even suggested that Tokyo's restrictive, anti-American policies qualified them as a trading "enemy," another exaggeration.

Take the issue of semiconductors. In 1989, U.S. companies were only able to gain 11 percent of the Japanese market—despite Tokyo's assurance that our share would rise to 20 percent by 1991. On February 15, less than two weeks on the job, I met with Ambassador Matsunaga to tell him, in effect, there was a new sheriff in town—and that I would be using every tool at my disposal to force concessions from Tokyo.

At the same time, one of the very first international challenges facing the new administration centered on the transfer of sensitive technology to Japan. For more than four years, we had been negotiating a joint effort to develop a new generation of fighter plane to help Japan patrol its shipping lanes and defend itself. When a tentative deal was first reached in November of 1988, many within the Commerce Department protested that we would reveal too much advanced aviation technology to Japan's defense contractors—so much so that Japan, in turn, would be able to develop a civilian aircraft industry that would compete with such U.S. producers as Boeing and McDonnell Douglas.

There was precedent for such concerns. In 1950, the Ford Motor Company allowed Eiji Toyoda of the Toyota Manufacturing group to tour their plant and copy their assembly line processes and other systems. It took a while, but today Toyota has overcome GM as the biggest car manufacturer in the world.

For his part, George Bush had firsthand experience watching the Japanese replicate American technology in the oil business. A genuine pioneer in the off-shore drilling industry, George had agreed to let a Japanese company come and study one of his rigs in the Gulf of Mexico during the late 1950s. They crawled all over the place making notes, and drawing diagrams and such. When he went to Japan the following year, George was greeted by a Japanese-made rig there that bore an eerie resemblance to his own back home.

With respect to the FSX deal in early 1989, the Japanese came to the bargaining table claiming to have a new radar-absorbing, or "stealth," material that could be used in the plane's wings and fuselage. My people thought their claim was extremely dubious. We couldn't come up with any specific evidence that they had such a design—tellingly, neither could they.

When the president called a special meeting of the National Security Council in the White House residence on Saturday, March 18, there were two schools of thought in the administration. Spearheading the argument for the hardliners was our new U.S. Trade Representative Carla Hills—who wanted Japan to receive American-made F-16s "off the rack," without the advanced devices and features—while State and Defense were content to let the deal go through as originally planned.

John Tower's nomination to head the Pentagon had, sadly, been defeated by the Senate a week before, so there was no defense secretary at the meeting. There were, however, plenty of generals bearing ribbons and medals. I recall being surprised at their lack of alarm over the terms of this deal—and its long-term implications. They didn't seem worried that, if you gave away that kind of technology, pretty soon you could have Japanese technology similar in capability to ours on the market, possibly being bought by our enemies and, in turn, used against American planes or forces.

I supported Carla's view, but having traded all my life knew there was going

In a Cabinet meeting, working with George Bush as the Cold War subsided to help open more markets to American goods and services.

to have to be a compromise. During the meeting, I delved into some of the technical aspects while arguing for a middle position whereby the transaction went through with certain safeguards in place to ensure the most crucial design secrets were not divulged.

After the meeting broke up and most of the attendees had left the residence, the president waved me over. Then, somewhat under his breath, he said, "Come on, Mosbacher, how the hell did you learn all this stuff? I've known you for thirty years!"

Defending my honor, I replied, "I've got some very good guys at Commerce who did a heck of a job briefing me." In fact, my first briefing on the FSX issue as secretary came just a week into my tenure, on February 10.

In the end, the president decided to go through with the deal with the safeguards I had prescribed. He also pledged to include the Commerce Department at the start of any new negotiations involving the exchange of military or technology secrets.

Incidentally, after Dick Cheney became defense secretary, the issue of technology transfer came up once again. This time, however, I was arguing for us to sell some computer technology to the Soviet Union. Of course, we had to prove

A private White House lunch with Vice President Cheney in May of 2008. We didn't always see eye-to-eye on every issue, but we remained good friends.

to our Export Control people that the Soviets or their bloc members wouldn't have access to sensitive technology that could be used against us. So we proved that, and they cleared the deal. Still, Cheney called me and maintained that we were making a mistake, giving the Soviets technology that could be used against American pilots. He even called a press conference to argue against our decision.

Having been publicly challenged, and never the shy and retiring type, I had my own press conference and responded to Cheney's concerns. "In case anyone is wondering," I said, "we don't want to sell the Soviets a top of the line product from Radio Shack or anywhere else—nor do we wish for them to be able to buy middle-tier technology. We want to sell them the cheapest computer technology possible, technology that is available at Radio Shack stores around the world." We had a list of the various products and their availability in cities around the world to back me up. My point was: either the Soviets were going to buy these readily available products from us, or from other countries. As long as it didn't negatively affect our national security, I wanted American companies to get that business.

As commerce secretary, I tried always to fight aggressively for American companies and their interests—and that included fighting for more access to foreign markets.

During my three years at the department, I made numerous statements outlining my views of my agency's role in the global economy; but perhaps the most comprehensive was the speech at the Detroit Economic Club in May of 1989. There, I said government and business should be partners—with the department's role to get "the stones, rocks, and other debris out of the way."

Foremost on my mind was our $130 billion trade deficit. Lest there be any doubt, I am an avowed free-trader. I believe in free and fair trade, yet I do not believe in unilateral free trade any more than I believe in unilateral disarmament. I thought we could recapture the lead from Japan and other economic competitors with what I called "an industry-led, business-government partnership to produce, in this country, consumer products of the future that drive American research and manufacturing."

To be clear, I did not go to Detroit to say our $130 billion trade deficit could be sharply reduced only if other nations would behave themselves, because the fact is our companies needed to get their acts together, as well. Too many of our auto and textile companies were clinging to outdated strategies concerning mass production, for example, and our technological weaknesses were manifest. The quality revolution being led by true American visionaries like David Kearns at Xerox and others was only then starting to take hold in boardrooms around the country, and I wanted to see more of it. "We need a strategy to innovate, produce, market, and sell world-class products in each and every industry," I urged.

Unfortunately, other members of the administration thought I was freelancing too much—and endorsing the same kind of industrial policy that Michael Dukakis had promoted during the 1988 campaign. What I wanted to see was more coordination and cooperation, not a government-funded initiative. Still, I was called to the White House for a woodshed meeting with the White House Chief of Staff John Sununu and the Director of the Office of Management and Budget Dick Darman.

John and Dick thought they could maybe rough me up and put a little fear in me, but after dealing with Pop nobody ever shook me up again. They laid into me, telling me in emphatic terms that I needed to clear these policy statements with them. "We don't need any unforced errors," they said in raised voices. I didn't much appreciate their tone, nor the implication that I had somehow screwed up. I held my ground, and told them I would damn well speak my mind when I knew I was on solid ground. I am not sure I responded properly to the sharing of their perspectives, a trait of mine dating back to my days at Choate. Maybe that's why I was drawn to John McCain during the 2008 campaign. He's very "individualistic," too.

During the summer of 1989, one of the most vexing domestic issues under my purview landed squarely on my desk with a thud. In 1988, Congress embedded a new regulation in the reauthorization of the Endangered Species Act, requiring shrimp boat operators in certain areas of the Gulf Coast and South Atlantic to start using something known as a "turtle extruder device" (TEDs) in their shrimp nets. The devices were specifically designed to let sea turtles caught in the shrimp nets escape instead of drowning. At the time, turtles were dying in these nets at a rate of about 11,000 a year. About 500 of those drowned turtles, however, were of a highly endangered species known as Kemp's Ridley.

The TED regulation arose out of years of debate in Congress; and as the May 1, 1989 deadline approached for the TEDs to be in place, I decided to issue a sixty-day "relaxation" of the law to give the shrimpers a little more time to purchase the special nets—which cost anywhere from $60 to $400. As that extended period was drawing to a close, a number of congressmen from the Gulf states came to see me to argue that the nets were getting clogged with sea grass and were otherwise dangerous to operate. So in early July, I extended the moratorium on enforcement while our department looked into their concerns. When I heard from our NOAA scientists a week later that even the least experienced captains and crews could safely operate the extruders and suffer a loss of no more than 5 percent of their shrimp, I decreed that, henceforth, the government would immediately begin enforcing the law of the land.

Then a modest amount of hell broke out.

I had always known from my days out on the waters of southeast Texas that the shrimp boat operators in the region—my aquatic "backyard," if you will—were a fiercely independent, but also tightly knit group. What I didn't know was that, unlike the shrimpers in the South Atlantic, the Gulf Coast shrimpers were willing to resort to violence and threats to preserve their way of doing business. As they saw it, the average shrimper could go for a year without catching a turtle, and seven years without catching a Kemp's Ridley. This was just another unnecessary regulation being forced on them by an uncaring government.

What these shrimpers didn't seem to appreciate was, with 12,000 boats operating, one Kemp's ridley turtle per boat every seven years was still a heavy toll in the eyes of the law.

In mid-July, as the TED law finally took effect, a group of shrimpers in Texas registered their protest by blockading a port along the Texas coast and threatening to kill anyone who tried to board their boats. Hundreds more trawlers blocked ship traffic in the Houston ship channel and other shipping lanes along the Texas Gulf Coast. At one point, there was even an attempted ramming of a Coast Guard vessel by shrimp vessels.

I was at Camp David with the Bushes and the rest of the Cabinet while everything was "hitting the fan" in Texas, and Sam Skinner, then secretary of transportation, was describing to me how ugly it had gotten. At the time, I was a half-hero to environmentalists, but a scourge to the shrimp people. So we tried another formulation requiring shrimpers to lift their nets every 105 minutes so that any trapped turtles could escape before they drowned. This measure didn't work, and in September we reinstated the original regulation requiring the TEDs as the law required.

Even then, some Gulf Coast operators said they would ignore the law.

I was so hated in some shrimping communities that eight or nine years after I left Washington and government, a stewardess working on the powerboat, *Hallelujah* (that I co-owned with Max Fisher) quit on me. When we entered a port city in Italy one day, the stewardess called home, and upon arriving back at the boat told the captain, "I cannot work on this boat with Mr. Mosbacher here."

The captain replied, "What you are talking about?"

"He almost ruined our family," she said. "We had to shut down our shrimp business for a long time because of him."

She just quit on the spot, and the captain reluctantly told me what had happened. Clearly, the strong feelings in that community died hard, and yet it is not clear what I could have done differently given the circumstances. As badly as I still feel for any business affected by that decision, I swore I would uphold the laws of our United States.

The turtle people eventually turned against me, too, even though the Kemp's Ridley turtles have staged an encouraging comeback. According to the U.S. Fish and Wildlife Service, the number of turtles nesting in Mexico grew by tenfold over the following decade.

That's the price of public leadership sometimes: you're damned if you do, *and* if you don't.

In August, meanwhile, Jimmy Baker and I—together with Treasury Secretary Nick Brady, Carla Hills, Attorney General Dick Thornburgh, Environmental Protection Agency Administrator William Reilly, and Bruce Gelb, the director of the U.S. Information Agency—traveled to Mexico to show our neighbors to the south that President Bush was serious about laying the groundwork for a

Pausing for a brief photo with Mexico's Carlos Salinas in April 1991 before another working session on NAFTA.

more productive relationship. Already, we had seen President Salinas and his government give us a few concrete signs they were intent on improving relations, too.

For example, Salinas proved he was committed to continuing his predecessor President Miguel de la Madrid's program of economic privatization. Salinas sold off hundreds of inefficient state-owned corporations to private investors and spent some of the proceeds on infrastructure and social services. He also took steps to open the protected Mexican economy to both foreign investment and foreign competition. In a short period of time, the Mexicans had moved to restructure their economy and reduce their trade barriers, which was a big development since Mexico was our third largest trading partner at the time.

I had already had a good meeting with Jaime Serra Puche, Mexico's Secretary of Commerce and Industrial Development, at my office in Washington in March. He was a very smart, and young, guy—at the time maybe forty or forty-one years old—and as we were getting acquainted, I kidded him that he had a better title than I did.

Jaime came in with a small team of guys, and though they were also fairly new on the job they laid out an ambitious series of plans to jump start the Mexican business community—and strengthen our economic ties. Among other measures, they were going to cut tariffs, cut the licensing fees and paperwork required to sell in their market, attack bribery, and pass a law to let foreign-made pharmaceuticals in without a huge tariff.

We had a long and informative talk that day, but when they left I turned to one of my guys and said, "These are some very smart guys, good guys, but if they claim they are going to do all that stuff they must be smoking marijuana." We laughed but agreed that if they could get some of their plans accomplished, we'd love to pursue it—and see where it led.

Sure enough, Jaime and his team started to deliver on their pledges, so we got serious about our end of the deal.

The agenda for our intense round of discussions in Mexico City in August centered principally on an old issue—drug enforcement—and a new one; namely, Mexico's economic prospects following a debt reduction agreement we had helped them negotiate just weeks before. As was the case throughout much of Latin America during the 1980s—the so-called "Lost Decade" for them—living standards in Mexico had dropped precipitously, partly because of the country's obligations to repay its massive foreign debt.

Helping Mexico and these other nations alleviate the tightening economic noose around their collective neck was the principal goal of the "Brady Plan"—a program announced in March of 1989 whereby the United States would help nations wishing to participate to rework their debt payments in exchange for their instituting tangible, meaningful financial reforms.

Mexico was the first to benefit from this innovative initiative, so the timing of our August trip was fortuitous. Suddenly, Mexico's way forward to sustainable economic growth and viability was not so far-fetched, or the delusional by-product of Acapulco Gold. During our discussions that August, as we realized the dramatic strides Mexico had made in a short time (boosted in significant ways by the United States), the low expectations tinged with cynicism that had traditionally attended Washington's attitude toward Mexico City gave way to a more ambitious view.

As Presidents Bush and Salinas had envisioned in their "Spirit of Houston" meeting shortly after both were elected, we could see a way for the United States and Mexico to eventually enter into a free-trade agreement similar to the one we had already struck with Canada in 1988. That August, the Mexican government had given us signals that they were willing to ensure greater access for American goods and services in Mexico, and beyond that, to start negotiating a formalized agreement in such areas as textiles, electronics, and autos.

Some trade and union critics back home were less impressed with this grand vision for a new free-trade pact. I remember how a leader at the Council of Foreign Relations firmly predicted it would take a minimum of ten years to complete a free trade agreement. Others predicted Mexico's nationalists would be very vociferous against an agreement—and that American labor unions would not want to compete with low-wage Mexican labor.

It would take hard work and persistence if we were to overcome the prevailing wisdom and doubters in both countries, but we made an important start in Mexico City that August. Two months later, on October 18, I publicly predicted that the United States and Mexico would eventually negotiate a free trade agreement. "We should not try to push them too fast, too hard," I said during testimony before the Senate banking committee, "but they [the Mexican government] are interested, extremely interested, in moving toward this."

Obviously, so were we.

In September I was back on the road, this time to Asia and Europe. The first stop on the fifteen-day trip was South Korea. At the time, given Korea's often contentious relationship with their neighbor just across the Korean Straits and the Sea of Japan, Seoul was eager to match Tokyo's move to build a new generation of fighter jets; and naturally, like Japan, they also wanted to acquire the most advanced technology they could.

On the table was a request from the Korean government for a commercially-licensed production program for their entire order of 120 fighter aircraft. This was cause for similar concerns as the Japan/FSX deal, because it would give the Koreans access to key software, avionics subsystems (such as the radar warning receiver), and weapons.

My job was to convince the Koreans that what they wanted was not necessarily what they needed. Having had several preliminary meetings in Washington with their ambassador, the Koreans knew I was coming to play the heavy—so they had rolled out the red carpet. When I arrived at the Ministry of Defense for the pivotal meeting, in fact, I was greeted with military honors—which, I later learned, made me one of the only non-heads-of-state to be accorded such treatment. I was also graciously received by President Rho and other key leaders.

Then it was down to business, as I settled into a deep wingback chair in the

Meeting with Korean President Roh Tae-woo at the Blue House in Seoul in September 1989. Relations with Korea, a strong ally, occasionally grew tense over trade matters.

second-floor conference room of the Defense Ministry. The Korean Minister of Defense sat at the other end, along with two translators.

Our thirty-minute meeting was not going well when, at the appointed time, my aide Fred Volcansek discreetly entered the room to alert me that it was time to go to the next appointment. I looked at Fred and moved my index finger downward, signaling him to sit down as we might be there a while longer.

"Well, Mr. Minister, I really believe we have to do this," I said, continuing our conversation.

Minister Yi replied, "Mr. Secretary, we want to build an F-X fighter, but we won't take F-16s off the shelf."

Not pleased with what I was hearing, I sank back in my deep wingback chair, looked at the minister, and said, "Well, then I guess I am going to have to go back to Washington and tell the president it's time to bring the boys home"— referring to the 75,000 American troops still stationed in Korea at the time.

Silence can be a valuable weapon during a negotiation, so I let the words hang in the air for a moment as the minister turned ash white.

"Mr. Secretary, how many F-16s are we talking about?" he finally asked. "We don't want to hear about the 75,000 troops we have in Korea heading home."

I was equally direct during a subsequent meeting with the Korean Minister of Trade Han Seung-soo, who is back in the Korean government as prime minister as I write this. Minister Han and I became good friends, but I explained we couldn't continue with the huge trade deficit we had. Then I used an argument I used many times.

"Obviously I didn't like it," I told Han, "but more importantly the Democrats who control the Congress won't like it—and they have the power to retaliate." The Democrats, I continued, "were not very good at or fond of free trade, generally speaking. Furthermore, if I have to go to Capitol Hill and report that South Korea was not amenable to opening their markets, the Democrats in power would just as soon cut off all trade with Korea."

Now, naturally, there was an element of bluster and bluffing in here—but also enough truth to make my claims seem plausible. Whatever it was, it worked.

For the record, let me add that I never cleared these negotiating tactics with the president. Had he ever caught wind, I am not sure how he would have reacted—except maybe to shake his head and say, "That's Mosbacher for you."

Seoul is truly a modern marvel, a modern-day Phoenix that rose from the ashes of war. To think the city was almost totally flattened to rubble by the Chinese during the Korean War, and was able to host the 1988 Summer Olympics some three decades later, was a remarkable achievement—a testament to the spirit and sense of industry of the Korean people. So after a busy morning of meetings, we got in the car and headed straight for Olympic Stadium.

As we entered the stadium, using the ramp that the athletes had used to march in, I was in awe of the sight—the sheer scope of the building. Then the massive scoreboard caught my eye, and there was a sign on it reading, "Welcome, Secretary Mosbacher." I loved it because, even though I had qualified for two different Olympic Games as an alternate (1968 and 1972), I would have hurt the team by accepting a slot that did not play to my strengths, so I chose not to participate. Thus, I had never marched in an Olympic ceremony.

After two very full days in Korea, it was on to Japan. As direct as I was with my hosts in Seoul, in Tokyo I was positively impolitic. At one point, I gave a speech comparing a joint study my department had done with Japan's ministry of trade on prices in Japan and the United States, and imports to both countries. The study found that the price of Japanese imports into our market was about half of the cost of U.S. goods imported into Japan—because of the restrictive Japanese tariffs and nontariff barriers.

So I got up in Japan and said, "Not only is this not what we consider to be fair trade, but for the Japanese housewives and mothers who need these goods, frankly, they're being gouged."

When I finished my speech, which was attended by the Japanese press, one of the reporters spoke up and said, "We are certainly touched by the secretary's concern for our mothers and housewives." His statement was dripping with sarcasm, and it was about as harsh as the Japanese would ever be in telling you off. They were not pleased.

Neither, I might add, was our ambassador, Mike Armacost. In traveling around the world, I usually found our ambassadors trying to smooth things over—and at times, behaving as if they represented their host country as much as they did America. I was much more prone to try to shake things up, make some direct points, and try to get action—so I am sure some of our diplomatic corps cringed when they heard I was coming their way.

My angst with Japan stemmed in large measure from the patently unfair practices whereby they were holding our Fed Ex packages that were being shipped through Japan to other countries. Even though Japan was a "transit country" for the packages—not the final destination—Japanese inspectors would open the packages and otherwise delay their shipment, causing a massive backlog and other problems. We really had to get them off a lot of these practices, and again I used Congress to help me do that.

I threatened my Japanese counterparts with going back to Capitol Hill to report how they would not change their "nontariff import restrictions." The term is important because the Japanese were not taxing us. Instead, they were using subtler methods to restrict U.S. commercial activity in the region. I would point this out to my counterparts in Tokyo, before musing about retaliating "the way Congressman Dingell wants, and just leave all those Japanese cars sitting on the docks here in Japan."

In the middle of all this, I vividly recall attending my first, and only, Sumo wrestling match—where the members of my traveling staff and I were privileged to sit in the Emperor's box. Frankly, I was worn out and didn't want to go, but it was a big deal that we had the Emperor's seats. In the end, I was glad I went.

The booth itself was beautifully adorned, but what I didn't expect was the fact that the winner of the match was an American, from Guam. I was very touched when they heard I was there and sent word that they would like to meet me. We shook their hands, and then we took a few pictures with him and the other wrestler. So I stood in the middle, and the guys kind of playfully crowded

Sandwiched between two Hawaiian-born sumo wrestlers, Fuauli Atisanoe and Jesse Kuhaulua, during my 1989 trip to Tokyo.

in beside me, looking tough. Right before the picture was snapped, though, I suddenly raised my elbows to get some breathing room—moving these two big guys a few inches.

Everybody was laughing, and the photo itself made *Time* magazine. I loved that picture because I thought it was somewhat emblematic of what I was trying to do in Japan—get some breathing room for our companies to compete in the tough Japanese market.

The final highlight of that interesting trip came from our stop in Poland, where the president had made a historic visit in July—answering Gorbachev's diplomatic PR gains in the West with his own masterful swing through East Europe. My trip was meant to continue building on the foundation of engagement and cooperation the president's trip had set in motion.

On September 20, we started our Poland visit with a courtesy call at Belvedere Palace with General Wojciech Jaruzelski, the prime minister and first secretary of the Communist Party. Of all the meetings I have had with foreign leaders, not the ministers but the heads of state, this was no doubt the most

With Lech Walesa in my Washington, DC, office. He had a charisma that easily transcended our language barrier.

unpleasant. First, General Jarulzelski has to be the single-most unattractive man I've ever seen in my life. His general bearing was menacing, with his thick glasses accentuating his yellowish eyes.

When he shook hands with me, moreover, there was no expression on his face. Jaruzelski knew he was on his way out, so he had no reason to spoil us with pleasantries. He also understood the real purpose of our trip was to go down to Gdansk to meet with the Solidarity movement leader, Lech Walesa, so he clearly had no interest in a dialogue, either. He sat there and lectured us for about twenty minutes about Poland, how he saw things needed to be, and why Solidarity was foolish not to join the communists in a grand coalition. He had no interest in hearing my views, so it was a nasty meeting.

When Jarulzelski finally paused to take a breath, I thanked him for his time, got up, and left.

A light snow had fallen by the time we reached Gdansk, but Walesa's welcome was far warmer than Jaruzelski's. The city itself was dank, and we didn't know where the entrance to the building was where Walesa kept his modest office. When we found the door, there were no lightbulbs in the entryway, there was trash all over the floor, and as we started walking up the stairs, the stench of urine overtook us. In this primitive setting, the 1983 Nobel Peace Prize winner was upstairs plotting his run for the Polish presidency.

Reaching the second floor, Walesa greeted us effusively at the door with his assistant. We shook hands and then stepped in and stood in front of the Solidarity flag for a picture. Walesa was wearing a blue blazer, a white shirt and tie, blue jeans, and tennis shoes. He was the picture of modesty, and yet this mystical, charismatic figure was in the midst of transforming his proud nation.

On top of that, Walesa had us in stitches. Mind you, he couldn't speak a word of English—everything we said was through the translator. He referred to the Soviet KGB officers who were harassing him, and made a swatting gesture around his face as if they were bees buzzing around. Most of all, it was mesmerizing to hear him describe the challenges Poland was facing.

While we were in Warsaw, we stayed at a Marriott Hotel that happened to be the first joint American business venture in Poland. Officially, the property had not been opened to the public, so we were the first people to stay there. Because there were no telephones, we had to run a line just to our operations center. Then, because the telephone system was so unreliable in Poland at that time—for example, it could take all day to complete an international phone call—the staff had to open a line to Washington and keep it open for the duration of our stay.

As the Velvet Revolution took hold in Czechoslovakia, Solidarity consolidated its gains in Poland, and the East German regime teetered on the precipice of implosion that fall, I believe the fulcrum of global attention shifted away from Moscow and the charismatic Soviet leader, Gorbachev, in favor of the West—to Washington in particular. With the "fall" of the Berlin Wall in early November, followed by the historic U.S.-Soviet meetings just off the coast Malta in early December—the so-called "sea-sick summit"—the tectonic plates of geopolitics were shifting in freedom's favor.

Leading the way forward, the world was coming to realize, was a steady, sure, and visionary leader named George Bush. Looking back, some may consider the remarkable historic events of 1989 and conclude that their positive outcome was foreordained. They would be wrong. Chinese philosophy observes that the acme of skill is *not* fighting and winning 100 battles, but winning without having to fight at all. For the sake of history, the point has to be made that it took a leader of George Bush's qualities, with his quiet but firm purpose, to help drive and manage the pivotal events of 1989 in delicate but decisive ways.

We weren't out of the woods in terms of the Cold War and the superpower conflict that had dominated the global agenda for four decades. Indeed, the stakes as we entered 1990 were perhaps even higher, as it appeared that our twilight struggle against imperial communism might, at long last, be winnable. But we had made an important start, and—as others have noted—applied some grease to the skids on which the antidemocratic forces would eventually be slid from power.

Historically, the Department of Commerce has been viewed as a political stockyard where fund-raisers and friends of the president are rewarded with a Cabinet appointment. As such, the stature of the department has lagged—often seen as clumsy, second-rate bureaucracy made up of "trade policemen, textile-quota administrators, and zealous antidumping enforcers," to cite one of the less enthusiastic assessments.[1] In fact, even though the Commerce posting had helped launch him to the White House in 1928, Herbert Hoover stated that the department "in the Washington social scale was next to the bottom at the dinner table. . . ."[2]

Yet prior to my time, some of the most capable and respected businessmen of the twentieth century had taken the post, including President Hoover, my fellow Houstonian Jesse Jones (who in a previous post at RFC was called the "second most powerful man in Washington" after FDR), and another native New Yorker, Averill Harriman. Not bad company, and in fact as I entered the job I felt confident that we could be productive and get things done at Commerce that would make a substantive contribution to the country's well-being.

The early book on me among the Beltway chattering class was that my personal relationship with the president would help me pursue, and achieve, a more ambitious agenda than most of my predecessors. At the same time, the media speculated that my friendship with Treasury Secretary Nick Brady and Secretary of State Jimmy Baker could be put to an early test. "Treasury, State, and Commerce share responsibility for trade and economic issues, and the three departments have often squabbled over policy," one *Business Week* story noted. "But if the Three Amigos can work together, the Bush Administration could

---

1. *The Yankee Trader: Why presidents should stay close to their U.S. trade representatives*, Greg Rushford/Rushford Report, February 2003.

2. During my three years at the department, President Bush came to visit me a handful of times in my beautiful, big office. We were gazing at the portrait of Herbert Hoover hanging over the fireplace during one of these visits, when I casually—and mischievously—asked George if he realized that Hoover had, in fact, gone directly from the Department of Commerce to the White House. The president appeared somewhat startled by the question at first, then broke out laughing.

Napping aboard Air Force One *in early 1992. George Bush loved to catch members of his team sleeping and signed this photo, teasing: "Keep up the great work as Secretary of Commerce."*

wind up with one of the strongest international economic teams Washington has seen in years."[3]

Like the president, Jimmy and I are competitive by nature—and there certainly were a few sharp but friendly policy disagreements during my three years at Commerce. Usually, he would accuse me of wearing my "protectionist hat," and I would countercharge that he was stuck up in his "ivory tower" at Foggy

3. Richard Fly, Steven J. Dryden, and Mark Ivey, "Mosbacher: Not Just Another Commerce Secretary; If Appointed, He Could Parlay His Friendship with Bush into Power," *Business Week*, December 12, 1988, 32.

Bottom. After he appeared on the February 13, 1989 cover of *Time* magazine, with a caption that called him "a gentleman who hates to lose," Baker inscribed it to me, writing, "To Bob, who hates to lose even more."

Some have suggested that I was not shy about using my relationship with the president to get my way. My plea? Guilty as charged. There's no question that my friendship with the president benefited the department and enabled me, first, to pursue some of his big ideas—such as NAFTA—and second, to actually get some ambitious things done. That's not to say our department won every policy dispute we entered during my tenure, however.

Early in 1990, in fact, the president chose Carla Hills and the U.S. Trade Representative's office to take the lead in negotiating the new U.S.-USSR trade treaty he had announced with Mikhail Gorbachev at the historic Malta summit. For weeks, I had been arguing that Commerce should spearhead those talks, given the department's expertise both in promoting nonstrategic Soviet trade and in managing the export controls that deny the Soviets high technology that could be militarily useful. Also bolstering my point was historical precedent: the last time we sat down with the Soviets to discuss trade (which was during the Nixon Administration), Commerce Secretary Pete Peterson represented the United States.

But Carla Hills, who is a trade lawyer and a tough negotiator in her own right, made a strong case, too. Though the trade representative's office was one of the smallest agencies, and had not had much of a role in East-West trade, Carla already had a global agenda leading our government's efforts not only to help conclude the Uruguay Round of international trade negotiations (the General Agreement on Tariffs and Trade), but also for coordinating trade policies toward Europe and Japan.

So both agencies competed to head up these historic negotiations; but once the president decided that the United States Trade Representative (USTR) would take the lead, that ended the debate and we moved to the next issue. Happily, as this one incident illustrated, there was nowhere near the friction between Commerce team and USTR that many suspected might emerge. As she put it after the president made that decision in early 1990, "We have worked and will continue to work hand in glove with Bob Mosbacher and his staff in this and in all matters. They are as essential to this process as USTR."

Carla Hills was always as classy as she was tough.

Our Commerce team didn't win every debate, but we weren't timid, shrinking violets about arguing for our point of view. That's the way it should have been; and as the weeks and months passed, our department was starting to change the common perception of the Commerce Department as an irrelevant, monolithic collection of number crunchers.

Indeed, even some in the media began to notice that Commerce was on the frontlines of a number of significant issues, and that my longtime personal relationship with the president had made a difference. One *Wall Street Journal* story suggested that, as secretary, I wielded a "rare degree of power for a commerce chief." The piece also quoted a senior Reagan administration official saying: "At cabinet meetings, he's like the 800-pound gorilla."[4] That prompted my predecessor Pete Peterson to send me a note saying: "I've heard of oxymorons before, but 'powerful' commerce secretary tops them all."

Truth be told, I loved the job—and did feel we were able to make a positive contribution to the nation as the ebb of the Cold War, and the onset of globalization, brought a new sense of urgency to economic matters. As the *Journal* had noted, I did believe that any action that benefited U.S. business in an increasingly global economy also enhanced national security. And, yes, in this I was flexible. Where free trade benefited U.S. industry, I was a free trader. Where other industries were helped by a modicum of government assistance, I was happy to use whatever authority and influence I had to intervene, and give them a friendly push.

Of course, the fact that George Bush was one of two presidents elected to serve a full term without party control in either house of Congress necessitated that his administration cultivate good relationships on the other side of the political aisle if we wanted to get progress on key issues. For example, Secretary of State Jimmy Baker worked effectively with Democratic leaders to strike a bipartisan consensus on our policy toward the Contras in Nicaragua even before the 1989 inaugural. In my case, I made sure to reach out socially and otherwise to congressional Democrats such as Representative John Dingell of Michigan, who ran the powerful House Commerce Committee and with whom I enjoyed a great friendship, as well as my fellow Texan Lloyd Bentsen.

Senator Fritz Hollings from South Carolina was another Democrat I enjoyed. He could be tough, but we got along well. In fact, this might be heretical to some Republicans, but at one point I went down to South Carolina to attend a fund-raiser for him. The Republican in that race didn't have a chance; and since Fritz chaired the Senate's Commerce Committee, it was an easy way for me to help strengthen our relations on Capitol Hill.

4. Peter Truell, "Bob Mosbacher Wields Rare Degree of Power For a Commerce Chief," *Wall Street Journal*, September 1, 1989.

Meeting with several members of the Massachusetts congressional delegation, led by Senators Kennedy (to my left) and John Kerry (to my right), about an economic development grant for a shipyard in Quincy. We worked hard to address as many requests as we could from Members of Congress.

Anyway, Hollings was a tough old goat, and often called me "General Mosbacher." "General Mosbacher," he would say in his thick low-country drawl, "how are you going to handle this problem?" He was a real southern gent.

One Democrat I didn't get along well with was Paul Sarbanes from Maryland. He was a prickly individual not given to social banter; and I was crossing my fingers many years later, in 2005, when my son Rob had to go before Sarbanes after President George W. Bush nominated Rob to lead the Overseas Private Investment Corporation.

Of course, I also enjoyed the Republicans with whom I worked. I remember at a holiday party one year, where I had been talked into playing Santa—costume and all—the venerable senator from South Carolina, Strom Thurmond, somehow ended up on my lap. I think I had already enjoyed a glass or two of holiday cheer—and I know darn well the senator, then ninety-eight years young or so, had helped himself to several refreshments as well.

After he landed with a thud, I asked him the only question that made sense at the time: "What do you want for Christmas, little boy?"

No question, my background and experiences as a businessman directly influenced how I approached my job as secretary. I have been a proud Republican all of my adult life, and I believe in the fundamental tenets of my party. But as secretary, I was even more interested in achieving results without ever abandoning our most basic principles.

For example, one of the projects we inherited from the Reagan administration involved a new weather satellite we were building with Ford aerospace. We were paying for it at Commerce, and once it was completed NASA would put it up into orbit.

One day, I asked for a status report on the project, and the folks from the weather bureau at NOAA kept saying, "No problem, Mr. Secretary. We've got it under control. Don't worry."

That fervent bit of reassuring notwithstanding, I've been in this world long enough to know that when somebody hands me a line like that, there's usually something wrong. When you get the feeling that something is wrong, I have learned, you dig harder.

What I had to pull out of these bureaucrats—with help from one of my closest and best aides, Preston Moore—was the fact that NOAA was almost two years behind getting the satellite up. Not only that, it was also way over budget.

Once I got my arms wrapped around the problem, I called the NOAA people back in and told them, "We're going to do something about this right now." They were perplexed that I could get so upset, but we were talking about billions of dollars, to say nothing of these important new weather satellites that could help save lives. (These satellites were a key step toward establishing the weather warning systems that farmers, mariners, and transportation officials rely on today.)

So I reached out to Bernie Schwartz, a great businessman who built up the Loral Corporation and had just acquired Ford Aerospace. Bernie was head of the whole thing, so I asked him to come see me. As the meeting in my spacious office got under way, Bernie's right-hand man started explaining how they were going to fix the problem. "We've got this going there, and we're doing this here," he explained.

Then, one of our lead guys from NOAA piped up, agreeing with the Ford man—"Yes, that's right, we're doing this and that together, and making good progress."

After a few minutes of this, I spoke up and said, "Thank you, gentlemen, for that presentation. Now if you wouldn't mind excusing yourselves so Bernie and I could visit in private for a moment."

One of the NOAA guys nervously spoke up, "But we would be happy to address any concerns. . . ."

I cut him off right there, looked him in his eyes, and gesturing to the door said, "Do you understand?"

They left.

As soon as the door closed, I turned to Bernie. "We've got to get this solved. We've got to get that satellite up. You've got to tell me precisely when you can do it, and how much it's going to cost."

Bernie had clearly been studying the problem, and immediately and confidently replied: "We can do it in three months."

"Great. Now how much are we talking about costs?"

"Three hundred million."

Now, that sounds like a ton of money, but considering the billions we had been wasting in the previous two years it was a bargain.

"Okay, Bernie," I replied, "but you realize if we don't get it done this time I'm going to have to let the relevant congressional leaders know what is happening. We're going to have to lay it all out for them, and there would no doubt be hearings. And to be clear, I'm not going to take the rap for this. So are you sure you can meet these terms?"

Bernie assured me he could, so we shook hands on the deal—and, happily, he held up his end of the bargain. I'm also happy to say we're friends to this day, which might strike some as odd considering he is a Democrat. But what you learn in the business world is not only to focus on results, but also the manner in which you conduct yourself. You don't get far in business unless you do what you say will get done—and treat your word as your bond.

So, yes, at times I had a bit of a culture clash with the career bureaucrats at the department, who were all fine people, but used to doing business a different way. That satellite project had become a typical Washington-style boondoggle, where the spending went on, and on, and on. We never thought there was any illegality involved, but all these years later I am still struck how the NOAA people didn't want to discuss the problem.

This particular episode exposed the fact that there was tremendous waste within NOAA, so I resurrected a civilian committee within Commerce that had long since been dormant to take a look at the agency's practices. Bill Carl, who knew boats as port chairman from Corpus Christi, served as a cochair along with John Bookout, the formidable head of Shell Oil who was likewise involved in their considerable transportation operations.

Once the rest of the committee was on board, they held a few hearings and about five months later prepared to issue their report. One night, I got a call from one of our chairs saying, "You're probably not going to like what we are ready to release in this report."

I asked for a synopsis, and he continued, "We think NOAA ought to get rid of a lot of their vessels and outsource a lot of their operations. You could halve the costs, and realize twice the efficiency."

I said, "No, if that's what you find, then publish it. Don't worry about me."

The truth is I was delighted with their findings, and suspected all along that that is what might be the result of the committee's study. So they went public, and the media paid some attention to it—giving it a modest splash.

Almost as soon as the report was released, however, every congressman whose district would be impacted by the proposed cutbacks—such as the elimination of a weather station—was against it. So they started fighting us.

There's an old saying that any government who robs Peter to pay Paul can count on the support of Paul every time; and frankly, I found this callous approach to how our public money is spent to be one of the most disappointing aspects to my time at Commerce. I always tried to view the spending of the department's money as if I was spending my own, and never could get used to the outright waste.

George Bush was no different. Early on in his administration—in an effort to show Congress, by example, that it was possible to cut government spending—President Bush challenged all of us who ran the departments to cut our budgets by 8 percent. Everybody said, "Yes, sir," but the truth is most did not take his instruction seriously.

Chalk it up to naiveté perhaps, or the fact that I had run a business and sat on the boards of others businesses, but when the head man says "cut the budget," you better damn well cut the budget—or start looking for new work.

So I went back to the department, and at one of our infamous Saturday morning meetings I reported the challenge given to us by the president. "We're going to have to cut our budget, and I would appreciate if you gave me your ideas how we can do it in the next two weeks."

Two weeks came and went with little in the way of progress, so at the next meeting I said, "You know you had two weeks to get me your ideas, and that's it—so get me your memos this week." Still, nothing happened, so at the very next meeting I said, "You all won't have to worry about it anymore. We'll be cutting your budget for you in my office, and we'll be cutting it by ten percent—not eight. So don't worry your pretty little heads about this anymore."

The response was almost deafening. "Oh no, we can do it Mr. Secretary—please," they pleaded. So I relented. "Okay, one more week . . . *but no more.*" They continued to kick and scream, but fortunately I had Preston Moore and Tom Collamore in my office to bear the brunt of these pleadings. "Tell the secretary this is the most important agency, or program, in the department—and we can't cut it," they would tell Preston. "The secretary cares too much about this," they urgently petitioned Collamore.

In the end, most of my bureau heads actually did as the president and I had asked, and none other than Dick Darman—the Office and Management Bureau chief, with whom I did not have the warmest of relationships—recognized later that Commerce was the only department to meet the president's challenge.

There was a key lesson in this experience for anyone who goes to Washington to serve in an agency, much less lead one. Nothing threatens a bureaucrat more than to cut their funding. It's the source of their power and, many maintain, their sense of self-worth. Inside the Beltway, real power comes from control—controlling a budget, controlling an area of policy-making. That's why most turf wars happen.

Meanwhile, as eventful as 1989 proved to be—highlighted by the Tiananmen Square uprising at one end of the spectrum, and the fall of the Berlin Wall on the other—1990 proved to be no less dramatic. A revolution of hope was spreading like wildfire throughout East and Central Europe; and everyday, the newspapers and TV reports seemed to carry news of some historic importance. If the Cold War had, in essence, frozen old methods and attitudes in place, the political chain reaction unfolding before our eyes in Europe quickly put the thaw to those societies long immobilized by the Cold War stalemate.

Having already had the chance to meet one of the leading revolutionaries of the time, Lech Walesa, I was also keen to size up the soft-spoken playwright and coauthor of the peaceful change in Europe, the new Czechoslovakian president, Vaclav Havel, at a White House dinner on February 20. Those were heady days of global transformation, and yet Havel's gentle demeanor completely disarmed me. How could a man so unassuming break the iron grasp of the Soviet Union?

Our conversations at the White House were encouraging enough that, six days later, I traveled to Prague to follow up on our discussions with the new Czech government. Ambassador Shirley Temple Black—perhaps THE most famous child actress in the world during my childhood who by then was also a respected diplomat—met me at the airport, and we drove together to the Embassy. During our ride, I confessed to Shirley that in the late 1930s when I was visiting Los Angeles with Pop, somebody at one of the studios tried to set me up on a blind date with her. I didn't go, I confided to Shirley, because I was only eleven or twelve years old, and was still too shy. "I must admit that not too many years later I thoroughly overcame any lingering shyness," I added. We enjoyed a good laugh over that.

From there, it was on to Germany in March, where the changes were even more pronounced. I had gone to Germany in October of 1989, and while the signs of political ferment at that historic time permeated the country, even then—just a few weeks before the Berlin Wall "fell"—no one dared publicly speak of its waning relevance.

What a big difference those five months made. There was an entirely different feeling in Germany—one of overriding excitement and optimism. Elsewhere, Europeans were stunned at the pace of events. Some were even openly questioning the wisdom of the drive being led by the president and Chancellor Kohl toward Germany's unification. In due course, Margaret Thatcher, Francois Mitterrand, and Gorbachev—three tough adversaries—would voice alarm at the prospect of a united Germany. To them, it was a matter of heeding the lessons of World War I and II: Germany could not be trusted.

George Bush disagreed strongly with this view. He felt the German people had suffered enough for the sins of the Third Reich; and besides, it was the stated objective of American foreign policy to see German unification restored. Early on, shortly after taking office, the president presciently predicted to our widely admired ambassador in Bonn, Vernon Walters, "I am convinced something will happen in Germany on my watch."

When events began to move, our commander-in-chief was ready to work—closely, immediately—with Kohl to secure Germany's unification within NATO.

George has since described the unification of Germany as the single-most important event to transpire during his presidency; and to be sure, it was one of his finest hours. The stakes couldn't have been higher, and George Bush's instincts, his gut, were dead-on accurate. It was presidential leadership at its finest to see him work with such strong-minded leaders as Thatcher and Mitterrand to assuage their concerns and bring them around to his position.

The president did the same during his May 1990 summit with Gorbachev in Washington, convincing the Soviet leader to permit that the Germans have the right of self-determination. East Germany, of course, had long been the crown jewel of the Warsaw Pact, so it was a stunning act of political courage by Gorbachev, one that affirmed Mikhail's commitment to his perestroika and glasnost programs of openness and reform.

In an interesting aside from that DC summit, I was mildly complaining to President Gorbachev that American companies were having a hard time gaining access to the USSR market because of the various layers of government and slow-moving bureaucrats in the centralized Soviet system. His reply caught me flat-footed. "You should know all about red tape," came his rejoinder through his interpreter, "you invented it." He was right . . . somewhat. The Commerce Department was one of the very first organizations to find a systematic use for red tape, employing it in the early days of the patent and trademark office as a way of marking the patents.

That incident showed how Gorbachev always did his homework; but as we discovered that fall, even the charismatic and brilliant leader was no match for the massive challenge he faced in trying to help the Soviet economy make the transition to a modern, market-driven economic engine capable of creating new businesses and new jobs.

Technically, our Moscow trip in early September 1990 was a "Presidential Development Mission," and traveling with me aboard the Air Force Boeing 707 bound for Moscow was a delegation of twenty American business leaders from various industries. As a result of their consultations during the May summit in DC, the president had, in turn, tasked me with finding a representative group of senior business leaders who could offer advice to Gorbachev as he attempted the Herculean feat of restructuring the USSR's moribund economy.

Our only stop on the way to Moscow was the U.S. Embassy in Helsinki, where President Bush had suggested he brief us on his way home from his hastily arranged one-day summit meeting with Gorbachev. That meeting, the second summit between the two leaders in 1990, was called in the aftermath of the Iraqi invasion of Kuwait as the president started to forge an unprecedented coalition to reverse that unprovoked aggression. The president understood the impact of the world community seeing the United States and its erstwhile superpower rival working on the same side against Saddam Hussein.

Arriving in Helsinki, we assembled at Ambassador John Weinmann's residence where the president emphasized that both he and Gorbachev had high hopes for our visit—and that time was of the essence. Despite a record wheat harvest that summer, he reported, no bread was available in Moscow. The Soviet economy was deteriorating daily, but he stressed that Gorbachev was not asking for direct government aid. Rather, he preferred to attract investment from the private sector, and considered American technology and management skills critical to his country's success.

The Soviets had a long way to go before they understood the ins and outs of a market economy, President Bush summarized, but he also noted how remarkable it was to hear a Soviet leader express such interest in the work of Adam Smith.

As our presidential briefing concluded, with the president heading back to Washington, I was walking with a number of these high-level American business executives to the cars when a voice came over the loudspeaker. "Secretary Mosbacher, just a moment," I heard the familiar voice say. I stopped what I was doing and directed my attention to the platform from which he had been speaking. Then, with a deadpan expression on his face, the president of the United States said: "Mosbacher, don't screw it up!"

I could see the teasing glint in my president's eye, but it wasn't clear if anyone else caught on.

Following the briefing, the president, President Gorbachev, and the rest of us were all heading straight for the airport at the same time. At one point, we noticed that our motorcade was passing Gorbachev's entourage on the far side of the highway. I remember these important American CEOs cheering rowdily, urging our driver to step on the gas and pass Gorby—which he proceeded to do, to the great delight of all.

If we beat Gorbachev to the airport, though, we had not beaten the Germans or the Japanese to Moscow—where companies from both countries were already quite active and visible.

We landed in Moscow after midnight on Sunday and jumped the next day into a very busy four-day schedule of meetings. Our agenda included a one-day excursion to Leningrad, and sessions with radical reformers such as Moscow's mayor, Gavril Popov; the Soviet Union's embattled Prime Minister, Nikolai Ryzhkov; and finally, Gorbachev. Interestingly, each of the leaders we consulted acknowledged that the USSR was in trouble, and that the crisis could be resolved only by sweeping changes. The direction was clear to all—the Soviet Union had to move from a controlled, command economy to a free and open system driven by market forces.

My friend Lod Cook, the chairman of Arco, observed at one point: "It's incredible to hear words like markets, profits, capital, and stocks repeated over and over in the halls of the Kremlin." Another friend, Don Marron, then of Paine Webber, later reported that one of the key Soviet advisors pulled him

Posing with the delegation of American business leaders I took to Moscow in September 1990.

aside and, in a hushed whisper, asked him to explain the difference between profit, revenue, and income.

The photos we had seen of Russians waiting in long lines to buy whatever food and other daily necessities they could find didn't prepare us for the shock of seeing it firsthand; and given the dire conditions we saw, many of my traveling companions felt the price of entry into the Soviet market was lower than it would ever be again.

But there were risks as well. During our first day, we joined the head of Pepsi Cola, Don Kendall, as he opened the first Pizza Hut in Moscow. I later learned that this same restaurant was later temporarily shut down, allegedly for health violations, in a power struggle between the radical Moscow City Council and the conservative District Council. Pizza Hut's problems underlined for us all just how confusing the political situation was in the USSR. At practically every step during our trip, I reminded our Soviet contacts of the obstacles that foreign investors face.

The highlight of our trip came on the final day, when we met for two hours with Gorbachev. Joining us were Jim Baker and his Soviet counterpart, Foreign Minister Eduard Shevardnadze. As we grappled with the issues, Gorbachev

Meeting Soviet President Mikhail Gorbachev in Moscow in September of 1990, with Jimmy Baker looking on.

encouraged a give-and-take, and his sense of humor flashed easily and often. He recognized that he had to start moving the Soviet empire toward a market economy, but at the same time he was determined to proceed cautiously. "To rush is to be irresponsible," he said at one point.

Perhaps as encouraging as anything I heard during that trip, I later learned that Soviet managers had left their factories and traveled to Moscow on over-night trains from Minsk, Lithuania, and as far away as the Kamchatka Peninsula on the Bering Sea. The sheer size of the turnout showed me that these soviet businessmen were eager to transform their state-run "companies" into efficient, modern enterprises.

Sadly, the optimism of that trip would soon give way to the grim reality that old habits and attitudes would indeed be tough to change. For example, I remember seeing these new kiosks they opened on Moscow street corners—with umbrellas, like the hot dog street vendors in New York. Those Moscow vendors were selling bananas and other fresh fruit from the West, and they were so popular you usually saw a line of people waiting. It was kind of exciting to see when I first encountered it, but when I went back the next time the vendors were gone.

I asked one of our embassy people, "What happened here? Did they make so much money they went into early retirement?" The guy I was with said, "No, they got shut down because 'some people' didn't think it was fair that these vendors were making a profit."

There was a genuine culture shock that came in the form of instilling a work ethic, and accepting the idea of profiting from your labors. Privately, I made a number of mental notes about my experiences in the Soviet Union, which only hardened my resolve never to do any business there in the region myself.

Happily, our efforts to make headway in Asia and the rest of the world proved less frustrating.

March of 1990 found me back to my old tricks—harassing my main nemesis Japan for more access to their markets. I had a chance to petition Prime Minister Kaifu during the hastily arranged mini-summit President Bush and he conducted in Palm Springs early in the month. Over the course of a nice dinner with President Ford, the Bushes, the Kaifus, and other VIPs at Walter and Lee Annenberg's home—as well as a round of golf at the Annenberg's Sunnyland estate—the president and I played good cop/bad cop, using a mixture of charm and straight talk to probe the Japanese leader for signs of openness.

Then on March 12, it was back to Tokyo for my second visit—to maintain the momentum the Palm Springs summit had initiated, and keep up the pressure. By then, I felt strongly that Japan's trade surpluses had "achieved a semi-permanent status" as I described it; and the two countries had agreed to address problems such as price collusion and other barriers to competition through a series of trade talks known as the "Structural Impediments Initiative."

During these talks, I detected a noticeable change in Japan's attitude since my visit the previous September. There were still plenty of hurdles for us to clear, and challenges to real progress, but I was no longer getting the same speech at every meeting. There were even differences of opinion among some Japanese leaders—which my team and I attributed to the fact that our discussions were progressing to a new level of seriousness.

I saw even more encouraging signs of economic growth that summer during a visit to Brazil and Chile. Already, the Brady Plan and a wave of privatization and other economic reforms had unleashed a surge of economic activity—and a growing sense of possibility to our south. During his visit to Washington in January of 1990, the young Brazilian president, Ferdinand de Collor, had brought a group of top Brazilian business leaders, and invited me to conduct a reciprocal visit that summer. As Brazil is Latin America's largest market, I instantly took President Collor up on his invitation. We subsequently added Chile to the itinerary, as it was perhaps the most modernized economy in Latin America at the time—and still is.

In tow with us as we set out on June 16 were nine U.S. corporate chiefs— most with operations in Brazil. During our three-day stop in Brazil, we got a firsthand look at the terrific challenge the Brazilians faced in radically restructuring an economy saddled by sky-high inflation and crippling debt. Then it was on to Chile, which was just emerging from the seventeen-year dictatorship of General Augusto Pinochet.

This was the fifth time in less than a year that I had invited business leaders to join me on my trade missions—trying to make sure they received fair treatment as bidders for big-ticket foreign contracts. Before then, it usually fell to U.S. state governors to take executives abroad in such a fashion. In contrast, most of our foreign competitors had long engaged in this practice of bringing corporate executives on trade and commerce missions.

July of 1990 brought a very special kind of homecoming, as the president decided to host the G-7 Economic Summit in our hometown, Houston. In between all of the official ceremonies, I decided to conduct a little informal diplomacy with Trade Ministers Muto, Helmut Hausmann, and Franz Andriessen from, respectively, Japan, West Germany, and the European Community. To help add to the authentic Houston flavor of our meetings, I decided to host a dinner that Saturday, July 7, for my honored guests at a restaurant called the Cadillac Bar.

I always enjoy going to this particular establishment because of its low-key, totally unpretentious atmosphere and the terrific Tex-Mex food. Of course, the Cadillac Bar was also famous, or maybe infamous, for the Tequila Shooter Girls who patrolled the dining room looking for patrons ready to let their hair down with a shot of tequila. These were not your usual shots dispensed by shot glass, mind you. If you ordered a shot at the Cadillac, the girls would walk up behind you, grab your forehead, yank your head back, and pour a healthy dose of Mexico's finest down your throat right out of the bottle. Then depending on how mischievous they were, they might spin you around or slap you on the forehead—as if the hooch alone wouldn't be disorienting enough.

When the president heard where I was planning to take my guests, he gave me a simple instruction: "Don't start World War III."

The Japanese trade minister, Kabun Muto, had really gotten into the spirit of the summit by turning out in full cowboy regalia—the hat, the shirt, the boots, the works. The other guests were in fine form, too, and everything was going smoothly when the shooter girls suddenly materialized—even though we had asked them to steer clear of our room. Next thing I know, they're getting ready to grab Europe's top trade man by the forehead and pull his head back for a shot of tequila. I remember thinking, "Oh my God, that WILL start World War III."

Fortunately, the girls were a little slow on the draw that day (but I wasn't) and an international incident was narrowly averted.

Another uncommon experience from the annals of personal diplomacy took place later that month in Thailand. I had already made productive stops in Hong Kong, Singapore, Indonesia, and Kuala Lampur in Malaysia, and was visiting Prime Minister Chatichai Choonhavan in Bangkok when he spontaneously insisted we play a quick game of golf. I protested, saying it had been too long since I had played, and besides that I didn't have the right clothes—but the prime minister was undeterred and assured me they could furnish everything I needed.

Nothing was unusual until I reached the practice tee to hit a few practice shots. As I was preparing to warm up, however, two attractive young ladies approached me—one with a parasol. When I bent down to tee up my first ball, the second young lady beat me to it—and proceeded to tee up every ball I needed.

Then as we walked to the first tee, the other young lady walked next to me, holding the parasol over my head so I wouldn't get too much sun. They were young and attractive ladies, but I soon discovered the Prime Minister's "caddies" were even lovelier. *It's good to be the king*, I thought, as my host arrived at the first tee.

During the fall of 1990, as he was simultaneously grappling with Saddam Hussein's invasion into Kuwait, the president and his negotiating team led by John Sununu, Dick Darman, and Nick Brady made a last-ditch effort to strike a budget deal with the congressional Democrats. All year long, the budget talks had provided a flash point for partisan acrimony, but a last-minute agreement was struck before the Fiscal Year elapsed that included Medicare cuts and spending curbs, as well as increased gasoline, tobacco, and alcohol tax increases—but, importantly, no income tax rate increase. It wasn't perfect, but it would meet the president's goal of dramatically improving the federal government's fiscal health.

As if to underscore the fairness of the plan, both conservatives and liberals in the House of Representatives revolted against their leaders and voted the bill down on October 6—resulting in a brief shutdown of the government excluding essential services. The bill that finally passed later that month, and the president signed on November 5, was not as good. The Medicare cuts and gas

As the sun set on the Cold War, it dawned for a new era of globalization. Meetings like this with Thai Prime Minister Chatichai Choonhavan in Bangkok made sure America was able to compete and win in the world market.

tax increases were smaller, and the very top income tax rate was eased up from 28 to 31 percent.

Most importantly, the package would reduce the deficit by $492 billion over five years and put tough new restrictions on spending.

Compromise tends to be a dirty word in many political circles these days, but the truth is: in 1990, as in every other year of his presidency, George Bush didn't have many attractive options if he wanted to get something done. Domestic policy is always more complicated and frustrating for a president than foreign policy, because on domestic policy you cannot act without first consulting your 535 "partners" on Capitol Hill who have strong opinions and demanding constituencies of their own. From 1989 to 1993, the Democrats controlled both chambers of Congress, a political reality that was reflected in the landmark pieces of legislation that did get passed on George's watch, such as the Americans with Disabilities Act and the Clean Air Act.

Would I add the 1990 budget to that list? Yes, I would. For one thing, it was the largest single deficit reduction package ever enacted—including the much-lauded budget agreements reached under President Clinton. Just as important, however, were the unprecedented spending caps that were placed on discretionary spending and the "pay as you go" discipline that would be enforced on all future tax cuts and entitlement increases.

Lost on most observers then, or since, was the fact that the deal laid the foundation for the prosperity of the 1990s. What mattered to most in Washington, naturally, was the "gotcha" politics of the deal—the fact that the deal constituted a violation of the "Read my lips" pledge.

The acrimony of the atmosphere in Washington was such that my late October road show to start touting the North American Free Trade Agreement with our Mexican partners came as a welcome relief. On Monday, October 22, Jaime Serra Puche and I, together with key team members, traveled to Dallas and Houston to launch what we called our "Partnership for Growth Week." The four days that followed passed in a blur of speeches and media interviews in San Antonio, New York City, Chicago, and Los Angeles.

Naturally, we were making this trip to the major media markets to make the point together that the agreement we were proposing would build up both the Mexican and American economies. At the time, Mexico was our third-largest trading partner, with $1 billion in trade in 1989. Every time a "maquiladora" (or Mexican corporation with special foreign investment and customs privileges) was set up in Mexico, I argued, it created jobs in the United States. In fact, a study by the Federal Reserve Board in Dallas released around that time estimated that 41,000 jobs had already been created in the United States because of the various maquiladoras.

During our tour, we also argued that free-trade agreement would take a lot of pressure off migrant workers and immigration coming into the United States as the Mexican economy started to grow and jobs became more plentiful. Finally, we made the point that NAFTA would make our countries more competitive in an increasingly interconnected global economy.

I was particularly pleased and proud that we started our U.S. tour in Texas—the front line with respect to Mexico. We knew we were embarking on a process that would take at least two years, maybe more, to complete, but I was particularly happy to know the benefits the deal would bring to Texas in particular . . . if we were successful. That first media blitz was well received, but in a way we knew our work was only just beginning. Still, it was exhilarating to see so much hard work begin to pay off.

The fall of 1990 also stands out in my memory for several family-related developments. First came a speech I made to the American Stock Exchange at the Mayflower Hotel in Washington. If I had to pick the single most poignant moment as Secretary of Commerce, that October day in our nation's capital might have been it. It had been some eighty years since Pop joined the Curb Market, seventy years since they moved inside, and about four decades since they changed the exchange's name to the AMEX—not long before Pop gave up his seat. It touched me deeply to hear many members detail how Pop had been an important and respected figure for much of their history. That afternoon, I confessed that the main reason I was standing there was directly attributable to the lessons that Pop had taught me not just about business, but about life itself.

Another one of the great family highlights from my time in Washington came when my son, Rob, earned the endorsement of the *Dallas Morning News*—one of the most respected newspapers not just in Texas, but in the country in my view—in his campaign for Texas lieutenant governor. At thirty-nine years of age, Rob had done a fantastic job of building a statewide campaign against a tough opponent—Bob Bullock, who had served sixteen years as the state's chief tax collector and financial officer.

Rob and Bob were running to succeed a true Texas legend, Lietutenant Governor Bill Hobby, who had presided over the Texas Senate for eighteen years. At least in the *Morning News'* view (a view that I shared), Rob had successfully presented himself as an outsider with new ideas while labeling Bullock the ultimate insider.

The paper said the following in their October 15 endorsement:

> At a time when Texas must look to the demands of the 21st century,
> Rob Mosbacher is the better choice to begin laying a forward-looking
> foundation for the state. He has solid proposals for economic development,
> job creation, minority entrepreneurship, government streamlining,
> education and ethics reform. Mr. Mosbacher called for management audits
> of every state agency long before Mr. Bullock jumped on that bandwagon.
> He has the capacity to bring efficiencies to state government, including
> plans for an informal cabinet-like structure so that heads of agencies will
> begin talking to one another. Additionally, Mr. Mosbacher is a man with a
> social conscience, the kind of new, young leader the state needs to cultivate.

Talk about proud fathers. My heart nearly burst out of my chest when I read this glowing summation of my fine son. Just as nice was what our First Lady, Barbara Bush, said two weeks later out on the stump with Rob in Dallas: "I think Texas needs a successful businessman who could cope, and . . . I can't think of anybody that could bring about better changes. . . ."

While Rob was working his heart out, and getting some high-powered help, I learned that not everyone was so supportive. While attending a fund-raiser in England at Blenheim Palace, I was visiting with a group that included Oscar and Lynn Wyatt, when Oscar started mouthing off how he was backing Bullock—with whom he had long been associated as a financial backer. As I listened to Oscar describe the race in the most slanted of ways, however, I was furious and felt insulted.

"Come on outside so we can settle this right now," I suggested to Oscar. I wanted to beat the daylights out of him.

Oscar quickly assessed the situation, which was escalating by the second, and leaned in and gave me a kiss smack on the lips. I just broke up. He had defused the situation and saved a friendship.

Back home, meanwhile, the Republican at the head of the Texas ticket, my friend Clayton Williams, was having a tougher time. He had started off his gubernatorial campaign against Ann Richards, the state treasurer, and had amassed a nineteen-point lead when his good ol' boy West Texas humor got him in trouble—and his lead started to evaporate. When a reporter asked him a question about the foggy weather, for example, "Claytie" likened it to rape: "It it's inevitable, just relax and enjoy it." That comment hurt him badly, particularly with women, who turned out to be a key part of Ann Richards' winning coalition.

Then after a televised debate with Richards, Claytie refused to shake hands. Richards seized upon this slight and used it to gently skewer Williams for the remainder of the campaign. In the end, our statewide GOP standard bearer suffered death by a thousand clever cuts. Never let it be said Ann Richards wasn't a shrewd politician.

Even though the candidates for Texas governor and lieutenant governor in each political party campaign separately—not part of a unified ticket—there is no question that Claytie's ongoing problems had created a downdraft on Rob's campaign. He ended up losing by seven points, and yet the day I spent campaigning with him in Tyler, Waco, and Houston the day before Election Day was one of my proudest moments as a father. I saw my son fighting for his beliefs, giving it his all, and handling himself with class.

While I had great respect and affection for Lieutenant Governor Bullock, I naturally felt then, and still do now, as if the better man lost that day in 1990. Undeterred, and true to form, Rob picked himself up and went on to find other positive ways to serve his state, his community, and eventually his country too.

Finally, two days after that tough election loss for our family, we got a shot in the arm when the news arrived that my daughter Kathi had eloped with a young man, Walter Cox, who she had been dating for some time. Of course, I had also eloped with Jane back in 1948, but the difference was that Kathi did not go to northern Georgia like I had—but to Austria instead.

Who says kids don't possess an amazing capacity to one-up their parents?

Chapter 19   ACTIONS, NOT JUST WORDS

As a mild tropical nightfall fell kindly and gently across Caracas, Venezuela, I was capping a full day of meetings and speeches by leading an American trade delegation over to Miraflores Palace for a night meeting with President Carlos Andres Perez. Built before the turn of the century and long the home of the Venezuelan president, Miraflores was a charming executive mansion. Like our own White House, it is smallish but dignified, perched upon a modest bluff overlooking the Caracas Valley below. Inside, the *palacio* showcases national treasures from furniture, to murals, to the works of classic Venezuelan painters such as Arturo Michelena, Cristobal Mendoza, Martín Tovar y Tovar, and Tito Salas.

Even though it was always among the most blessed South American countries in terms of natural resources—particularly oil—Venezuela had struggled to manage that wealth. During the drive into Caracas from the airport, I saw how the hillsides were choked with shantytowns and thousands of shacks—their rusty, worn tin roofs dully reflecting the sun.

Now in his second stint as president, Perez was under public fire stemming from the economic difficulties his nation faced. Yet, though he was under political siege, so much so that he would be forced to survive two coup attempts the following year, his genial demeanor prevailed during our private meeting in his office. Next door, our delegation and the Venezuelan trade minister waited in the large and ornate Salon de Espejos.

Not long into my private meeting with President Perez, one of his aides silently, efficiently appeared in the room and handed him a note—which Perez, somewhat irritated at the interruption, placed in his lap without reading. We continued our conversation; but after a few minutes the aide returned, whispered somewhat urgently in Perez's ear, and gestured to the unread note in his lap.

Perez paused to take up the small card, and studied its contents. His demeanor, which had been friendly and warm, took on a more sober, somber visage. Gone was the easy smile.

"Mr. Secretary," Perez finally said, "your government has initiated the air campaign against Iraq. The United States is at war."

I had known the war was coming—we all did. George Bush had been very up front with the American people, with Iraq, and the global community that Saddam Hussein's unprovoked aggression against Kuwait would not be permitted to stand. The only question in mid-January 1991 was the precise hour when Operation Desert Shield to defend the rest of Arabian peninsula would became Operation Desert Storm to liberate Kuwait.

Still, the news that we had indeed crossed that dangerous rubicon—that a state of war now existed—startled me. It was hard to believe Saddam had so misjudged the United States, much less his chances to prevail. Moreover, it saddened me to recognize that many lives would be lost on both sides of the conflict—including innocent victims.

Given the gravity of the situation, I felt compelled to express my strongly felt belief that Kuwait must be liberated, and Saddam not permitted to profit from his reckless disregard for the rule of international law. "Iraq's aggression against a free nation should be unacceptable to every free nation," I emphatically told Perez. "I can assure you we take this situation very, very seriously."

"You're right," Perez quickly added, without hesitation. "Saddam must exit Kuwait." Later that night, Perez took to the Venezuelan airwaves to offer his full support for the coalition's efforts in Desert Storm. What a stark contrast that memory presents in light of today's regrettable leadership in Caracas, and the state of relations between our two nations today.

I returned to Washington the following afternoon, heading straight from the airport to the White House for the administration's first meeting as a wartime Cabinet. Secretary Cheney and General Colin Powell, the chairman of the joint chiefs, had already briefed the public about our initial, encouraging success; and the president had already briefed congressional leaders that morning. What was most striking to me about that afternoon Cabinet session was not the content of our discussion—the president was not going to get into operational specifics—but the calm, determined manner I saw my friend demonstrate as the weight of the world was placed squarely on his shoulders.

In my view, January 1991 was perhaps the most dramatic month official Washington had seen since the fall of Saigon in April of 1975. America was once again at war, our economy was struggling, and the streets of Washington were filled with demonstrators beating drums and chanting their ominous predictions about "50,000 war dead." The stakes could hardly have been higher for the administration.

There had been a strenuous public debate leading up to Desert Storm, and occasionally someone on either side would say something sensationalistic or

Surveying the devastation of the Kuwaiti oil fires in the wake of Desert Storm with Congressman Bob Dornan from California and the Kuwaiti Ambassador to the United States, Sheikh Saud Nasir al-Sabah, in March of 1991. Georgette is to my left.

inflammatory. Most disturbing of all to me, however, was the meddling of an old Texas friend, Oscar Wyatt, who had made a ton of money on oil deals with the Iraqi government. Accompanied by John Connally, Wyatt defied the White House and U.S. policy by traveling to Baghdad before the war—to try and win the release of the American and British hostages being held at the time. Instead, Oscar and Connally were used for enemy propaganda purposes by Saddam and came home empty-handed.

Unfortunately, even after we soundly defeated Iraq in 1991, Oscar remained dedicated to his relationship with Saddam. In October of 2007, he pleaded guilty and was imprisoned for paying a $200,000 kickback to Saddam Hussein in 2001—in clear violation of the United Nations' Oil for Food program. As shameful as that was, it was Oscar's behavior during a risky time for our troops in 1991 that I never forgot. In fact, at a State Department reception a few years ago, Oscar came up to a group of us who stood there talking. He tried on several occasions to greet me somewhat flippantly, which I repeatedly tried to ignore. Finally Oscar said, "Bob, are you such a big shot that you don't talk to your friends?"

"Not at all, I just don't talk to *&#%@!s," I said, referring to the fact that I thought Oscar's actions lacked loyalty to our country.

Others, like Oscar, also bet on the wrong horse in Desert Storm. There in the region, King Hussein of Jordan (a disappointing surprise) and the Palestine Liberation Organization's Yassir Arafat (a predictable disappointment) also sided with Saddam against the coalition; while closer to home the *Washington Times* newspaper ran several "Hall of Shame" stories recapping some of the most dire, and wrong-headed, predictions made (mostly by Democrats like Ted Kennedy) in the run-up to the war.

More importantly, winning the way we did—by keeping our word and abiding by the United Nations resolutions authorizing the liberation of Kuwait—we saw how, for the first and maybe only time, the UN Security Council worked as its founders envisioned. With George Bush, Jim Baker, Brent Scowcroft, and others doing such a masterful job of forging an unprecedented international coalition, the Security Council responded by serving for once as a forum for action, not obstruction; and in the end, the rule of international law was upheld.

The reason I had gone to Venezuela, and led numerous other trade missions during my time as secretary, was because I knew we had to open new markets and boost our exports to get our economy going again—and keep it growing. In fact, we now know it was just two months later, in March of 1991, when the economy did technically emerge from a brief and shallow recession, bouncing back largely on the strength of our exports. We've seen the same thing happen here in the twenty-first century as well, which simply reinforces my belief that free and fair trade is the only way we can remain an economic superpower.

During late 1990 and early 1991, we developed a program called the National Export Initiatives (NEI) whereby our department conducted seminars all over the country aimed at spreading the word of opening markets around the world. In February of 1991, for example, we took a team of senior trade officials from seven or eight government agencies to Minneapolis to start a series of how-to lessons for businesses wishing to do more exporting. These were great for teaching the public how to take advantage of government resources, but let me add they were also great team-building within the government, too. These sessions forced us to get our act together.

Before we were done, we conducted several dozen NEI sessions in every part of the country—including a May 1991 session in Boston led by none other than the president of the United States.

Another important program that came out of this push to open new markets was the Trade Promotion Coordinating Committee, or TPCC. After a year or so, my team and I realized that each federal department, in essence, had its own trade agenda. They conducted their own trade missions, often with conflicting messages and goals, and mixed results at best. I thought there should be a mechanism to help the administration coordinate between the Cabinet departments and other senior administration representatives as we engaged new potential trade partners.

When we petitioned the president to put this TPCC in Commerce, he granted the request within twenty-four hours. Thus was born the first presidential-level coordinating group promoting trade.

Of course, looking back, the NEI and TPCC efforts weren't the sexiest or highest profile things we did during my time, but in my view both efforts made a contribution to the nation's well-being. They helped reduce redundancy and waste, and that struck me as plain, old-fashioned good government—the football equivalent of good blocking and tackling.

Later, during the Clinton administration, while we were discussing how to move NAFTA through the Congress, my successor Ron Brown took the occasion to tease me just a little. "You could have done a lot more to grab headlines, and get attention for the department," he said, sitting in the large office—and behind the desk—I used to occupy. Ron was kidding, but in all seriousness that's not how I approached my job as secretary. I was there to see that the president's agenda was carried out. If things went well, the president was supposed to get the credit—it was his agenda, after all. If things went wrong, however, we were supposed to fix the problems in the departments.

Along the way, I did occasionally seek to focus media attention on our efforts at Commerce—where and when I thought it was appropriate. On the heels of a good U.S tour in October of 1990 to promote the free trade agreement with Mexico, on April 16 I set off on a six-day tour of Mexico with my friend Jaime Serra Puche and others to gin up support for NAFTA south of the Rio Grande. When all was said and done, we visited Mexico City, Merida, Vera Cruz, Monterrey, Chihuahua, and finally Huatulco.

It was a heartening experience to visit with the various Mexican business leaders, entrepreneurs, and citizens who saw not only a fair agreement being offered, but hope of a better future. No question, there were those who also harbored doubts about NAFTA—and even suspicions. Some thought the treaty was a clever U.S. dodge whereby we would snatch up Mexico's oil industry and other vital pieces of their economy.

I am sad to say that, on both sides of the border, the passage of time has done precious little to abate the Oliver Stone-like conspiracy theory, particularly as it relates to questions of sovereignty. Even today, despite the thousands of new businesses and millions of jobs it has created, some insist NAFTA is a Trojan horse. In Mexico, some still believe Big Business will use NAFTA to buy up Mexican oil companies, while here at home some on the far right think NAFTA is part of a conspiracy whereby American sovereignty is jettisoned in favor of the creation of a "North American Union"—like the European Union. Nothing could be more absurd.

As it was, following a successful tour through Mexico, the battlefield to see NAFTA become a reality shifted to Capitol Hill—where we would have to start not only the lobbying for "fast track" authority, but also the long and laborious process of drafting a bill that reflected the direction that both Mexico and the United States wanted to go. There was a passing of the torch of sorts at this point, because that's when Carla and her USTR office took the baton to start writing the treaty as a completed deal. From the outset, Carla had been more committed to the Uruguay Round of the General Agreement on Tariffs and Trade (GATT), but as NAFTA gained momentum and legitimacy, she got fully on board and proved why she was one of the most respected trade lawyers in the country.

With the NAFTA chugging down the tracks toward a vote, other countries and leaders were clearly taking notice. In fact, I considered it a high compliment when our stalwart ally, Turkish President Turgut Ozal, suggested hammering out a free trade agreement with us during my visit to see him in June of 1991. Ozal was very forward-thinking, bordering on brilliant. He was in a jovial mood during our official meeting at the Harbiye Ordu Evi military headquarters in Istanbul, and our fruitful discussions continued after he invited me down to his seaside home in Kemer, just outside the resort town of Antalya, with my traveling companions Chesley Pruet and Layton Stewart.

While we were there, Chesley declared he wanted to do parasailing—then he challenged me to follow suit. Never one to duck a dare, I accepted. It was fun, but afterwards President Ozal gave me hell, saying, "Suppose something happened to you? I would have to call the president and say, 'I'm sorry we killed your secretary of commerce.'"

As interesting and fun as he was—President Ozal could name all fifty U.S. states, and every capital city—he was also very heavy. Too heavy, it turned out, for his short stature. In fact, we first met in 1987 in Houston when he underwent a triple-bypass surgery at Methodist Hospital. So I was a little surprised that

With Turkish President Turgut Ozal in the resort town Kemer, June of 1991. Chesley Pruet, who accompanied me, had his back to the camera.

weekend to see him indulging in the most fattening dishes covered in cheese, to which he invariably added salt. "Mr. President," I finally said, "the doctors in Houston would be pretty mad at you if they saw all of this."

Turgut laughed. "I know they would. Isn't it horrible?"

Tragically, he died less than two years later of heart failure.

Ozal was not only easy to like, but also to respect—particularly since he took a real risk in allowing coalition aircraft overflight rights and access to key air bases during the liberation of Kuwait. That was a particularly tough decision for someone leading a predominantly Muslim nation; yet under Ozal's leadership, Turkey was always a staunch, reliable member of NATO.

During the summer of 1991, an issue involving the 1990 Census finally came to a head—requiring me to make another unpopular call. As I indicated earlier, the census is a recurring political nightmare, erupting at the start of every decade to make the life of the commerce secretary as complicated as any problem he or she is likely to face.

The census is politically sensitive because, at least in 1990, an estimated $60 billion in federal assistance was to be divvied up, and federal and state legislative districts were to be redrawn, based on the results of our count. That federal money, and those congressional and state seats, were destined to go where we found people. For example, as it was originally conducted, the 1990 Census was going to cost Pennsylvania and Wisconsin (which had fewer people, as we saw it) one congressional seat each, while giving one each to Arizona and California (which had gained more citizens).

The difficulty you have in conducting a totally accurate census is many people live in illegal housing—or no housing at all—while others live with friends or family, or are simply avoiding any contact with the government.

The original 1990 Census counted 248.7 million people living in the United States; but shortly thereafter experts in our census bureau used a new survey technique to sample 165,000 households—and the findings of that exercise led them to believe we had missed roughly five million people. Despite the findings of this brand new survey, however, the evidence was inconclusive on whether an adjustment would improve the bureau's numbers on how the population was shared among states, cities, and even within neighborhoods. Moreover, it did not show any improvement in terms of overall accuracy.

The paradox is that, in attempting to make the actual count more accurate by an adjustment, we might be making the "shares" less accurate. Added to that, an adjusted set of numbers could disrupt the political process and create paralysis in the states that were working on redistricting or had already completed it. The country had never before used statistical formulas to adjust the decennial count, and as I said in my announcement, I was uncomfortable proceeding "on unstable ground in such an important matter of public policy."

I was not inclined, at that time, to abandon a 200-year tradition of how we actually count people.

My decision was instantly condemned as groundless and politically motivated by our opponents on Capitol Hill and by plaintiffs (mostly U.S. cities) in a three-year-old lawsuit trying to force me to adjust the count. Mostly it was political posturing. To give you an idea: before the controversy fully erupted, I invited New York City Mayor David Dinkins to have lunch with me at the Department. We had a very pleasant visit, during which the mayor said we had missed a bunch of areas. "Well, Mayor, we certainly don't want to miss anyone," I assured him, "so why don't we send a team out into the field with yours to see what we missed?"

As it turns out, we hadn't missed a damn thing. The New York team was counting burned-out city blocks in the Bronx and other places.

Unfortunately, the extra effort we had made in New York didn't stop Mayor Dinkins from calling my decision "nothing less than statistical grand larceny. The census is the very cornerstone of our democratic system. If we fail to do our best to ensure all Americans are counted, we are failing to live up to the promise of our democracy."[1]

For all the rhetorical bombast in the opposition, I did have my defenders. In the House, I recall how a well-spoken Pennsylvania congressman named Tom Ridge defended me, and our department, and added an eloquent voice of reason to the debate. Meanwhile in the Senate, Herb Kohl, a Democrat from Wisconsin and head of the Senate panel overseeing the census, said he believed I made a decision with "the fairest and most honest judgment" possible, given the time constraints.

Most important, however, was the unanimous verdict by the United States Supreme Court—handed down in March of 1996—that supported my position, affirming that I had made a "reasonable decision in an area where technical experts disagree." I hasten to add that the Clinton administration supported my position when the lawsuit made it to the high court for review in 1995, though they also announced they would employ the new method of statistical sampling when they conducted the 2000 Census.

A poignant postscript came during the research for this book, one that took my appreciation for the importance of the census to a deeper and more personal level. During our research, we relied on the work of "enumerators" like Eugene Wipfler and James Leonard in 1880, and men like Henry Hopter in 1900, as we attempted to piece together the earliest days of the Mosbacher clan here in America.

I can only imagine the sight that Hopter found on June 7, 1900, for example, when he bounded up the stairs leading to 265 East 106th Street, and encountered thirty-three-year-old Louis Mosbacher and his twenty-eight-year-old bride Babette, together with my then-three-year-old father and his eight-month-old sister, Hattie. Before he moved down the street to interview the Dulanys, Levisons, and Schloseens, I wonder if Hopter noticed if my aunt was crawling yet. Pop was surely talking by then, but had his unique vocabulary started to evolve? Was the grandmother I never met in good health?

Finally, it is a matter of some irony that my grandfather doesn't appear in the 1890 Census, at least not that I could find, so it appears he may have been one of the "undercounted" big city residents that was so much at issue 100 years later.

While I am grateful that nine Supreme Court justices eventually found that my July 1991 decision regarding the census was above politics, the very next

1. Felicity Barringer, "U.S. Won't Revise 1990 Census, Says Chief of Commerce," *New York Times,* July 16, 1991.

month saw me getting pulled directly into the middle of the 1992 campaign. On Saturday morning, August 3, I met with the president and his other political advisors at Camp David to start planning in earnest for what we all knew, even back then, would be a tough reelection bid.

Since November of 1990, and even before, I had been rumored as one of the key figures who would help organize and run the '92 campaign—but as 1991 progressed, the prospects of what was a sure win just after Desert Storm, with the president popularity at record-high levels, started to dim. The economy, which had technically already emerged from recession, was still limping along, while unemployment stood at 6.9 percent and would continue to creep up through its peak of 7.8 percent in June of 1992.

Most troubling to me at the time was the credit crunch—whereby overextended banks were tightening their loan policies, leaving struggling companies starved for operating capital. The president and I had seen company after company wither on the vine in Texas during the oil bust of the 1980s, and during the summer of 1991 I was very concerned about seeing it happen again nationally.

Timing being everything in life, we were in the immediate aftermath of the Savings and Loan crisis—a time when bankers were still viewed with some suspicion, particularly by regulators. Every loan officer had in their mind the nightmare vision of standing before a congressional committee, raising their right hand, and then withstanding a public flogging for any loan they made that turned bad.

As a result of the tightening credit markets, some of us in the administration—like Vice President Dan Quayle—were starting to hear from business friends and leaders across the country. Properties weren't moving, the construction sector was stalling, and worst of all, small- and medium-sized businesses and manufacturers were gasping for air. These were the people we relied on to get some growth back into the economy.

"I'm no expert," the venerable political reporter David Broder opined in the *Washington Post* of the situation, "but to me that smells like economic trouble for the country and political headaches for George Bush."[2] David was right. The country still faced some tough challenges, and the president was very concerned—and not just because his political fortunes hung in the balance. He read his mail; and he traveled the country extensively, getting firsthand reports from business owners.

2. David Broder, "Economic Trouble, Political Headaches; When overextended banks suddenly tighten their loan policies, the economy bellyflops," *Washington Post,* August 18, 1991.

I had a raging case of heartburn, as well. As it related both to the economy and the campaign, I felt very strongly that we had to act—and we had to act fast.

Yet, at the time, some of the president's other key economic advisors did not share my sense of urgency. That summer, for example, OMB Director Dick Darman, Chief of Staff John Sununu, and my friend Nick Brady all argued that we were in recovery—and the president simply needed to sit tight to let things move his way. Their prescription was to do as little as possible, which I thought was a mistake.

Technically, Darman, Sununu, and Brady were correct—but they didn't recognize that the prevailing perception around the country was that we were still in a recession. As the unemployment numbers rose, so did widespread public fears.

As we moved into the fall of 1991, moreover, George Bush was starting to get his teeth kicked in for not extending unemployment benefits. The charge was either that no one in the administration knew people were in trouble, or they simply didn't care—and neither view was particularly helpful to the president's prospects for reelection.

I felt I owed my friend a frank assessment, so shortly after we traveled to Houston for his first '92 reelection fund-raiser, I shared my concerns. When just the two of us were riding together in the car, I made my case for urgent, immediate action on the economy.

"The situation is getting bad," I told the president. "You have to do something now."

As he listened intently, however, I could see he was not going to let my gloomy predictions go unchallenged. "Okay, if you're right," he fired back, "then why does everybody else think we are coming out of this recession and there is no reason to do anything reckless?"

My frustration with the do-nothing crowd came spilling out. "If it weren't for their attitude," I said, referring to Darman, Sununu, and Brady, "we wouldn't have this problem."

"Are you telling me that you think three guys caused the recession?"

"No, sir, but I think they sure as hell exacerbated it."

Plainly stated, I made a pain in the ass of myself. I pushed so hard on several different instances that fall I am sure people—including me—wonder why I wasn't fired. I wanted the president to go to the country, tell them he heard their concerns, and that, furthermore, he had a plan to help them through their tough times. In essence, I was advocating what in hindsight many might refer to as a Bill Clinton-like "I feel your pain" gambit.

"People out there need to see that you understand their problems," I finished.

George Bush had staked a large part of his presidency on the 1990 budget deal, which was the largest deficit-reduction legislation ever passed—and, for the first time, imposed real cuts on Congress' discretionary spending.

In turn, however, the president's hands were somewhat tied in terms of what the federal government could do to augment the nascent cycle of economic growth then under way through tax cuts. Nevertheless, to the extent possible, I felt strongly that he needed to make sure the people knew he was doing everything he could. Even if we had to go out and promote some half-measures as full solutions, we had to give voters the appearance that we were addressing their core concerns about jobs and wages.

Specifically, I argued that we should fight for tax relief for any company, large or small, that would create new jobs.

Finally, the president said, "Okay, darn it, if you feel so strongly that I ought to be saying something about this, give me something. You guys write a speech there at Commerce." For the record, I do not think the president disagreed with me, but I also believe he was getting a lot of conflicting advice—a fact that underscored the complexity of his predicament.

A few days later, I ran into John Sununu at the White House. "Are you happy?" he asked as we passed in the hallway. "You finally won this fight. He's going to make your speech."

I was pleased, but having been given the ball I knew we had to do something with it. My team and I worked over the Thanksgiving holiday to fashion a speech that conveyed a more proactive economic message, and on December 3, 1991 the president unveiled it in Florida during a visit with employees at a Tropicana Products Inc. facility. While there, he said the following:

> We can't sit back and hope for the best. We all know that too many people are having a tough time right now. I'm hearing about it in conversations with working people. I'm reading hardship stories in the letters people write. . . . I do understand, and I am concerned. I really want to help. . . .

Among the remedies we put out there were a capital gains tax cut, and new IRA regulations letting first-time homebuyers use those retirement savings to get a piece of the American Dream. Again, it was not the big tax cut or other dramatic measure we would have liked to have touted, but it at least gave us a peg or two on which to hang our hat.

"I'm determined to leave no stone unturned in an effort to promote economic growth," the president added. While the speech lacked soaring rhetoric, it was plain-spoken and direct—and a great deal better, in my view, than the emerging narrative being promoted by our political opponents that we were "out of touch" and didn't care.

Unfortunately, just as we were getting out of the gate with this newer, more aggressive approach on the economy, personnel changes and the attendant turmoil within the administration meant our message had no legs. The same day the president spoke in Florida, the increasingly embattled John Sununu—who had become a lightning rod for controversy, and a routine target for journalist Ann Devroy of the *Washington Post*—submitted his resignation as chief of staff. Sam Skinner, who had been the transportation secretary, was named to replace Sununu.

This "regime change" helped to temporarily snuff out any momentum I had hoped to get with this new message and strategy. By the time we came back to it, Pat Buchanan on the right—and seven Democrats on the left—were pummeling the president for not doing enough to get the economy going. How the other economic advisors could look at what was happening and not see the damage being inflicted on the president still escapes me. Looking back now, I am convinced that those missteps in 1991 directly contributed to the administration's defeat a year later. Watching those developments had to have an alluring impact on Ross Perot back in Texas—to say nothing of Pat Buchanan and Bill Clinton, already on the campaign trail.

Two days after the Sununu shake-up, on December 5, I joined President Bush in the White House press briefing room where he announced my appointment as the general chairman of his reelection effort, working together with Bob Teeter as the chief strategist, businessman Fred Malek as the campaign manager, and longtime Washington hand Charlie Black as the senior advisor. Others, such as Vice President Quayle and campaign hands Mary Matalin and Rich Bond, were also slated to play key roles.

Teeter and I had met with the president in the Oval Office the morning before; and as the plans for a three-headed campaign structure started to be finalized, I was committed to making the situation work. Normally, I was a big believer that only one person can be in charge at a time. That's why, back in 1988, I was one of the most ardent proponents of bringing Jim Baker over from Treasury as the '88 campaign chief.

In fact, our new campaign team did not get off to an auspicious start. The afternoon after the press conference, a struggle emerged as to who would get top billing on the press release. Poor Marlin Fitzwater, the administration's affable and able press secretary, got caught in the middle as Teeter and I took turns telling him how the release should read. Coming from the business world, I was naturally taken aback that someone would suggest placing the chief strategist before the chairman in the pecking order, but that was a sign of struggles yet to come.

Missing from this line-up, of course, was Lee Atwater—the feisty and flamboyant political in-fighter who died tragically earlier in 1991 following a yearlong fight against brain cancer. The vacuum created by Lee's loss would be felt time and again in the months ahead, as the 1992 Bush-Quayle campaign struggled to find our footing.

Still, standing with the president in the small, somewhat cramped White House briefing room that December day, I was grateful for his confidence in me, optimistic of our ultimate success, but clear-eyed as to the difficulties we would face.

I was also struck by the bittersweet realization that I would soon be leaving the Department of Commerce after nearly three eventful, challenging, and rewarding years. I've been asked why I made the decision to leave Commerce, and the answer sounds so corny that I hesitate committing the reason to paper. In truth, I left because I thought I owed it to the president to help him be reelected. George Bush had asked me to help, and as usual I was powerless to refuse my friend who had done so much for our country, and for me.

I had accomplished some important things at Commerce. In this, I was lucky to have all of those terrific, talented people around me, like my deputy secretary Rock Schnabel and my personal assistant Evan Hughes—who did such great work and helped in so many ways. Thanks to their help, we got NAFTA out of the gate, and helped the president usher in a "new world order" marked by the steady march of free markets around the world. We didn't win every battle we waged with Japan, within the administration, or even within our department (with the career bureaucrats who promised to outlast us). I wish we had done more to help get the ball rolling on the president's vision for a hemispheric free-trade zone, and that I had been more effective advocating for action on the economy.

Still, the world had changed in such profound ways during those three years that I can only look back now in wonder. At the time, though, there was no time for such navel-gazing. Soon, it would be my job to make sure the man most responsible for bringing the global community to the threshold of this new and more hopeful era earned four more years to lay the foundation for the future.

Chapter 20 DON'T LET THEM PUT YOU OUT FRONT

As a rule, running doctors and nurses are a bad sign; but throw in a state dinner, and the sight of running medical personnel can cause instant alarm. It was the evening of January 8, 1992, the tenth day of a twelve-day trip to Asia. Together with the president and first lady—and a contingent of some two dozen business leaders—we had already traveled to Australia, Singapore, and South Korea to push for greater access in these international markets for American goods and services. Now in Japan, we were clearly saving the toughest case for last.

For years, the Japanese had gained market share here in the United States by overcharging their domestic consumers at home, then cutting the prices on the goods they exported to us. In December of 1991, in fact, my department found that Japanese automakers had been "dumping" minivans on our market at artificially low prices. Coupled with a $41 billion trade deficit with Japan, and rising unemployment, the main purpose of this trip was to send a message to Tokyo that the status quo was no longer acceptable.

To be candid, the trip was also undertaken at my urging to send an equally clear message to American voters that the Bush administration was fighting to create more jobs through foreign trade. "Every billion dollars of goods sold overseas creates 20,000 American jobs," I said on *Meet the Press* on the eve of our Asia travels, hoping to frame the context of the debate.

This trip was a swan song of sorts for me at Commerce, but also the opening gambit of the 1992 campaign—and a chance for me to help spur the administration to take a more proactive stance on the economy.

The night of January 8, Prime Minister Kiichi Miyazawa hosted a formal dinner at his official residence, but the evening was not getting off to a smooth start. After I went through the receiving line at a predinner reception, the president turned to me and asked, "How are you feeling, pal?" I was feeling fine, but he clearly was not. Like a ton of people on the trip—including a bunch of the media traveling with us—the president had caught an intestinal bug. At the reception, he appeared pale and drained. The truth is, he shouldn't have been going to dinner, and Barbara was encouraging him not to go—but as George Bush saw it,

At far left next to Treasury Secretary Nick Brady, President Bush and Japanese Prime Minister Kiichi Miyazawa address American and Japanese business leaders on January 8, 1992. The President was fighting to honor his scheduled commitments despite a stomach virus that overtook him later that night.

he could not cancel. "It would be too embarrassing for the Japanese," he said. As usual, he was putting the feelings and concerns of others ahead of his own.

At dinner, I was seated next to Barbara on the dais with the two leaders, Deputy Prime Minister Watanabe, and a couple of the ministers. The dinner had just started when suddenly I saw one of the White House nurses racing full speed down the aisle toward the head of the table. It startled me, and instinctively I looked over to see if there was an attack on the president.

About the time my eyes fell on him, he just slumped over.

Oh my God, he's had a heart attack, I thought as I grabbed Barbara's hand. She stood to go over, and I went with her. After a few tense moments, we heard the president joke, "Why don't you just roll me under the table and let me sleep it off?" Assured by the doctors that the president would be fine—he would be taken back to his room, not the hospital—Barbara immediately took over.

"I can't explain what happened to George, because it has never happened before," she explained to the crowd, "but I'm beginning to think it's the ambassador's [Mike Armacost] fault. He and George played the Emperor and the Crowned Prince in tennis today, and they were badly beaten. And we Bushes aren't used to that. So he felt much worse than I thought."

It was pure grace and class under difficult circumstances. Everybody loved it; instantly, a wave of relief swept over the room.

Of course, after the president fell ill, the media went into one the first of many feeding frenzies we would encounter in 1992. That night, the White House had agreed to allow an unmanned camera in the room to capture just the toasts, but since it was left on, the camera also captured the leader of the free world getting sick. Naturally, with such footage of global news value, the Japanese broke their agreement and shared that footage with the waiting world. After that, any hope we had of driving a message back home that we were getting traction on trade issues—and creating badly needed jobs—evaporated.

Lost in this feeding frenzy was the fact that we were, in fact, making tangible headway toward gaining greater access to Japan's markets—and that was, in turn, helping to create more jobs in America. On our first day in Japan, for example, we choppered down to Kashihara outside of Osaka to help open the second Toys "R" Us store permitted in Japan. There with us that day was my new Japanese counterpart, Kozo Watanabe of Ministry of International Trade and Industry, as well as Ambassador Armacost, Toys "R" Us Chairman Charles Lazarus, and other local dignitaries.

The news that Toys "R" Us was opening stores in Japan had not been universally welcomed there. Concerned that these large-scale stores and their cheaper prices might drive smaller companies out of business, Japanese officials had been using red tape and regulations to delay their applications—and those of other American companies—for up to a decade or more in some cases.

In Toys "R" Us' case, they had also met opposition in Japan because of their business model. The company cut out the "middle man" by buying many of its products directly from factories, thus circumventing Japan's arcane distribution system. Accordingly, it was reported that this high-profile debut had created "panic," leading at least one toy store owner to shut their doors even before the Toys "R" Us location had opened. Still, the chain's debut had been warmly embraced by wary Japanese consumers—as we could tell from the 5,000 local citizens who turned out to wave small Japanese and American flags during the ceremony.

Our team had worked for over a year to help Toys "R" Us get a toehold in the tough Japanese market, so I felt pretty good that day as I watched my president and one of our leading businesses celebrate what we all hoped was the start of a new and better chapter in our trade relations.

Also hoping for a sea change in Japan's position on market access were the heads of the three biggest auto manufacturers in the U.S. traveling with us—Lee Iacocca of Chrysler, Red Poling from Ford, and the General Motors chairman, Bob Stempel. As my team and I designed the delegation for this trip, the idea was to get a sizeable group of top business leaders with interests in Asia, particularly Japan, and with the president leading us, make it akin to a trade mission on steroids. At the time, auto-related goods accounted for three-fourths of our $41 billion trade deficit with Japan, so these auto leaders simply had to be invited as I saw it.

When he saw that I wanted to bring all three automakers, however, the president's very able national security advisor, Brent Scowcroft, said, "God, Bobby, can't you just take one?"

"We could do that," I replied, "but the other two companies would be mad they weren't included. They would think we were giving special treatment."

Adding to the urgency, U.S. auto sales were in a slump, and the month before we left General Motors Corporation had announced plans to close twenty-one plants and lay off 74,000 workers. It was a tough time in the industry, and we had to show those workers we weren't going to roll over and play dead while the Japanese were getting away with economic murder.

Against that background, the stakes were plenty high when I went into my meeting with trade minister Kozo Wantanabe to discuss the lack of official action to open Japan's car markets and drop other legal restrictions on foreign business. I was growing very impatient because this was well-tread ground. We had raised it three or four times in previous meetings, with little result. It seemed we were just going around in circles.

As Mike Ferron handed me the talking points, I looked over at Tom Collamore. "I think we've been here before, sir," Tom said, smiling. We had all had enough, and as we entered the ornate room and sat down I realized we had to change our tactics. We had tried cajoling; we had tried direct confrontation. Now, after giving it some serious forethought, I decided it was time for more drastic measures.

As the meeting began, we exchanged the customary pleasantries, but in short order it became pretty clear that little had changed in Japan's position. Unable and unwilling to endure more stonewalling, I blew my top.

I started by recounting the number of times we had covered Japan's untenable

During frank negotiations like this session with Korean military leaders, I was not shy about leveraging America's tremendous sacrifice and investments in pursuit of global security to win more favorable terms from our allies on market access, trade deals, or, as in this case, the procurement of U.S. military equipment.

policies, and how they had always promised changes that never came. "This is what they want me to say," I said sharply as I threw the talking points across the table, "but what I'm going to say to you is, I want this fixed and I want it fixed now. I'm tired of all this foot-dragging."

Then I abruptly stood up and walked out.

It was later reported that our trade talks that day were "polite but unproductive." Not quite. This was not textbook behavior on a presidential trip, but it moved the ball. Before we left Japan, the president had extracted a Japanese pledge to buy an additional $10 billion in American auto parts each year by 1995—a plan that would create 200,000 new jobs in America.

This was exactly the kind of news I was hoping the Asia trip would generate, but once again this positive development was followed by a significant setback that wiped out our message. We returned home to the news that the unemployment rate had risen to 7.1 percent in December, the highest rate in six years. A total of 2.3 million jobs had been lost since the recession began in 1990.

In politics, perception is the coin of the realm, and perception is largely dictated by the news media. For all the positive gains we made, and there were a few, the 1992 Asia trip was widely reported as a net negative for the president. For example, within hours of returning from Japan, Lee Iacocca made a speech at the Detroit Economic Club defending his industry and his employees.

Lee was tired, and still angry, both at the Japanese and media criticism of the trip. Unfortunately, some reporters also interpreted his remarks as being critical of the administration, and after reading the reports the president was understandably angry. "I thought you said Iacocca was going to be okay," he said to me. Lee had, in fact, told me the trip had been helpful in his view, so I called to ask what happened. He sent me the transcript of his speech; and upon reading the speech, it was clear, at least to me, that his comments had been taken out of context.

Here's how Lee started his speech:

> This was a historic trip, and let me start by saying President Bush set a very important precedent. He took some heat here and in Japan for dragging along a business delegation. The Japanese didn't know what to make of it, except something had changed.
>
> What's changed is that economics finally made it to the front of the plane along with the generals and the admirals and the Foggy Bottom types. In the past, we weren't even invited to ride coach. The president just tore a page from Japan's book. Their leaders have always taken business leaders on missions like this because they've always put economics first.
>
> Now, we're doing that. . . .

Lee's remarks weren't all sweetness and light, of course. Always a straight-shooter, he went on to say that the deals we had cut were "from a Detroit perspective a weak start—but a start."

"This trip didn't resolve this country's trade problems with Japan," he summarized. "Nobody expected it to. You cannot resolve in three days problems that have developed over twenty years. But it did bring those problems to a head. And frankly, that's been long overdue."

Another vote of gratitude came from Jim Robinson III, CEO of American Express: "This is the first time the U.S. has come out united—the Commerce Department, the Treasury, the President, the business community—to declare that trade is a national priority on a par with our security interests. For better or worse, we have crossed that line in the sand."

In the aftermath of the trip, since it was my idea, it fell to me to go on the weekend TV shows to defend it to a cynical beltway press corps. One typical line of questioning was, "Has George Bush stooped to becoming a car sales-man?" My view was that, if he was a salesman of sorts, he was in pretty darn good company. Margaret Thatcher in Great Britain, President Roh in South Korea, Francois Mitterrand in France, and Helmut Kohl in Germany were all known to go to bat for their domestic auto producers, so why not the president of the United States? Shouldn't he be interested in his country's economy—and not just autos, but homes, electronics, and other core consumer goods as well?

The Washington media didn't want to hear it, but I was perfectly content to sit there and make the point that, yes, the president had been willing to roll up his sleeves, and get out there selling U.S. jobs and services overseas.

Looking back, I suppose the way that trip turned out—the way it was nega-tively reported in the media—was the biggest disappointment of my time in the administration. I didn't care that it was a black eye for me personally. What pained me the most was that it was deemed to have hurt the president. Other than that, I didn't give a damn. I felt that way all the way through my time in Washington. I always did what I thought was right, and tried never to hurt or embarrass the president. Those were two key rules I had for myself.

Incidentally, after one of the in-studio TV interviews that weekend following the trip, I was chatting off-camera about the campaign with one of the produc-ers. We were having a friendly give-and-take, but the banter turned chilly when he candidly confided: "You know, we think that you ought to be vulnerable this year. We think we've got a chance of beating you."

There was something about the way this member of the supposedly indepen-dent news media said it—"we" think we have a chance of beating "you"—that spoke volumes about the us-versus-them media mind-set at that time. Together with Pat Buchanan's full-throated primary challenge on the right, and six or seven Democrats wailing away on the left, to me it seemed as if our campaign would soon be taking off into gale-force headwinds.

The president didn't officially declare his candidacy for reelection until Feb-ruary 12, but the situation in New Hampshire—site of the first contested pri-mary, where Buchanan had the support of the influential *Manchester Union Ledger* newspaper—was deteriorating fast enough to where we had to get our as-yet undeclared candidate up there for a full day of campaign stops a month early, on January 15.

Shortly after accepting my appointment as campaign chairman, I had pub-licly acknowledged the political reality that the New Hampshire race was "very close" and that "right now, I'd be happy to win it." Some White House aides had previously said they did not expect Buchanan to get much more than 20 percent of the vote; but I was wary of seeing the firebrand columnist "win" in the eyes of the media by beating expectations.

Coming out of the gate, one of the fundamental problems we faced stemmed from the campaign's structure. With three leaders at the top—me, along with Bob Teeter as chief strategist responsible for overall tone and direction, and Fred Malek as campaign manager overseeing nuts and bolts of daily operations—it was never fully clear to the media, any of us, or anyone else as to who was in charge. Most campaigns usually develop "camps" and encounter power struggles for control of the campaign, and ours was no exception. As a result, it often appeared that we were speaking out of both sides of our mouths.

For example, in December, the campaign and the White House publicly disagreed about the wisdom of cutting taxes for the middle class. Then early in 1992 someone leaked the idea of a $300-a-person, onetime tax rebate that made no sense politically or economically. This concept was immediately criticized by supply-siders like Jack Kemp and disowned by deficit hawks like Dick Darman. Such public infighting not only underscored the divisions within our inner circle about how much should be done to revive the economy, it also undermined confidence in the administration overall.

Another issue that opened a rift within the party surfaced shortly after the reelection campaign was officially announced. On February 13, I met at the Bush-Quayle headquarters in Washington with leading members of the gay and lesbian community to hear their views on funding for AIDS treatment, anti-gay and lesbian discrimination, and other issues.

No question, at that time the relationship between the Republican Party and the gay community was antagonistic at best, and had recently been exacerbated by extreme elements on both sides. The activist group Act-Up, for example, had routinely harassed President Bush, his family, and indeed the entire town of Kennebunkport, Maine during their trips there. The group's protests occasionally involved noisy crowds marching through the small town and throwing condoms as they demanded more federal funding for AIDS research—even though we were already spending $4.25 billion on AIDS programs. In fact, the $1.8 billion earmarked for AIDS research in 1992 was more than we spent on cancer and heart disease, which claimed far more lives at that time.

And yet, for not doing as the protestors demanded, the president and his administration were branded—unfairly, I contend—as uncaring bigots.

On the other hand, listening to the bombastic rhetoric, particularly coming out of the Buchanan campaign and other gay-baiting candidates seeking to stoke GOP passions, it was not hard to understand why many in the gay community were concerned about the tone of the overall campaign even in those early stages.

I have always viewed politics as the art of inclusion—not exclusion—so when my daughter Dee approached me about taking this meeting, it made sense. We invited Urvashi Vaid, the executive director of the National Gay and Lesbian Task Force, along with several peers and colleagues, to give me a briefing so I could hear their concerns firsthand. We met for twenty-five minutes, and had what I think both sides felt was an open, frank, and respectful conversation.

Afterwards, the Task Force put out a press release that described our discussion as a "historic meeting—believed to be unprecedented in recent memory . . . a groundbreaking moment. . . ." They were appreciative of the meeting; and while I tried to assure them that George Bush would never stand for anyone on his campaign saying or doing anything to diminish any American, I didn't promise them anything in terms of policy. For example, we still didn't see eye-to-eye with respect to AIDS funding, or openly gay men and women serving in the military.

It was a candid exchange of views, and after it was over I moved on to the other big issues we faced—not thinking I had just given life to the newest, and ugliest, of campaign wedge issues.

A few weeks later, however, on the eve of the eight GOP Super Tuesday primaries, Pat Buchanan took direct aim at me, and that specific meeting, while he was crisscrossing Mississippi and Louisiana.

"This is not consistent with the pro-family agenda," Buchanan said of my meeting. "What I would like to see from Mr. Bush is at least a statement that Mr. Mosbacher doesn't represent us [Republicans], and that he went off on a lark." In Pat's worldview, the president's campaign had no business even talking to a segment of our society that had concerns involving discrimination—something that should be abhorrent to every American.

By that time, however, Buchanan had already put enough political pressure on the White House to fire the head of the National Endowment of the Arts, John Frohnmayer, for several grants the agency had made that Buchanan characterized as "pornographic and blasphemous." Not anxious to let him get traction on yet another political front, the White House understandably sought to distance the president from this new controversy.

At the campaign, we didn't have the same ability to sidestep the issue; and I was grateful when the president's campaign press secretary, Torie Clarke, backed me up, noting that: "Mr. Buchanan is trying to incite feelings of fear and hatred that shouldn't be part of the political process."

As for me, I was more direct in calling Pat's comments "bigoted."

With no prospect of a primary victory anywhere on the horizon, the Buchanan campaign was already starting to "circle the drain" when he set his gun sights on me. Pat was throwing a few final political Hail Marys—trying to score some cheap points by throwing evangelicals and working-class conservatives some red meat on cultural issues. Understanding his motivations is not the same as condoning them, of course. That sequence of exchanges with Buchanan was one of the ugliest turn of events I experienced, not just in 1992—already an unhappy year—but in my sixty years in Republican politics. Looking back, it still simmers my blood.

As the spring wore on, it grew increasingly clear to me and most everyone watching the campaign that the Bush-Quayle reelection effort was not getting the kind of traction we needed. We had badly misjudged the corrosive impact of the Buchanan campaign, and the intraparty divisions Pat exposed—together with our sluggishness to address the economic woes people felt with a cohesive message backed by a credible plan—in turn created the opening for Ross Perot to jump into the race as an independent, which he did in February.

In short order, the wrong Texas businessman—Perot—was leading in most national polls and threatening to blow the race wide open.

Not helping matters on the Bush-Quayle front, to be candid, was the ongoing power struggle that evolved between Bob Teeter and me for control of the campaign. By 1992, Bob Teeter had established himself as one of the very best pollsters in politics, but a pollster is only one part of a broader campaign team—and after working in so many national campaigns I think Bob viewed 1992 as his big chance to run the whole show. I loved Bob but, to be honest, didn't feel he was suited to running a presidential campaign—which he was clearly trying to do despite my best efforts to make the situation work.

An even closer Teeter friend and supporter from Michigan—former President Ford—privately voiced a similar opinion about Bob's 1992 role. "Bob is a good pollster," the former president told journalist Tom DeFrank during a May 1993 interview, "but he isn't necessarily a good political strategist. He can get whatever answers are out there in the field, but there is a big difference between getting information and then utilizing."[1]

So there we were: I was unhappy with Bob, and he was not apt to see things my way. The trouble was that Teeter wasn't alone in his disregard for the business types who raise the money so they can afford to buy TV ads. *You go raise*

1. Thomas M. DeFrank, *Write It When I'm Gone* (New York: Berkley Books, 2007), 178.

the money, and we'll handle the hand-to-hand combat. That's the way a lot of political guns feel.

Incidentally, my highly successful and accomplished friend Fred Malek experienced the same treatment when he jumped from the political operative role he had fulfilled in campaigns past to the fund-raiser side of things in the McCain 2008 campaign. "My political IQ has dropped 100 points in the eyes of the experts," he sighed to me at one point during the McCain campaign, citing the way the younger operatives treated him.

Politics isn't all attack dogs and sound bites. There are a lot of good and capable people who get involved on the finance side for the simple reason that they want to help the country, and more often than not they are mistreated by the political gurus. I remember one 1992 briefing in particular when I was selling an audience on George Bush's sterling qualities when one of these experts whispered to me, "That's enough, Mossy—these folks want some red meat."

No question, my background as a fund-raiser cut against me in 1992; but in the end it was the campaign's three-headed structure that proved most unworkable—and I bear some responsibility for that. The president gave three of us a job, and clearly we weren't getting it done. We failed him, to be blunt, and knowing that hurts more that I can bear.

For example, during the late spring of 1992, while I was advocating for Jim Baker to take over as White House chief of staff and help right our political ship, Bob Teeter and Fred Malek sided together against such a move.

"It would have been wiser if we had teamed up with Bob, because Mosbacher was moving in the right direction," Malek said in an interview for this book recently. "He had advocated in the right direction when he was secretary to address the economy more forcefully, but was out-voted by the other advisors. Then in the spring of 1992, Mosbacher was trying to get structural changes made on the campaign to no avail because he wasn't getting support. But he was right."

Bob Teeter, God rest his soul, told me the same thing before he died; and only someone who has experienced the gut-wrenching ups and downs of a presidential campaign can appreciate how much these comments mean.

For his part, the president knew we were in trouble, but was never one to panic. If changes were to take place, he signaled to me at the time, they would come sometime around the convention in Houston, in August.

In the meantime, we continued to be split over how to answer the Perot candidacy. Some of us weren't sure he would survive past Labor Day. But others, like Vice President Quayle, along with Teeter and Malek, thought he would still be standing in November.

Little did we know that we were both right.

Just as quickly as he surged into contention in national polls, Perot flamed out in mid-July. By then, he had balked at buying TV advertising or other campaign staples like yard signs—a bizarre way to run a campaign, for sure. Fortunately for us, the internal infighting in the Perot operation was even worse than ours had been, and their campaign literally came apart at the seams.

For most of 1992, until Jimmy Baker came back as White House chief of staff in late August, I had the same helpless sensation I had felt when Pop cut my jib sheet during that childhood race. There we sat, falling further and further behind. For a full year, I had been pressing first the president's economic advisors, and then my compatriots on the campaign, for more action on the economy—for more action in general. We had become far too reactive, letting outside events dictate the action.

We were hoping the GOP convention would help us change that.

Traditionally, political conventions present candidates a terrific chance to change the debate and the media narrative, and to recast themselves before the public. To be sure, we had our work cut out for us leading into Houston that August. Riding the wave created both by the Perot withdrawal and their own convention in New York City, the smooth-talking Governor Clinton and his newly-minted running mate, Senator Al Gore from Tennessee, had surged to a twenty-point lead.

As we headed into the 1992 convention in Houston, we knew we had a daunting task to try and reel in the surging Clinton-Gore ticket, but our experience from 1988 gave us a sense of hope. Indeed, those of us who know George Bush best know he is a gamer. After a summer of discontent, we knew he would be going all-out.

The Baker announcement also offered a boost to the president's supporters and troop morale throughout the reelection effort. After Jimmy moved from the State Department back over to the White House, we made changes in the campaign structure and Baker indicated the best way I could help then was to direct all fund-raising for the Republican Party. As it was, the president's campaign was about to receive $76 million in public financing; but funds elsewhere were running perilously low.

When Jimmy called and asked me to handle the party fund-raising, to be honest, I confided that I felt frustrated and beaten up after a year of constantly

Rob and I discuss logistics with Bill Harris, who managed the 1992 GOP Convention at the Astrodome in Houston. (Photo courtesy Buster Dean)

advocating for us to do things that, too often, never got done. Baker heard me out, but was not going to take no for an answer. "Bobber," he started. "Remember when you said that if I went back to the White House, you would do anything I asked? Well, anything is here."

Then Baker really put the screws to me. He did the one thing he knew would seal my fate. He put the president on the phone. "I am confident we can win this thing, Bob," the president said, "but I need you to do this. It would mean everything to Bar and me."

Thus ended any doubt about what I would be doing with my immediate future.

With just nine weeks left until Election Day, things looked pretty bleak from the finance side. The party's Victory '92 operation—which was expected to raise $46 million for state party needs, advertising, and get-out-the-vote activities— had pulled in only $5 million. Meanwhile, the Presidential Trust Fund, which supported daily campaign operations, was only $2 million toward its $10 million goal.

With Baker back at the helm, other pieces of the puzzle started to fall into place as well. Adman extraordinaire Roger Ailes agreed to take over "special projects," and Craig Fuller went back to reprise his 1988 role as chief of operations. At that time, polls showed Bill Clinton leading by ten to fifteen points, as our convention bounce appeared to taper off. Then came reports that economic growth slowed in the second quarter to a 1.4 percent rate, compared with a healthier 2.9 percent growth rate in the first three months of the year.

This was not the kind of economic storyline we needed heading into the stretch run.

In short order, however, the president's staff changes started to show signs of paying off. Baker sharpened the campaign's message, tightened control of the White House and campaign staffs, and overhauled decision-making procedures. As *Time* magazine reported at the time: "What used to involve a series of meetings and what one senior official derided as groupthink that resulted in drift, boiled down to a very simple reality: What Baker says, goes."[2]

In fact, in early September, our campaign announced a package of programs under the heading of the "Agenda for American Renewal." After a full year of pushing and prodding, the campaign finally had a cohesive economic message complete with several enticing elements—not the least of which was President Bush's goal to help double our GDP to be the first $10 trillion economy in history. Finally, we were painting a compelling picture of the future that would appeal to voters.

Going into the final weekend, in fact, we had closed the gap with the Clinton-Gore ticket to one point—and with solid news about the economy starting to come out, the momentum was shifting to our side. That's when the independent counsel investigating the Iran-Contra affair, Lawrence Walsh, essentially reindicted Reagan's defense secretary Cap Weinberger just four days before the election. Even worse, Walsh included an already discredited allegation about then-Vice President Bush in his report. It was pure dirty politics at its worst: a four year-old story, the definition of "old news," propagated with the help of a clearly biased national news media.

To have worked so hard, against such a series of bizarre and discouraging events all year long, only to have the election snatched away by one of the sleaziest acts in modern politics . . . well, let's just say the depths of my disregard for Lawrence Walsh's conduct in late October 1992 knows no bounds.

The release of the Walsh report erased any momentum we were gaining, and four days later the Bush-Quayle ticket was defeated for reelection by Clinton-Gore.

2. Susan Page and Timothy Clifford, "Campaign '92 Tactics," *Newsday*, September 7, 1992.

274 ★ Don't Let Them Put You Out Front

Of course, in addition to the challenges I've already outlined, there were numerous other causes leading to the 1992 election outcome: an able campaign run by Governor Clinton; an economy that recovered too late to change the public perception that things actually were getting better; and a cadre of Washington- and New York-based editors and producers who proved anything but objective and impartial observers of events.[3]

George Bush, of course, would never stoop to blaming anyone other than himself for the '92 loss, but I would put him last on any list. He held firm to his principles, even when the easy thing would have been to jettison them. He stayed loyal to his vice president, who had been nothing but loyal to him. He put off engaging in partisanship, even when many of us vehemently disagreed with his decision. And in the end, it bears repeating, he still almost pulled it out.

All the while, even as he was locked in mortal political combat, George Bush still managed to focus on tending to the people's business. In the midst of his final leg of politicking in early October of 1992, in fact, George Bush took yet another decisive act of forward-looking leadership that should be remembered by future generations. Together with Mexican President Carlos Salinas and Canadian Prime Minister Brian Mulroney, he looked on as Carla Hills—together with Jaime Serra Puche and Trade Minister Michael Wilson of Canada—initialed the North American Free Trade Agreement at a ceremony in San Antonio. The deal still required congressional approval to become law, but that signing ceremony took us a vital step closer to realizing a $6 trillion common market comprising 360 million people and stretching 5,000 miles from the Yukon in the north to the Yucatan peninsula in the south.

Just as important, NAFTA offered the real hope of job creation and economic growth that would strengthen each of our societies in important ways.

That's why, if I picked one thing that I was proudest of from my time at Commerce, it was helping the president conceive and sell the NAFTA. We faced plenty of political criticism as we set out to realize the vision, and we would face even more pushback as we moved to help finalize the deal after leaving Washington, but sixteen years later I remain convinced we did the right thing,

3. According to a January 1993 *Washington Journalism Review* article, the *Washington Post's* ombudsman, Joann Byrd, examined the newspaper's photos, stories, and headlines during the last seventy-three days of the campaign and concluded they were "very lopsided" in Clinton's favor. An April 1996 poll released by the Freedom Forum, meanwhile, found that the wide majority of Washington newspaper reporters and news bureau chiefs consider themselves liberals or moderates and voted for Bill Clinton in 1992.

Exchanging a few warm words with Baroness Thatcher during a 2002 trip to London.

despite ominous predictions of some kind of "sucking sound" of Americans' jobs headed south.

Throughout 1992, I was always amazed that someone as smart as Ross Perot could be against the NAFTA deal. Tellingly, during one of the political debates involving the president, Governor Clinton, and Ross, I walked up to Perot during one of the breaks and had the following exchange.

"Ross, how are you?" I inquired.

"Oh, Bob, nice to see you."

"You, too, Ross," I answered, "but I am puzzled over something. How can you be against NAFTA, a successful businessman like you are?"

"Well, I'm not really against it," he said. "It's just the way they're presenting it."

Right.

Though George Bush is too modest to do so for himself, he had other accomplishments that history will note as well. For example, historians such as Michael Beschloss and journalists such as Jon Meacham have cited the 1990 budget deal as a case study in political courage that laid the foundation for the prosperity of the 1990s. That's pretty good recognition.

Furthermore, on ending the Cold War without a shot being fired between the superpowers, and realizing both the the peaceful liberation of Central and Eastern Europe and German unification within NATO, George Bush earned the gratitude of tens of millions of people. No less than Mikhail Gorbachev declared at President Bush's eightieth birthday party in Houston that, "Today, I can say with certainty that of all my counterparts in the world arena George Bush was the best."

During the Bush 41 administration, the United States was more respected, sought after, and even beloved around the world than any time before or since—and that's principally due to the way George H. W. Bush conducted himself as our president. President Reagan, great and loved as he was here at home—he was so popular, and deservedly so—was not held in the same high regard and esteem globally. For every Margaret Thatcher who loved him, there was a Francois Mitterrand who viewed Reagan with a tad more suspicion.

Not so with George H. W. Bush. For one thing, he knew many of his fellow leaders before he made it to the White House. But once he rose to the "mountaintop of American politics" (as he has frequently called the presidency), those same leaders knew he was tough, straightforward, honest, but also someone who would listen to—and consider—their views. And for that reason, as never before or since, I think America reached a zenith in international respect and friendship.

Chapter 21 WHEN ALL IS SAID AND DONE,
THERE'S NOTHING LEFT BUT FAMILY

January 20, 1993 dawned bright and brisk, and the political pall that had been cast over our lives seemed to lift as the 747 formerly known as "Air Force One" took off from Andrews Air Force Base for one last trip—this one bringing George and Barbara Bush, and the rest of their extended political family, back to Houston and home. With the Democrats controlling the White House *and* both chambers of Congress, it felt good to get out of Dodge. The Clinton Inauguration festivities had been tough to watch, as they proved a constant reminder of a campaign that we could—and should—have won. The bitterness of that experience still lingered; yet the majesty and solemnity of the inauguration ceremony that day served as a cathartic reminder that our beloved republic was resilient and would indeed survive.

The flight that afternoon to Houston was remarkably cheerful under the circumstances, with small amounts of friendly banter and discussions of the future. What melancholy we felt remained largely below the surface, though a few let their tears bubble up. When they did, the president was quick to wrap an arm around and comfort them.

In fact, for some time after the 1992 election, George tried to comfort me—and I know he did the same with many others. Usually, we would be talking about something else when his expression turned forlorn and he would suddenly, softly lament, "I let you down." You could hear the genuine pain in his voice. Ours is not the most introspective generation, and I think these unsolicited mea culpas were George's way of coming to terms with what he perceived as a public rejection. He hated leaving his mission unfinished; he didn't like seeing the beltway pundits proved right; but most of all, I think, he abhorred the thought of letting anyone who worked or voted for him down.

The fact that he was trying to assume responsibility was vintage Bush, but the truth is he didn't let us down. It was his team that failed him, and the country, in 1992.

After the Bushes received a very warm welcome home at Ellington Air Force Base, we said our goodbyes and took our separate paths back into private life. Driving home, I knew I was turning the page from one fulfilling chapter to the next; and once again I was confronted with my good fortune. Unlike most who leave a presidential administration, I knew I was going to get my old job back heading Mosbacher Energy—though the vote among my colleagues and family might have been close had it come to that.

After four years in Washington, I was ready to dive headfirst back into my company. Absence makes the heart grow fonder, as the saying goes, and I truly missed the business—the deals, studying the different plays. I missed making tough decisions such as whether to spend millions of dollars you might lose if you got a "duster," or as my friend Chesley Pruet used to say, "the suitcase sand." (That meant if your test sand came back with saltwater, it was time to plug your well, pack your suitcase, and move on to the next prospect.)

Hope springs eternal for the Texas oilman. There is a certain truth to the myth that if you cut a Texan with a knife, he bleeds half crude oil. Once you get the business in your bloodstream, you can never get it fully out.

I was doubly fortunate because, while I was in Washington those four years, my son Rob had kept Mosbacher Energy going in an oil market that was still fairly soft since the price had taken a nosedive to $10 a barrel in the mid-1980s. Despite a brief spike in the price of oil following the Iraqi invasion of Kuwait in 1990, the price of a barrel of crude oil hovered around $20 between 1989 and 1993—well off the highs of roughly $38 a barrel we had seen in the late 1970s and early 1980s.[1]

I was itching to get back into the company—to try and help kick things into higher gear—and helping me, advising me, mentoring me almost from the beginning was my old friend Max Fisher. Max began calling me on a daily basis, offering wise advice. If Pop couldn't be there to act as a trusted sounding board, this was the next best thing in my view. Max was the next most influential figure in my life.[2]

One of the things Max urged me to do, for example, was to go back to focusing on those drilling areas, particularly in the United States, where I had made money in the first place. I relied on Max to the point that after I started dating my wife Mica some years later, he helped guide me to a success there as well!

Back at the company's helm, we also started exploring more international

1. Except for the brief Iraq-related spike in 1990, it would be twenty-two years—from 1982 to 2004—before the price of a barrel of oil would get back up to the $30s.

2. Now that Max is gone, my heroine just might be Roberta McCain, John's mother, who at ninety-six years young bought a car during a recent trip to Europe after she was informed she was too old to rent one. Now that is spunk!

With our dear family friend and personal mentor, Max Fisher, who advised and helped me in so many ways.

deals. The fall of the Soviet Union and the end of the Cold War helped to open up a number of new and potentially promising markets. Based on my visits to Russia while at Commerce, I was not keen on doing any business there; but the demise of the superpower conflict clearly removed a lot of barriers and tensions that had made certain parts of the world essentially off-limits in terms of conducting business deals during the Cold War.

One of the best deals we closed was in Venezuela. I have long maintained that it is better to be lucky than smart, and in this case we managed to get into

Venezuela, develop production, and sell out of that venture before Hugo Chavez assumed the Venezuelan presidency in 1999.

Incidentally, I'll never forget a private 1999 meeting I arranged for Chavez, who was the president-elect at the time, in Houston with former President George H. W. Bush. During their conversation, Chavez laid out a series of grand and altruistic plans for his presidency, and at the conclusion of his remarks he asked "41" what he thought. "Well, Mr. President," George said, "that sounds very interesting, but it seems we are more often judged by our actions, and not just our words."

After entering office, of course, Chavez proceeded to erode the country's legal framework, nationalizing and confiscating foreign oil projects, and taxing oil profits—to say nothing of what he has done to weaken human rights and democratic institutions in and around Venezuela. He is a sad, disgraceful figure within the world community.

Elsewhere in Latin America, meanwhile, we drilled a well with Duke Energy in Peru, with my friends Chesley Pruet and Max Fisher also taking a small piece. That turned out to be a very expensive deal, roughly a $12 million dry hole—what we call an "open by mistake" well.

Mosbacher Energy was also active in England, Indonesia, and Tunisia and had several oil and gas projects in India as well. In fact, we won the concession to develop an offshore field with 333 billion cubic feet of gas southeast of Chennai that we subsequently sold after a frustrating experience. India is the world's largest democracy, but unfortunately it is also a place where it can be agonizingly slow to get anything done.

Closer to home, we have had projects both in western and eastern Canada, including an offshore field called Terra Nova off Newfoundland and the Sable Island field off Nova Scotia. We thought Terra Nova would go on stream in the mid-1990s, but it didn't happen until 2002—at least eight years behind schedule, and at three times the cost. The good news is we have been producing up to 140,000 barrels per day, and the Sable Island has been producing up to 350,000,000 cubic feet of gas per day. When these projects were being built, for billions of dollars, I was afraid we had too big a percentage. Now that they are on stream and making money, naturally, I think our part is too small. That's life.

In February of 1993, just a month after returning to Houston, I also signed a contract with the energy company Enron. I had known Ken Lay, the CEO, since the early 1970s, and had served on the Enron board in the mid-1980s after the merger between Houston Natural Gas and InterNorth, a Nebraska pipeline company, led to its creation. Ken wanted me to come back on the board, but

I didn't think that was proper so we found a different configuration, where I would advise on various international deals with the right to take a piece of the action. That evolved into my becoming a consultant to the company. My esteemed friend, Jim Baker, did the same thing.

As I immersed myself in Enron's balance sheet and reacquainted myself with its operations portfolio, it was clear something had changed in the way the company did business. Starting in 1991, Enron became the first major energy company that would, upon closing a deal, book all of the profits they expected to make over the full term of the agreement in that first year. In other words, they started "marking to market" on their deals, which was legal under federal law. In fact, that was a recent accounting change that Enron had lobbied to enact.

For example, if Enron expected to derive, say, $10 million a year in income for ten years on a certain project, they would put the full $100 million in income, discounted at a fairly low rate, in that first year's earnings. I became increasingly dismayed at this practice. My experience in Canada with the Terra Nova project—eight years behind schedule, and over budget—demonstrated the problem with booking profits before they happen. Large and complex projects undertaken in remote areas and rough terrain rarely pan out exactly the way they are drawn up in stately wood-paneled boardrooms. There are too many variables—too many things that can, and often do, go awry. As a general rule, I have found that most complex projects take at least twice as long to start making money as the developers think.

Jimmy Baker and I talked several times over 1993 into 1994, as we became uncomfortable with the company's accounting. Although Enron's international business was booming at the time, and although a number of other companies were starting to use the same "mark-to-market" technique, I eventually decided it was entirely unrealistic. So I pulled the ripcord and terminated my consulting arrangement after a little over a year, as did Jimmy—who had reached a similar conclusion.

By that time, my relationship with Ken was already on the rocks. We had a major falling out over an offshore drilling deal off the west coast of India. Both Mosbacher Energy and Enron were vying for the project, until Ken came to me and said: "Don't worry if we get it and you don't, because I'll still bring you in on our piece of the deal. In fact, why don't you just drop out and you can have a part of ours?" We never discussed a specific percentage, but it sounded like a good idea to me so we shook hands and Mosbacher Energy pulled out.

After Enron won the contract, Ken called to inform me, "The guy who runs our oil and gas subsidiary is balking at giving you the piece we discussed, and I can't get him to budge." Ken was trying to make it sound like this person at the subsidiary didn't work for him, but in truth he was stiffing me. It would have been one thing had Ken come back to me and said they could only give me a small percentage, because—as I said— we had not talked specifics.

That was a real falling out for us, one that accelerated my leaving the company, and probably had something to do with Rob's hiring one of Enron's top developers, Jim Steele, to help manage our power projects.

Despite this disappointment, I was saddened and shocked to watch as Enron collapsed in 2001. It was an international business scandal of the highest order—Fortune 100 companies don't disappear everyday—but for many of us here in Texas it was also a personal tragedy as we saw so many friends, so many loyal employees, so many of our fellow Houstonians adversely affected.

I had known Ken Lay a long time, and always found him a very generous and caring individual. How he started believing all the B.S. that he and his company were putting out, however, still dismays me. As younger people say these days, he drank the Kool-aid. It was a sad ending for someone who, I thought in the beginning, had all the right instincts.

As I was tending to my day job back in the energy business, the pull of trade issues and policy brought me back into the national political arena on several occasions. In October of 1993, former presidents Gerald Ford, Jimmy Carter, Ronald Reagan, and George Bush formed a commission to help President Clinton in the final drive to win congressional approval for NAFTA. George, together with former Presidents Carter and Ford, had already appeared with President Clinton the previous month at a White House ceremony supporting NAFTA; and they were tasking former United Nations Ambassador Andrew Young and me to serve as national chairmen of this new commission. The goal was to assemble all living former U.S. secretaries of state, as well as business executives such as Microsoft Chairman Bill Gates and former Chrysler CEO Lee Iacocca, plus luminaries like former Speaker of the House Tip O'Neill and former Federal Reserve Chairman Paul Volcker to urge adoption for the treaty.

My job was essentially to work the phones—to call friends on Capitol Hill on both sides of the political aisle, stress the benefits of the deal, and try to answer any concerns. The lobbying we did that fall was, for me, a labor of love. As a businessman, I knew the treaty would create jobs. As a Texan, I knew it would help strengthen our neighbor to the south, Mexico, and give their citizens more hope for the future, too. And as a free-trade globalist, I believed that passing the NAFTA would be a helpful stepping-stone toward realizing George Bush's vi-

A little rest and relaxation with former CNN anchor Lou Dobbs and actor Michael York. Lou was an early supporter of NAFTA and its clear benefits to the United States; but in time, his views on international trade grew more populist and, perhaps, ratings-driven.

sion of a hemisphere that was united in common ideals—rooted in democratic capitalism.

Was NAFTA perfect? Heck no—no treaty that big and complex is. But it did deliver positive results almost as soon as President Clinton signed it into law on December 8, 1993. In fact, one of the most interesting endorsements came from a friend of mine, anchor Lou Dobbs, who hosted CNN's *Moneyline* for many years. I appeared with Lou on his show in 1997 as we marked the three-year anniversary of NAFTA, and before the interview even started Lou, who is now among the most vocal critics of NAFTA and trade in general, had this assessment:

> The Clinton administration tomorrow will unveil its report on the three years of NAFTA. It will reveal that the highly politicized treaty has increased cross-border trade by 45 percent, leading to a loss of a little

more than 100,000 jobs[3] in the United States, hardly the dire economic consequences that NAFTA's opponents had originally predicted, given that the U.S. economy has created almost seven million jobs since NAFTA took effect. . . .

I am not sure what happened to my friend Lou after he briefly returned to CNN and became one of the ardent detractors of just about anything to do with Mexico. True, the Mexican government has plenty of shortcomings when it comes to fighting the drug lords and promoting border security, to say nothing of helping us curb illegal immigration. Maybe it was the almighty pursuit of ratings, but before he left CNN again I often found Lou's rhetoric counterproductive—and certainly *not* the respectful dialogue we need to establish to actually address these and many other issues of importance.

In January of 1995, the Clinton administration led a bipartisan push to help Mexico recover from their currency crisis that saw the peso sink to historic lows very early in the administration of President Ernesto Zedillo. As the peso lost its purchasing power and robbed Mexico of its ability to repay loans mostly held by U.S. banks, it left U.S. banks dangerously exposed—threatening to bring them down along with the entire Mexican economy.

When asked, I was happy to join a press conference given by Clinton Treasury Secretary Robert Rubin—along with my former administration colleague, Brent Scowcroft—in urging Congress to extend a sizeable loan to Mexico City. "Mistakes have been made," Brent said, referring to the Mexican government. "But when the barn is on fire, one doesn't focus on how the fire was made before calling the fire department."

I added: "There is virtually no choice. We must go forward with this."

Fortunately, Congress did act quickly, and a certain catastrophe was avoided. Unfortunately, my friend Jaime Serra Puche—with whom I had worked so closely on NAFTA, and who had been appointed finance and public credit minister in the new Zedillo administration—was unfairly tagged with the blame for the crisis and forced out of office. Most of the problems that led to the crisis were approved and implemented under President Salinas; but as the song says, they were going to "punish the monkey, and let the organ grinder go."

I had another outburst of bipartisanship in 1997, when I supported President Clinton's drive to get Congress to renew fast-track legislation, which would authorize the president to negotiate international trade agreements on which

3. I strongly dispute this figure. In the first few years alone, NAFTA created hundreds of thousands of jobs.

Congress would vote up or down *without amendments*. My desire to help President Clinton jump-start the trade issue was borne of concern. Since the promising 1994 Miami summit, when the proposed trade initiative was renamed the Free Trade Area of the Americas, the United States had largely withdrawn from its leadership role on liberalized trade.

As a result, a "southern cone" group called "Mercosur"—originally comprising Brazil, Argentina, Uruguay, and Paraguay—sprang up, and started to fill the vacuum left by Washington's inaction. The MERCOSUR group started by offering Chile and Bolivia associate membership status, which created a market of 220 million potential consumers with a combined gross domestic product of about $1 trillion—more than twice the economic output of ASEAN, the Association of Southeast Asian Nations. Then they planned free trade talks with Colombia, Venezuela, Ecuador, and Peru. I thought they were well on their way to establishing a South America Free Trade Area as a counterweight to NAFTA. From there, they could strike deals with the European Union, the Central American Common Market, and even Mexico and Canada.

By then, I was chairing the Americas Society and the affiliated Council of the Americas, so it was my job to help inform the public about the politics, economies, and cultures of countries in the Western Hemisphere while promoting economic integration with free trade and investment. But again, doing so was a labor of love. I felt a sense of duty and determination to help support and enhance those things I helped set in motion— and which I thought would help our nation.

I was not the only Mosbacher staying active on issues affecting the general welfare, however. In April of 1997, I watched with great pride as Rob, then forty-six years old, announced he was running for mayor of Houston. The announcement ended months, if not years, of speculation over Rob's political future. He had also been mentioned as a possible candidate for Texas Governor in 1994, and was everyone's short list for all the top jobs in the state.

By then, Rob had more than earned his stripes and paid his dues as a political activist and fund-raiser. He was seen as an extremely capable business leader, serving at the time on nineteen nonprofit boards and ten civic boards—including board chairman of the world-renowned Methodist Hospital and the local chapter of the American Red Cross. Together with his service on several state boards, the question heading into the 1997 Houston city election wasn't whether Rob was qualified or could get the job done. There was also no question surrounding what motivated Rob to run for mayor—he had consistently, and selflessly, given of his time to help lead numerous community-oriented projects to

Celebrating NAFTA's tenth anniversary with Canada's Brian Mulroney, George Bush, and Carlos Salinas. I continued to press for free and fair trade after leaving Washington.

help the less fortunate. His opponents could, and did, accuse Rob of being born to a wealthy family and promoting business-friendly policies; but they couldn't credibly charge that he didn't care about helping people.

"We all are blessed or cursed with circumstances at birth that we can't control, and I have been blessed," Rob told the *Houston Chronicle* in August of 1997. "I think the question is: What have you done with it? Did you take it for granted? Did you view it as something that was some entitlement?"

No, the only question hanging over Rob's run for mayor was whether someone with his Republican credentials could attract enough support in a Democrat-leaning city to beat a nationally-known African American candidate, Lee P. Brown, who had just left the Clinton White House. Brown had served as police chief in Houston and New York before entering the Clinton administration as the drug czar. Of course, Houston city races are technically nonpartisan, but right off the bat the 1997 mayor's race had an undeniable partisan undercurrent to it.

Two case studies that offered hope for Rob's chances that year were Rudy

With veteran newsman Walter Cronkite aboard Rhapsody *during a trip to Martha's Vineyard in 1999.*

Giuliani in New York and Richard Riordan in Los Angeles, who had successfully convinced big-city urban voters they could trust a conservative to run City Hall. Clearly, this offered a model to follow; and together with his campaign team and backed by a blue-chip group of financial supporters such as the Port of Houston chairman Ned Holmes, developer Walter Mischer, and investor Charles Miller, Rob dove into the campaign headfirst. "The challenge of our next mayor is how we build on [Houston's] economic momentum and extend it to every corner of our city," Rob said, as he laid out one of the central ideas behind his candidacy.

My friend George Bush later confided how it was much worse for him as a father when either of his politically-active sons were attacked by opponents and media critics, but I didn't worry nearly as much during 1997 because, as I saw it, most of the attacks against Rob were either totally irrelevant—such as his privileged upbringing—or totally absurd, such as the suggestion that Rob would have to run to me for advice when making decisions as mayor.

To their credit, the *Houston Chronicle* also discounted these flimsy attacks when they endorsed Rob during both the general election in November, and the run-off election that followed in December. Quoting from their first endorsement:

> . . . Mosbacher combines the right mix of business acumen, fiscal
> conservatism, education, experience, accomplishment, integrity,
> communications skills, energy and a sincere caring about Houston. . . .
> His resume has much to recommend him, including substantive political
> activism, business success and a long and broad involvement in the civic
> and charitable life of Houston. It is clear that he cares about the city
> and its people and, stereotypes about wealth and privilege aside, he has
> demonstrated his caring in ways more long-standing and meaningful than
> mere politically motivated token resume-building. . . .

To counter Rob's well-managed campaign, Lee Brown brought President Clinton, Vice President Al Gore, and other Democratic Party leaders to town to inspire voters to favor Brown. No question, as other observers noticed at the time, Brown also benefitted from a citizen-driven measure to end affirmative action that was also placed on the November ballot. This gave liberals and minority voters another source of motivation to turn out, and after the votes were counted in the first round of voting on November 4, Brown finished with 42 percent of the vote while Rob placed second in a four-man field with 29 percent.

The December run-off was a two-man affair, Rob versus Lee Brown. I am biased, of course, but Rob was a far better debater, a better candidate, and offered a more compelling vision of Houston's future. To their credit, however, the Brown team did a terrific job turning their voters out to the polls a second time, and when the dust settled Rob had managed to corral more than 47 percent—with Brown coming in under 53 percent. Once again, I knew in my heart that the better man had not won, but having suffered through a few agonizing losses with men like George Bush and Gerry Ford I knew that went with the territory.

All you can do, which Rob did magnificently, is get up, dust yourself off, and get on with life. Luckily for Houston, Rob almost immediately threw himself back into both his business activities, as well as his civic endeavors—and in the years ahead went on to lead the Greater Houston Partnership, the Salvation Army, and help countless other meaningful causes.

For my civic engagement, I was offered a wonderful opportunity to rejoin the board of visitors at the M. D. Anderson Cancer Center—the hospital that had treated Jane with such great care and skill, and today is recognized as perhaps THE leading cancer research and treatment hospital in the world.

First Pooch Millie eavesdropping on my conversation with Barbara Bush, America's most beloved First Lady. She is the brightest Point of Light for her leadership on family literacy.

Of course, I was all the more delighted when George Bush came on the board and served as its chairman for two years—a remarkable act on his part. No question, one of the great highlights of my time with M. D. Anderson came in June 1999, when I chaired what one news report called "the largest charitable fund-raising event of its kind in U.S. history." To help George and Bar celebrate their seventy-fifth and seventy-fourth birthdays, respectively, we gathered their family and about 3,000 of their friends at Houston's Astroarena—and raised $10.1 million for M. D. Anderson. The event that night was headlined by Hollywood Republicans (Arnold Schwarzenegger, Bruce Willis) and entertainers ranging from the Oak Ridge Boys, to Van Cliburn, to the Ballet Hispanico of New York.

Earlier that week, George did something that has become a matter of routine for him: he celebrated a milestone birthday with a parachute jump, exiting the aircraft and free-falling from nearly 5,000 feet before floating down to the lawn of the George Bush Presidential Library on the campus of Texas A&M University. This was the third parachute jump of George's life. The first came during World War II, when his torpedo plane was shot down in the Pacific. The second came in 1997, in Yuma, Arizona.

Raising that $10.1 million was particularly fulfilling because every penny went to fund the George and Barbara Bush Endowment for Innovative Cancer Research at the hospital. Like me, the Bushes had a deeply personal reason for enlisting in the war against cancer: their three-year-old daughter, Robin, died of leukemia in 1953.

It had been almost thirty years since I had lost Jane, but also on my mind that night was my brother Bus, who also succumbed to cancer on August 13, 1997. Growing up, Bus had a very fair, reddish-blonde complexion. Given the amount of time he spent in the sun throughout his life, he was a particular risk for the skin cancer that first developed on his lip, eventually metastasized and spread. He was seventy-five.

Bus was an extremely talented and smart man—and as he showed throughout his sailing career, he had some exceptional leadership qualities. Bus could be wonderful, charming, and even sweet, but he could also be difficult, a "sharp-eyed perfectionist," as the *New York Times* described him in their obituary. He did not suffer fools gladly.

Looking back, there is a sadness that my brother and I were so often at odds, but we had our fun moments, too. When we were both young adults, for example, we secretly raced against each other out on Long Island Sound a couple of times. These matches were spirited, intense. At the time, there was speculation as to which of us was, in fact, the better sailor—but we pledged we would never divulge the results, not even to Pop.

I am not about to break my word now.

Less than a year after we lost Bus, I experienced another family death of sorts when my marriage to Georgette ended in divorce. I do not have much more to add to what Georgette has written in her two books that touch on our relationship, except to say our fourteen years together were filled with excitement, fun, and—obviously—our fair share of rough patches. That happens when two strong-willed personalities come together.

In the end, Georgette wanted to live in New York full-time, and spent most of her time there. I love New York City, but Houston has been my home since 1948. Most of my family is here, along with friends and my business. After a while, Georgette and I simply grew apart; and I wish her nothing but the best.

Dealing with these two personal losses, Bus and Georgette, was not a happy time, as you might imagine. Yet the sailing gods intervened in my life once again—this time introducing me to a lovely woman with whom I wanted to spend more and more time.

It was a party being thrown for my friend, sailing legend Buddy Melges, at Houston's Bayou Club. The event sponsor was responsible for managing

Still dating at the time, Mica and I prepare for an ill-fated afternoon cruise on Babe. *Despite poor planning on my part, I still got the girl in the end!*

the guest list of 200 to 300, and when she asked Buddy if he had anyone he wanted on the VIP list, he immediately piped up: "Have you invited my buddy, Mosbacher?"

"Well, I don't know," she replied.

"Oh, you can just call him and tell him it's for me," Buddy suggested. "Make sure he comes out."

So I did—and not only did I see my old sailing friend Melges, that's where I also first met the beautiful and engaging Mica McCutchen. We instantly hit it off, and had great fun visiting at the party. At one point I thought I detected a spark. I was a little gun-shy, and it was several weeks before I called her. She was jogging at the Houstonian Hotel, and when we got together later she was still in her jogging clothes. As I recall, my opening line was admittedly less than romantic: "You know," I said, "most women I know would have gone to a lot of trouble to fix themselves up, but that's an ugly brown jacket."

I recovered from that awkward start, thankfully, and before long Mica and I decided to go to Green Turtle Cay in the Bahamas for a weekend getaway. My good friend and sailing buddy Tommy Dickey offered us his sailboat, *Babe*, to use, which was moored nearby on Man o' War Cay, so we rented a Boston

Whaler to get there. We had a great sail, and at the end of the day headed home to Green Turtle.

Unfortunately, the motorboat we were renting had no fuel gauge, and halfway back, as the sun was setting, we ran out of gas. With no other option, and no radio or cell phone, Mica and I tied up at a deserted island called No-Name Cay. We had no hope of being rescued that night because after sunset no one moves in Bahamian waters, and we had no food or other provisions except wine. So we slept there in our rented 15-foot Boston Whaler, and were rescued the next morning.

Mica's mother, Jane, couldn't believe we had run out of gas, and neither could my kids. In fact, my family was so shocked they gave me ship-to-shore radios for future use. As for Mica, she was a really good sport about my screw-up, and I suppose that's when we really clicked as a couple.

As it turns out, my sloppy performance as a seaman on that first trip together was a minor warm-up test for our relationship because a short time later I was diagnosed with prostate cancer. Fortunately, we caught it early during my annual heart and blood test; but despite the positive prognosis I was suddenly hit with my mortality. I called Mica from the doctor's office, and told her it felt like I had been kicked in the stomach. The very mention of the word "cancer" scares the hell out of everyone, and it took Mica's caring intervention to help me snap out of this fog I had gone into, and to make getting better a priority.

Within a few weeks, I opted for radiation therapy and dutifully showed up every morning at 6:45 A.M. to be first in line for my treatments. For the first four or so weeks, I was doing just fine. My energy level was still high, so I did something I would not advise to anyone else. After my treatments, I would go to the office for a full day's work. By the time I got to week five or six, I was wiped out. Mica said, "Mossy, you'll get well if you stop and rest."

Fortunately, I came through that treatment with a positive outcome, but that experience did more than restore me to good health. It also showed to me that I had a very special, strong, and caring woman in my life—someone I needed by my side. Mica and I got engaged in April of 2000 on our way to a Houston Astros game. We married that July 20 (Mica's birthday) in a very private ceremony at my home—a surprise to our guests, who thought it was a birthday dinner.

To be honest, I never really had what you might call a real wedding, so it meant a great deal for me to have my family and friends there—with Rob serving as my best man. I had eloped with Jane, after all, and gone to the Justice of the Peace with Sandra and Georgette. I wanted to get this one right. Given the importance that faith has come to occupy in my life, it was also important to me

With our fantastic kids at Odyssey Academy, the charter school we opened in Galveston, thanks to some talented and dedicated educators. It remains one of my proudest accomplishments.

to have a minister present, and for that we turned to Dave Peterson of Memorial Drive Presbyterian and Charlie Shedd, who had baptized me so many years before.

Afterwards, I broke out a very special wine, La Tache, for the celebratory dinner, and a lovely singer, Yvonne Washington, sang a few George Gershwin tunes by request, adding to the magic of that night.

I certainly never had a hard time staying active, but Mica makes life fun— and she keeps me grounded. Every once in a while, if I suggest that she do something a certain way, she'll fire back: "I'm sorry, Mr. Secretary, but I'm not working for you." We worked hard to blend our families.

Most of all, my wife has a heart of gold. A few years ago, a young Hispanic boy was viciously assaulted by a couple of local teenagers. He was beaten badly and sodomized. It was classified as a hate crime, and after she read the news Mica called the family, offered some kind words of encouragement, and helped them financially. She is always doing things like that—not for credit or attention, but because she is a deeply caring and sensitive person.

Around the time this tragedy was reported, in fact, Mica came up with the idea for a bridge called "Harmony Arc" to be built in Houston—spanning Buffalo Bayou between Allen Parkway and Memorial Drive. Including an installation by Jaume Plensa depicting universal figures in harmony, the bridge design features a visual sleight of hand: a twisted archway at its center that from afar will make it appear impossible to cross. However, when pedestrians or bikers are closer, they will see the bridge is easily passable. From one vantage point, moreover, the "twisted arc" will frame the Houston skyline. To me, it is a beautiful metaphor—race relations are awkward at best in situations where one group keeps another at a distance. It is only after we come together as Texans and Americans that hurtful stereotypes and false perceptions fall by the wayside.

The Harmony Arc is an inspired idea on Mica's part, and naturally I admire her for that. It's been an honor for me simply to get out of her way, and watch her make this wonderful vision a reality.

Another important project we undertook together involved the 2008 presidential election.

In November 2008, Senator Barack Obama of Illinois prevailed over my good friend, and a great American, Senator John McCain of Arizona to be elected the forty-fourth president of the United States of America. Though there wasn't a Bush on the national ticket for only the second time since 1980, Mica and I had more than a passing interest.

We had dinner with John McCain at a Washington event benefiting the Reagan Library in 2006. That night, I told John I would be with him if he ran for president; but privately I told Mica I had no interest in jumping in with both feet. So we did a few little things, like the time Mica hosted a "Women for McCain" tea. Both Cindy and John came, but we didn't ask for contributions. The folks in the campaign thought we were nuts, but oftentimes you have to give the relationship between the prospective giver and the candidate time to grow.

Unfortunately, not enough donors were coming on board, and as John's poll numbers gradually sank during the first half of 2007 his fund-raising started to dry up with it. When the wheels finally came off, and the campaign asked me to come onboard, I told Mica: "I feel I have to help this man. He is a good man and the right candidate. He is what our country needs."

We did a lot of soul-searching before I answered, because it meant that we would be working long hours, and traveling back and forth to Washington. It was exactly what I had *not* wanted to do, but once again I felt the tug of public service drawing me back to the arena.

Finally, in August 2007, I formally joined the McCain effort as general

Mica and me with Gary and O. J. Shansby (r.) and John McCain at Sedona during the 2008 campaign. Victory was not to be for the McCain-Palin ticket, but I couldn't have been prouder to stand behind this genuine American hero.

campaign chairman—coming onboard at perhaps John's darkest hour. Mica joined as the Women for McCain national chairwoman. John was down in the polls at the time; his fund-raising was *de minimus* behind his top competitors; and there had just been a serious staff shake-up involving his campaign manager Terry Nelson and senior strategist John Weaver. Generally speaking, they seemed to be barely hanging on by their fingertips, with the first January 2008 primary contests fast approaching.

Despite the bleak condition of his political operation, John defiantly declared that even if the campaign ran out of money he would get in the middle seat in coach, continue his campaign alone, and press ahead telling people the truth. How could you not admire that?

My enthusiasm was somewhat abated, however, when I went to my first campaign budget meeting at the McCain headquarters and discovered how much debt we had—against no assets. Our 2007 third-quarter finance report showed us with $3.4 million on hand and debts totaling $1.7 million. The trouble was, another $1.8 million of that money had been raised for, and legally had to be dedicated to, the general election. So this report meant we essentially had no cash on hand. Even with the general election money factored in, we still owed about $94,000.

The slide toward a negative cash flow had been months in the making. During the first quarter of 2007, for example, the McCain operation spent more than any other campaign on staff payroll—a whopping $1.6 million, versus $1.1 million for their next-closest competitor, former Massachusetts Governor Mitt Romney.

On top of that, the McCain camp had chartered two planes on a long-term basis, which was far more expensive than using commercial air travel. The plane leases were clearly executed on the assumption that John was a shoo-in to win the nomination; but as he started to lag badly in the polls, and fund-raising took a dive, the campaign's financial burn rate was too high. I don't blame John for that—the candidate shouldn't have to delve into such details—but rather, I think the McCain campaign staff had been infected with a case of "front-runner's disease." Or as Pop would call it: "Big shot-itis."

Already, the campaign had been forced to lay off much of the staff, while cutting the pay of its senior members and contemplating the drastic measure of accepting federal matching funds during the primary. We needed to find other savings immediately, so working with the lawyers we got out of those ill-advised plane leases.

Then I got on the phone and called every state finance chairman, every city finance chairman, and every cochair to tell them what the situation was—to their credit, not one of them quit during these dark days. I'll never forget that, and neither will John McCain. We really had some great people who were committed to the process, the candidate, and the country.

We were desperate for cash back then. Campaign manager Rick Davis would nervously check the bank account every day. When checks came in he would walk them immediately to the bank. In June 2008 Mica and I rented an apartment in Washington—the only husband and wife team working together in finance.

Meanwhile, the finance team—led by Tom Loeffler; Fred Malek; Susan Nelson, the finance director; and Brian Haley, the deputy finance director—was trying to pick up supporters one-by-one. Day after day, week after week, Susan fed me names and numbers, and I'd make the call. Then she would nervously pace the floor waiting to see if the caller would take the call. On it went, and by the time the final call had been made and the final arm had been twisted, we had raised $419 million—with all but $35 million of it coming in 2008. Rick Davis later said that the finance team was the only part of the campaign that worked like a well-oiled machine.

Most important to the McCain revival, however, was the way John shined throughout the fall of 2007 during the many GOP debates. To us—and a growing number of primary voters—he seemed more real, more in command, than his able competitors. Added to that, when all seemed lost, John made the decision to simply "go to New Hampshire and tell the truth," as he put it. It was a big gamble, but it paid off.

The 101 town hall meetings he held gave Granite State Republicans, an independent and knowledgeable group, maybe the truest sense of John McCain the man.

Of course, John had also repeatedly gone to Iowa and told the truth there, too, but most corn farmers don't like it when you argue against ethanol subsidies. John also went to Michigan and bluntly told the unions and auto executives that their lost manufacturing jobs were not coming back—and that they had to reform their industry, while we retrained their workers.

I was particularly pleased with the way John refused to pander to the fear and ignorance of the isolationists and others by declaring himself an unabashed free trader.

During the primary, he maybe hacked a lot of people off, but I admired the way John McCain leveled with the American people and let the chips fall where they may. That's called leadership; and that's what Republican primary voters responded to in handing John one of the most remarkable come-from-behind nomination victories in modern political history.

Only months before, he was dead in the water—as if his jib sheet had been cut, too. It took courage, adherence to principle, and sheer dedication to his cause to put the wind back into his sails, and carry him into the Minneapolis GOP Convention where he was confirmed as our standard bearer against a tough field of competitors.

Unfortunately, the general election that followed would not feature a similar comeback story. That fall is where the seas turned ugly for the old Navy warrior and his campaign.

In his very gracious concession speech on November 4, John assumed full responsibility for the outcome of the election. His statement that crisp, clear Arizona night was nothing short of magnanimous, and helped our country start to come together after a tough campaign.

Like everyone else, I share the view that, when the economy tanked and the stock market went into its nosedive, our chances went with it. I also give great credit to the Obama campaign, which did an effective job of tying John to the George W. Bush administration. The president and, to a lesser extent his party, get the credit or the blame for the economy—right or wrong. For six years, President Bush "43" had done a magnificent job keeping our economy growing despite the 9/11 attacks and two costly wars; but markets work in cycles, and George W. Bush's historic span of job creation and economic growth ran its course at precisely the worst time.

As important as anything leading to his defeat, however, I believe John McCain was ill-served by a small coterie of political professionals who, in my view, routinely put their own interests ahead of the candidate they were supposed to serve.

For example, within this small group, everyone fancied themselves a policy expert with all the answers. Not only that, they tended to treat the rest of us from the business world like village idiots. Even though we had people who had built businesses and hospitals and schools, had done remarkable things for their communities, and had contacts those guys could only dream about, these top political guys clearly felt they were too busy and important to return calls.

I had to push them to do regular meetings with economic and foreign policy experts—you know, the people who actually knew what they were talking about. Toward the end of the campaign, for example, after the economy took over as THE pivotal issue, they had John running all over the place, ranting about firing the Securities and Exchange Commission head Chris Cox, and generally appealing to the lowest common denominator. They tried to turn the maverick into a populist, but it didn't work.

Meanwhile, I had been pushing for weeks for John to do a meeting with leading economists and CEOs like Fred Smith at Fed Ex and the respected former GE head Jack Welch to show he was serious about fixing these big problems. As usual, the inner group either ignored the suggestion or said, "We're already doing that." So I finally called John directly, and after he heard my pitch said, "You're absolutely right." We did the big economic meeting in Ohio, but it was done at the last minute.

You cannot do campaign events like that once and hope that it penetrates. It's a big country, and we were up against a disciplined and well-financed opponent. The campaign's job was to come up with a credible and cohesive argument to elect John McCain—and to keep repeating it. We had to find a compelling alternative to the Obama mantra "change we can believe in," and then drive that message home. We never did.

Another problem, as I saw it, involved the campaign's inexcusable lack of Hispanic outreach. John McCain has been a heroic voice of common sense on the divisive issue of immigration; and as a result, he was perhaps the only Republican with a shot at winning the Hispanic vote. Instead, we ended up with around 33 percent. Why? It turned out the three or four people who were running the McCain campaign couldn't do everything, so the idea to have John reach out and cultivate votes in the Hispanic community also withered on the vine.

Nobody has all the answers, so why not be inclusive? That's the way you should run everything. The smartest guy in the world still doesn't know everything. In the end, I am sad to say, this was a clear-cut example of a few Washington egos wanting to be seen as the hero. The problem is that their exclusive management style came at the expense of "our" candidate—and the 57 million Americans who were supporting the McCain cause.

Worst of all, perhaps, was the shameful treatment meted out to Governor Palin even before Election Day, with nameless sources trying to pin the loss on her surprise selection as the vice presidential running mate. Maybe that's what you have to do when you're a Washington lobbyist, and you have to start explaining to your clients what went wrong—and why you're still the go-to guy. You start leaking to your media friends, who are all too eager to help you dish the inside campaign dirt.

That's the seedy side of politics I hate the most.

Still, at eighty-two, I am more philosophical than I used to be. Maybe I am mellowing with age, maybe I have enough scars from previous political wars, but I wish everyone with whom I worked well. It's a peculiar business, politics—and Lord knows, I have made my share of mistakes.

Now I hope the future holds more time with Mica and my family. I recall how Pop often said: "When all is said and done, there's nothing left but family."

I'm biased, naturally, but couldn't be prouder of Dee, Rob, Kathi, and Lisa. They're generous and kind, witty and fun, smart and principled. Each, in their own way, is also accomplished and respected.

Dee has directed several award-winning and thought-provoking documentaries, including her 1994 film, *Straight from the Heart*, which was nominated for an Academy Award. She also continues to work as a psychiatrist in San Francisco.

Rob recently added another chapter of public service to his distinguished career, serving as president and CEO of the Overseas Private Investment Corporation in Washington, where he earned rave reviews from foreign leaders

Mica describes me as her first true love, while she is my last true love. (Photo courtesy of Alexander's Fine Portrait Design)

My sister Barbara and I revisit one of our family's favorite restaurants in New York City.

One of the great blessings of my eighty-two years has been seeing our grandkids grow and develop into fine young men and women. In the back row, Lisa and Downing's twins Whitney (left) and Parker flank Peter, while sitting are Jane, Bayly, and Meredith. (Photo courtesy of Alexander's Fine Portrait Design)

Rob and I sharing a really good laugh before Kathi's wedding in 2006. Mere words cannot describe my pride in him.

Nanette and Dee can rightly boast the longest relationship in our family. The tension that once marked our relationship has long since given way to joy.

With daughters Lisa, left, and Kathi. Looking at them reminds me just how lucky I have been in life.

and, most importantly, the forty-third president of the United States who appointed him.

My daughter Kathi, meanwhile, has one of the most advanced food minds, and palates, in the country—having studied with foodie icons James Beard in Greenwich Village and Chef Ken Lo in London, and at the venerable Le Cordon Bleu in Paris. Trust me, what Kathi does not know about food is not worth knowing. The icing on the cake is that she is a truly wonderful daughter, to boot.

Then there is my baby girl, my Lisa, who somehow finds the time to get involved with so many wonderful causes while raising a beautiful family. She is a true Point of Light, and a remarkable wife and mother.

Of course, the highest compliment I could pay my kids is drawn from the highest standard of decency I know. For the positive and caring way they have lived their lives, my son and daughters are a wonderful tribute to their mother, Jane Pennybacker Mosbacher. She left this world much too soon; but just as Jane lit up every room she entered, she also imbued her children with the same grace and good humor that endeared her to all.

As for me, I hope God gives me more days and nights with Mica listening to Frank Sinatra and cooking spaghetti dinners. Hopefully, there is still more time to get out on the sailboat where we can look out at the open expanse of beautiful iridescent blue sea—or the majesty of the night sky illuminated by the moon and stars. And of course I still get lost looking into Mica's eyes.

Mica describes me as her first true love; while to me, she is my last true love. I feel truly blessed to share this happy time in my life with her, my stepson Cameron, and now Cameron's beautiful bride Brittanie and their child Donald Cameron Duncan IV (Donnie), born in October of 2008. Just recently, Mica and I even baby-sat Donnie, and I am happy to report that both the child—and the grandparents—survived the experience.

Then in January of 2009, following what I suspect was my last visit to the White House for a very moving Points of Light event honoring George and Barbara Bush, Mica and I decided to have doctors investigate some persistent stomach pains I had been having. They performed an endoscopic ultrasound that, unfortunately, produced a diagnosis of pancreatic cancer.

This time, it was Mica who felt she had been run over by a truck—and that was before we found out the cancer had spread to the liver.

Long a master of my own fate, like Pop I have now lost control of my life except for making my own medical decisions. What matters most now is time spent with family and friends. I find great comfort, and hope, in my faith and know that after a lifetime of charging forward—of going to windward—that I can let down my sails, ride through this storm, and still make it to safe harbor in the end.

I have been in enough rough seas as a sailor and know that blue skies always follow a storm.

The reason why maybe gets back to that summer day so many years ago in the backseat with Pop, and that enduring lesson he taught me about my good fortune. It's better to be lucky than to be smart, as life has taught me, and for my family and friends, for the challenges and opportunities that have come into my life, and for the many chances I have had to serve this wonderful country, I've been—by far—the luckiest guy I know.

Epilogue   ALREADY WHERE I WANT TO BE

Many, many years ago—almost half a century ago—my friend and banker, Ben Love, came to see me regarding a loan I wanted to take out. "Bob," he said somewhat coyly after we exchanged pleasantries, gesturing to my loan application in his hand, "I need a statement before we can complete this transaction."

Ben, of course, meant a financial statement—but Mosbacher Energy was a privately-held company, and Ben was aware that we never shared our internal numbers. As advised by Pop more than half a century ago, I also never put my name on a loan. I would pledge certain properties as collateral, but not the entire "nut."

"I'll give you a statement," I said, as Ben braced himself. "I'm confident!"

My statement did not go over well with Ben, who was one of the strongest, toughest, most successful bankers I have known. As a person, he was a great friend, and when he liked you—and believed in you—he would go the extra mile for you. Ben had been in the Air Force as an elite navigator, he had been shot at and almost shot down. He was a hard-driver on his employees, but he never asked them to do anything he wouldn't have done himself.

As a young businessman, my outlook tended to be optimistic. Much of that was due to the fact that I was blessed early in my career with some success, and a great deal of good fortune. Even when we hit an expensive dry hole or some other setback, I always felt better days lay ahead if we worked harder than everyone else.

In that regard, I was a little different than Pop. His life experience taught him always to worry about survival, about the future. As Emil Mosbacher's fortunate son, in contrast, I had the comparative luxury of taking calculated, manageable risks, confident of my family's welfare.

Now in the autumn of life, my confidence in the future is undiminished, which is not to say I believe that future will be free of new troubles and travails. After the hard-fought 2008 campaign, like all Americans, I wish the forty-fourth president of the United States well. We face some serious economic and geopolitical challenges, and President Obama must succeed in leading our nation in addressing them.

Sharing a laugh with President George W. Bush during a Free Trade Agreements push on Feb. 26, 2008, in the Eisenhower Executive Office Building in Washington, DC. From the left are former Defense Secretary William Cohen, yours truly, former Commerce Secretary Bill Daley, the president, and former White House Chief of Staff Mack McLarty. (White House photo by Chris Greenberg)

As important as anything, I hope America will not turn inward, and away from the world, as we continue to confront those threats to our shared future. The U.S. economy can, and will, remain the world's leading economy throughout the twenty-first century, provided we *not* heed the protectionists and isolationists, and withdraw or pull back from the global market.

The United States is, generally speaking, a free-trade nation because it is a policy that has worked demonstrably well for us. Much of our economic growth in modern times has been tied to our exports.

For free trade to succeed, however, it must also be fair—a two-way street.

Remember the outcry in the late 1980s when the Japanese bought a majority interest in Rockefeller Center? There was both great fear that they would end up controlling the United States, and widespread anger that they had been able to buy a symbol of New York and America. As it turned out, it was a good sale for the American owners—and, for those who are interested, the property is back under American ownership.

More recently, when the China National Offshore Oil Company offered in 2005 to buy the American oil company, Unocal, a backlash erupted over the concept of a foreign company controlling one of our energy producers. The critics were worried that China could then potentially drive up the price of oil and start an invasion of our energy supply. Never mind that Unocal was a midsized energy company—certainly not a critical cog in our national energy machine.

A year later, in 2006, a similar furor quickly emerged when Dubai Ports World, a state-owned company based in the United Arab Emirates—a modern, progressive, and stable country that also happens to be a friend of the United States—announced its intent to acquire businesses in six major American seaports. Critics of this deal, including leading members of Congress, successfully attacked the idea, saying it would weaken national security—which they had to know was absurd at best, and bigoted at worst. Just as disappointing, the collapse of that deal sent a terrible message that we were willing to limit foreign investments in our country based on emotion and ignorance, not facts and reason.

Perhaps worst of all, and of much greater importance, in 2008 the United States Congress, under Speaker Pelosi's union-dominated leadership, refused to consider granting free trade status to Colombia—despite the fact that Colombia is openly pro-American, a courageous ally in the battle against narco-traffickers, and a key counterweight to the contemptible leadership in Venezuela.

My point in citing these examples is that, moving forward, I hope our nation will set a different course, veering away from a counterproductive direction that restricts trade or investments here. I recognize that U.S. businesses and workers face subsidized competition around the world—including Italy's steel industry and, of course, Airbus, subsidized by much of Europe—but the only way we can fix these problems, and ensure our continued prosperity, is to stay engaged in the global economy. Besides, the world still looks to America, with all our challenges, to lead by example. They expect it.

Despite our detractors around the world, the United States is still the "last, best hope of mankind"—a beacon of freedom and opportunity that will continue to draw economic and political refugees like my grandfather and grandmother no matter the risks involved. Indeed, every day there are overcrowded boats filled with scared sons and daughters, brothers and sisters, and mother and fathers heading through the surf and into the Gulf of Mexico—trying to reach our shores. There are tired migrant workers trekking across the deadly desert scrub of north Mexico, hopping on freight trains, doing whatever it takes to enter the land of opportunity.

Yes, the pull of America is as strong as ever; and it's time, particularly for my party, to recognize not only the self-evident fact that our immigration system is broken, but that it is going to require a comprehensive—and humane—approach to fix it. Eventually, we are going to have to wake up to the fact that Hispanics are no different from the Irish, German, Chinese, Italian, Jewish, and other immigrants in times past who came here escaping destitution and seeking a better life.

In other words, we should heed the lessons of the Know Nothing Party, which during the 1850s rode a wave of anti-immigrant sentiment to some regional political success. Their hardening attitude was part of the political backlash against the three million German and Irish immigrants—most of them Catholic—who poured into America through our ports at midcentury. Fearing the impact of the new arrivals, the Know Nothings gained momentary political favor in select cities by denouncing the so-called "popery" of the new immigrants, seeking to delay their citizenship and to deny them voting rights. In some northern cities, there were even bloody anti-Catholic riots.

In her terrific book, *Team of Rivals*, historian Doris Kearns Goodwin notes how the first and greatest Republican of them all, Abraham Lincoln, disdained the discriminatory beliefs of the Know Nothings. "As a nation, we began by declaring *all men are created equal . . .*" Lincoln said at the time. "When Know Nothings get control, it will read 'all men are created equal except [slaves], and foreigners and Catholics.'"[1]

Xenophobia didn't find a place in the party of Lincoln during our Republic's hour of maximum peril—on the eve of our Civil War. If we are to avoid seeing the GOP reduced to a regional faction, it should have no place in the party of Lincoln today.

Let me add one final thought, this one about energy. Having been in the oil and gas business for close to sixty years, I have seen the wild gyrations of the market. In 1986 and then again in 1999, the price of a barrel of oil sank to $10—a modern low-water mark—but in early 2008 it went to $144 a barrel. The lesson Pop helped me learn is that you can always hope for the best, but you must be prepared for the worst—and be in a position to survive the $10 times, while also enjoying the $140 oil times.

On a long-term basis, over the next twenty years, I do not see how the price of oil can do anything but rise. As the world economy grows, the global demand for oil and gas will continue to surge, particularly in countries like India and China with huge populations that are just beginning to buy cars.

I think we are right to try to find renewable sources of energy of all sorts—as well as nuclear—because someday, not a day I will see, but sometime in the next fifty years the world will change from oil and gas over to a combination of sources we are working on now, and some we cannot envision. However, anyone who thinks this fundamental change from fossil fuels like oil and gas and clean coal (or converted to gas) is going to happen before 2030 is not being realistic. They're dreaming.

One of the key impediments to progress is that Congress seems unable to act on this issue, even after oil spikes to well above $100 a barrel. The long-term vision, and sustained commitment, demanded to reduce our dependence on carbon-based energy has proven to be beyond our collective political will so far. If that holds true, our energy problems are only going to get worse before real solutions are enacted.

That said, I believe we are lucky to be Americans, and it is our joy and a duty to keep our democracy working—to do our part. I have tried to do just that; but now, as the sun sets on my life, I look forward to more time out on the water— and more time with Mica and my family.

Many years ago, we were sitting on the back of a friend's deep-sea trawler enjoying post-race drinks off the coast of California. We were cruising along at a leisurely pace when one of the smart-aleck members of our crew asked how fast the trawler would go. "Eight or nine knots," replied the skipper.

"No, I know that's what we're doing right now," our soon-to-be-former crew member sarcastically pressed, "but how fast does she go when you really open her up?"

"Let me tell you, boy," the skipper replied, "I don't know where you're hurrying to get to, but when I'm on my boat I've already gotten to where I want to be."

I feel the same way.

Sailing is still a great sport for the aficionados, the people who love it, but for the general public the only sailing event they cover these days is the America's Cup—along with the odd round-the-world race. The rest of the big events, like the Volvo Ocean Race, are lucky to get even a small mention in most newspapers. That's a shame, because sailing is a great way for people, and kids, to learn to live in the elements. It teaches you about the sea and the dangers that can lurk in and around it. At least as important, it teaches you about the sky, the weather— and it offers us physical activity.

Since leaving Washington, I did not jump back into competitive racing like I had in the past, but a few recent experiences stand out. In October of 2004, we rented a house in St. Tropez and I sailed in the seventy-fifth anniversary of the

Assaulting the "royal lap" after sailing with King Juan Carlos, Mica, and the Duke and Duchess of Arion.

Dragon Class with George Francisco. King Constantine and the event organizers had kindly invited us over, and we manned one of the 167 boats they had in the field. I tried not to take it too seriously, and finishing in the top third as we did was a decent showing—though I found I still did not like losing. Old habits die hard.

I also enjoyed participating in several "masters" events in San Francisco Bay—a class of events where the skipper has to be at least sixty years of age and won a national or international championship. My last time out in a master's event, at age eighty, we finished third.

Whether racing in some of these fun regattas, or even tinkering around with a little sunfish sailboat, I am totally at peace out on the water—and particularly when my family is with me.

A few years ago, I was hunting in rainy and cold conditions, trudging through the damp South Texas brush and fending off the 45-degree chill. As night was falling, it became dark enough that our group couldn't see which direction we were headed. When I declared that we were going dead east, the hunting guides with us disagreed. After they consulted their little compass, however, they were mildly surprised to discover we were heading due east.

I knew the wind was from the east, and because I could feel it equally on my cheeks that meant we were heading straight into it. Everybody probably can sense these things, but it just registers with me. Thanks to sailing, it always has. I can look at a flag somewhere and tell how hard the wind is blowing, and from what direction. So along with Texas crude, I guess there is some saltwater pulsating through these veins as well.

That's why, when I am on the water, I've already gotten to where I want to be.

It's the challenge and pleasure combined. It's the association you have with some of the finest and nicest people alive. For me, it's a feeling of being one with the sea and the wind—and most of all with my Pop, the unforgettable father who got me started, and helped make all I am possible.

INDEX

Abercrombie, Josephine, 154
Abercrombie, "Mr. Jim," 79, 154
Ackerman, Betty, 81–82, 131
Act-Up, 267
Agenda for American Renewal, 273
Agnew, Spiro, 158
AIDS, 267
Ailes, Roger, 191, 192, 272
Airbus, 307
Aladdin Oil Company, 47
Alexander, Margaret, 149
All-American Air Races, 47
Aller (steamship), 9
Altmayer, Mortimer, 25
American Association of Retired Persons, 196
American Express, 265
American Red Cross, 285
American Stock Exchange, 19, 91, 243
Americans with Disabilities Act, 242
America's Cup, 9, 104, 109–10, 112, 183, 309
Americas Society, 285
Ames, Nancy, 130
Anderson, John, 168
Anderson, John G., 51
Andriessen, Franz, 129
Annenberg, Lee, 238
Annenberg, Walter, 238
Aquino, Corazon, 156–57
Arafat, Yassir, 249
Armacost, Mike, 219, 262
Armstrong, Anne, 159
ASEAN, 285
Association of Southeast Asian Nations, 285
Atlantic Class, 65–66
Atwater, Lee, 191, 192, 259
Atwell, George J., Jr., 47
automobile industry, 211, 260, 263, 264, 297

Babbitt, Bruce, 187
Baker, Howard, 164, 165, 166, 166n, 168, 183
Baker, James A., 159, 160, 168, 177–79, 192, 198,
    213, 258
  as campaign chairman for Ford, 150–51, 170
  as Commerce Secretary, 147, 151
  friendship with R. Mosbacher, 6, 125, 131, 134,
    150, 224–26
  investment in Hollywood Marine Inc., 155,
    155n

  involvement with Enron, 281
  as Secretary of State, 224, 227, 236, 249
  as White House Chief of Staff, 270–73
Baker, Mary Stuart, 131, 134
Baldridge, Mac, 198
Bank of America, 30
Barry, Desmond, 119
Bartholdi, Frédéric-Auguste, 9
Beard, James, 303
Benny, Jack, 80
Bentsen, Lloyd, 125, 158, 187, 204, 227
Bergen, Jack, 30–31
Berghaus, Erwin, 69
Berlin, Dick, 53, 54, 75
Berlin Wall, 232, 233
Berman, Camille, 87–88
Berman, Wayne, 205
Bertron, Jimmy, 118
Beschloss, Michael, 275
Bethlehem Steel, 24
Biden, Joe, 187
Billingsley, Sherm, 35
Birch Society, 116–117
Black, Charlie, 258
Black, Shirley Temple, 232–33
Black Panthers, 134
Blakely, William, 119
Block, Edward, 47
Bloomingdale, Samuel, 51
Boch, Norman, 86
Boeing, 208
Bond, Alan, 183
Bond, Rich, 165, 188, 258
Bookout, John, 231
Boskin, Michael, 201
Botkin, Henry, 40
Bowen, Jack, 97, 157
Boyles, Howard, 86
Boyles, Jimmy, 86
Bradley, E. R., 38, 46
Bradley's Beach Club Casino, 38
Brady, Michael Joseph ("Mike"), 51
Brady, Nick, 192, 213, 224, 240, 256
Brady Plan, 215, 238
Brazil, 238–39
Breen, Jon, 165
Bremen (steamship), 27
Bren, Don, 195–96

Britt, Glenn M., 47
Broder, David, 255
Bromfield, Charles, 47
Brown, David Garland, 71
Brown, Lee P., 286, 288
Brown, Ron, 250
Bruce, George, 47
Buchanan, Pat, 258, 266, 268–69
Buchwald, Art, 130
Buck, E. O., 99
bull markets, 28–29
Bullock, Bob, 243, 245
Bureau of Economic Statistics, 202
Burke, Jackie, 83
Burns, Charlie, 35
Bush, Barbara, 79, 115, 117, 134, 165, 169, 193–94,
    244, 260–61, 277
Bush, Columba, 169
Bush, Fred, 149
Bush, George Herbert Walker, 79, 115–117, 125,
    130, 134, 143, 146, 159, 162, 177–79, 198, 222,
    224–27, 231, 277, 282, 287
  attitude toward German unification, 233
  Birch Society and, 117
  campaigns, 160–62, 164–69, 184–97, 266–76
  candidacy, 159–61
  as chairman of M. D. Anderson Cancer
      Center, 289
  as chairman of RNC, 194
  fund-raising, 194–95
  legislation passed under, 242–43
  oil drilling, 208
  Persian Gulf War, 246–48
  reelection, 184, 258
  as representative, 122–23
  Robert A. Mosbacher's relationship with,
      xi–xii
  run against Howard Baker, 164, 165, 166
  United Nations posting, 158
  as vice president, 155, 171
  visit to Japan (1992), 260–62
Bush, George Walker, 205, 228
Bush, John Ellis ("Jeb"), 169
Bush, Marvin, 165
Bush, Prescott, 117
Buss, Adele, 84
Butler, Butch, 122
Byrd, Joann, 274n

Cadel, John, 53
Cadillac Bar, 239
Callaway, Bo, 147
Campaign Reform Act, 196

Canada:
  free-trade agreement, 216
  oil fields, 280
Carbone, Liz, 32, 139, 174
Carl, Bill, 230
Carmody, Arthur, 77, 119
Carter, James Earl ("Jimmy"), 152, 155, 159, 172,
    282
Census (1990), controversy, 252–54
Central American Common Market, 285
Cerf, Bennet, 39
Chambers, Fred, 117, 125
Chase, 99
Chavez, Hugo, 280
Cheney, Richard Bruce ("Dick"), 209–10, 247
Chile, 238–39
China National Offshore Oil Company, 307
Choate School, 50, 62–64, 71, 86
Choonhavan, Chatichai, 240
Christian Coalition, 190
Chrysler, 263
Cinco de Mayo Field, 96–99
Cinco Ranch, 154
Claremont Liberation Army, 135
Clarke, Thomas A., 47
Clarke, Torie, 268
Clean Air Act, 242
Cleveland, Grover, 9
Cliburn, Van, 289
Clifford D. Mallory Cup. See Mallory Cup
Clinton, William Jefferson, 118, 196–97, 242,
    250, 258, 271, 273, 274, 282–85
  support for Lee Brown, 288
Coastal Corporation, 99
Cochran, Charles, 201
Cockrell, Alan, 121
Cohen, Bill, 164
Cold Spring Harbor Beach Club, 60
Cold War, 223, 227, 232, 276, 279
Coleman, Sylvan, 30
Collamore, Tom, 205, 232, 263
Collor, Ferdinand de, 238
Common Cause, 196
Compton, Betty, 37
Congressional Leadership Committee, 160
Connally, John, 158–60, 162, 164–65, 168, 173,
    248
Conner, Dennis, 183
Consolidated America Life Insurance Com-
    pany, 125
Cook, Lod, 235
Coolidge, Calvin, 28
Council of Economic Advisors, 144

Council of the Americas, 285
Courtelis, Alec P., 194
Cox, Chris, 298
Cox, Ed, 79
Cox, John, 117
Cox, Walter, 245
Crane, Phil, 168
Cronkite, Walter, 170
Crosby, Bing, 44
Cuba, 39–40
Cullen, Hugh Roy, 78, 96
Cunningham, Briggs, 65, 110
Curb Market. *See* New York Curb Market
Curbstone Brokers (Sobel), 24
Cushing, Harvey, 43
Czechoslovakia, 222

Dallas Morning News, 243–44
Dandy, Walter, 43
Danforth, John, 205
Daniel, Price, 116, 118
Darman, Dick, 211, 232, 240, 256, 267
Davies, Marion, 53
Davis, Arthur, Jr., 59, 60
Davis, Pat, 64
Davis, Rick, 296
de Collor, Ferdinand, 238
DeFrank, Tom 269
de la Madrid, Miguel, 214
Demaret, Jimmy, 83
de Menil, Dominique, 88
de Menil, John, 88
Department of Commerce and Labor, 201,
    224–32
Desert Shield, 247
Desert Storm, 247, 255
Detroit Economic Club, 211
Devroy, Ann 258
Dickey, Tommy, 139, 291
Dingell, John, 227
Dinkins, David, 253
Dobbs, Lou, 283
Dole, Robert Joseph, 167, 190, 191
Dow Jones Index, 28
Drachman, Roy, 33
Dragon Class World Championship, 126–29,
    309–10
Dragon Olympic trials, 140
*Drilling Ahead: The Quest for Oil in the Deep
    South, 1945–2005* (Cockrell), 121
Dubai Ports World, 307
Dukakis, Michael, 187, 188, 189, 196, 211
Duke Energy, 280

Duncan, Brittanie, 304
Duncan, Cameron, 304
Duncan, Donald Cameron, 304
Duncan, George, 51
Duncan, John, 182
DuPont, Pete, 191
Durant, William, 27, 30
Durante, Jimmy, 44

Earhart, Amelia, 47
Eisenhower, Dwight D., 113, 116, 117, 118
Elkins, Jim, Sr., 154
Elvstrom, Paul, 139
Endangered Species Act, 212
Energy Policy and Conservation Act, 144
energy sector:
    controls, 144–45
    deregulation of, 144–45
    tax breaks, 180
Enron, 96, 280–82
Esperson Drug Store, 87
European Union, 285

Fanjul, Jose ("Pepe"), 202
Farmer, Robert, 187–88, 189, 196
Farrell, Johnny, 50
Farren, J. Michael, 205
Fatio, Maurice, 47
Fay, Albert, 103, 104–5, 116
Fay, Ernie, 103, 104–5
Federal Election Campaign Act Amend-
    ments, 147
Federal Election Commission, 187n
Federal Reserve Act, 20
Federal Trade Commission Act, 20
Fernandez, Ben, 168
Fisher, Max, 146, 177, 194, 278, 280
Fitzgerald, Jennifer, 178
Fitzwater, Marlin, 258
Flagler, Henry, 46
Flagler, Mary, 46
Florida Gas, 157
Ford, Gerald R., 143–52, 158–61, 170, 238, 269,
    282, 288. *See also* President Ford Committee
Ford Motor Company, 208, 263
Fraenkel Oil and Gas, 86
Francisco, George, 107, 128
free trade, 211, 215–16, 243, 259
Free Trade Area of the Americas, 285
Freedom Forum, 274n
Freeman, Norman, 108
Freireich, Emil, 130
Frohnmayer, John, 268

Fuermann, George, 78
Fuller, Craig, 192, 273
Fund for Limited Government, 160

G-7 Economic Summit, 239
Gable, Clark, 44
Gall, Bob, 137
gangsters, 37–38
Ganzi, Wally, Jr., 194
Gartrell, Nanette, 136–37
Gates, Bill, 282
gay community, 267–68
Gelb, Bruce, 213
General Agreement on Tariffs and Trade, 226, 251
General Motors Corporation, 27, 30, 263
geologists, 84–86, 94, 96
George and Barbara Bush Endowment for Innovative Cancer Research, 290
George Bush Presidential Library, 289
Gephardt, Dick, 187
Germani, Ben, 82, 83
Germany, 233, 276
Gerry, Lloyd, 147, 152
Gerry, Robert, 147, 152
Gershwin, George, 39–43, 47, 51, 175
Gershwin, Ira, 43
Gershwin, Leonore, 43
Getty Oil, 121
Gimbel, Adam, 39
Gimbel, Bernard, 39, 51
Giuliani, Rudy, 286–87
glasnost, 234
Gleason, Jack, 166–67
globalization, 227
Gold, Vic, 168
Goldwater, Barry, 117–18, 191
Goodwin, Doris Kearns, 308
Gorbachev, Mikhail, 201, 222, 226, 233–37, 276
Gore, Al, 187, 271, 278
Governor's Cup, 106–7
Graham-Paige (private equity firm), 30
Gramm, Phil, 183–84
Great Depression, 4, 27, 100. *See also* stock market crash (1929)
Greater Houston Partnership, 288
Greenspan, Alan, 144, 150
Gray, Shapleigh, 85, 96
Grubbs, Ned, 47, 62–63
Grumman Aircraft Corporation, 30

Hagen, Walter, 51
Haig, Alexander, 191

Halbouty, Michael T., 94–96
Haley, Brian, 296
Han, Seung-soo, 218
Harkins, Hank, 86, 93
Harlem, 2
Harmony Arc, 294
Harriman, Averill, 224
Harrison, Dan, 79
Hart, Gary, 187
Hausmann, Helmut, 239
Havel, Vaclav, 232
Hearst, William Randolph, 53
Hennessy, Jack, 194
Henson, Peter, 57
Herring, Bob, 96
Hershey, Jake, 106
Heyward, DuBose, 41
Hild, Herb, 57
Hills, Carla, 201, 208, 213, 226, 251, 274
Himmler, Heinrich, 67
Hines, Gerry, 182
Hobby, Bill, 243
Hollings, Fritz, 227–28
Hollywood Marine Inc., 155
Holmes, Ned, 287
Holocaust, 67–69
Holt, Bobby, 194
Hood, Ted, 104
Hoover, Herbert, 28, 100, 224,
Hope, Bob, 44
Hopter, Henry, 254
Hotel Corporation of America, 30
Houston: Land of the Big Rich (Fuermann), 78
Houston Natural Gas, 96, 280
Howland, Grace, 70
Hughes, Evan, 259
Humble Oil, 78
Hunt, H. L., 96, 113, 115
Hussein (King of Jordan), 249
Hussein, Saddam, 234, 240, 247–49
Hutcheson, Thad, 116, 139

Iacocca, Lee, 263, 265, 282
immigrants, 21, 308
  epidemics among, 17
  living conditions, 14–15, 17
Inland Steel Company, 19
International Dragon Association, 126n
International Yacht Racing Union, 57n
InterNorth, 96, 280
Iran-Contra Affair, 227, 273
Iraq, 234, 246–48, 278
Isotta Fraschini (car), 54–55

Jackson, Jesse, 187
Japan:
  imports, 218–19
  trade relations with, 206–9, 211, 216, 238,
    259–64
Jaruzelski, Wojciech, 220–21
Jayred, Wally, 96
John Birch Society, 116–117
Johnson, Harry T. F., 53, 75
Johnson, "Honey," 75
Johnson, Lady Bird, 62
Johnson, Lyndon Baines, 62, 113, 118, 134, 158
Johnson, Muriel ("Honey"), 53
Johnson, Warren, 53
Johnston, Robert, 80
Jolson, Al, 44
Jones, Jerry, 147
Jones, Jesse, 99–100, 224
Juan Carlos, King, 128, 179

Kaifu, Toshiki, 238
Kearns, David, 211
Kemp, Jack, 184, 191, 267
Kemp's Ridley (turtle), 212–13
Kendall, Don, 36
Kennedy, John F., 46, 112, 113, 118, 158
Kennedy, Joseph P., 29, 46, 50
Kennedy, Robert F., 113
Kennedy, Ted, 249
Kent State, 134
Kickerillo, Vincent, 153–54
Kilroy, Bill, 79, 118, 119
King, Martin Luther, Jr., 113, 122, 134
Kirkwood Drilling, 93
Kissinger, Henry, 148
Knapp, Arthur, 57, 71
Knickerbocker Yacht Club, 59–60
Know Nothing Party, 308
Kohl, Helmut, 233, 266
Kohl, Herb, 254
Kolliba, Homer, 93
Korean War, 218
Kravis, Henry, 194
Kriendler, Jack, 35–36
Kriendler, Pete, 36
Kuhn, Loeb, and Co., 25
Kuwait, 234, 240, 247, 278

Laird, Mel, 148
Lamarr, Hedy, 80
Lamour, Dorothy, 80
Larchmont Yacht Club, 60
Lawrence, Berdon, 155

Lay, Kenneth, 96, 157, 280–82
Lazarus, Emma, 10
Lazarus, Mike, 262
Leavitt, Arthur, 179
Lee, Thomas Jefferson, 71
Leonard, James, 254
Levi, Philip, 25
Liedtke, Bill, 113, 115
Lincoln, Abraham, 308
Lindbergh, Anne Morrow, 38
Lindbergh, Charles, 38
Livermore, Jesse, 29, 30
Lo, Ken, 303
Locomobile, 30, 31
Loeffler, Tom, 296
Lollobrigida, Gina, 140–41
Lombard, Carol, 44
Long, Meredith, 87
Long Island Sound International Class, 71
Louisiana Land and Exploration, 31
Love, Ben, 181, 305
Love Petroleum, 121
Lucas, Anthony, 78
Lusitania, 15
Lynn, Bill, 57

Madoff, Bernard, 23
Madrid, Miguel de la, 214
Magnolia Petroleum Company, 79
Magritte, Rene, 88
Malcolm X, 134
Malek, Fred, 258, 267, 270–71, 296
Mallory Cup, 56, 107–9
Manhasset Bay Race Week, 101
Mann, John, 90
Marcos, Ferdinand, 156–57
Marcos, Imelda, 156–57
Marcus, Stanley, 79
Marron, Don, 194, 235
Masterson, Peter, 103, 105, 107
Matalin, Mary, 258
Mathias, Bob, 149
Matsunaga, Nobuo, 207
Matthews, Scott, 60
Maxim's, 87–88
Maxwell, Cooch, 57
Mayo, John, 92–93
McCain, John, 211, 294–99
McCain, Roberta, 278n
McCarthy, Glenn H., 80
McCormick, Edward, 24
McDevitt, Dobie, 82–83
McDonnell Douglas, 208

McIntyre, Marvin W., 43
McNamara, Don, 105
M. D. Anderson Cancer Center, xii, 130,
  288–90
Mdivani, David, 53
Meacham, Jon, 275
Mears, Arthur D. ("Downing"), Jr., 153, 185
Mears, Bayly, 185
Mears, Lisa Mosbacher, 126, 132, 149–50, 153,
  185, 303
Mears, Parker, 185
Mears, Whitney, 185
Mecom, John, 79
Meehan, Michael, 28
Melges, Buddy, 108–9, 183, 290–91
Mendell, Bill, 85, 93, 94, 96, 97
Mendoza, Cristobal, 246
Mercer, Henry, 110
Mercosur (regional trade agreement), 285
Merman, Ethel, 44
Methodist Hospital, 285
metric system, 206
Mexico:
  economy, 215–16, 284–85
  NAFTA, 226, 242–43
  U.S. relations with, 213–16
Michelena, Arturo, 246
Michigan Republican Party, 146
Midvale Steel and Ordinance Company, 19
Miller, Charles, 287
Miller and Company, 25
Mischer, Walter, 287
Mitchell, Abe, 51
Mitterrand, Francois, 233, 266
Mizner, Jim Addison, 46
Mondale, Walter, 195
Moore, Preston, 229, 232
Morgan, Henry, 110
Morton, Rogers, 147, 151
Mosbacher, Babetta, 12, 17, 18, 254
Mosbacher, Barbara, 5, 44, 55, 162, 164
Mosbacher, Bruce, 154
Mosbacher, Catherine, 185
Mosbacher, Diane ("Dee"), 5, 81, 89, 132–36,
  166, 174, 268, 299
Mosbacher, Emil ("Bus"), Jr., 38, 50, 52, 55, 130,
  153, 164, 166, 290
  as Chief of Protocol under Nixon, 124, 136, 140
  naval career, 66–67
  sailing career, 57–61, 101, 110–12
Mosbacher, Emil, Sr., 35, 54–55, 137, 175, 198, 305
  advice from, 78, 92, 98, 137
  as broker, 19–20

childhood, 2–7, 12
death, 177–78
early career, 2–7, 13
friendships, 29, 39–44
gambling, 31, 38
golfing, 50–53
illness, 175–76
Jewishness, 6
North American Steel investigation, 19, 24–26
in Palm Beach, 46–50
Porgy and Bess, financing of, 40–42
real estate dealings, 32–33
relationships with employees, 138–39
religious beliefs, 17
risk-taking by, 33, 81
as "runner," 20–21
sailing, 56–61
security measures taken by, 39
"survival instinct," 18, 33, 34
as trader, 31
Mosbacher, Georgette Paulsin-Muir, 182–83,
  290, 292
Mosbacher, Gertrude, 46–47, 75, 162–64
Mosbacher, Hannchen, 10
Mosbacher, Jane (daughter of Robert Mos-
  bacher Jr.), 185
Mosbacher, Jane Pennybacker, 71–77, 80–81,
  99, 106, 126–32, 245, 288, 290, 292, 303
Mosbacher, Johanna ("Hattie"), 12, 17, 254
Mosbacher, Karoline, 67, 68
Mosbacher, Kathryn ("Kathi"), 17, 44, 132, 153,
  163, 245, 303
Mosbacher, Lisa. See Lisa Mosbacher Mears
Mosbacher, Louis, 9–13, 254
Mosbacher, Mendel, 10
Mosbacher, Meredith, 185
Mosbacher, Mica McCutchen, 166n, 278,
  291–95, 299, 304, 309
Mosbacher, Patricia Ryan, 38, 130
Mosbacher, Peter Clark, 185
Mosbacher, Robert A., Jr., 5, 89, 132, 166, 174,
  185, 198, 278, 299, 303
  campaign for Texas lieutenant governor,
  243–45
  mayoral run, 285–88
  nomination to Overseas Private Investment
  Corporation, 228
  senate run, 183–84
Mosbacher, Robert A., Sr.:
  attitude toward energy policy, 308–9
  attitude toward free trade, 211, 259, 282–83,
  306–7
  attitude toward immigration, 308

as board member of M. D. Anderson Cancer
   Center, 288–90
business career, 75–100, 153–57, 180–82
   Enron, involvement with, 280–82
   return to Mosbacher Energy, 278–82
childhood, 4–5, 34, 46–50, 70
diagnosis with pancreatic cancer, 304
education:
   Choate School, 50, 62–64, 71, 86
   Washington and Lee University, 71
marriages:
   Georgette Paulsin-Muir, 182–83, 290, 292
   Jane Pennybacker, 71–77, 80–81, 99, 106,
      126–32
   Mica McCutchen, 166n, 278, 291–95, 299,
      304, 309
   Sandra Smith Gerry, 140–42, 147, 152–53,
      182, 292
political career, 113–25
   allegations against, by Gleason, 167
   appointments under, 205
   budget negotiation, 231–32, 240, 242
   as chairman of the Americas Society, 285
   confirmation hearings, 204
   dignitaries and, 232–43
   as finance chairman for George H. W. Bush,
      160–62
   as finance chairman for Gerald Ford, 143–52
   financial policies, 256–58
   friendship with James A. Baker, 6, 125, 131,
      134, 150, 224–26
   as fund-raiser for George H. W. Bush, 184–86
   as general campaign chairman for John Mc-
      Cain, 294–99
   as general chairman of G. H. W. Bush re-
      election, 258
   George H. W. Bush's relationship with, xi–xii,
      5, 226, 227
   media relations, 265–66
   NAFTA, 226, 242–43, 250–51, 259, 274–75,
      282–85
   1990 Census, controversy, 252–54
   1992 campaign, 255–59
   oil policy, 179–81
   Persian Gulf War, 246–48
   regulation of shrimping industry, 212–13
   as Republican, 115–18, 145–46
   resignation, 259
   responsibilities of office, 203–4
   support for Nixon, 113–15, 123–25
   trade policy, 210–11, 227, 249–51
   as U.S. Secretary of Commerce, 6, 198–245
   visit to Japan (1992), 261–66

   sailing career, 56–61, 65–66, 71, 101–12, 128,
      139–40, 290–92, 309–10
Mosbacher, Sandra Smith Gerry, 140–42, 147,
   152–53, 182, 292
Mosbacher Energy, 83, 85, 93, 117, 121, 156, 159,
   178, 305
   geologists, 84–86
   oil crisis of 1980s, 181–82
   oil drilling, 278–80
   oil exploration in Canada, 184–85
Mosbacher Properties, 75
Mulroney, Brian, 274
Murchison, Clint, 79, 96–98
Muto, Kabun, 239

Naffziger, Howard, 43
NAFTA, 226, 242–43, 250–51, 259, 274–75,
   282–85
NASA, 229
National Bank of Commerce, 99
National Endowment for the Arts, 268
National Export Initiatives, 249–50
National Gay and Lesbian Task Force, 268
National Oceanic and Atmospheric Adminis-
   tration, 204
National Petroleum Council, 179
NATO, 276
Nazism, 11
Nelson, Susan, 296
Nelson, Terry, 295
New York:
   German population, 13, 16–17
   immigrants, 14–15, 17
   Jewish population, 15
   tenements, 14–15
New York Commercial, 20
New York Confidential, 37
New York Curb Market, 19, 20–24, 31, 91, 243
   and immigrants, 21
   as self-regulated institution, 21
   stock market crash (1929) and, 27–30, 32
New York Stock Exchange, 21
   stock market crash (1929), 27–29, 32
Nicaragua, 227
Nice, Harry, 43
Nielson, Gerald B., 90
Nixon, Richard M., 113–15, 117, 123–25, 147,
   152, 158
NOAA, 204, 229–31
North, Lowell, 139
North American Free Trade Agreement. See
   NAFTA
North American Sailing Championship, 56

North American Steel, 19, 24–26
North Atlantic Treaty Organization, 276
North Central Texas Oil Company, 77, 119

Oak Ridge Boys, 289
Obama, Barack, 197, 294
O'Day, George, 104
O'Dell, Bob, 149
O'Donnell, Peter, 117
Ogilvy, Stan, 57
O'Gorman, Patrick, 57
oil:
  barges, 155
  crisis of 1980s, 180–81
  drilling, 92–98, 117, 121, 180–81, 208
  exploration in Canada, 184–85, 280
  industry, 78–79, 307
  in Philippines, 156
  prices, 180–81, 278, 308
  refineries, 155
Oil for Food program, 248
Olaf V, 106
Old Ocean, 79
O'Neill, Tip, 282
OPEC oil embargo, 144
Operation Desert Shield, 247
Operation Desert Storm, 247, 255
Overseas Private Investment Corporation, 228, 299, 303
Ozal, Turgut, 251–52

Packard, David, 146, 147
Palin, Sarah, 299
Pallay, George, 43
Palm Beach, Florida, 46–50
Pan American airlines, 54
Pan Am Production Co., 156
pari-mutuel betting, 31
Parr, George, 92
Parsley, Bob, 86
Paul, Ron, 183
Payne, Leon, 79
Pebble Beach Golf Club, 207
Pelosi, Nancy, 307
Pennybacker, Claude, 72
perestroika, 234
Perez, Carlos Andres, 246
Perot, Ross, 172–73, 258, 269, 270–71, 275
Perry, Charlotte, 59
Persian Gulf War, 246–48
Peterson, Dave, 292–93
Peterson, Pete, 226, 227
Petroleum Club, 94

PFC. See President Ford Committee
Pinochet, Augusto, 239
Poland, 220–22
Poling, Red, 263
political conventions, 169–70
Popov, Gavril, 235
Porgy and Bess, 40–42
Powell, Colin, 247
President Ford Committee, 143–44, 147–51
Presidential Trust Fund, 272
Pressler, Larry, 167
Prohibition, 35–37
Pruet, Chesley, 119–22, 157, 177, 251, 280
Pruitt, Bert, 48
Puche, Jaime Serra, 214–15, 250, 274, 284

Quayle, Dan, 189, 255, 258, 271
Quezon, Manuel L., 54

Ray, Ted, 51
RCA Radio, 28–29
Reagan, Ronald, 178, 179, 180, 183, 195, 276
  appointment of R. Mosbacher to Secretary of Commerce, 201
  assassination attempt, 171
  NAFTA, support for, 282
  1968 campaign, 124
  1976 campaign, 145, 146, 150
  1980 campaign, 159, 162, 164–72
  1984 campaign, 184
Reagan Library, 294
Reed, Gordon, 102
Reed, Lawrence S., 102–6, 122
Reilly, William, 213
Reinach, Udo, 50
Remick, Dave, 85
Republic Iron and Steel Company, 19
Republican National Finance Committee, 145–46
Reston, Scotty, 162
Rho, Tae-woo, 216, 266
Richards, Ann, 244–45
Richardson, Elliott, 151
Richardson, Sid, 79, 96, 113, 158
Rickenback, Thomas, 59
Ridge, Tom, 254
Rio Grande Pipeline, 96
Riordan, Richard, 287
Roberts, John, 155
Robertson, Pat, 190–91
Robinson, Jim, 265
Rockefeller, John D., 46
Rockefeller, Nelson, 142

Rockefeller Center, 207
Romney, George, 124
Romney, Mitt, 296
Roosevelt, Franklin D., 117, 224
Roosevelt, Julian ("Dooley"), 104
Rowan Drilling Company, 99
Rubesemum, Sandy, 64
Rubin, Robert, 284
Runyon, Damon, 37
Ryzhkov, Nikolai, 235

Safire, Bill, 159
sailing. See also specific races
  career of R. Mosbacher, 56–61, 65–66, 71,
    101–12, 128, 139–40, 290–92, 309–10
  going windward, 1–2, 311
Salas, Tito, 246
Salinas, Carlos, 214, 274
Salvation Army, 288
Sarazen, Gene, 51
Sarbanes, Paul, 228
Saville, David, 128
Scandinavian Gold Cup, 104
Schiff, Mortimer L., 25, 47
Schnabel, Rock, 259
Schraaft (club), 37
Schwab, Susan, 205
Schwartz, Bernard, 229–30
Schwarzenegger, Arnold, 289
Scowcroft, Brent, 249, 263, 284
Scovill Cup, 60
Sears, Henry, 110
Securities and Exchange Commission, 298
"Senator Straddle" (ad campaign), 191
Sharp, Dudley, 122
Shattuck, Frank, 37
Shedd, Charlie, 132, 293
Sheldon, Jim, 71
Shevardnadze, Eduard, 236
Shields, Cornelius ("Corny"), Sr., 56, 110
Shivers, Allan, 118
"shorting" stocks, 27n, 30
shrimping industry, 212–13
Simon, Bill, 144, 148
Simon, Paul, 187
Singer, Paris, 46
Skarzynski, Michael, 205
Skinner, Sam, 213, 258
Skouras, Spyros ("Spiro"), 63
Slight, Fred, 147
Smackover Play, 121
Smith, Adam, 235
Smith, Cardella, 81, 133–34

Smith, Fred, 298
Smith, Jesse, 59
Smith, Lloyd, 84, 140
Smith, Randy, 172, 177
Smullyan, Clint, 30
Sobel, Robert, 24
Sofia, Princess, 128
"soft" money, 187n, 188, 197
Soling Olympic trials, 140
Soling World Championship, 139
South Korea, 216–18
South Rio Grande Valley Gas Company, 98
Southern Ocean Racing Conference, 106
Soviet Union. See USSR
Sparkman & Stephens, 103
Sports Illustrated, 110
St. Petersburg-Miami Handicap, 107
Standard Oil, 46, 156
Stanford, R. Allen, 23
Stanolind Co. of Indiana, 79
Star Class, 57
Stassen, Harold, 168
Statue of Liberty, 9–10
Steele, Jim, 282
Stempel, Bob, 263
Stephens, Olin, 103
Stern, Stanley, 60
Stewart, Layton, 251
stock market crash (1929), 27–30, 32
Stork Club, 35–36
Stowers, Ann, 71
Strake, George, 86
Sturrock, Jock, 112
Summers, George, 49, 54
Sununu, John, 191, 211, 240, 256, 257, 258
Swift, Kay, 41
Sykes, Howard A., 47

Taft, Robert, 116
"taxpayer" property, 32
Team of Rivals (Doris Kearns Goodwin), 308
Team 100 program, 195–96
technology:
  in global economy, 202–3
  Japan and, 207–8, 216
  Soviet Union and, 209–10, 226, 234–35
Teeter, Bob, 190, 191, 192, 258, 267, 269, 270–71
tenements, 14–15
Tet Offensive, 113
Texas, oil industry, 78–79
Texas A&M University, 289
Texas Commerce Bank, 99, 181
Texas Congressional Boosters, 146

Texas Corinthian Yacht Club, 103, 126
Texas Democratic Party, 119
Texas Gulf Producing Co., 102
Thatcher, Margaret, 233, 266
Thornburgh, Dick, 213
Thurmond, Strom, 228–29
Tiananmen Square, 232
Tilden, Samuel, 24
Tovar y Tovar, Martin, 246
Tower, John, 118–19, 159, 183, 208
Townhouse Operation fund, 166–67
Toyoda, Eiji, 208
Toyota Manufacturing, 208
Toys "R" Us, 262
Trade Promotion Coordinating Committee, 249–50
Turkey, trade relations with, 251–52
Turner, Stan, 59
Turner, Ted, 109
turtle extruder device, 212
21 (club), 35–36

Ueberroth, Peter, 201
Umlauf, Charles, 87
United Nations' Oil for Food program, 248
United Nations Security Council, 249
United States Trade Representative, 226
University Computing Company, 115
Unocal, 307
Untermyer, Samuel, 19, 24–26
U.S. Fish and Wildlife Service, 213
U.S. Oil and Gas Association, 179
U.S. Steel, 27, 30
USSR:
  economy, 234–38
  trade relations with, 209–10, 226
USTR, 226

Vaid, Urvashi, 268
Vanderbilt, Harold ("Mike"), 110
Vardon, Henry, 51
Venezuela, 246, 249, 279–80
Vietnam War, 113, 122, 134
Volcansek, Fred, 217
Volcker, Paul, 282

Walesa, Lech, 221–22, 232
Walker, Jimmy, 37

Wallace, George, 134
Wallace, Henry, 100
Walsh, D. D., 71
Walsh, Lawrence, 273
Warburg, Paul, 41
Washington, Yvonne, 293
Washington and Lee University, 71
Watanabe, Kozo, 261–63
Watergate scandal, 124, 145
Weaver, John, 295
Weicker, Lowell, 167–68
Weinberger, Cap, 273
Weinmann, John, 234
Welch, Jack, 298
Welch, Louis, 130
Welch, Robert, 117
West, J. M., 78
Wheeler, Michael, 153
Wheless, William ("Fishback"), 154
White, Jim, 121
White, Mark, 160
Whiton, Herman F. ("Swede"), 102, 103
Williams, Clayton, 244–45
Williams, Ted, 191
Willis, Bruce, 289
Willkie, Wendell L., 205
Wilson, Michael, 274
Winchell, Walter, 36, 37
Winchester, Roy, 113, 115
Wipfler, Eugene, 254
Woodstock, 134
Woodward, Bob, 155
World War I, 11, 15, 20, 28
World War II, 67–69
Wyatt, Lynn, 244
Wyatt, Oscar, 99, 244, 248
Wyly, Charles, 115
Wyly, Sam, 114–15

Yarborough, Ralph, 117, 124–25
Young, Andrew, 282
Young, John, 201
Young Socialist Alliance, 136

Zapata Offshore, 117
Zeckendorf, "Big Bill," 64
Zedillo, 284
Zilboorg, Gregory, 42